M000113171

*The Little Big*

# PASTA, RICE & MORE
# COOK BOOK

*The Little Big Pasta, Rice & More Cook Book*
was created and produced by McRae Books Srl
Borgo Santa Croce, 8 – Florence (Italy)
info@mcraebooks.com
Publishers: Anne McRae and Marco Nardi

Project Director: Anne McRae
Design: Marco Nardi
Text: Carla Bardi, Mollie Thomson, Sara Vignozzi, Rosalba Goffré,
Editing: Helen Farrell, Antony Shugaar
Photography: Studio Lanza, Studio Cappelli, Mauro Corsi, Leonardo Pasquinelli, Gianni Petronio, Lorenzo Borri, Stefano Pratesi
Home Economist: Benedetto Rillo
Artbuying: McRae Books, Arianna Cappellini
Layouts: AdinaStefania Dragomir, Giampietro Bruno
Repro: Fotolito Toscana, Florence

The publishers would also like to thank Ceramiche Bellini (Ginestra Fiorentina), Ceramiche Virginia (Ginestra Fiorentina), Ceramiche Bitossi (Montelupo), Ceramiche Bartolini (Montelupo), and Ceramiche Taccini (Montelupo) who kindly lent props for the photography.

ISBN 88-89272-32-5
Printed and bound in China

---

### GENERAL INFORMATION
The level of difficulty of the recipes in this book is expressed as a number from 1 (simple) to 3 (difficult).

*The Little Big*

# PASTA, RICE & MORE COOK BOOK

McRae Books

# Contents

# LONG
# PASTA

# TYPES OF LONG PASTA

Spaghetti is the classic long dried pasta shape and its name is almost synonymous with pasta itself in some parts of the world. But there are many other delicious long shapes, ranging in size from tiny cappellini, through the various widths of spaghetti, to the much thicker bucatini and ziti which are hollow inside. Some long pasta shapes, such as linguine or reginette, are flattened, while others, like fusilli lunghi, are spiralled or curved. Some broader types, such as reginette, have fluted or scalloped edges. Long pasta generally works well with smooth, olive oil based sauces that can be twirled with ease around a fork. This chapter has more than 70 ideas for delicious sauces; in most cases we have indicated a specific type of long pasta to use in each recipe but almost all can be served with any long pasta with spectacular results.

Ziti

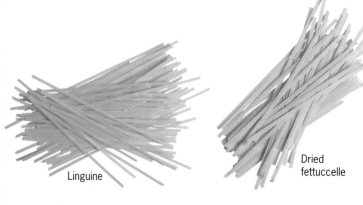

Linguine

Dried
fettuccelle

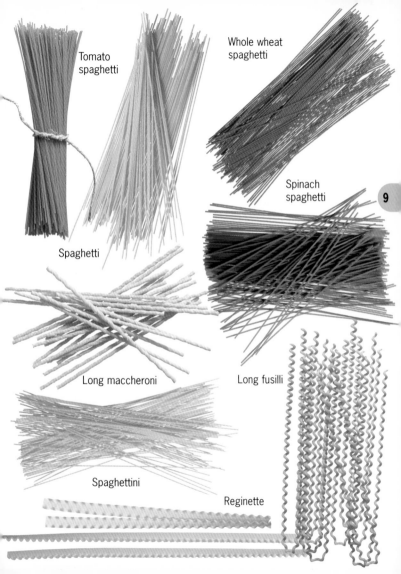

Tomato spaghetti

Whole wheat spaghetti

Spinach spaghetti

Spaghetti

Long maccheroni

Long fusilli

Spaghettini

Reginette

# SPICY SPAGHETTI WITH PANCETTA AND ONION

C ook the pasta in a large pan of salted, boiling
water until al dente. • Meanwhile, heat the oil in
a medium saucepan over high heat. • Sauté the
chile pepper and pancetta until browned. Remove
the pancetta and set aside. • In the same
saucepan, sauté the onion for 8–10 minutes over
medium heat. Return the pancetta to the saucepan
and let it flavor the onion. • Drain the pasta and
add to the sauce. • Season with parsley and
Pecorino. Toss well and serve.

*Serves: 4–6*

*Preparation: 10'*

*Cooking: 15'*

*Level of difficulty: 1*

- 1 lb/500 g
  spaghetti
- 4 tbsp extra-virgin
  olive oil
- 1 dried chile
  pepper, crumbled
- 5 oz/150 g
  pancetta, coarsely
  chopped
- 1 white onion, finely
  chopped
- 1 cup/100 g finely
  chopped parsley
- 2 cups/250 g
  freshly grated
  Pecorino cheese

# SPAGHETTI WITH CALAMARI

Serves: 4–6

Preparation: 10'

Cooking: 55'

Level of difficulty: 1

- **8 small calamari, cleaned**
- **2 onions, finely chopped**
- **2 cloves garlic, finely chopped**
- **4 tbsp extra-virgin olive oil**
- **3 cups/750 g peeled and chopped canned tomatoes**
- **salt and freshly ground black pepper to taste**
- **1 lb/500 g spaghetti**

Cut the calamari crosswise into thin half circles. • Heat the oil in a large frying pan. Add the onion and garlic and sauté over medium heat until they begin to change color. • Add the calamari and tomatoes. Season with salt and pepper. Turn the heat down low, cover, and simmer for about 45 minutes, or until the calamari are tender. • Cook the spaghetti in a large pot of salted, boiling water until al dente. Drain well and place in a heated serving dish. Toss with the sauce and serve hot.

# SPAGHETTI WITH FRESH TOMATOES AND LEMON

C ook the spaghetti in a large pot of salted, boiling water until al dente. • While the pasta is cooking, peel the tomatoes, cut them in half, and squeeze out as many seeds as possible. Chop coarsely and place in a bowl. • Finely chop the garlic and basil together. Add to the tomatoes and season with salt and pepper (the salt will help the basil to keep its bright green color). • Pour in the lemon juice and oil and mix well. • Drain the pasta and place in a heated serving dish. Pour the sauce over the top and toss vigorously. • Serve hot.

Serves: 4–6

Preparation: 10'

Cooking: 12'

Level of difficulty: 1

- **1 lb/500 g spaghetti**
- **1¹/₂ lb/750 g ripe tomatoes**
- **1 clove garlic**
- **20 fresh basil leaves**
- **salt and freshly ground black pepper to taste**
- **freshly squeezed juice of 1 large lemon**
- **¹/₂ cup/125 ml extra-virgin olive oil**

# BUCATINI WITH CAPERS AND OLIVES

Cook the bucatini in a large pot of salted, boiling water until al dente. • In a large skillet, sauté the garlic and parsley in the oil over medium heat until the garlic starts to color. • Stir the olives and capers into the sauce and cook over low heat for 2–3 minutes. • Drain the pasta and place in the skillet. • Toss with the capers and olives over medium-high heat for 2 minutes. • Place in a heated serving dish and sprinkle with the Pecorino. • Serve hot.

14

*Serves: 4–6*

*Preparation: 10'*

*Cooking: 15'*

*Level of difficulty: 1*

- 1 lb/500 g bucatini
- 4 tbsp extra-virgin olive oil
- 2 cloves garlic, finely chopped
- 3 tbsp finely chopped parsley
- 1 cup/100 g pitted and chopped black olives
- 3 tbsp capers
- $^1/_3$ cup/45 g freshly grated Pecorino cheese

# SPAGHETTI WITH TUSCAN PESTO

*Serves: 4–6*

*Preparation: 10'*

*Cooking: 12'*

*Level of difficulty: 1*

- 1 lb/500 g spaghetti
- 1 large bunch fresh basil leaves
- 2 cloves garlic
- 15 walnuts, shelled
- 3 tbsp pine nuts
- $^1/_2$ cup/125 ml extra-virgin olive oil
- salt and freshly ground black pepper to taste
- 6 tbsp freshly grated Pecorino cheese

Cook the spaghetti in a large pan of salted, boiling water until al dente. • While the pasta is cooking, chop the basil, garlic, walnuts, and pine nuts in a food processor. Gradually add the oil as you chop. • Transfer to a small bowl. Stir in the cheese and season with salt and pepper. • Drain the pasta and place in a heated serving bowl. • Add the pesto and toss gently. Serve hot.

# SPAGHETTI WITH BLACK TRUFFLES

**C**ook the spaghetti in a large pan of salted, boiling water until al dente. • Wash the truffles in warm water, scrubbing the surfaces carefully. Dry well and grate finely. • Heat the oil in a small, heavy-bottomed saucepan until fairly hot. Remove from the heat and add the truffles. Mix well. • Return to very low heat and add the garlic and anchovies. Squash the anchovies with the back of a fork so that they dissolve in the oil. Stir until the oil is well-flavored with the garlic. Take care that the garlic doesn't burn and that the oil never boils. Remove from the heat. Taste and season with salt and pepper, if needed. • Drain the pasta and place in a heated serving dish. Pour the truffle sauce over the top, toss well, and serve.

Serves: 4–6
Preparation: 15'
Cooking: 12'
Level of difficulty :1

- **1 lb/500 g spaghetti**
- **5 oz/150 g black truffles**
- **6 tbsp extra-virgin olive oil**
- **2 cloves garlic, cut in half and lightly crushed**
- **4 anchovy fillets**
- **salt and freshly ground black pepper to taste**

16

# SPAGHETTI WITH CHEESE AND PEPPER

Cook the pasta in a large pan of salted, boiling water until al dente. • Drain the pasta, leaving just a little more water than usual. This will help to melt the cheese and will prevent the pasta from sticking together. • Transfer the spaghetti to a large heated serving dish. Sprinkle the Pecorino over the top. Cover with a generous grinding of pepper and toss for 1–2 minutes. • Serve at once.

*Serves: 4–6*

*Preparation: 5'*

*Cooking: 15'*

*Level of difficulty: 1*

- 1 lb/500 g spaghetti
- 2 cups/250 g freshly grated Pecorino cheese
- freshly ground black pepper to taste

# SPAGHETTI WITH GARLIC AND OIL SAUCE

*Serves: 4–6*

*Preparation: 5'*

*Cooking: 15'*

*Level of difficulty: 1*

- **3 cloves garlic, lightly crushed**
- **¹/₂ cup/125 ml extra-virgin olive oil**
- **1 lb/500 g spaghetti**
- **freshly ground black pepper to taste**

Cook the pasta in a large pan of salted, boiling water until al dente. • Heat the oil in a frying pan and sauté the garlic until pale gold. • Drain the pasta and transfer to the frying pan with the garlic and oil. Season with a generous grinding of pepper. • Toss over high heat for 1 minute. Serve hot.

# SPAGHETTINI WITH RAW ARTICHOKES

Clean the artichokes, cutting off the stalks, removing all the tough outer leaves, and slicing about 1 inch (2.5 cm) off the tops. Cut in half, and remove any fuzzy choke. • Cut the artichokes into very thin slices. Place in a bowl of cold water with the lemon juice to soak for 15 minutes. • Drain well, and dry carefully with a clean cloth. Place in a large serving bowl (large enough to hold the pasta too). Season with salt and pepper and drizzle with the oil. • Cook the pasta in a large pan of boiling, salted water until al dente. • Drain well and transfer to the bowl with the sauce. Add the Parmesan, toss vigorously, and serve.

*Serves: 4–6*

*Preparation: 15'*

*Cooking: 10'*

*Level of difficulty: 1*

- **8 small, fresh artichokes**
- **juice of 1 lemon**
- **salt and freshly ground black pepper to taste**
- **4 tbsp extra-virgin olive oil**
- **1 lb/500 g spaghettini**
- **2 oz/60 g Parmesan cheese, in flakes**

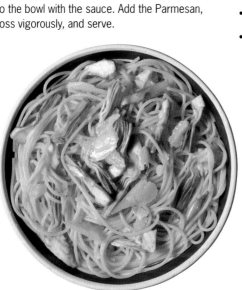

# REGINETTE WITH BASIL SAUCE

*Serves: 4–6*

*Preparation: 15'*

*Cooking: 15'*

*Level of difficulty: 1*

- 2 large potatoes, diced
- 6 oz/180 g green beans, cut in lengths
- 1 lb/500 g reginette
- 50 fresh basil leaves
- 2 tbsp pine nuts
- 4 tbsp freshly grated Parmesan cheese
- 6 tbsp extra-virgin olive oil
- 2 cloves garlic
- salt and freshly ground black pepper to taste

Bring a large pan of salted water to the boil and add the potatoes and beans. Boil for 2–3 minutes, then add the pasta. • Meanwhile chop the basil, pine nuts, cheese, oil, and garlic in a food processor until smooth. • Place in a large serving bowl (large enough to hold the pasta too). Drain the pasta and vegetables, reserving 3 tablespoons of the cooking water to add to the sauce. • Put the pasta, vegetables, and cooking water into the bowl with the sauce and toss vigorously. • Serve hot.

# SPAGHETTI WITH ASPARAGUS

*Serves: 4–6*

*Preparation: 20'*

*Cooking: 45'*

*Level of difficulty: 1*

- 1¹/₂ lb/750 g asparagus
- 4 tbsp extra-virgin olive oil
- 2 cloves garlic, finely chopped
- 1 lb/500 g firm-ripe tomatoes, peeled and seeded
- salt to taste
- 1 lb/500 g spaghetti
- 8 tbsp freshly grated aged Pecorino cheese

Remove the tough woody pieces off the bottoms of the asparagus stalks and peel the rest. Cut into short sections, keeping the tips apart. • Heat the oil in a large frying pan. Sauté the asparagus stalks over medium heat for 5 minutes. • Add the garlic and tomatoes and season with salt. Cover and cook over low heat for 15 minutes. • Add the asparagus tips, and cook for 10 minutes more, or until the asparagus is tender. • Cook the pasta in a large pan of salted, boiling water until al dente. • Drain and add to the asparagus sauce. Sprinkle with the Pecorino, toss well, and serve.

# LINGUINE WITH FAVA BEANS

P od the beans and set aside in a bowl of cold
water. • Cut the cloves of garlic in two and
place in a frying pan with the rosemary, half the
butter, and the oil. Sauté until the garlic begins to
change color. • Remove the garlic and rosemary.
Lower the heat to medium, add the onion, and
sauté until soft. • Drain the fava beans and add to
the frying pan with the stock. Season with salt and
pepper. • Cook over medium-low heat for about 20
minutes, or until the beans are tender, stirring from
time to time. • Cook the linguine in a large pot of
salted, boiling water until al dente. Drain well and
place in a heated serving dish. • Pour the sauce
over the pasta and toss with the Parmesan and the
remaining butter. Serve hot.

*Serves: 4–6*

*Preparation: 20'*

*Cooking: 45'*

*Level of difficulty: 1*

- 3 lb/1.5 kg fava/
  broad beans, in
  their pods
- 2 cloves garlic
- 3 sprigs fresh
  rosemary
- 4 tbsp butter
- 4 tbsp extra-virgin
  olive oil
- 1 large onion, finely
  chopped
- 1 1/2 cups/375 ml
  Beef stock (see
  page 955)
- salt and freshly
  ground black
  pepper to taste
- 1 lb/500 g linguine
- 1/3 cup/45 g
  freshly grated
  Parmesan cheese

# BUCATINI WITH PANCETTA AND SPICY TOMATO SAUCE

Sauté the pancetta and onion in the oil in a large frying pan over medium heat until the onion is transparent. • Add the tomatoes and red pepper flakes. Season with salt and pepper and cook over medium-low heat until they reduce, about 15 minutes. • Meanwhile cook the bucatini in a large pot of salted, boiling water until al dente. Drain and transfer to the frying pan. • Toss with the sauce over medium heat for 2 minutes. • Place in a heated serving dish and sprinkle with the Pecorino. • Serve hot.

| | |
|---|---|
| Serves: | 4–6 |
| Preparation: | 15' |
| Cooking: | 30' |
| Level of difficulty: | 1 |

- 6 oz/180 g pancetta, diced
- 1 onion, finely chopped
- 2 tbsp extra-virgin olive oil
- 1 1/2 lb/750 g tomatoes, canned, and chopped
- 1 tsp red pepper flakes
- salt and freshly ground black pepper to taste
- 1 lb/500 g bucatini
- 1/2 cup/60 g freshly grated Pecorino cheese

# ZITI WITH CHERRY TOMATOES, PESTO, AND RICOTTA CHEESE

Serves: 4–6
Preparation: 20'
Cooking: 45'
Level of difficulty: 1

- 1 lb/500 g ziti
- 1 lb/500 g cherry tomatoes
- 4 tbsp extra-virgin olive oil
- 2 cloves garlic, finely chopped
- 12 oz/350 g very fresh Ricotta cheese, well drained
- 1 quantity Pesto (see page 948)
- salt and freshly ground black pepper to taste
- fresh basil leaves, to garnish

Break the ziti into short lengths and cook them in a large pot of salted, boiling water until al dente. • While the pasta is cooking, rinse the cherry tomatoes and cut them in halves or quarters, depending on their size. • Heat the oil in a large frying pan and sauté the garlic for 2–3 minutes. • Add the tomatoes and cook over low heat for 5 minutes. • Drain the pasta and transfer to a heated serving dish. • Add the Ricotta, pesto, and tomatoes. Season with salt and pepper. • Toss gently, garnish with the basil, and serve.

# ZITI WITH SAUSAGE AND RICOTTA CHEESE

Prick the sausages all over with a toothpick. • Sauté in a pan with the oil, bay leaf, onion, and garlic for 5 minutes. • Drizzle with the wine and cook until it has evaporated. • Add the tomatoes, marjoram, and parsley. Season with salt and pepper cook over medium heat for 25–30 minutes. • Remove the sausages, cut into small pieces, and return to the pan. • Meanwhile, cook the ziti in a large pan of salted, water until al dente. • Drain and transfer to a heated serving dish. Spoon the sauce over and top with the Ricotta. • Serve hot.

*Serves: 4–6*

*Preparation: 20'*

*Cooking: 35'*

*Level of difficulty: 1*

- **14 oz/400 g fresh Italian sausages**
- **2 tbsp extra-virgin olive oil**
- **1 bay leaf**
- **1 onion, finely chopped**
- **2 cloves garlic, chopped finely**
- **$^1/_2$ cup/125 ml white wine**
- **1 lb/500 g coarsely chopped canned tomatoes**
- **1 tbsp finely chopped marjoram**
- **1 tbsp finely chopped parsley**
- **salt and freshly ground black pepper to taste**
- **1 lb/500 g ziti**
- **4 oz/125 g Ricotta cheese, drained**

# BUCATINI WITH TOMATOES, ALMONDS, AND FRIED BREAD

*Serves: 4–6*

*Preparation: 15'*

*Cooking: 20'*

*Level of difficulty: 1*

- **1 medium onion, finely chopped**
- **4 tbsp extra-virgin olive oil**
- **1 lb/500 g coarsely chopped canned tomatoes**
- **salt and freshly ground black pepper to taste**
- **3 oz/90 g almonds**
- **4 thick slices day-old firm-textured bread, cut in cubes**
- **1 lb/500 g bucatini**
- **³/₄ cup/75 g freshly grated Pecorino cheese**

Sweat the onion in a frying pan with 1 tablespoon of oil for 10 minutes. • Add the tomatoes and season with salt and pepper. Cover and cook over low heat for 20–25 minutes. • Toast the almonds in a small frying pan over low heat. Remove from heat and chop coarsely. • Sauté the bread in a frying pan with the remaining oil until crisp and brown. • Cook the bucatini in plenty of salted, boiling water until al dente. Drain and transfer to a heated serving bowl. Pour the sauce over the top. Sprinkle with the almonds, bread, and Pecorino. Serve hot.

# SPAGHETTI WITH ZUCCHINI AND CHEESE

Heat the oil in a large frying pan and sauté the zucchini until golden brown. Drain on paper towels to eliminate excess oil. Set aside in a warm oven. • Melt the butter in a medium saucepan and add the Gorgonzola and cream. Stir with a wooden spoon, mixing in the Ricotta and Parmesan. Cook over very low heat, stirring continuously, until smooth and creamy. Season with salt and pepper. • Meanwhile, cook the pasta in a large pan of salted, boiling water until al dente. • Transfer to the pan with the cheese sauce and sauté over high heat for a few moments, tossing gently. • Add the zucchini and remove from heat. • Dust with pepper and serve immediately.

Serves: 4–6

Preparation: 20'

Cooking: 20'

Level of difficulty: 1

- 4 tbsp extra-virgin olive oil
- 1 1/4 lb/600 g zucchini/ courgettes, cut in thin rounds
- 1 tbsp butter
- 5 oz/150 g Gorgonzola cheese, chopped
- 3/4 cup/200 ml fresh heavy/double cream
- 3 1/2 oz/100 g Ricotta cheese, drained
- 1/3 cup/50 g freshly grated Parmesan cheese
- 1 lb/500 g spaghetti
- salt and freshly ground white pepper to taste

# BUCATINI WITH SPICY BROCCOLI SAUCE

*Serves: 4–6*

*Preparation: 15'*

*Cooking: 30'*

*Level of difficulty: 1*

- 2 heads broccoli, weighing about 1¹/₄ lb/600 g
- 1 lb/500 g bucatini
- 6 tbsp extra-virgin olive oil
- 4 tbsp finely chopped parsley
- 4 tbsp finely chopped basil
- 2 cloves garlic, finely chopped
- 1–2 dried chile peppers, crumbled
- pinch of ground cinnamon
- ³/₄ cup/75 g freshly grated Pecorino cheese
- salt to taste

Divide the broccoli into small florets and chop the stalks into small cubes. • Cook in a large pan of salted, boiling water for 10 minutes, or until tender. • Drain the broccoli, reserving the cooking water. • Return the water to the pan and add the pasta. • Meanwhile, heat the oil in a large frying pan and sauté the parsley, basil, garlic, and chile pepper over high heat for 3–4 minutes. • Sprinkle with the cinnamon and add the broccoli. Simmer for a few minutes over medium heat, stirring often. • Drain the pasta when cooked al dente, and transfer to the pan. Sauté for 2–3 minutes, tossing gently. • Sprinkle with the Pecorino and serve immediately.

# SPAGHETTINI WITH BOTTARGA

Boil the spaghettini in a large pan of salted, boiling water until it is cooked al dente. • Drain well and toss quickly in a large frying pan with the garlic, parsley, and oil. • Sprinkle with the bottarga, season with pepper, and serve hot.

*Serves: 4–6*

*Preparation: 10'*

*Cooking: 10–15'*

*Level of difficulty: 1*

- 1 lb/500 g spaghettini
- 2 cloves garlic, finely chopped
- 2 tbsp finely chopped parsley
- $3/4$ cup/200 ml extra-virgin olive oil
- $1^1/_2$ oz/45 g of freshly grated bottarga (dried mullet or tuna roe)
- freshly ground black pepper to taste

# BUCATINI WITH BREAD CRUMBS

*Serves: 4–6*

*Preparation: 15'*

*Cooking: 15'*

*Level of difficulty: 1*

- ¹/₂ cup/125 ml extra-virgin olive oil
- 10 anchovy fillets
- 1 lb/500 g bucatini
- 4 oz/125 g fine dry bread crumbs
- 1 tbsp each capers and chopped black olives
- salt and freshly ground black pepper to taste

Heat half the oil in a small, heavy-bottomed pan and add the anchovies. Stir until they dissolve into the oil. • Cook the pasta in a large pot of salted, boiling water until al dente. • Heat the remaining oil in another pan and toast the bread crumbs in it for 5 minutes. • Drain the pasta and place in a heated serving dish. Add the bread crumbs, capers, olives, and oil and toss. Drizzle with the anchovy sauce. Toss again and serve.

# BAVETTE WITH OCTOPUS AND ZUCCHINI

U se a sharp knife to chop the octopus into small pieces. • Heat 4 tablespoons of oil in a large frying pan and sauté the garlic for 2–3 minutes. • Add the octopus, cover, and cook over medium-low heat for 25 minutes, stirring often. • Add the zucchini, parsley, and stock to the pan and cook for 15 minutes. Season with salt and pepper.
• Cook the bavette in a large pan of salted, boiling water until *al dente*. • Drain well and add to the pan with the octopus. • Season with a generous grinding of pepper and the remaining oil. Toss gently and serve hot.

Serves: 4–6
Preparation: 25'
Cooking: 50'
Level of difficulty: 1

- 1 1/4 lb/600 g octopus, cleaned
- 6 tbsp extra-virgin olive oil
- 3 cloves garlic, finely chopped
- 10 oz/300 g zucchini/courgettes, cut in half lengthwise and thinly sliced
- 2 tbsp finely chopped parsley
- salt and freshly ground black pepper to taste
- 1/2 cup/125 ml Vegetable Stock (see page 956)
- 1 lb/500 g bavette

# SPAGHETTI WITH TUNA AND TOMATO SAUCE

Sauté the garlic and parsley n the oil in a large frying pan over medium-low heat for 2 minutes. • Add the tomatoes, season with salt, and cook for 4–5 minutes. • Mix in the tuna, stir, and turn off the heat immediately. • Cook the spaghetti in a large pot of salted, boiling water until al dente. • Drain well and transfer to a heated serving dish. Toss gently with the sauce and serve hot.

*Serves: 4–6*

*Preparation: 15'*

*Cooking: 15'*

*Level of difficulty: 1*

- $1/2$ cup/125 ml) extra-virgin olive oil
- 2 cloves garlic, finely chopped
- 3 tbsp finely chopped parsley
- 24 cherry tomatoes, cut in half
- 8 oz/250 g tuna packed in oil, drained and flaked
- salt to taste
- 1 lb/500 g spaghetti

# LINGUINE WITH MINT AND LEMON

U se a sharp knife to remove the lemon zest (outer, yellow part only) in a long spiral.
• Blanch the lemon zest in boiling water for 2 minutes. Drain and slice very thinly. • Squeeze the lemon juice and set aside. • Place the tomatoes, lemon zest, lemon juice, mint, salt, chile pepper, if using, and oil in a large serving bowl. • Set the sauce aside for 1 hour to flavor.
• Cook the linguine in a large pan of salted, boiling water until *al dente*. • Drain the pasta and place under cold running water to cool. • Drain well and add to the bowl with the sauce. Toss gently and serve.

*Serves: 4–6*

*Preparation: 15' + 1 h to rest the sauce*

*Cooking: 15'*

*Level of difficulty: 1*

- **1 untreated lemon**
- **1 lb/500 g cherry tomatoes**
- **20 mint leaves, torn**
- **salt and freshly ground white pepper to taste**
- **1 fresh chile pepper, sliced (optional)**
- **1 lb/500 g linguine**
- **2 scallions/spring onions, cleaned and very thinly sliced**

# FESTONATI WITH GARLIC, BELL PEPPERS, AND ZUCCHINI

Serves: 4–6

Preparation: 20'

Cooking: 1 h

Level of difficulty: 1

- 1 head fresh garlic
- 1¼ lb/600 g zucchini/ courgettes
- 6 tbsp extra-virgin olive oil
- salt and freshly ground black pepper to taste
- ½ red bell + ½ yellow bell pepper/ capsicum, cleaned and cut into small pieces
- 4 tomatoes, peeled, seeded, and chopped
- 1 lb/500 g festonati
- 1–2 tbsp finely chopped fresh herbs (thyme, marjoram, basil)

Preheat the oven to 300°F/150°C/gas 2. • Wrap the garlic in aluminum foil and bake for about 45 minutes. • Trim the zucchini, cut in half, remove the seeds, and slice into small pieces. • Heat 3 tablespoons of oil in a large frying pan and sauté the zucchini for 3 minutes. Season with salt and pepper. • Add a ladleful of hot water from the pasta pan, cover, and cook over low heat for 10 minutes. • Unwrap the garlic and mash in a small bowl.• Add the garlic, remaining oil, bell peppers, and tomatoes to the zucchini and sauté over medium-high heat for 5 minutes. • Meanwhile, cook the pasta in a large pan of salted, boiling water until al dente. • Drain the pasta and transfer to the pan with the sauce. • Toss gently, sprinkle with the herbs, and serve.

# SPAGHETTI WITH SCAMPI AND OLIVE PESTO

Place the pine nuts in a large frying pan over medium-high heat and toast until golden brown. Do not add any oil or other fat to the pan; the pine nuts will brown beautifully without it. • Chop almost all the olives (reserve a few whole to garnish), 4 tablespoons of pine nuts, the parsley, and 6 tablespoons of oil in a food processor until smooth. Season with salt and pepper. • Heat the remaining oil in a large frying pan and sauté the scampi pieces and garlic over high heat for 5 minutes. • Meanwhile, cook the spaghetti in a large pan of salted, boiling water until al dente. • Drain well and add to the pan with the scampi. Add the pesto, reserved whole olives, and remaining pine nuts and toss gently over medium heat for 2–3 minutes. • Serve hot.

*Serves: 4–6*

*Preparation: 20'*

*Cooking: 20'*

*Level of difficulty: 1*

- **6 tbsp pine nuts**
- **4 oz/125 g pitted black olives**
- **large bunch fresh parsley**
- **$1/2$ cup/125 ml extra-virgin olive oil**
- **salt and freshly ground black pepper to taste**
- **12 scampi, shelled, deveined, and cut in sections**
- **1 clove garlic, finely chopped**
- **1 lb/500 g spaghetti**

46

# LINGUINE WITH DRIED TOMATOES AND CAPERS

Cut the fresh tomatoes in half or in quarters and squeeze them gently to remove the seeds. Sprinkle lightly with salt and leave to drain for 10 minutes. • Heat the oil in a heavy-bottomed saucepan over low heat. Add the dried tomatoes and cook over low heat for a few minutes before adding the fresh tomatoes, capers, garlic, and pepper flakes. Season with salt. Simmer for 20 minutes. • Cook the spaghetti in a large pan of salted, boiling water until al dente. • Drain and place in a heated serving dish. Toss with the tomato sauce and serve hot.

*Serves: 4–6*

*Preparation: 20'*

*Cooking: 35'*

*Level of difficulty: 1*

- **2 lb/1 kg tomatoes, peeled**
- **salt to taste**
- **4 oz/125 g dried tomatoes, finely chopped**
- **1 lb/500 g linguine**
- **4 tbsp capers**
- **1 clove garlic, peeled but whole**
- **6 tbsp extra-virgin olive oil**
- **$1/2$ tsp red pepper flakes**

# ZITI WITH LEEKS AND TOMATOES

*Serves: 4–6*

*Preparation: 25'*

*Cooking: 40'*

*Level of difficulty: 1*

- 4 tbsp extra-virgin olive oil
- 2 cloves garlic, finely chopped
- 2 large leeks, thinly sliced
- 1 1/2 lb/750 g tomatoes, peeled and chopped
- salt and freshly ground black pepper to taste
- 1 lb/500 g ziti
- 7 oz/200 g Scamorza (or other smoked) cheese, diced

Heat the oil in a large frying pan and sauté the garlic for 2–3 minutes. Add the leeks and sauté for 5 more minutes. • Add the tomatoes and season with salt and pepper. Cook over medium-low heat for 25–30 minutes, or until reduced. • Cook the pasta in a large pan of salted, boiling water until al dente. • Drain well and add to the pan with the cheese. • Toss gently over medium heat for 1–2 minutes. • Serve hot.

49

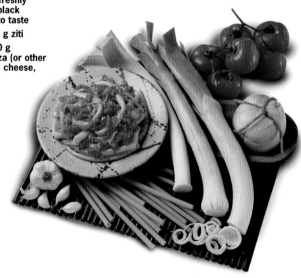

# BUCATINI WITH SWORDFISH AND HERBS

Clean the swordfish, removing the skin and the large central bone. Cut into bite-sized pieces.
• Place in a large flat-bottomed bowl and drizzle with the lemon juice. Set aside for 5 minutes.
• Heat the oil in a large frying pan and sauté the garlic, parsley, fennel seeds, and chile pepper for 3–4 minutes. • Add the swordfish and pistachios. Season with salt and place over high heat until the pieces of fish are cooked. • Meanwhile, cook the pasta is a pan of salted, boiling water until al dente.
• Drain well and add to the pan with the swordfish.
• Toss gently over medium heat for 2 minutes.
• Serve hot.

*Serves: 4–6*

*Preparation: 20'*

*Cooking: 20'*

*Level of difficulty: 1*

- **1 large thick slice of swordfish, weighing about 1 lb/500 g**
- **juice of 2 lemons**
- **6 tbsp extra-virgin olive oil**
- **2 cloves garlic, finely chopped**
- **2 tbsp finely chopped parsley**
- **1 tsp fennel seeds, lightly crushed**
- **1 red chile pepper, sliced**
- **4 tbsp pistachios**
- **salt to taste**
- **1 lb/500 g bucatini**

# BAVETTE WITH SALMON AND LIME

Serves: 4–6
Preparation: 10'
Cooking: 15'
Level of difficulty: 1

Cook the pasta in a large pan of salted, boiling water until al dente. • Meanwhile, heat the oil in a large frying pan over high heat. Sauté the garlic, chile pepper, and parsley for 2–3 minutes. • Add the salmon and sauté for 5 minutes. • Drain the pasta and add to the frying pan. • Add the lime juice and zest and season with salt and pepper. • Toss gently and serve.

52

- 1 lb/500 g bavette
- 4 tbsp extra-virgin olive oil
- 2 cloves garlic, finely chopped
- 1 chile pepper
- 1 tbsp finely chopped parsley
- 12 oz/350 g fresh salmon fillets, cut in thin strips
- juice and finely grated zest of $1^1/_2$ limes
- salt and freshly ground black pepper to taste

Serves: 4–6

Preparation: 15'

Cooking: 20'

Level of difficulty: 1

- **large bunch wild fennel**
- **5 tbsp extra-virgin olive oil**
- **1 large onion, finely chopped**
- **4–6 strand saffron, crumbled**
- **4 tbsp raisins**
- **4 tbsp pine nuts**
- **salt and freshly ground black pepper to taste**
- **8 oz/250 g fresh sardines, cleaned, heads removed**
- **1 lb/500 g bavette**

# BAVETTE WITH SARDINES

Cook the wild fennel in a large pan of salted, boiling water for 10 minutes. Drain, reserving the cooking water. • Heat the oil in a large frying pan and sauté the onion and saffron for 7–8 minutes, or until the onion is soft. • Add the raisins, pine nuts, salt, and pepper and sauté for 5 minutes. • Add the sardines and a little of the reserved cooking water and cook for 5 more minutes, stirring often. • Cook the pasta in the reserved cooking water until al dente. Drain and add to the pan. • Toss gently and serve.

# HOT AND SPICY
# SPAGHETTI FRITTATA

*Serves: 4–6*

*Preparation: 25' + 30'
    to drain Mozzarella*

*Cooking: 35'*

*Level of difficulty: 1*

- 8 oz/250 g
  **Mozzarella cheese**
- **salt and freshly
  ground black
  pepper to taste**
- 6 tbsp **extra-virgin
  olive oil**
- 2 cloves **garlic,
  finely chopped**
- 1 lb/500 g
  **tomatoes, peeled
  and coarsely
  chopped**
- small bunch of
  **basil, chopped**
- 3 oz/90 g **spicy
  salami, peeled and
  cut in thin slices or
  small cubes**
- 1 lb/500 g
  **spaghetti**
- 5 **eggs**
- 2 tbsp **finely
  chopped parsley**
- $^1/_2$ cup/60 g
  **freshly grated
  Pecorino cheese**

Slice the Mozzarella and place in a colander. Sprinkle with salt and let drain for 30 minutes.
• Heat half the oil in a large frying pan and sauté the garlic for 3–4 minutes. • Add the tomatoes, season with salt and pepper, and cook over medium heat for 10 minutes. • Stir in the basil.
• Meanwhile, cook the spaghetti in a large pan of salted, boiling water until al dente. • While the pasta is cooking, beat the eggs in a large bowl with the parsley, and half the Pecorino. Season with salt and pepper. • Drain the spaghetti and run quickly under cold water. Drain well and add to the bowl with the eggs. Add the tomato sauce and toss well.
• Heat the remaining oil in a large frying pan. Add half the spaghetti mixture, spreading it evenly over the bottom of the pan. • Cover with the salami, Mozzarella, and remaining Pecorino. Top with the remaining spaghetti mixture and cook over medium-low heat for about 5 minutes, or until the egg is hardening and the bottom is becoming crispy. • Use a plate to help you turn the frittata and cook on the other side. • Serve hot or at room temperature.

# LINGUINE WITH PESTO AND BAKED CHERRY TOMATOES

Preheat the oven to 350° F/180° C/gas 4. •
Place the cherry tomatoes on a baking sheet,
sliced side up, and drizzle with 2 tablespoons of
oil. Lightly dust with salt and pepper. • Bake for
15 minutes. • Chop the basil, Parmesan, garlic,
almonds, and remaining oil in a food processor
until smooth. Season with salt and pepper.
• Cook the pasta in a large pan of salted, boiling
water until al dente. • Drain well and place in a
heated serving dish. • Add the pesto and baked
tomatoes and toss gently. • Serve hot.

*Serves: 4–6*

*Preparation: 25'*

*Cooking: 30'*

*Level of difficulty: 1*

- 1$^1$/$_2$ lb/750 g cherry tomatoes, cut in half
- 6 tbsp extra-virgin olive oil
- salt and freshly ground white pepper to taste
- 2 oz/60 g fresh basil
- $^1$/$_2$ cup/60 g freshly grated Parmesan cheese
- 2 cloves garlic, peeled
- 1$^1$/$_2$ oz/45 g peeled almonds
- 1 lb/500 g linguine

# BUCATINI WITH TOMATO AND ONION SAUCE

Heat the oil in a large frying pan and sauté the onions for 5 minutes. Add the pancetta and sauté for 5 more minutes. • Add the tomatoes and cook for 10 minutes. • Pour in the wine, season with salt and pepper, and cook for 10 more minutes. • Cover and cook over medium-low heat for about 1 hour, stirring frequently. • Cook the pasta in a large pan of salted, boiling water until al dente. Drain well and transfer to a heated serving dish. • Pour the sauce over the top. Toss well and serve hot.

*Serves: 4–6*

*Preparation: 25'*

*Cooking: 1 h 30'*

*Level of difficulty: 1*

- **4 tbsp extra-virgin olive oil**
- **1¹/₄ lb/600 g onions, cut in thin rings**
- **1 lb/500 g ripe tomatoes, peeled and chopped**
- **5 oz/150 g pancetta, diced**
- **salt and freshly ground black pepper to taste**
- **¹/₂ cup/125 ml dry red wine**
- **1 lb/500 g bucatini**

# BAVETTE WITH BROCCOLI AND PINE NUTS

*Serves: 4–6*

*Preparation: 25'*

*Cooking: 30'*

*Level of difficulty: 1*

- 1$^1$/$_2$ lb/750 g broccoli
- $^1$/$_2$ cup/125 ml extra-virgin olive oil
- 2 cloves garlic, finely chopped
- 8 tbsp pine nuts
- 1–2 dried chile peppers, crumbled
- salt to taste
- 1 lb/500 g bavette

Rinse the broccoli and divide into small florets. •
Heat the oil in a large frying pan and sauté the
garlic until pale gold. • Add the pine nuts, chile
pepper, and salt and cook over low heat. •
Meanwhile cook the pasta in a large pan of salted,
boiling water. • About 5 minutes before the pasta
is cooked, add the broccoli. • Drain the pasta and
broccoli together when the pasta is cooked al
dente. Place in a heated serving dish. • Pour the
sauce over the top. Toss well and serve.

# FESTONATI WITH VEGETABLES

Heat the butter in a medium frying pan and sauté the leeks for 3–4 minutes. • Add the water, season with salt and pepper, and cook for about 10 minutes, or until the leeks are very tender. • Add the cream and leave over very low heat. The sauce should thicken and reduce as you cook the other vegetables and the pasta. • Clean the artichoke by trimming the stem, pulling down and snapping off all the tough outer leaves, and cutting off the top third of the leaves. Cut in half and remove any fuzzy choke with a sharp knife. Cut in small cubes. • Heat the oil in a large frying pan and sauté the garlic, artichoke, zucchini, and carrot over medium heat for 10 minutes, or until tender. • Meanwhile, cook the pasta in a large pan of salted, boiling water until al dente. • Drain and add to the pan with the artichoke mixture. Add the leeks sauce and toss gently over low heat for 2–3 minutes. • Serve hot with the Parmesan passed separately.

*Serves: 4–6*

*Preparation: 30'*

*Cooking: 30'*

*Level of difficulty: 1*

- 3 tbsp butter
- 2 large leeks, thinly sliced
- 4 tbsp water
- salt and freshly ground black pepper to taste
- ³/₄ cup/180 ml heavy/double cream
- 3 tbsp extra-virgin olive oil
- 2 cloves garlic, finely chopped
- 1 artichoke
- 2 zucchini/ courgettes, diced
- 1 carrot, diced
- 1 lb/500 g festonati
- 4–8 tbsp freshly grated Parmesan cheese

# PASTA WITH BEANS AND BROCCOLI

S oak the beans overnight in a large bowl of cold water. • Drain and cook in a large saucepan of water with the bay leave, 1 clove of garlic, the celery, and 2 tomatoes for 1–2 hours, or until tender. Season with salt 5 minutes before removing from the heat. • Drain the beans, removing the bay leaf, celery, garlic, and tomato skins. Set aside. • Heat 2 tablespoons of oil in a large frying pan and sauté the chopped garlic for 2–3 minutes. Add the tomatoes. Season with salt and pepper and cook over medium heat for 10–15 minutes. • Cook the broccoli in a pan of salted, boiling water for 8–10 minutes, or until tender but still crunchy. Drain well and set aside. • Cook the pasta in a large pan of salted, boiling water until very al dente (2–3 minutes less than the cooking time indicated on the package). • Drain the pasta. • Heat the remaining oil in a small frying pan and fry a cupful of pasta over high heat until browned and crispy. • Meanwhile, place the remaining pasta in the pan with the tomato sauce. Add the beans and broccoli and toss gently for 2–3 minutes. • Divide the pasta and sauce among 4–6 individual serving dishes and top each one with a little of the fried pasta mixture • Serve hot.

*Serves: 4–6*

*Preparation: 30' + time to soak beans*

*Cooking: 30' + 1–2 h to cook beans*

*Level of difficulty: 2*

- **12 oz/350 g dried cannellini or white kidney beans**
- **1 bay leaf**
- **2 cloves garlic, 1 whole and 1 finely chopped**
- **1 stalk celery**
- **12 tomatoes, 2 whole, and 10 peeled and chopped**
- **salt and freshly ground black pepper to taste**
- **4 tbsp extra-virgin olive oil**
- **1 lb/500 g broccoli, in small florets**
- **1 lb/500 g spaghettini or dried tagliolini**

# SPAGHETTI WITH ARUGULA, CHILE, AND GARLIC

C ook the spaghetti in a large pan of salted,
boiling water for 10 minutes. • Add the arugula
and continue cooking until the pasta is al dente. •
While the pasta is cooking, heat the oil in a large
frying pan and sauté the garlic, chile peppers, and
anchovies, if using, for 2–3 minutes. Do not let the
garlic burn. • Drain the pasta and arugula and add
to the pan with the garlic and oil. Season with salt.
• Toss gently and serve hot.

*Serves: 4–6*

*Preparation: 15'*

*Cooking: 15'*

*Level of difficulty: 1*

- **1 lb/500 g spaghetti**
- **1 large bunch arugula/rocket**
- **6 tbsp extra-virgin olive oil**
- **4 cloves garlic, finely chopped**
- **1–2 dried chile peppers, crumbled**
- **4–6 anchovy fillets**
- **salt to taste**

64

# SPAGHETTI WITH LEMON AND BOTTARGA

Serves: 4–6
Preparation: 20'
Cooking: 15'
Level of difficulty: 1

- 1 lemon
- 4 tbsp butter
- 2 oz/60 g bottarga
- scant $^1/_2$ cup/ 100 ml Vegetable Stock (see page 956)
- 1 lb/500 g spaghetti
- 2 tbsp salted capers, rinsed
- 1 tbsp finely chopped marjoram

Peel the lemon. Place the peel in a small pan of water and bring to a boil. Remove from heat and cut in thin strips. • Cut the fruit into thin wedges. • Melt the butter in a large frying pan and add the bottarga. Drizzle with stock and cook for 5 minutes over medium-low heat. • Meanwhile, cook the pasta in a large pan of salted, boiling water until al dente. • Drain and add to the pan with the bottarga.• Add the lemon peel and wedges, capers, and marjoram. Season with salt. • Toss gently for 2 minutes. • Serve hot.

# SPAGHETTI PUGLIA-STYLE

Heat the oil in a large frying pan to very hot. Add the chile peppers and a tomato and cook for 2–3 minutes. • Add all the tomatoes one by one, cooking each one as you go. Season with salt and pepper and remove the chile peppers. • Cook the pasta in a large pan of salted, boiling water until al dente. • Drain the pasta and add to the pan with the tomatoes. • Add the basil and Pecorino, toss well, and serve immediately.

Serves: 4–6

Preparation: 20'

Cooking: 30'

Level of difficulty: 1

- $^1/_2$ cup/125 ml extra-virgin olive oil
- 2 large red chile peppers, whole
- 2 lb/1 kg San Marzano (oval) tomatoes, peeled, seeded, and cut in half lengthwise
- salt and freshly ground black pepper to taste
- 1 lb/500 g spaghetti
- 10 leaves basil, torn
- 1 cup/120 g freshly grated aged Pecorino cheese

# ZITI WITH TOMATO AND GREEN BEANS

Cook the beans in a large pan of salted, boiling water. • After about 5 minutes, add the ziti and cook until the pasta is al dente and the beans are tender. • Drain well and toss with the tomato sauce. • Garnish with the Ricotta salata and serve.

*Serves: 4–6*

*Preparation: 15' + time to make Tomato sauce*

*Cooking: 15'*

*Level of difficulty:1*

- 1 quantity Tomato Sauce (see page 950)
- 2 lb/1 kg green beans, cleaned
- 1 lb/500 g ziti
- 2 oz/60 g Ricotta salata, in flakes, to serve

# BUCATINI WITH EGGS AND ARTICHOKES

*Serves: 4–6*

*Preparation: 20'*

*Cooking: 35'*

*Level of difficulty: 1*

- **4 tbsp extra-virgin olive oil**
- **1 onion, finely chopped**
- **3 oz/90 g pancetta, thinly sliced**
- **4 artichokes**
- **salt to taste**
- **1 cup/250 ml dry white wine**
- **1 cup/250 ml water**
- **2 eggs**
- **1 lb/500 g bucatini**
- **1/2 cup/60 g freshly grated Pecorino cheese**

Heat the oil in a large frying pan and sauté the onion and pancetta for 5 minutes. • Clean the artichokes as explained on page 20. Slice thinly. • Add the artichokes to the pan and cook for 10 minutes. • Add the wine and cook until it has evaporated. • Season with salt and add the water. Cook for 15 minutes, or until the artichokes are tender. • Cook the pasta in a large pan of salted, boiling water until al dente. • Meanwhile, beat the eggs in a small bowl with salt. • Drain the pasta and add to the pan with the artichoke sauce. Add the eggs and Pecorino, toss over high heat for 3 minutes, and serve.

# SPAGHETTI WITH MEATBALLS

Prepare the tomato sauce. • Place the beef in a bowl and stir in the onion, egg, parsley, salt, and pepper. Mix well and shape into balls about the size of small walnuts. • Roll the balls in the flour. • Heat the oil in a large frying pan and fry the meatballs over medium-high heat for 10 minutes, or until browned all over. • Add the tomato sauce and basil to the pan and cook for 10–15 minutes more over low heat heat. • Meanwhile, cook the spaghetti in a large pan of salted, boiling water until al dente. • Drain the pasta and add to the pan with the meatball sauce. Toss over medium heat for 2–3 minutes. • Serve hot with the Parmesan sprinkled over the top.

Serves: 4–6

Preparation: 25' + time to make sauce

Cooking: 30'

Level of difficulty: 1

- 1 quantity Tomato Sauce (see page 950)
- 1 lb/500 g ground lean beef
- 1 small onion, finely chopped
- 1 egg
- 2 tbsp finely chopped parsley
- salt and freshly ground black pepper to taste
- 1/2 cup/75 g all-purpose/plain flour
- 6 tbsp extra-virgin olive oil
- fresh basil leaves
- 1 lb/500 g spaghetti
- 6 tbsp freshly grated Parmesan cheese

# SPAGHETTI WITH FRIED EGGS

Cook the spaghetti in a large pan of salted, boiling water until al dente. • While the pasta is cooking, heat 2 tablespoons of oil in a large frying pan and fry the eggs. • Drain the pasta and toss in a heated bowl with the cheese and remaining oil. Season with salt and pepper. • Divide the pasta among 4–6 individual serving dishes. Top each dish with an egg and serve.

*Serves: 4–6*

*Preparation: 10'*

*Cooking: 15'*

*Level of difficulty: 1*

- 1 lb/500 g spaghetti
- 4–6 tbsp extra-virgin olive oil
- 4–6 eggs
- 1/2 cup/60 g freshly grated Parmesan cheese
- salt and freshly ground black pepper to taste

# SPAGHETTI WITH SPICY CHERRY TOMATO SAUCE

*Serves: 4–6*

*Preparation: 15'*

*Cooking: 20'*

*Level of difficulty: 1*

- 2 lb/1 kg cherry tomatoes, cut in half
- 1 lb/500 g spaghetti
- $^1/_2$ tsp red pepper flakes
- fresh basil leaves, torn
- $^1/_2$ cup/125 ml extra-virgin olive oil
- salt and freshly ground black pepper to taste

Place the tomatoes in a bowl with the garlic, pepper flakes, and basil. • Heat the oil in a large frying pan over high heat and add the contents of the bowl. Cook for 5–6 minutes, gently stirring with a wooden spoon at frequent intervals. Season with salt and remove from heat. • Cook the spaghetti in a large pot of salted, boiling water for about 8–10 minutes. • Drain the spaghetti and add to the tomato mixture in the pan. Cook for about 5 minutes more over high heat, stirring well, so that the tomato sauce is absorbed by the pasta as it finishes cooking. • Serve at once.

# SPAGHETTI WITH PESTO AND SUMMER VEGETABLES

Serves: 4–6

Preparation: 15'

Cooking: 25'

Level of difficulty: 1

- **4 tbsp extra-virgin olive oil**
- **3 zucchini/ courgettes, diced**
- **1 yellow bell pepper/capsicum, cleaned and diced**
- **6 large tomatoes, diced**
- **1 red chile pepper, sliced**
- **salt and freshly ground black pepper to taste**
- **1 lb/500 g spaghetti**
- **1 quantity Pesto (see page 948)**

Heat the oil in a large frying pan and sauté the bell pepper and zucchini for 5 minutes over high heat. • Add the tomatoes and chile pepper and season with salt and pepper. Sauté for 10 minutes, or until the vegetables are tender. • Cook the spaghetti in a large pan of salted, boiling water until al dente. • Drain the pasta and add to the pan with the vegetables. Add the pesto and toss over medium heat for 2 minutes. • Serve hot.

# LINGUINE WITH TOMATOES AND CAPERS

Heat the oil in a large frying pan and sauté the onion, capers, and oregano for 5 minutes, or until the onions have softened. • Add the tomatoes, chile pepper, and parsley. Season with salt and pepper. Cook for 15 minutes, or until the tomatoes have reduced. • Cook the spaghetti in a large pan of salted, boiling water until al dente. • Drain the pasta and toss with the sauce in the pan for 2 minutes. • Serve hot.

*Serves: 4–6*

*Preparation: 15'*

*Cooking: 15'*

*Level of difficulty: 1*

- **4 tbsp extra-virgin olive oil**
- **1 onion, finely chopped**
- **4 tbsp salted capers, rinsed**
- **1 tsp dried oregano**
- **6 large tomatoes, peeled and chopped**
- **1 chile pepper, finely chopped**
- **2 tbsp finely chopped parsley**
- **1 lb/500 g linguine**
- **salt and freshly ground black pepper to taste**

# SPAGHETTI WITH PANCETTA

Serves: 4–6

Preparation: 15'

Cooking: 25'

Level of difficulty: 1

- 6 oz/180 g pancetta, cut in thin strips
- 2 cloves garlic, finely chopped
- 5 oz/150 g day-old bread, cut in cubes
- 4 tbsp extra-virgin olive oil
- 1 lb/500 g spaghetti
- 2 tbsp finely chopped parsley
- salt and freshly ground black pepper to taste
- 1 cup/120 g freshly grated Pecorino cheese (optional)

Place the pancetta and garlic in a large non-stick frying pan and sauté until crisp. Scoop the pancetta out of the pan and keep warm. • Place the bread in the pan with 2 tablespoons of oil and cook until golden brown. • Meanwhile, cook the spaghetti in a large pan of salted, boiling water until al dente. • Drain the pasta and add to the pan with the bread. Add the pancetta, parsley, remaining oil, and Pecorino, if using. Season with salt and pepper. Toss over medium heat for 2 minutes. • Serve hot.

# BAVETTE WITH MUSHROOMS

Clean the mushrooms carefully and cut the larger ones into small pieces. • Sauté the onion in the oil in a frying pan, covered, over low heat for 20 minutes. Season with salt and add the garlic and chile. • Increase the heat and pour in the wine. • Add the mushrooms and sauté over high heat for a few minutes. • Stir in the tomatoes, basil, and parsley and cook for about 10 minutes. Season with salt. • Cook for about 10 minutes, or until the mushrooms are tender. • Cook the pasta in salted boiling water until al dente. Drain and add to the pan with the sauce. • Toss gently for 2 minutes and serve hot.

*Serves: 4–6*

*Preparation: 30'*

*Cooking: 40'*

*Level of difficulty: 1*

- 1 lb/500 g mixed mushrooms (porcini, shitaake, champignons, etc)
- 1 onion, finely chopped
- 4 tbsp extra-virgin olive oil
- salt to taste
- 2 cloves garlic, finely chopped
- 1 dried hot chile pepper, crumbled
- 4 tbsp dry white wine
- 12 cherry tomatoes, coarsely chopped
- 1 bunch fresh basil, torn
- 1 tbsp finely chopped parsley
- 1 lb/500 g bavette or other long pasta

# BAVETTE WITH ASPARAGUS, PANCETTA, AND GINGER

*Serves: 4–6*

*Preparation: 15'*

*Cooking: 20'*

*Level of difficulty: 1*

- 1 lb/500 g asparagus
- 4 tbsp extra-virgin olive oil
- 3 oz/90 g diced pancetta
- $^1/_2$ tbsp finely grated fresh ginger
- salt to taste
- 1 lb/500 g bavette
- $^1/_2$ cup/60 g freshly grated Parmesan cheese

Trim the tough bottoms off the asparagus stalks. • Cook in salted, boiling water for 10 minutes, or until tender. • Chop into short lengths. • Heat the oil in a large frying pan and sauté the pancetta and ginger for 5 minutes. • Add the asparagus and cook for 5 minutes. Season with salt. • Meanwhile, cook the spaghetti in a large pan of salted, boiling water until al dente. • Drain the pasta and add to the pan with the asparagus and pancetta. Toss over medium heat for 2–3 minutes. • Serve hot with the Parmesan sprinkled over the top.

# SPAGHETTI WITH SEAFOOD

Scrub the mussels and clams and soak them in cold water for 1 hour. • Clean the squid and cuttlefish. Chop the bodies into rounds and the tentacles into short pieces. • Do not peel the shrimp tails. • Pour 3 tablespoons of the oil into a large frying pan, add the mussels and clams, and steam open over medium heat. This will take about 10 minutes. Discard any that have not opened.
• Heat 6 tablespoons of the oil in a large frying pan and sauté the garlic, parsley, and red pepper flakes for 2 minutes over medium heat, taking care not to brown. • Add the squid and cuttlefish. Season with salt and pepper, cook briefly, then add the wine.
• Cook for 12 minutes, then add the shrimp tails.
• After 5 minutes add the clams and mussels (if preferred, extract the mollusks from their shells, leaving just a few in the shell to make the finished dish look more attractive). Mix well and cook for 2 minutes more. Turn off the heat, cover, and set aside. • Meanwhile, cook the spaghetti in a large pan of salted, boiling water until al dente. Drain, and add to the pan with the seafood sauce. Toss for 1–2 minutes over medium-high heat. • Transfer to a heated dish and serve immediately.

*Serves: 4–6*

*Preparation: 30' + time to soak shellfish*

*Cooking: 15'*

*Level of difficulty: 1*

- 10 oz/300 g each clams and mussels in shell
- 10 oz/300 g squid, cleaned and dried
- 10 oz/300 g cuttlefish
- 10 oz/300 g shrimp/prawn tails, washed and dried
- $1/2$ cup/125 ml extra-virgin olive oil
- 2 cloves garlic, finely chopped
- 3 tbsp finely chopped parsley
- 1 tsp red pepper flakes
- $1/2$ cup/125 ml dry white wine
- salt and freshly ground black pepper to taste
- 1 lb/500 g spaghetti

# LONG FUSILLI WITH LEEKS

Prepare the leeks by discarding the outer leaves and cutting off almost all the green part. Slice in thin wheels. Set aside. • Combine the butter, oil, onion, and garlic in a frying pan and sauté over medium heat until the onion turns pale gold. Add the pancetta and stir until it browns. • Add the leeks and boiling water and simmer over low heat until the leeks are very tender. Season with salt and pepper. • Add the egg yolks and sugar and stir vigorously. Remove from heat. • Cook the fusilli in a large pot of salted, boiling water until al dente. Drain well and transfer to a heated serving dish. Toss with the sauce and sprinkle with Pecorino. • Serve hot.

Serves: 4–6
Preparation: 10'
Cooking: 20'
Level of difficulty: 1

- 10 leeks
- 2 tbsp butter
- 4 tbsp extra-virgin olive oil
- 1 onion, finely chopped
- 2 cloves garlic, finely chopped
- 4 oz/125 g pancetta, diced
- 1 cup/250 ml boiling water
- salt and freshly ground black pepper to taste
- 2 egg yolks
- dash of sugar
- 1 lb/500 g fusilli lunghi
- 6 tbsp freshly grated Pecorino cheese

# BUCATINI WITH PANCETTA, CHEESE, AND PARSLEY

Cook the pasta in a large pan of salted, boiling water until al dente. • Meanwhile, heat the oil in a medium saucepan over high heat. • Sauté the chile pepper and pancetta until browned. Remove the pancetta and set aside. • In the same saucepan, sauté the onion for 8–10 minutes over medium heat. Return the pancetta to the saucepan and let it flavor the onion. • Drain the pasta and add to the sauce. • Season with parsley and Pecorino. Toss well and serve.

*Serves: 4–6*

*Preparation: 10'*

*Cooking: 20'*

*Level of difficulty: 1*

- 1 lb/500 g spaghetti
- 4 tbsp extra-virgin olive oil
- 1 chile pepper
- 5 oz/150 g pancetta, coarsely chopped
- 1 white onion, finely chopped
- 1 cup/100 g finely chopped parsley
- 2 cups/250 g freshly grated Pecorino cheese

# SPAGHETTINI SORRENTO-STYLE

*Serves: 4–6*

*Preparation: 20'*

*Cooking: 1 h 10'*

*Level of difficulty: 1*

- **6 tbsp extra-virgin olive oil**
- **10 green olives, pitted and sliced**
- **6 cloves garlic, finely chopped**
- **8 anchovy fillets**
- **2 fresh chile peppers**
- **2 tbsp capers packed in salt, rinsed**
- **$^1/_2$ cup/125 ml dry white wine**
- **$1^1/_2$ lb/800 g canned tomatoes**
- **salt and freshly ground black pepper to taste**
- **1 lb/500 g spaghettini**

Heat the oil in a large frying pan and sauté the olives, garlic, anchovies, chile peppers, and capers for 3–4 minutes. • Pour in the wine and cook until it has evaporated. • Add the tomatoes and 2 ladlefuls of hot water. Season with salt and pepper. Cover and cook over very low heat for about 1 hour, stirring often and adding more hot water if the sauce dries out. • Cook the pasta in a large pan of salted, boiling water until al dente. • Drain well and add to the pan with the sauce. • Toss well and serve immediately.

# SPAGHETTI WITH ORANGE

C ook the pasta in a large pot of salted boiling water until al dente. • Heat the oil in a large frying pan over medium heat. Add the garlic and anchovies. Let the anchovies dissolve gently, taking care not to burn them. Add the bread crumbs and cook 2–3 minutes. Pour in the wine and cook until evaporated. • Add the oranges and their juice. Cook for 2 minutes over high heat. Season with the salt. • Drain the pasta and place in a heated serving dish. Spoon the sauce over the top. Toss gently, sprinkle with the parsley, and serve.

*Serves: 4–6*

*Preparation: 15'*

*Cooking: 15'*

*Level of difficulty: 1*

- **1 lb/500 g spaghetti**
- **6 tbsp extra-virgin olive oil**
- **2 cloves garlic, finely chopped**
- **8 anchovy fillets**
- **2 tbsp fine dry bread crumbs**
- **4 tbsp dry white wine**
- **4 oranges, peeled and cut into segments (use blood oranges if available)**
- **salt to taste**
- **1 tbsp finely chopped parsley**

# SPAGHETTI WITH SEAFOOD SAUCE

Serves: 4–6

Preparation: 30' + 1 h to soak shellfish

Cooking: 35'

Level of difficulty: 2

Soak the mussels and clams in cold water for 1 hour. • Chop the squid and cuttlefish into bite-sized chunks. • Put half the oil in a large frying pan, and cook the mussels and clams until open. Discard any that do not open. Extract the mollusks. Leave a few in their shells to garnish. • Heat two-thirds of the remaining oil in the frying pan and sauté the garlic, parsley, and pepper flakes. Add the squid and cuttlefish. Season with salt and pepper, cook briefly, then add the wine. Cook for 12 minutes, then add the scampi. After 5 minutes add the clams and mussels. Mix well and cook for 2 minutes more.

• Meanwhile, cook the spaghetti in a large pan of salted, boiling water until al dente. Drain and add to the pan. Toss for 1–2 minutes over high heat.

- **10 oz/300 g each mussels and clams, in shell**
- **10 oz/300 g each squid, and cuttlefish, cleaned**
- **10 oz/300 g scampi**
- **4 oz/125 ml extra-virgin olive oil**
- **2 cloves garlic, finely chopped**
- **3 tbsp finely chopped parsley**
- **1 tsp red pepper flakes**
- **$^1/_2$ cup/125 ml dry white wine**
- **salt and freshly ground black pepper to taste**
- **1 lb/500 g spaghetti**

Serves: 4–6

Preparation: 15'

Cooking: 30'

Level of difficulty: 1

# SPAGHETTI WITH CRAB MEAT

- **2 cloves garlic, finely chopped**
- **1 tbsp finely chopped parsley**
- **4 tbsp extra-virgin olive oil**
- **14 oz/400 g fresh or frozen crab meat**
- **1¹/₂ lb/750 g peeled and chopped tomatoes**
- **salt and freshly ground black pepper to taste**
- **1 lb/500 g spaghetti**

In a large frying pan, sauté the garlic in the olive oil until it begins to color. • Add the crab meat and cook for 2–3 minutes. • Remove the crab meat and add the tomatoes. Season with salt and pepper and cook over medium heat for about 25 minutes, or until the sauce reduces. • Cook the spaghetti in a large pan of salted, boiling water until al dente. • Drain well and transfer to the pan with the tomatoes. • Add the crab meat, toss well, and serve hot.

# SPAGHETTI WITH CRAWFISH

Clean and shell the crawfish, reserving the heads, and cut into 2-inch (4-5-cm) pieces. Rinse and dry the crawfish and set aside. • To make the stock, put the heads, bunch of parsley, carrot, celery, half the chopped onion, tomatoes, and bay leaf into a large pan of salted water. Cover and bring to a boil over medium heat. When the water begins to boil, lower the heat and move the lid so the pan is only partially covered, and cook for 45 minutes. Turn off the heat. • Heat the oil in a large frying pan and sauté the chopped parsley, garlic, and remaining chopped onion over low heat for 5 minutes. • Add the crawfish and cook for 7–8 minutes. • Pour in the white wine and cook until it evaporates. • Take a few of the crawfish pieces out of the pan and remove the hard part. Discard this, and mash the flesh with a fork. Return to the pan; this will give the sauce added flavor. • Drain the stock and discard the heads and other ingredients then return to the pan and bring to a boil over medium heat. • Cook the spaghetti in the boiling stock until al dente then drain. • Add the cooked spaghetti to the sauce and toss over high heat. Serve immediately.

*Serves: 4–6*

*Preparation: 25'*

*Cooking: 1 h*

*Level of difficulty: 1*

- 2 lb/1 kg crawfish (freshwater crayfish)
- 1 bunch parsley
- 1 carrot
- 1 stalk celery
- 1 medium onion, chopped
- 4 tomatoes, peeled but left whole
- 1 dried bay leaf
- 6 tbsp extra-virgin olive oil
- 6 tbsp finely chopped parsley
- 2 cloves garlic, finely chopped
- $1/2$ cup/125 ml dry white wine
- salt to taste
- 1 lb/500 g spaghetti

# SPAGHETTI WITH DUBLIN BAY PRAWNS

*Serves: 4–6*

*Preparation: 20'*

*Cooking: 25'*

*Level of difficulty: 2*

- 1 lb/500 g Dublin Bay prawns
- 5 tbsp extra-virgin olive oil
- 2 cloves garlic, finely chopped
- 1 tbsp finely chopped parsley
- 2 small dried chilies, crumbled
- salt to taste
- $^1/_2$ cup/125 ml dry white wine
- 1 lb/500 g spaghetti

Clean the prawns but do not remove the shells. • Heat the oil in a large frying pan and sauté the garlic, parsley, and chile for 2–3 minutes over low heat. Increase the heat slightly and add the prawns. Season with salt and mix well. • Moisten with the wine, allow to evaporate, and cook for 8 minutes. Turn off the heat and cover the pan. • Meanwhile, bring a large pan of salted water to a boil over medium heat and cook the spaghetti until al dente. Drain well and place in the pan with the sauce. Toss well for 2 minutes over medium heat. • Serve immediately.

# SEA AND MOUNTAIN SPAGHETTI

S oak the clams and mussels in a large pan of cold water for 1 hour. • Place the clams and mussels in a large pan over high heat and steam until opened. Turn off the heat, discarding any that have not opened. Extract the mussels and clams from their shells and place in a bowl. • Strain the liquid in the pan through into a large bowl. • Heat the oil in a large frying pan and sauté the parsley and garlic for about 5 minutes. • Drain the porcini mushrooms and add to the pan. After about 10 minutes add the tomato. Cook for 10 more minutes then add the mollusks. Check the seasoning and add more salt if necessary. • Pour in the strained cooking liquid and cook for 5 minutes. • Meanwhile, cook the spaghetti in a large pan of salted boiling water until al dente. • Drain well and add to the pan with the sauce. Toss over high heat for 2–3 minutes. • Transfer to a serving bowl and serve immediately.

*Serves: 4–6*

*Preparation: 30'*
*+ 1 h to soak*
*shellfish*

*Cooking: 25'*

*Level of difficulty: 1*

- 1 lb/500 g clams
- 1 lb/500 g mussels
- 6 tbsp finely chopped parsley
- 3 cloves garlic, finely chopped
- 6 tbsp extra-virgin olive oil
- 2 oz/60 g dried porcini mushrooms, soaked in warm water for 15 minutes
- 2 large tomatoes, chopped
- salt to taste
- 1 lb/500 g spaghetti

# BAVETTE WITH WEDGE SHELL CLAMS

Soak the clams in a large bowl of warm salted water for 1 hour. • Transfer to a large saucepan and cook until all the shells are open. Discard any that do not open. Filter the liquid and set aside. • Sauté the garlic and parsley in the oil in a large frying pan until pale gold over high heat. • Pour in the wine and let it evaporate. • Mix the tomato sauce and reserved cooking liquid. Add to the sauce and lower the heat. • Add the clams and cook for 2–3 minutes. Season with salt. • Cook the pasta in a large pan of salted, boiling water until al dente • Drain and add to the sauce, adding 2 tablespoons of cooking water if needed. • Toss well and serve hot.

*Serves: 4–6*

*Preparation: 15' + 1 h to soak shellfish*

*Cooking: 15'*

*Level of difficulty: 1*

- 2 lb/1 kg wedge shell (or other) clams
- 2 cloves garlic, finely chopped
- 1 tbsp finely chopped parsley
- 6 tbsp extra-virgin olive oil
- 1/2 cup/125 ml dry white wine
- 1/2 cup/125 ml tomato sauce, store-bought or homemade
- salt to taste
- 1 lb/500 g bavette

# CAPPELLINI WITH BRANDY AND HERBS

Heat the oil in a large frying pan and sauté the onion and garlic until they begin to color. • Add the herbs and cook for 2–3 minutes. • Pour in the brandy and cook for 2–3 more minutes. • Meanwhile, cook the cappellini in a large pot of salted, boiling water until al dente. • Drain well and place in the pan with the sauce. Season with salt and pepper and sprinkle with the cheese. • Toss over high heat for 2 minutes. • Serve hot.

*Serves: 4–6*

*Preparation: 15'*

*Cooking: 15'*

*Level of difficulty: 1*

- **4 tbsp extra-virgin olive oil**
- **1 medium onion, finely chopped**
- **2 cloves garlic, finely chopped**
- **1 lb/500 g cappellini**
- **1 tbsp each finely chopped sage, mint, rosemary, bay leaves, parsley**
- **5 tbsp brandy**
- **salt and freshly ground black pepper to taste**
- **1 cup/125 g freshly grated Parmesan cheese**

# LINGUINE WITH GREEN BEANS, POTATOES, AND BASIL SAUCE

Serves: 4–6

Preparation: 20'

Cooking: 30'

Level of difficulty: 1

- 1¹/₂ lb/750 g green beans, cleaned and cut into lengths
- 3 medium new potatoes, peeled and diced
- 1 quantity Pesto (see page 948)
- 1 lb/500 g linguine
- 4 tbsp butter
- 4 tbsp freshly grated Pecorino cheese
- 4 tbsp freshly grated Parmesan cheese

Cook the beans and potatoes in a large pot of salted, boiling water until tender. • Take them out with a slotted spoon and use the same water to cook the pasta. • While the pasta is cooking, prepare the pesto. Add 2 tablespoons of boiling water from the pasta pot to make it more liquid. • When the pasta is cooked al dente, drain and place in a heated serving dish. • Toss with the pesto, butter, and vegetables. Sprinkle with the cheeses and serve hot.

# SPAGHETTI WITH PANCETTA AND FRESH MARJORAM

Sauté the pancetta in the oil in a saucepan until translucent. • Remove the pancetta and set aside. • Sauté the onion in the same saucepan until softened. • Add the tomatoes and cook over high heat until they reduce, about 25 minutes. Add the pancetta. • Cook for 5 minutes, add the marjoram, and remove from heat. Season with salt and pepper. • Cook the pasta in a large pan of salted, boiling water until al dente. • Drain well and transfer to a heated serving dish. Toss with the sauce, sprinkle with the Pecorino, and serve hot.

*This delicious dish comes from Umbria, in central Italy, where it is served throughout the year.*

Serves: 4–6
Preparation: 20'
Cooking: 30'
Level of difficulty: 1

- 6 oz/180 g pancetta, cut into small cubes
- 4 tbsp extra-virgin olive oil
- 1 large onion, finely chopped
- 1 1/2 lb/750 g tomatoes, peeled, seeded, and coarsely chopped
- 1 small bunch marjoram, finely chopped
- salt and freshly ground black pepper to taste
- 1 lb/500 g spaghetti
- 1/2 cup/60 g freshly grated Pecorino cheese

# BUCATINI WITH SPICY CHILE OIL

Process the chile peppers with the garlic and oil in a food processor until very finely chopped. • Heat the oil in a large frying pan over medium heat and add the chile mixture. • As soon it begins to sizzle, remove from the heat and season with salt. • Cook the pasta in a large pan of salted, boiling water until al dente. • Drain and add to the chile oil. Toss well and serve.

104

*Serves: 4–6*

*Preparation: 10'*

*Cooking: 15'*

*Level of difficulty: 1*

- • 4 spicy red chile peppers, chopped
- • 4 cloves garlic, finely chopped
- • $^1/_2$ cup/125 ml extra-virgin olive oil
- • salt to taste
- • 1 lb/500 g bucatini

# SPAGHETTI WITH WILD ASPARAGUS

*Serves: 4–6*

*Preparation: 30'*

*Cooking: 45'*

*Level of difficulty: 1*

- 1¹/₂ lb/750 g wild asparagus
- 4 tbsp extra-virgin olive oil
- 2 cloves garlic, finely chopped
- 1 lb/500 g firm-ripe tomatoes, peeled and seeded
- salt to taste
- 1 lb/500 g spaghetti
- 6 tbsp freshly grated Pecorino cheese

Remove the woody part of the asparagus, peel the rest of the stalk, and cut into short sections. Separate the tips. • Sauté the asparagus stalks in the oil in a frying pan over medium heat for 5 minutes. • Add the garlic and tomatoes and season with salt. Cover and cook over low heat for 15 minutes. • Add the asparagus tips, and cook for 15 minutes more, or until the asparagus is tender. • Cook the pasta in a large pan of salted, boiling water until al dente. • Drain and add to the asparagus sauce. Sprinkle with Pecorino, toss well, and serve.

# SPAGHETTI WITH BEEF AND TOMATO SAUCE

Heat the oil in a large saucepan and add the slices of beef, tomatoes, parsley, garlic, and capers. Cook over low heat for 1 hour. • Season with salt and pepper. • Cook the pasta in a large pan of salted, boiling water until al dente. • When the sauce is ready carefully remove the slices of meat. • Drain the pasta and add to the saucepan with the sauce. • Toss gently and serve the pasta with its sauce. The very tender slices of beef can be served afterward as a second course.

Serves: 4–6

Preparation: 15'

Cooking: 1 h

Level of difficulty: 1

- 6 tbsp extra-virgin olive oil
- 14 oz/400 g sliced beef
- 1 lb /500 g firm-ripe tomatoes, coarsely chopped
- 3 tbsp finely chopped parsley
- 2 cloves garlic, finely chopped
- 1 tbsp capers, packed in salt, rinsed
- 1 lb /500 g spaghetti
- salt and freshly ground black pepper to taste

# SPAGHETTINI WITH MUSHROOMS

Serves: 4–6

Preparation: 30'

Cooking: 45'

Level of difficulty: 1

- 1¹/₄ lb/625 g mixed mushrooms (porcini, white, champignons)
- 1 onion, finely chopped
- 6 tbsp extra-virgin olive oil
- salt to taste
- 2 cloves garlic, finely chopped
- 1 dried hot chile pepper, crumbled
- 6 tbsp dry white wine
- 12 cherry tomatoes, coarsely chopped
- 1 tbsp finely chopped basil
- 1 tbsp finely chopped parsley
- 1 lb/500 g bavette

Clean the mushrooms very carefully and cut the larger ones into small pieces. • Sweat the onion in the oil in a frying pan over low heat for 20 minutes. Season with salt and add the garlic and chile. • Increase the heat and pour in the wine. • Add the mushrooms and sauté over high heat for a few minutes. • Stir in the tomatoes, basil, and parsley and cook for about 10 minutes. Season with salt. • Cook for about 10 more minutes, or until the mushrooms are tender. • Cook the pasta in a large pan of salted, boiling water until al dente. • Drain and add to the sauce. Toss well and serve hot.

# NEAPOLITAN-STYLE FUSILLI

Sauté the onions, carrots, celery, garlic, and pancetta in the oil in an earthenware casserole over high heat until lightly golden. • Add the meat and sear all over. • Increase the heat and pour in the wine and tomato concentrate mixture. Cover and cook over low heat for 1 hour. • Add the tomatoes and basil and season with salt and pepper. • Simmer, partially covered, over low heat for about 2 hours, or until the meat is tender, adding the stock if the sauce begins to dry. • Cook the pasta in a large pan of salted, boiling water until al dente. • Drain and transfer to a large bowl with the salami and half the sauce. • Arrange one-third of the pasta in a baking dish and spread with one-third of the Ricotta. Sprinkle with Pecorino and more sauce. Continue to layer the pasta, sauce, Ricotta, and Pecorino until all the ingredients are in the dish. Serve hot. • Serve the meat thinly sliced as a main course.

*Serves: 4–6*

*Preparation: 25'*

*Cooking: 3 h 35'*

*Level of difficulty: 2*

- **3 red onions, finely chopped**
- **2 carrots, finely chopped**
- **2 stalks celery, finely chopped**
- **2 cloves garlic, crushed but whole**
- **6 oz/180 g diced pancetta**
- **4 tbsp extra-virgin olive oil**
- **2 lb/1 kg stewing beef, in 1 piece**
- **1 lb/500 g long fusilli pasta**
- **²/₃ cup/150 ml dry white wine**
- **4 tbsp tomato concentrate/puree dissolved in 4 tbsp dry white wine**
- **3 lb/1.5 kg tomatoes, peeled and finely chopped**
- **1 small bunch fresh basil, torn**
- **salt and freshly ground black pepper to taste**
- **scant 1 cup/200 ml Beef Stock (see page 955)**
- **6 oz/180 g diced salami**
- **14 oz/400 g Ricotta cheese**
- **6 tbsp freshly grated Pecorino cheese**

# SPAGHETTI WITH MUSSELS

Soak the mussels in a large bowl of warm salted water for one hour. • Transfer to a large saucepan, drizzle with the wine, and cook until they open up. Discard any that do not open. Filter the liquid and set aside. • Leave eight mussels in their shells. Shell the rest and chop the flesh coarsely. • Sauté the garlic, parsley, and shelled mussels in the oil in a frying pan. Season generously with pepper and let simmer for 4–5 minutes. • Remove the mussels and set aside covered with a plate to keep them warm. • Add the filtered liquid from cooking the mussels to the pan and bring to a boil. • Cook the pasta in a large pan of salted, boiling water until al dente. • Drain and finish cooking in the boiling cooking liquid from the mussels. • Add all the mussels, toss well, and serve hot.

Serves: 4–6

Preparation: 15' + 1 h
to soak mussels

Cooking: 25'

Level of difficulty: 1

- 2$^1$/$_2$ lb/1.25 kg mussels, rinsed and ready for cooking
- 6 tbsp dry white wine
- 2 cloves garlic, finely chopped
- 1 small bunch parsley, finely chopped
- $^1$/$_2$ cup/125 ml extra-virgin olive oil
- salt and freshly ground black pepper to taste
- 1 lb/500 g spaghetti

# SPAGHETTI WITH SUN-DRIED TOMATOES

Pour the oil from the sun-dried tomatoes into a frying pan. Heat over low heat and add the tomatoes. Sauté briefly and season with chile pepper and salt. • Cook the pasta in a large pan of salted, boiling water until al dente. Drain and add to the pan. Sprinkle with the basil. • Serve the spaghetti hot with the cheese sprinkled over the top.

| |
|---|
| Serves: 4–6 |
| Preparation: 10' |
| Cooking: 15' |
| Level of difficulty: 1 |

- **14 oz/400 g sun-dried tomatoes packed in oil, finely sliced**
- **dried chile pepper**
- **salt to taste**
- **1 lb/500 g g spaghetti**
- **10 leaves fresh basil, torn**
- **12 tbsp freshly grated Caciocavallo or Fontina cheese**

# SPAGHETTI WITH TUNA AND CAPERS

*Serves: 4–6*

*Preparation: 10'*

*Cooking: 15'*

*Level of difficulty: 1*

- **4 tbsp capers packed in salt**
- **7 oz/200 g tuna packed in oil, drained**
- **1 bunch fresh mint**
- **¼ tsp red pepper flakes (optional)**
- **4 tbsp extra-virgin olive oil**
- **salt to taste**
- **1 lb/500 g spaghetti**

Rinse the capers under cold running water and place in a small saucepan. Add enough water to cover and bring to a boil. Drain the capers, rinse them again, and pat dry on paper towels.
• Chop the tuna, capers, mint, and chile pepper, if using, in a food processor. • Transfer to a large bowl and mix in the oil. Season with salt.
• Cook the pasta in a large pan of salted, boiling water until al dente. Add 4 tablespoons of cooking water to the sauce. • Drain the pasta and toss with the tuna sauce, adding more cooking water if needed.

# SPAGHETTI WITH ZUCCHINI

Rinse the zucchini under cold running water. Cut into rounds or slice them lengthwise. • Heat the oil in a large deep frying pan until very hot. Fry the zucchini in 2 or 3 batches for 5–7 minutes each, or until the zucchini are golden brown. Drain on paper towels. Season with salt and cover with a plate to keep them warm. • Cook the pasta in a large pan of salted, boiling water until al dente. Drain and sprinkle with Pecorino. Top with the fried zucchini, basil, and a drizzle of oil. Add a little cooking water if needed. • Toss well and serve hot.

*Serves: 4–6*

*Preparation: 15'*

*Cooking: 25'*

*Level of difficulty: 1*

- **1 lb/500 g zucchini/ courgettes**
- **2 cups/500 ml oil, for frying**
- **salt to taste**
- **1 lb/500 g spaghetti**
- **6 tbsp freshly grated Pecorino cheese**
- **10 leaves fresh basil, torn**

# SPAGHETTI WITH LOBSTER

Sauté the onion in the oil in a large frying pan for 10 minutes. • Add half the parsley and the tomatoes. Cook for 15–20 minutes, or until the tomatoes have broken down. • Season with salt and add the lobster meat. Simmer for 10 minutes. • Cook the pasta in a large pan of salted, boiling water until al dente. Drain and add to the pan. Toss well so that the pasta absorbs the flavors of the sauce. • Serve in individual dishes and sprinkle with the remaining parsley.

118

*Serves: 4–6*

*Preparation: 30'*

*Cooking: 45'*

*Level of difficulty: 1*

- **1 onion, finely chopped**
- **6 tbsp extra-virgin olive oil**
- **2 tbsp finely chopped parsley**
- **14 oz/400 g firm-ripe tomatoes, peeled and chopped**
- **salt to taste**
- **14 oz/400 g lobster meat, cut into large chunks**
- **1 lb/500 g spaghetti**

# SPAGHETTI WITH CLAMS

S oak the clams in cold water for 1 hour. • Put the clams, white wine, and 2 tablespoons of the oil in a large frying pan and sauté until the clams are open. • Remove the clams, discarding any that have not opened, and set aside. Put the cooking liquid in a bowl and set aside. • Combine the remaining oil and garlic in the same skillet and cook until the garlic begins to change color. • Add the tomatoes and cook over medium heat for about 5 minutes. • Pour in the clam liquid. Season with salt and pepper. Cook for 15 more minutes, or until the sauce has reduced. • Add the clams and parsley, and continue cooking for 2–3 minutes. • Cook the spaghetti in a large pot of salted, boiling water until al dente. Drain and transfer to the skillet with the sauce. • Toss for 1–2 minutes over medium-high heat, and serve.

*Serves: 4–6*

*Preparation: 15' + 1 h to soak clams*

*Cooking: 30'*

*Level of difficulty: 1*

- 1 1/2 lb/750 g clams, in shell
- 4 tbsp extra-virgin olive oil
- 4 tbsp dry white wine
- 2 cloves garlic, finely chopped
- 4 large ripe tomatoes, peeled and chopped
- salt and freshly ground black pepper to taste
- 1 tbsp finely chopped parsley
- 1 lb/500 g spaghetti

# SPAGHETTI WITH LEMON, CREAM, AND CHILE PEPPER

Grate the zest of one of the lemons and cut the fruit into small pieces. Squeeze the juice from the other lemon. • Sauté the garlic in the oil in a heavy-bottomed pan until it begins to color. • Add the cream, salt, and lemon zest and pieces and cook over medium heat for 4–5 minutes. • Add the lemon juice and cook for 2–3 minutes more. • Meanwhile, cook the spaghetti in a large pot of salted, boiling water until al dente. • Transfer to the pan with the cream. Add the chile pepper and Parmesan, toss well, and serve.

122

*Serves: 4–6*

*Preparation: 15'*

*Cooking: 20'*

*Level of difficulty: 1*

- **1 clove garlic, finely chopped**
- **1 cup/250 ml heavy cream**
- **salt to taste**
- **3 oz/90 g freshly grated Parmesan cheese**
- **1 spicy green or red chile pepper, sliced**
- **1 lb/500 g spaghetti**

# SPAGHETTI WITH SMOKED PANCETTA AND EGG

Serves: 4–6

Preparation: 5'

Cooking: 15'

Level of difficulty: 1

- 1 lb/500 g spaghetti
- 2 cloves garlic, lightly crushed but whole
- 4 tbsp extra-virgin olive oil
- 6 oz/180 g diced bacon
- 4 fresh eggs
- $2/3$ cup/90 g freshly grated Parmesan cheese
- salt and freshly ground black pepper to taste

Cook the spaghetti in a large pot of salted, boiling water until al dente. • Meanwhile, sauté the oil, garlic, and pancetta in a frying pan over medium heat until the pancetta is golden brown but not crisp. Remove the pan from heat and discard the garlic. • In a mixing bowl beat the eggs, Parmesan, Pecorino, and salt until well mixed. Set aside. • Drain the pasta and place in a heated serving dish. Add the egg mixture and toss. • Return the pan with the pancetta to high heat for 1 minute. Pour the hot oil and pancetta over the pasta and egg, and toss well. • Grind a generous amount of black pepper over the top and serve.

# SHORT
# PASTA

# TYPES OF SHORT PASTA

All the short pasta shapes in this chapter are commercially-made and dried using hard durum wheat flour. There are hundreds of different types of short pasta; about 65 percent of all pasta sold in Italy today falls into this category. It includes some old favorites, such as penne, maccheroni, ruote, farfalle, fusilli, and conchiglie, many of which are now also available in flavored or colored versions. This is a selection of the most common short pasta types.

Penne rigate

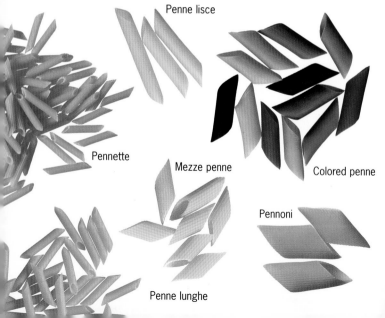

Penne lisce

Pennette

Mezze penne

Colored penne

Pennoni

Penne lunghe

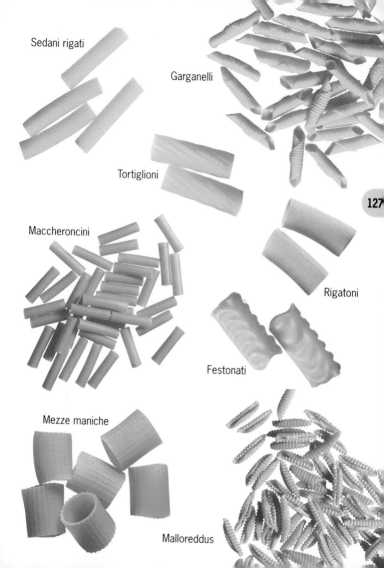

Sedani rigati

Garganelli

Tortiglioni

Maccheroncini

Rigatoni

Festonati

Mezze maniche

Malloreddus

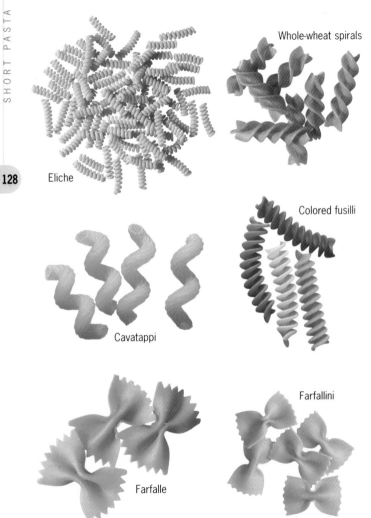

Whole-wheat spirals

Eliche

Colored fusilli

Cavatappi

Farfallini

Farfalle

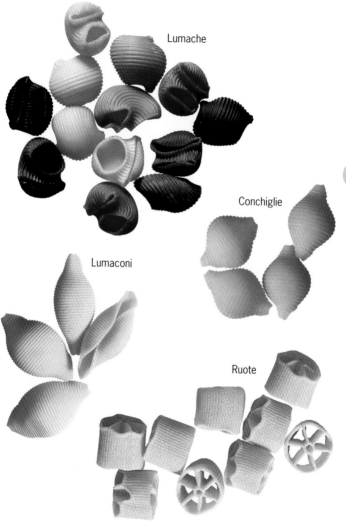

Lumache

Conchiglie

Lumaconi

Ruote

# WHOLE WHEAT PENNE WITH CELERY AND GORGONZOLA

Clean the celery by removing the tough outer stalks. Reserve a few of the leaves, and chop the tender inner stalks into small pieces. • Melt the butter in a large frying pan and sauté the celery stalks for 3–4 minutes. • Add the vegetable stock, cover, and cook over low heat for 10 minutes, or until tender. Season with salt and pepper and remove from the heat. • Beat the creamy Gorgonzola with the milk in a small saucepan. Cook over low heat until the cheese has melted. • Cook the pasta in a large pan of salted, boiling water until *al dente*. • Finely chop the reserved celery leaves. • Drain the pasta and transfer to a heated serving bowl. • Pour the Gorgonzola sauce over the top, and sprinkle with the celery leaves, walnuts, and spicy Gorgonzola. • Toss gently and serve.

*Serves: 4–6*

*Preparation: 20'*

*Cooking: 20*

*Level of difficulty: 1*

- 1 celery heart, tough outer leaves removed, sliced
- 2 tbsp butter
- $^1/_2$ cup/125 ml Vegetable Stock (see page 956)
- salt and freshly ground black pepper to taste
- 8 oz/250 g creamy Gorgonzola cheese
- $^1/_2$ cup/125 ml milk
- 1 lb/500 g whole-wheat/wholemeal penne
- 3 oz/90 g shelled walnuts, chopped
- 3 oz/90 g spicy Gorgonzola cheese, diced

# BAKED FUSILLI WITH CHEESE

Preheat the oven to 450°F/230°C/gas 7. • Cook the pasta in a large pan of salted, boiling, water until al dente. • Drain and return to the pan. Add the cheese and cream and season with salt and pepper. Set aside to rest for 2–3 minutes. Line an ovenproof baking dish with the pancetta and scatter with the rosemary. Cover with the pasta and bake for 10 minutes. Serve hot.

132

*Serves: 4–6*

*Preparation: 15'*

*Cooking: 25'*

*Level of difficulty: 1*

- 1 lb/500 g fusilli
- 8 oz/250 g freshly grated Bagoss (or Fontina) cheese
- 4 tbsp heavy/ double cream
- salt and freshly ground black pepper to taste
- 8 thin slices pancetta (or bacon)
- 8–10 sprigs fresh rosemary

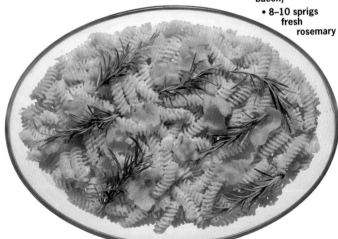

# WHOLE-WHEAT RIGATONI WITH PECORINO CHEESE

*Serves: 4–6*

*Preparation: 15'*

*Cooking: 25'*

*Level of difficulty: 1*

- 1 lb/500 g whole-wheat/wholemeal rigatoni
- 2 potatoes, diced
- 7 oz/200 g young Pecorino cheese
- $1/2$ cup/125 ml full cream milk
- 4 tbsp butter
- salt and freshly ground black pepper to taste
- $3/4$ cup/60 g freshly grated Parmesan cheese

Cook the rigatoni and potatoes in a large pan of salted, boiling water. • Place the Pecorino, milk, and butter in the top of a double boiler and cook until the cheese has melted. Season with salt and pepper. • Drain the pasta and potatoes when the pasta is cooked al dente. • Pour the cheese sauce over the pasta, sprinkle with the Parmesan, mix well, and serve.

# FLORENTINE-STYLE PENNE

*Serves: 4–6*

*Preparation: 25'*

*Cooking: 1 h 20'*

*Level of difficulty: 1*

- **4 tbsp extra-virgin olive oil**
- **1 medium onion, finely chopped**
- **1 small carrot, finely chopped**
- **1 small stick celery, finely chopped**
- **2 tbsp finely chopped parsley**
- **14 oz/400 g ground lean beef**
- **$^1/_2$ cup/125 ml full-bodied, dry red wine**
- **$1^1/_2$ lb/800 g canned Italian tomatoes, coarsely chopped**
- **salt and freshly ground black pepper to taste**
- **1 cup/250 ml Beef Stock (see page 955)**
- **1 lb/500 g penne**
- **1 cup/150 g freshly grated Parmesan cheese**

Heat the oil in a large frying pan and sauté the onion, carrot, celery, and parsley together for 4–5 minutes. • Add the meat and cook until lightly browned, breaking up any lumps that may form as it cooks. • Pour in the wine and cook until the alcohol has evaporated. • Add the tomatoes and season with salt and pepper. Stir well and simmer for 5 more minutes. • Add 2–3 tablespoons of the stock, cover and simmer for at least 1 hour, stirring in a little more stock at intervals to keep the sauce moist (but not sloppy). • Cook the pasta in a large pan of salted, boiling water to a boil until just al dente. • Drain well and add to the sauce. Toss gently and leave for 5 minutes so that the pasta is coated thoroughly with the rich sauce and has absorbed its flavors. • Turn off the heat, stir in the Parmesan and serve at once.

# RIGATONI WITH ZUCCHINI

C ook the rigatoni in a large pot of salted, boiling water until al dente. • In a large frying pan, sauté the garlic in the butter and oil until it starts to change color. Add the zucchini and pepper flakes. Sauté over high heat until the zucchini begin to turn golden brown. • Lower heat, cover the pan with a lid, and simmer until the zucchini are just tender. Season with salt and pepper. • Drain the pasta and place in a heated serving dish. • Add the zucchini, parsley, and Parmesan, and toss well. Serve hot.

Serves: 4–6

Preparation: 10'

Cooking: 25'

Level of difficulty: 1

- 1 lb/500 g rigatoni
- 3 tbsp butter
- 3 tbsp extra-virgin olive oil
- 2 cloves garlic, finely chopped
- 6 zucchini, sliced in thin wheels
- 1 tsp crushed red pepper flakes
- salt and freshly ground black pepper to taste
- 3 tbsp finely chopped parsley
- 6 tbsp freshly grated Parmesan cheese

# MACCHERONI WITH ONION SAUCE

*Serves: 4–6*

*Preparation: 10'*

*Cooking: 45'*

*Level of difficulty: 1*

- 5 large onions, thinly sliced
- 4 tbsp butter
- 4 tbsp extra-virgin olive oil
- salt and freshly ground black pepper to taste
- 1 cup/250 ml dry white wine
- 2 tbsp finely chopped parsley
- 6 tbsp freshly grated Parmesan cheese
- 1 lb/500 g maccheroni

Sauté the onions in a skillet with the butter and oil over medium heat until they begin to change color. Season with salt and pepper. • Turn the heat down to low, cover, and simmer for about 40 minutes, or until the onions are very soft. • Uncover and add the wine. Turn the heat up to medium and stir until the wine evaporates. Remove from heat. • Cook the pasta in a large pot of salted, boiling water until al dente. Drain well and place in a heated serving dish. • Pour the onion sauce over the top. Add the parsley and Parmesan and toss well. Serve hot.

# FUSILLI WITH PESTO, CREAM, AND TOMATOES

**M**ix the pesto and tomato sauce in a large bowl. Stir in the cream until well blended. • Cook the pasta in salted, boiling water until al dente. • Heat the serving bowls with 1 tablespoon of the cooking water from the pasta. Discard the water. • Drain the pasta and transfer to the warmed bowls. Add the sauce, toss well, and serve. • Serve hot.

*Serves: 4–6*

*Preparation: 10'*

*Cooking: 15'*

*Level of difficulty: 1*

- **1 quantity Pesto (see page 948)**
- **1 cup/250 ml homemade (see page 950) or store-bought Tomato sauce**
- **6 tbsp heavy/ double cream or 2 tbsp Mascarpone cheese**
- **1 lb/500 g fusilli**

138

# PENNE WITH RICOTTA

P lace the Ricotta in a bowl large enough to hold the pasta as well. Stir in the nutmeg, lemon zest, Parmesan, and oil. • Cook the pasta in a large pan of salted, boiling water until al dente. • Add about 2 tablespoons of the pasta water to the Ricotta, then season with salt and pepper. • Drain the pasta and add to the Ricotta mixture. • Toss well and serve hot.

Serves: 4–6
Preparation: 15'
Cooking: 25'
Level of difficulty: 1

- **14 oz/400 g fresh Ricotta cheese**
- **dash of nutmeg**
- **1 tbsp finely grated lemon zest**
- **6 tbsp freshly grated Parmesan cheese**
- **4 tbsp extra-virgin olive oil**
- **1 lb/500 g penne**
- **salt and freshly ground black pepper to taste**

# PIPETTE RIGATE WITH SICILIAN PESTO

*Serves: 4–6*

*Preparation: 15' +*
*1 h 30' to drain*
*tomatoes and chill*
*sauce*

*Cooking: 15'*

*Level of difficulty: 1*

- 2 tbsp capers, salted
- 1¹/₂ lb/750 g ripe tomatoes
- salt to taste
- 4 tbsp extra-virgin olive oil
- 1 tsp red pepper flakes
- 1 clove garlic, finely chopped
- 1 tsp dried oregano
- 1 lb/500 g pipette rigate

Rinse the capers under running cold water to remove the salt. Dry well. • Cut the tomatoes in half. Use a knife to remove the seeds. Sprinkle with a little salt and lay upside down in a colander to drain for 30 minutes. • In a bowl (large enough to hold the pasta later), mix the oil, red pepper flakes, capers, garlic, and oregano. • Cut the tomatoes in cubes and add to the mixture. Refrigerate for 1 hour. • Cook the pasta in a large pan of salted, boiling water until al dente. • Drain and add to the bowl with the sauce. • Toss well and serve hot.

# MACCHERONI WITH MUSSELS

*Serves: 4–6*

*Preparation: 30' + 1 h to soak the mussels*

*Cooking: 30'*

*Level of difficulty: 1*

- **4 lb/2 kg mussels, in shell**
- **³/4 cup/180 ml dry white wine**
- **2 cloves garlic, finely chopped**
- **1 fresh chile pepper, finely chopped**
- **1 tbsp finely chopped parsley**
- **6 tbsp extra-virgin olive oil**
- **3 lb/1.5 kg firm-ripe tomatoes, peeled and coarsely chopped**
- **salt to taste**
- **1 lb/500 g maccheroni**

Soak the mussels in a large bowl of cold water for 1 hour. • Drain and scrub well. • Place 2 tablespoons of wine in a large saucepan and add a handful or two of mussels. Cover and cook over high heat until they open. Remove from the pan and let cool. Repeat until all the mussels are open. Discard any that do not open. • Remove most of the mussels from their shells, leaving a few in their shells to garnish the serving dish. • Sauté the garlic, chile, and parsley in the oil in a large frying pan until the garlic is pale gold. • Pour in the remaining wine and cook until it evaporates. • Stir in the tomatoes and cook over high heat until the tomatoes have broken down, about 5 minutes. • Season with salt. • Add the shelled mussels and cook for 5 minutes more. Remove from the heat. • Cook the pasta in a large pan of salted, boiling water until *al dente*. • Drain and transfer to a serving dish. Add the sauce and toss well. Garnish with the mussels with shells on and serve.

# FARFALLE WITH VODKA AND CAVIAR

Cook the farfalle in a large pot of salted, boiling water until al dente. • In a large frying pan, melt the butter over low heat and add the vodka and lemon juice. • Stir in the salmon and caviar. Cook over medium-low heat for 2–3 minutes. Add the cream, and season with salt and pepper. Remove from heat. • Drain the pasta well and add to the pan with the salmon. • Toss well over medium heat and serve.

144

*Serves: 4–6*

*Preparation: 5'*

*Cooking: 15'*

*Level of difficulty: 1*

- 1 lb/500 g farfalle
- 4 tbsp butter
- 4 tbsp vodka
- juice of 11/2 lemons
- 4 oz/125 g smoked salmon, crumbled
- 4 tsp caviar
- 4 tbsp light/single cream
- salt and freshly ground black pepper to taste

# GARGANELLI WITH CREAMY SAUSAGE SAUCE

*Serves: 4–6*

*Preparation: 20'*

*Cooking: 30'*

*Level of difficulty: 1*

- 1 onion, finely chopped
- 1 tbsp butter
- 14 oz/400 g Italian sausages
- 3/4 cup/180 ml heavy/double cream
- 1/8 tsp freshly grated nutmeg
- salt and freshly ground black pepper to taste
- 1 lb/500 g garganelli
- 4 tbsp freshly grated Parmesan cheese

Sauté the onion in the butter in a frying pan over low heat until translucent. • Add the sausages, crumbling them with a fork and sauté until well browned. Add the cream and let it reduce over very low heat for about 20 minutes. • Season with nutmeg, salt, and pepper. • Cook the pasta in salted, boiling water until *al dente*. • Drain and add to the sauce. • Sprinkle with the Parmesan, remove from the heat, and dot with the remaining butter. Serve hot.

# FUSILLI WITH SPINACH, SWISS CHARD, AND POACHED EGGS

Bring a large pan of salted water to a boil and add the Swiss chard, spinach, and pasta.
• In a separate wide frying pan bring 2 quarts (2 liters) of unsalted water to a boil with the vinegar. • Break the eggs delicately into the boiling liquid. Lower the heat, cluster the white around the yolk with a spoon, and cook the eggs for 3–4 minutes. • Drain one egg at a time with a slotted spoon, and holding each egg in the slotted spoon, plunge it for a few seconds into a bowl of cold water in to stop the cooking process. Drain again, and set aside, keeping warm. • Drain the pasta and vegetables and transfer to a heated serving dish. Top with the eggs. Drizzle with the butter and sprinkle with cheese, if liked. • Season with salt and pepper and serve.

146

*Serves: 4–6*

*Preparation: 15'*

*Cooking: 15'*

*Level of difficulty: 1*

- 1 lb/500 g Swiss chard, cleaned and coarsely chopped
- 12 oz/350 g spinach, cleaned and coarsely chopped
- 1 lb/500 g fusilli
- 8 tbsp white wine vinegar
- 4–6 eggs, straight from the refrigerator
- 6 tbsp melted butter
- 3/4 cup/75 g aged freshly grated Pecorino cheese (optional)
- salt and freshly ground white pepper to taste

# FARFALLE WITH RADICCHIO AND GOAT'S CHEESE

Sauté the onion in 3 tablespoons of the oil. •
When the onions are tender, add the radicchio
and season with salt and pepper. Sauté for a few
minutes, then add the beer. • When the beer has
evaporated, add the goat's cheese and stir well,
softening the mixture with the milk. • Cook the
pasta in a large pan of salted, boiling water until
cooked al dente. • Drain well and add to the pan
with the sauce. • Toss for a few minutes, drizzle
with the remaining oil, and serve.

*Serves: 4–6*

*Preparation: 15'*

*Cooking: 25'*

*Level of difficulty: 1*

- 1 onion, thinly
  sliced
- 7 tbsp extra-virgin
  olive oil
- 1 large head
  (or 2 small)
  Trevisian radicchio,
  cut in strips
- salt and freshly
  ground black
  pepper to taste
- 4 tbsp light beer
- 4 oz/125 g soft
  fresh goat's cheese
- 2 tbsp milk
- 1 lb/500 g farfalle

148

# PASTA WITH RAW ZUCCHINI, PECORINO CHEESE, AND MINT

*Serves: 4–6*

*Preparation: 15'*

*Cooking: 25'*

*Level of difficulty: 1*

- **6 very fresh small zucchini/courgettes**
- **1 tbsp lemon juice**
- **salt and freshly ground black pepper to taste**
- **6 tbsp extra-virgin olive oil**
- **6 fresh mint leaves**
- **1 lb/500 g penne**
- **4 oz/125 g fresh Pecorino cheese, cubed**

Cut the zucchini in julienne strips and place them in a bowl (large enough to hold the pasta as well). • Add the lemon juice, salt, pepper, oil, and mint leaves. Stir well and let sit for about 20 minutes. • Cook the pasta in a large pan of salted, boiling water until cooked al dente. Drain well and place in the bowl with the zucchini. Toss well, add the Pecorino cheese, toss again, and serve

# FUSILLI WITH VEGETABLES

Serves: 4–6

Preparation: 20'

Cooking: 30'

Level of difficulty: 1

- 6 tbsp extra-virgin olive oil
- 1 red onion, peeled and thinly sliced
- 1 celery heart, cleaned and chopped
- 1 eggplant/ aubergine, peeled and diced
- 1 yellow bell pepper/capsicum, cleaned and cut in small squares
- salt and freshly ground black pepper to taste
- 8 small tomatoes, sliced
- 1 lb/500 g fusilli
- 6–8 basil leaves, torn (optional)
- 2 oz/60 g Ricotta salata cheese, crumbled

Heat 4 tablespoons of oil in a large frying pan and sauté the onion over high heat for 3 minutes. • Add the celery, eggplant, and bell pepper. Season with salt and pepper and stir well. Cover and cook over medium heat for 20 minutes, or until the vegetables are almost tender. • Add the tomatoes and continue cooking, uncovered, for 5 minutes. • Cook the pasta in a large pan of salted, boiling water until *al dente*. • Drain well and add to the frying pan with the vegetables. Add the Ricotta and basil, if liked, toss gently, and serve.

# CAVATAPPI WITH SHRIMP AND ASPARAGUS

Heat half the oil in a large frying pan and cook the asparagus tips and shallots until tender. Season with salt and pepper. • Heat the remaining oil in another frying pan and cook the shrimp over medium heat for 4–5 minutes. • Meanwhile, cook the pasta in a large pot of salted, boiling water until al dente. • Drain well and add to the pan with the asparagus. Add the shrimp and toss well. • Serve hot.

*Serves: 4–6*

*Preparation: 15'*

*Cooking: 25'*

*Level of difficulty: 1*

- **8 oz/250 g shrimp tails**
- **4 tbsp extra-virgin olive oil**
- **12 oz/350 g asparagus tips**
- **2 shallots, sliced**
- **salt and freshly ground black pepper to taste**
- **1 lb/500 g cavatappi**

# CONCHIGLIE WITH ARTICHOKE SAUCE

*Serves: 4–6*

*Preparation: 15'*

*Cooking: 25'*

*Level of difficulty: 1*

- **8 artichokes**
- **4 tbsp extra-virgin olive oil**
- **1 lb/500 g conchiglie**
- **2 cloves garlic, finely chopped**
- **3¹/₂ oz/100 g black olives**
- **1 tbsp capers**
- **salt and freshly ground black pepper to taste**
- **2 tbsp finely chopped parsley**

Clean the artichokes by removing the tough outer leaves and trimming the stalks. Cut in half and remove any fuzzy choke with a sharp knife. Slice thinly. • Heat the oil in a large frying pan and sauté the garlic until soft. Add the artichokes, olives, and capers. Season with salt and pepper and cook over medium heat for 10 minutes, or until tender. • Meanwhile, cook the pasta in a large pot of salted, boiling water until al dente. • Drain well and add to the pan. Add the parsley, toss for 2–3 minutes, then serve at once.

# PENNE WITH CANTALOUPE, CREAM, AND PARMESAN

*Serves: 4–6*

*Preparation: 10'*

*Cooking: 30'*

*Level of difficulty: 1*

- 1 lb/500 g penne
- 1 small clove garlic, very finely chopped
- 1 tbsp extra-virgin olive oil
- 1 cup/250 g heavy/ double cream
- 1/2 cup/125 ml Marsala wine
- 1 small, ripe cantaloupe/rock melon, peeled and chopped in small cubes
- salt and freshly ground black pepper to taste
- 6 tbsp freshly grated Parmesan cheese

Cook the pasta in a large pot of salted, boiling water until al dente. • In a heavy-bottomed saucepan, sauté the garlic in the oil for 2–3 minutes. Pour in the cream and Marsala, then add the cantaloupe. Simmer for 8–10 minutes. Season with salt and pepper. • Drain the pasta, toss with the sauce, and place in a heated serving dish. • Sprinkle with the Parmesan, toss well, and serve.

# FARFALLE WITH CANTALOUPE

Peel the cantaloupe and chop finely. • Cook the cream, port, and garlic in a large frying pan over medium heat for 5 minutes. • Add the cantaloupe, season with salt and pepper, and simmer for 10 minutes. • Meanwhile, cook the pasta in a large pot of salted, boiling water until al dente. • Drain well and transfer to a heated serving dish. Pour the cantaloupe cream over the top and sprinkle with the Parmesan. • Toss well and serve.

Serves: 4–6

Preparation: 15'

Cooking: 20'

Level of difficulty: 1

- 1 small cantaloupe/rock melon
- 1 cup/250 ml heavy/double cream
- $^1/_2$ cup/125 dry Port wine
- 1 clove garlic, finely chopped
- salt and freshly ground white pepper to taste
- 1 lb/500 g farfalle
- 4 oz/125 g freshly grated Parmesan cheese

# GARGANELLI WITH ROMAGNOL MEAT SAUCE

*Serves: 4–6*

*Preparation: 15'*

*Cooking: 45'*

*Level of difficulty: 1*

- 3 oz/90 g butter
- $^{1}/_{2}$ onion, 1 small carrot, finely chopped
- 2 tbsp finely chopped parsley
- 5 oz/150 g chicken livers, coarsely chopped
- 5 oz/150 g beef, coarsely chopped
- salt and freshly ground black pepper to taste
- 4 tbsp dry Marsala wine
- 8 oz/250 g tomatoes, peeled and chopped
- $^{1}/_{2}$ quantity Béchamel sauce (see page 946)
- dash each nutmeg and cinnamon
- 2 cups/500 ml Beef Stock (see page 955)
- 2 oz/60 g prosciutto
- 1 lb/500 g garganelli

Melt two-thirds of the butter in a large, heavy-bottomed pan and sauté the onion, carrot, and parsley for 5 minutes. • Add the chicken livers and veal, season with salt and pepper and sauté for 5 more minutes. • Stir in the Marsala then add the tomatoes, béchamel, nutmeg, and cinnamon. Cook on medium-low heat for 30 minutes, adding stock to keep the sauce liquid. • Sauté the prosciutto in the remaining butter and add to the sauce 5 minutes before removing from heat. • Meanwhile, cook the garganelli in a large pan of salted, boiling water until al dente. • Drain well and place in a heated serving dish. • Pour the sauce over the top, toss well, and serve.

# PENNE WITH FRESH TUNA AND GREEN BEANS

Serves: 4–6

Preparation: 25'

Cooking: 25'

Level of difficulty: 1

- 6 tbsp extra-virgin olive oil
- 2 cloves garlic, whole but lightly crushed
- 14 oz/400 g fresh tuna fillets, bones removed, coarsely chopped
- salt and freshly ground black pepper to taste
- 14 oz/400 g French beans/ green beans
- 6 large firm, ripe tomatoes
- 2 tbsp finely chopped fresh oregano
- $^1/_2$ cup/125 ml dry white wine
- 1 lb/500 g penne

Heat 4 tablespoons of the oil in a large frying pan and sauté the garlic until pale golden brown. Remove and discard the garlic. • Add the tuna and sauté for 5 minutes. Season with salt and pepper. • Add the green beans, tomatoes, half of the oregano, and the wine and cook over medium-high heat for 10 minutes, stirring often. • In the meantime, cook the pasta in a large pan of salted, boiling water until al dente. • Drain the pasta and add to the pan with the tuna sauce. Add the remaining oregano and oil and toss over high heat for 1–2 minutes. • Serve hot.

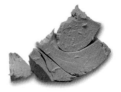

# WHOLE-WHEAT FUSILLI WITH TOMATO AND ARUGULA

C ook the pasta in a large pan of salted, boiling water until *al dente*. • Meanwhile, heat 4 tablespoons of oil in a large frying pan and sauté the onion and scallions for 3–4 minutes. • Add the anchovies and stir until dissolved in the oil. • Add the cherry tomatoes and arugula with 2 tablespoons of cooking water from the pasta pan. Season with salt and pepper and cook over high heat for 3–4 minutes. • Drain the pasta and add to the pan. • Drizzle with the remaining oil, season with pepper, toss gently, and serve hot.

160

*Serves: 4–6*

*Preparation: 20'*

*Cooking: 20'*

*Level of difficulty: 1*

- 1 lb/500 g whole-wheat/wholemeal fusilli
- 6 tbsp extra-virgin olive oil
- $1/2$ small onion, finely chopped
- 2 scallions/spring onions, thinly sliced
- 2–4 anchovy fillets
- 1 lb/500 g cherry tomatoes, cut in half
- 1 small bunch arugula/rocket, chopped
- salt and freshly ground black pepper to taste

# MALLOREDDUS WITH LAMB SAUCE

Heat the oil in a heavy-bottomed saucepan and sauté the onion, garlic, and rosemary for 5 minutes. • Add the lamb, season with salt and pepper, and sauté until nicely browned. • Add the tomatoes, cover the pan and simmer for at least 2 hours. • Cook the malloreddus in a large pan of salted, boiling water until al dente. • Drain and add to the pan with the sauce. Toss well, sprinkle with the Pecorino, and serve hot.

162

Serves: 4–6

Preparation: 25'

Cooking: 2 h 15'

Level of difficulty: 1

- 6 tbsp extra-virgin olive oil
- 1 onion, finely chopped
- 4 cloves garlic, finely chopped
- 2 tbsp finely chopped rosemary
- 2 lb/1 kg lamb, cut from the leg and finely chopped with a knife
- salt and freshly ground black pepper to taste
- 1 lb/500 g peeled and chopped tomatoes
- 1 lb/500 g malloreddus
- 4 oz/125 g freshly grated Pecorino cheese

# PENNE WITH PEAS, PANCETTA, AND ONIONS

Serves: 4–6

Preparation: 15'

Cooking: 35'

Level of difficulty: 1

- **6 tbsp extra-virgin olive oil**
- **5 oz/150 g pancetta, cut in small pieces**
- **4 medium onions, finely chopped**
- **1 lb/500 g fresh or frozen peas**
- **salt and freshly ground black pepper to taste**
- **1 lb/500 g penne**

Heat the oil in a large frying pan and sauté the pancetta for 2 minutes. • Add the onion and sauté until soft. • Stir in the peas and simmer over low heat for about 20 minutes, or until the peas and soft and imbued with the flavor of the onions. Season with salt and pepper. • Meanwhile, cook the pasta in a large pot of salted, boiling water until al dente. Drain well and add to the pan with the sauce. • Toss briefly and serve hot.

# CONCHIGLIE WITH VEGETABLES AND HERBS

Serves:: 4–6

Preparation: 20'

Cooking: 20'

Level of difficulty: 1

- 6 tbsp extra-virgin olive oil
- 1 white onion, coarsely chopped
- 2 tbsp finely chopped mixed herbs (rosemary, marjoram, thyme, oregano, basil)
- 1 red bell pepper/capsicum, cleaned and cut in squares
- 1 yellow bell pepper/capsicum, cleaned and cut in squares
- 1 large zucchini, cut in cubes
- 7 oz/200 g Ricotta cheese, drained
- salt and freshly ground black pepper to taste
- 1 lb/500 g conchiglie

Heat 4 tablespoons of oil in a large frying pan and sauté the onion and herbs for 5 minutes. • Add the red and yellow bell pepper and zucchini diced vegetables and season with salt and pepper. Cover the pan and cook for 10–15 minutes, stirring often. • Cook the pasta in a large pan of salted, boiling water until *al dente*. • Drain the pasta, reserving $1/2$ cup (125 ml) of the cooking water. Add the pasta to the pan with the vegetables. Add the Ricotta and a generous grinding of black pepper. Drizzle with the remaining oil. • Toss gently and serve.

# CAVATELLI WITH PANCETTA AND BROCCOLI

Bring a large pan of salted water to a boil and blanch the broccoli for 5 minutes. Drain well, reserving the water. Return the water to the boil and add the pasta. • Heat the oil in a large frying pan and sauté the garlic, pancetta, and parsley for 3–4 minutes. • Add the broccoli and garbanzo beans and cook over high heat for 5–7 minutes, stirring constantly. • Add the red pepper flakes and season with salt and pepper. • Drain the pasta and add to the pan with the broccoli sauce. Toss gently over medium heat for 2 minutes. • Serve hot.

*Serves: 4–6*

*Preparation: 20'*

*Cooking: 25'*

*Level of difficulty: 1*

- **14 oz/400 g broccoli florets**
- **1 lb/500 g cavatelli**
- **4 tbsp extra-virgin olive oil**
- **2 cloves garlic, finely chopped**
- **4 oz/125 g pancetta, cut in small strips**
- **2 tbsp finely chopped parsley**
- **8 oz/250 g cooked garbanzo beans/ chick-peas**
- **1 tsp red pepper flakes**
- **salt and freshly ground black pepper to taste**

# MACCHERONI WITH ANCHOVIES AND CAPERS

Heat 2 tablespoons of the oil in a small saucepan over low heat. Add the anchovies and stir until they dissolve. Remove from the heat and set aside. • Sauté the garlic, capers, and chile in the remaining oil in a large frying pan until the garlic is pale gold. • Meanwhile, cook the pasta in salted boiling water until al dente. • Drain and add to the frying pan. Add the anchovies and oil, toss gently, and serve hot.

Serves: 4–6

Preparation: 15'

Cooking: 20'

Level of difficulty: 1

- $^1/_2$ cup/125 ml extra-virgin olive oil
- 6 anchovy fillets packed in oil, rinsed and finely chopped
- 3 cloves garlic, finely chopped
- 2 tbsp capers packed in salt, rinsed
- dried chile pepper, to taste
- 1 lb/500 g maccheroni

# MACCHERONCINI WITH PEAS, SAUSAGE, AND SAGE

Serves: 4–6

Preparation: 30'

Cooking: 45'

Level of difficulty: 1

- 1 small onion, finely chopped
- 1 tbsp butter
- 1 tbsp tomato purée
- 7 oz/200 g Italian sausage, crumbled
- $^1/_2$ cup/125 ml heavy/double cream
- 1 clove garlic, finely chopped
- 1 small bunch fresh sage
- 2 tbsp extra-virgin olive oil
- 2 cups/250 g fresh or frozen peas
- $^1/_4$ tsp sugar
- 1 cup/250 ml boiling water
- salt and freshly ground black pepper to taste
- 1 tbsp finely chopped parsley
- 1 lb/500 g maccheroncini
- 6 tbsp freshly grated Parmesan cheese

Sauté the onion in the butter in a medium saucepan over medium heat for 5 minutes. • Add the tomato sauce and sausage. • Pour in the cream and cook over low heat for 15 minutes. • Sauté the garlic and sage in the oil in a frying pan until the garlic is pale gold. • Stir in the peas, sugar, and hot water. • Cook, adding more water if needed, until the peas are tender. • Season with salt, add the parsley, and remove from the heat. • Cook the pasta in salted, boiling water until al dente. • Drain and add to the sauce. • Sprinkle with the Parmesan and serve hot.

# MACCHERONI WITH BROCCOLI AND TUNA

Rinse the broccoli under cold running water. Cut the stem into small chunks and divide the tops into florets. Use the broccoli leaves as well, coarsely chopped. • Cook the broccoli in a large pan of salted water for 5 minutes, then drain well, reserving the cooking water. • Bring the cooking water back to the boil and add the pasta. • Meanwhile, heat 4 tablespoons of the oil in a large frying pan and sauté the onion for 5 minutes. • Add the tuna, chile pepper, and thyme, and season with salt and pepper. Pour in 1 scant cup (200 ml) of cooking water from the pasta, and simmer over low heat for 10 minutes, or until the pasta is cooked al dente. • Drain the pasta and add to the pan. Toss gently for a few minutes. • Drizzle with the remaining oil and serve hot.

*This healthy dish is also very good when made with whole-wheat (wholemeal) pasta.*

170

*Serves: 4–6*

*Preparation: 20'*

*Cooking: 25'*

*Level of difficulty: 1*

- 1 lb/500 g broccoli (or cauliflower)
- 1 lb/500 g maccheroni
- 6 tbsp extra-virgin olive oil
- 1 large onion, finely chopped
- 8 oz/250 g tuna, packed in oil, drained
- 1 dried chile pepper, crumbled
- 1 tbsp finely chopped fresh thyme (or 1 tsp dried thyme)
- salt and freshly ground black pepper to taste

# PENNE WITH PISTACHIOS AND BLACK OLIVES

Place the pistachios in a food processor and chop finely. • Heat the oil in a large frying pan and sauté the onion with the pistachios and cream. Season with salt. • Cook the pasta in a large pan of salted, boiling water until al dente. • Drain well and add to the frying pan with the sauce. • Add the olives and the Parmesan cheese and toss gently for 2 minutes over high heat. • Transfer to a heated serving dish and sprinkle with the bread crumbs and the extra chopped pistachios.
• Serve hot.

*Serves: 4–6*

*Preparation: 25'*

*Cooking: 20'*

*Level of difficulty: 1*

- **6 oz/180 g shelled pistachios**
- **4 tbsp extra-virgin olive oil**
- **1 onion, finely chopped**
- **4 tbsp heavy/ double cream**
- **salt to taste**
- **1 lb/500 g penne**
- **4 oz/125 g pitted black olives, sliced into rounds**
- **$^2/_3$ cup/100 g freshly grated Parmesan cheese**
- **4 tbsp extra shelled pistachios, coarsely chopped, to garnish**

# FARFALLE WITH SPRING ONIONS AND PANCETTA

Place half the the garbanzo beans in a food processor and chop coarsely. • Heat the oil in a large frying pan and sauté the scallions over medium heat for 3–4 minutes. • Add the pancetta and sauté for 2 minutes. • Add the cabbage and stock and cook over low heat for 10 minutes, stirring often. • Season with salt and pepper and add both the whole and chopped garbanzo beans. Cook for 5 more minutes. • Meanwhile, cook the pasta in a large pan of salted, boiling water until *al dente*. • Drain and add to the sauce. • Toss gently and serve.

174

*Serves: 4–6*

*Preparation: 15'*

*Cooking: 20'*

*Level of difficulty: 1*

- 7 oz/200 g cooked garbanzo beans/ chick peas
- 2 tbsp extra-virgin olive oil
- 2 scallions/green onions, finely chopped
- 3 oz/90 g pancetta, diced
- 8 oz/250 g Savoy cabbage, shredded
- ²/₃ cup/150 ml Vegetable Stock (see page 956)
- salt and freshly ground black pepper to taste
- 1 lb/500 g farfalle

# SPICY TOMATO FUSILLI

*Serves: 4–6*

*Preparation: 20'*

*Cooking: 25'*

*Level of difficulty: 1*

- **4 tbsp butter**
- **2 tbsp extra-virgin olive oil**
- **1 onion, finely chopped**
- **2 cloves garlic, finely chopped**
- **1¹/₄ lb/600 g canned tomatoes**
- **4 tbsp white wine**
- **1 bay leaf**
- **salt to taste**
- **2 red bell peppers/ capsicums, chopped**
- **dried red chile pepper to taste**
- **1 lb/500 g fusilli**
- **8 basil leaves, torn**

Heat the butter and oil in a large frying pan and sauté the onion and garlic for 10 minutes.
• Add the tomatoes, wine, and bay leaf. Season with salt and bring to a boil, stirring. Cover and cook for 1 hour over very low heat, stirring occasionally. • Twenty minutes before the sauce is cooked, add the bell pepper and chile pepper. • Cook the pasta in a large pan of salted, boiling water until *al dente*. • Drain and transfer to a heated serving bowl. • Remove the bay leaf from the sauce and pour over the pasta. Sprinkle with the basil and toss gently. If liked, add more chile pepper. • Serve hot.

# PENNE WITH WILD FENNEL, TUNA, AND PINE NUTS

*Serves: 4–6*

*Preparation: 20'*

*Cooking: 25'*

*Level of difficulty: 1*

- 12 oz/350 g wild fennel
- 5 tbsp extra-virgin olive oil
- 1 onion, finely chopped
- 2 cloves garlic, finely chopped
- 1 tbsp capers, packed in salt, rinsed
- 2¹/₂ oz/75 g pine nuts
- 12 oz/350 g tuna, packed in olive oil, drained
- 6 tbsp dry white wine
- salt to taste
- 1 dried chile pepper, crumbled
- 1 lb/500 g penne
- fresh basil leaves, torn, to garnish (optional)

Trim the fennel and rinse well in cold running water. • Blanch the fennel for 5 minutes in a saucepan of salted, boiling water water. Drain well, reserving the cooking water, and chop coarsely. • Heat the oil in a large frying pan and sauté the onion and garlic for 5 minutes. • Add the fennel, capers, and pine nuts and sauté for 5 minutes. • Add the tuna and sauté for 2–3 minutes more, breaking the tuna up with a fork. • Drizzle with the wine and cook until it has evaporated. • Season the sauce with salt and chile pepper, then pour in ¹/₂ cup (125 ml) of the reserved cooking water. • Meanwhile, cook the pasta in the remaining reserved cooking water until al dente. • Drain well and add to the frying pan with the sauce. Toss gently and remove from the heat. • Garnish with the basil, if using, and serve hot.

*If you can't find wild fennel, substitute with the same amount of Swiss chard.*

# FUSILLI WITH SMOKED SALMON, CREAM, AND DILL

C ook the pasta in a large pan of salted, boiling water until al dente. • In the meantime, heat the butter and cream in a large frying pan. Add the salmon and season with salt and pepper. Stir over medium heat until the sauce reduces a little. • Drain the pasta well and add to the pan with the sauce. Toss gently and sprinkle with the dill. • Serve hot.

*Serves: 4–6*

*Preparation: 15'*

*Cooking: 15'*

*Level of difficulty: 1*

- **1 lb/500 g fusilli**
- **12 oz/350 g smoked salmon, chopped in small pieces**
- **6 tbsp butter**
- **$^{1}/_{2}$ cup/125 ml heavy/double cream**
- **salt and freshly ground black pepper to taste**
- **1 bunch fresh dill, finely chopped**

178

# PENNE WITH CAULIFLOWER

*Serves: 4–6*

*Preparation: 15'*

*Cooking: 30'*

*Level of difficulty: 1*

- 1 cauliflower, weighing about 1 1/2 lb/750 g
- salt and freshly ground black pepper to taste
- 1 lb/500 g penne
- 3 cloves garlic, finely chopped
- 6 tbsp extra-virgin olive oil
- 2 tbsp finely chopped parsley

Divide the cauliflower into the head and stalk. Peel and chop the stalk coarsely. • Fill a large saucepan with cold water and add the cauliflower stalks. • Bring to a boil and add salt and the cauliflower heads. Cook for 5 minutes. • Add the pasta and cook until al dente. • Sauté the garlic in the oil in a frying pan over medium heat until the garlic is pale gold. • Remove from the heat. Add the parsley. • Drain the pasta and cauliflower and add to the sauce. Season with a grinding of black pepper, toss gently, and serve.

# PENNE WITH TOMATO SAUCE AND TURKEY ROLLS

Cut the turkey in thin slices. Gently pound the slices with a meat tenderizer. • Season the turkey meat lightly with salt and pepper. Sprinkle with the garlic, cheese, and parsley. • Carefully roll each slice up into a small roll, fastening each one with a toothpick. • Heat the oil in a frying pan and sauté the onion until translucent, about 5–7 minutes. • Add the turkey rolls and brown gently on all sides. • Pour in the wine and cook until it has evaporated. • Add the tomato sauce, cover, and cook over low heat for about one hour. Add water or stock to the pan during cooking if the sauce dries out too much. • About 15 minutes before the sauce is ready, cook the pasta in a large pan of salted, boiling water until al dente. • Drain well and transfer to a heated serving dish. • Pour the sauce over the top, tossing gently. • Serve hot.

Serves: 4–6

Preparation: 30'

Cooking: 1 h + 15'

Level of difficulty: 2

- 14 oz/400 g turkey thigh or breast
- salt and freshly ground black pepper to taste
- 2–3 cloves garlic, thinly sliced
- 3 oz/90 g Pecorino cheese, in flakes
- 2 tbsp finely chopped parsley
- 4 tbsp extra-virgin olive oil
- 1 onion, finely chopped
- $^1/_2$ cup/125 ml dry white wine
- 1 quantity Tomato Sauce (see page 950)

# CONCHIGLIE WITH GARLIC, CAULIFLOWER, AND CHILE

182

Divide the cauliflower into bite-sized florets and dice the stalk into small cubes. Cook in boiling water until half cooked (about 7 minutes). Drain and set aside. • Combine the oil, butter, and onion in a large frying pan and sauté until the onion is transparent. Add the garlic and crushed chilies and sauté until the garlic begins to change color. • Add the cauliflower pieces and cook over medium-low heat for 8–10 more minutes, or until the cauliflower is tender. Season with salt and pepper. • Cook the conchiglie in a large pot of salted, boiling water until al dente. • Drain well and transfer to the pan. Toss the pasta and sauce together over medium heat for 2–3 minutes. • Serve hot.

Serves: 4–6
Preparation: 10'
Cooking: 25'
Level of difficulty: 1

- 1 large cauliflower
- 4 tbsp extra-virgin olive oil
- 3 tbsp butter
- 1 medium onion
- 4 cloves garlic, finely chopped
- 1 tsp crushed chilies
- salt and freshly ground black pepper to taste
- 1 lb/500 g conchiglie

# PENNE WITH FRESH PEAS

*Serves: 4–6*

*Preparation: 30'*

*Cooking: 30'*

*Level of difficulty: 1*

- 4 tbsp extra-virgin olive oil
- 1 medium white onion, thinly sliced
- salt and freshly ground white pepper to taste
- 2 cups/500 ml Beef or Vegetable Stock (see pages 955 or 956)
- 1 lb/500 g penne
- 1 lb/500 g shelled fresh peas

Heat the olive oil in a large frying pan and sauté the onion until translucent, about 5–7 minutes. • Add the peas and season with salt and pepper. Cover and simmer over medium-low heat for 10 minutes. • Uncover the frying pan and pour in the stock. Turn the heat up to medium and cook for 5–10 minutes, or until the peas are

*Add extra flavor by adding 2 tablespoons of finely chopped mint just before removing from the heat.*

very tender. • Meanwhile, cook the pasta in a large pan of salted, boiling water until al dente. • Drain well and add to the pan with the sauce. • Toss gently for 1–2 minutes. • Serve hot.

# FUSILLI WITH SPINACH AND ONION SAUCE

Heat 2 tablespoons of oil in a large frying pan and sauté the onions, capers, and anchovies over low heat for 5 minutes. Add 2 tablespoons of hot water and cook over low heat for 10 minutes.
• Blanch the spinach in a little salted, boiling water for 3–4 minutes. Drain well. • Meanwhile, cook the pasta in a large pan of salted, boiling water. • Heat the remaining oil in a large frying pan and sauté the garlic until pale golden brown. Discard the garlic and add the spinach to the oil. • Drain the pasta, and add to the pan with the spinach. • Toss gently for 1 minute. • Top with the onion sauce, olive, and parsley, and serve hot.

- $^1/_2$ cup/125 ml extra-virgin olive oil
- 3 onions, thinly sliced
- 8–10 anchovy fillets
- 2 tbsp capers, packed in salt, rinsed
- 1 lb/500 g fusilli
- 2 lb/1 kg spinach, chopped
- 2 cloves garlic, whole but crushed
- $^2/_3$ cup/60 g black olives
- 1 tbsp finely chopped parsley

186

Serves: 4

Preparation: 30'

Cooking: 45'

Level of difficulty: 1

- 1 onion, coarsely chopped
- 2 large potatoes, peeled and coarsely chopped
- 3 tomatoes, coarsely chopped
- 3 cloves garlic, 1 whole and 2 finely chopped and coarsely chopped
- 1 lb/500 g Swiss chard, cleaned
- salt and freshly ground black pepper to taste
- 4 tbsp extra-virgin olive oil
- 8 oz/250 g ditalini
- 3/4 cup/90 g freshly grated Pecorino cheese

# DITALINI WITH VEGETABLES

Bring a large saucepan of water to the boil with the onion, potato, 1 tomato, and whole clove of garlic. Add the Swiss chard and season with salt. Cook for 20 minutes, or until the chard is tender. Drain, reserving the cooking water. • Sauté the remaining garlic in the oil in a large frying pan until pale gold. • Add the remaining tomatoes and sauté for 10 minutes. • Season with salt and add the chard and other vegetables. • Meanwhile, bring the reserved cooking water to a boil and cook the pasta until al dente. • Drain and add to the pan with the vegetables. • Toss gently, sprinkle with the Pecorino, and serve hot.

# TROFIE WITH SPICY FAVA BEAN SAUCE

C ook the Catalogna chicory in a large pan of salted, boiling water for 5 minutes, then add the pasta. • In the meantime, heat 4 tablespoons of oil in a large frying pan and sauté the garlic until pale golden brown. • Add the fava beans and chile pepper. Season with salt and pepper, cover, and cook over medium-high heat. • Drain the pasta and chicory and add them to the pan with the fava bean sauce. • Add the tomatoes and drizzle with the remaining oil. Season with a little more salt and pepper, if liked. Toss gently over low heat for 2–3 minutes. • Serve hot.

*Serves: 4–6*

*Preparation: 15'*

*Cooking: 25'*

*Level of difficulty: 1*

- 8 oz/250 g Catalogna chicory, coarsely chopped
- 1 lb/500 g dried trofie
- 6 tbsp extra-virgin olive oil
- 3 cloves garlic, finely chopped
- 12 oz/300 g frozen fava/broad beans
- dried chile pepper, crumbled, to taste
- salt and freshly ground black pepper to taste
- 16–20 cherry tomatoes, diced

# SPIRALS WITH GREEN BEANS AND TUNA

Cook the beans in salted water for 10 minutes. Drain and cut into 1-inch (2.5-cm) pieces. • Heat the oil in a large frying pan and sauté the onion for 5 minutes. • Add the beans to the pan and season with salt and pepper. Partially cover and simmer over low heat for 10 minutes. • Cook the pasta in a large pan of salted, boiling water until al dente. • Place the tuna in a heated serving dish and crumble with a fork. • Drain the pasta and add to the dish with the tuna. Pour the bean and onion mixture over the top and sprinkle with the thyme and marjoram. • Toss gently and serve hot.

Serves: 4–6

Preparation: 20'

Cooking: 30'

Level of difficulty: 1

- 1 lb/500 g green beans
- 6 tbsp extra-virgin olive oil
- 1 large onion, finely chopped
- salt and freshly ground black pepper to taste
- 1 lb/500 g spirals
- 8 oz/250 g tuna, packed in oil
- 1 tbsp each finely chopped fresh thyme and marjoram

# FUSILLI WITH CHEESE AND ZUCCHINI

*Serves: 4–6*

*Preparation: 15'*

*Cooking: 25'*

*Level of difficulty: 1*

- **4 tbsp extra-virgin olive oil**
- **1 lb/500 g zucchini /courgettes, diced**
- **4 shallots, finely chopped**
- **salt and freshly ground white pepper to taste**
- **1/2 cup/125 ml dry white wine**
- **1 lb/500 g fusilli**
- **1 cup/250 ml heavy/double cream**
- **5 oz/150 g Fontina cheese, diced**

Heat the oil in a large frying pan and sauté the zucchini and shallots for 7–8 minutes. • Season with salt and pepper. Drizzle with the wine and cook until it evaporates. • Meanwhile, cook the pasta in a large pan of salted, boiling water until al dente. • Add 1/2 cup (125 ml) of water from the pasta pan to the zucchini sauce and cook over high heat. • Add the cream, cheese, and well-drained pasta and toss over high heat for 2–3 minutes. • Serve hot.

# RUOTE WITH ARTICHOKES AND SUN-DRIED TOMATOES

C lean the artichokes by pulling down and snapping off the tough outer leaves. Trim the stalk and cut off the top third of the leaves. Cut the artichokes in half and remove any fuzzy choke. Chop finely. • Cook the pasta in a large pan of salted, boiling water until al dente. • In the meantime, heat the oil in a large frying pan and sauté the onion for 5 minutes. • Add the anchovies and stir until they have dissolved in the oil. • Add the sun-dried tomatoes and artichokes and drizzle with $^1/_2$ cup (125 ml) of cooking water from the pasta pan. Cook over high heat for 5 minutes. Season with salt and pepper. • Drain the pasta and add to the pan. Toss over high heat for 2–3 minutes. • Serve hot, sprinkled with the Parmesan.

*Serves: 4–6*

*Preparation: 20'*

*Cooking: 20'*

*Level of difficulty: 1*

- **2 artichokes**
- **1 lb/500 g ruote**
- **6 tbsp extra-virgin olive oil**
- **1 large onion, finely chopped**
- **24 sun-dried tomatoes, packed in oil, chopped**
- **8 anchovy fillets, packed in oil**
- **salt and freshly ground black pepper to taste**
- **1 cup/120 g freshly grated Parmesan cheese**

# FARFALLE WITH WALNUT PESTO

Blanch the walnuts in boiling water for 1 minute. Drain and remove the tannic peel. • Cook the farfalle in a large pan of salted, boiling water until al dente. • Chop the walnuts finely in a food processor. • Place in a large bowl with the sugar, cinnamon, and lemon zest. • Drain the pasta and add to the bowl with the walnut pesto. • Toss gently and garnish with the extra walnuts. • Serve hot.

*Serves: 4–6*

*Preparation: 20'*

*Cooking: 20'*

*Level of difficulty: 1*

- **10 oz/300 g shelled walnuts**
- **1 lb/500 g farfalle**
- **2 tbsp brown sugar**
- **$^1/_2$ tsp ground cinnamon**
- **grated zest of $^1/_2$ lemon**
- **20 extra walnuts, shelled and cut in half, to garnish**

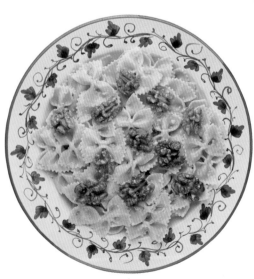

# PENNE WITH TOMATO AND BASIL SAUCE

Serves: 4–6

Preparation: 15'

Cooking: 30'

Level of difficulty: 1

- 1¹/₂ lb/750 g peeled and chopped tomatoes
- fresh basil leaves, torn + extra to garnish
- 2 cloves garlic, finely chopped
- 6 tbsp extra-virgin olive oil
- salt and freshly ground black pepper to taste
- 1 lb/500 g penne
- 6 tbsp freshly grated Parmesan cheese

Place the tomatoes, torn basil, garlic, oil, salt, and pepper in a medium saucepan over medium heat. Partially cover the pan and cook for 25 minutes. Stir often with a wooden spoon. • Cook the pasta in a large pan of salted, boiling water until al dente. • Drain the pasta and transfer to the saucepan with the sauce. Toss well. • Serve hot, sprinkled with the Parmesan, and garnished with the extra basil.

# FUSILLI WITH RICOTTA BALLS AND CELERY

*Serves: 4–6*

*Preparation: 20'*

*Cooking: 25'*

*Level of difficulty: 1*

- 1 lb/500 g **Ricotta cheese, drained**
- 8 tbsp **freshly grated Parmesan cheese**
- $2/3$ cup/100 g **all purpose/plain flour**
- **salt and freshly ground white pepper to taste**
- 2 tbsp **parsley, chopped finely**
- 1 **egg yolk**
- 6 tbsp **extra-virgin olive oil**
- 1 large **celery heart**
- **juice of 1 lemon**
- 10–12 **shelled walnuts, coarsely chopped**
- 4 tbsp **stock**
- 1 clove **garlic, finely chopped**
- 1 lb/500 g **fusilli**
- $1/2$ cup/75 g **fine dry bread crumbs**

Preheat the oven to 400° F/200° C/gas 6. • Place the Ricotta and Parmesan in a large bowl with the flour, salt, pepper, parsley, and egg yolk. Mix well, then shape into balls the size of large marbles. • Transfer the balls to an oiled baking dish, drizzle with 2 tablespoons of oil, and bake for 10 minutes. • Divide the celery in two and process half of it with the lemon juice, walnuts, and stock in a food processor until smooth. • Slice the remaining celery into short lengths. • Heat the remaining oil in a large frying pan and sauté the chopped celery and garlic for 5 minutes. • In the meantime, cook the pasta in a large pan of salted, boiling water until al dente. • Drain well and add to the frying pan. Add the processed celery mixture and toss over medium heat for 2 minutes. • Add the bread crumbs and transfer to a heated serving bowl. • Add the Ricotta balls and toss gently.
• Serve at once.

# RUOTE WITH TOMATO PESTO

Serves: 4–6
Preparation: 10'
Cooking: 1 h 15'
Level of difficulty: 1

- 1 lb/500 g tomatoes
- 1 lb/500 g ruote
- 6 tbsp extra-virgin olive oil
- 45 leaves basil
- 1 clove garlic
- 4 tbsp pine nuts + extra to serve
- 1 cup/120 g freshly grated Pecorino
- salt to taste

Preheat the oven to 240°F/120°C/gas 2. • Blanch the tomatoes in a pan of boiling water for 1 minutes. Drain and peel. Cut in half. • Bake the tomatoes in the oven for 1 hour. • Chop the basil, garlic, and pine nuts in a food processor until smooth. • Place in a bowl with the cheese. Season with salt. • Chop the tomatoes coarsely and add to the pesto. • Cook the pasta in a large pan of salted, boiling water until al dente. Drain and add to the bowl with the pesto. • Toss gently, sprinkle with the extra pine nuts, and serve.

| | |
|---|---|
| Serves: 4–6 | |
| Preparation: 15' | |
| Cooking: 25' | |
| Level of difficulty: 1 | |

# PENNE WITH PESTO AND ZUCCHINI

- 6 tbsp extra-virgin olive oil
- 1 onion, thinly sliced
- 2 tbsp water
- 4 large zucchini/courgettes, thinly sliced
- 6–8 zucchini/courgette flowers
- 1 bunch basil
- salt and freshly ground black pepper to taste
- 2 tbsp pine nuts
- 1 lb/500 g penne

Heat 1 tablespoon of oil in a large frying pan and add the onion and water. Cook over medium-low heat for 5 minutes. • Add the zucchini and cook for 10–15 minutes. • Rinse and clean the basil. Chop in a food processor with the remaining oil and pine nuts. • Chop the zucchini flowers. • Cook the pasta in a large pan of salted, boiling water until al dente. • Drain well and place in a heated serving dish. Add the sauce and zucchini flowers and toss gently. • Serve hot.

# SPIRALS WITH BEANS AND BASIL

Heat 6 tablespoons of the oil in a large frying and and sauté the onion and chile pepper for 6–8 minutes, or until the onion is translucent.
• Trim the green beans and cut into short lengths.
• Add the green beans and fava beans to the frying pan with the onion. Season with salt and pepper and cook over medium-high heat for 10 minutes, stirring continuously. • In the meantime, cook the pasta in a large pan of salted, boiling water until al dente. • Drain the pasta and add, together with $^1/_2$ cup (125 ml) of cooking water, to the pan with the beans. • Toss over medium heat with the basil and remaining oil for 1–2 minutes. • Serve hot.

*Serves: 4–6*

*Preparation: 25'*

*Cooking: 25'*

*Level of difficulty: 1*

- $^1/_2$ cup/125 ml extra-virgin olive oil
- 1 large onion, coarsely chopped
- 1 green spicy chile pepper, finely chopped
- 10 oz/300 g French beans/ green beans
- 1 lb/500 g small fava beans, peeled
- salt and freshly ground black pepper to taste
- 1 lb/500 g spirals
- 12 leaves fresh basil, torn

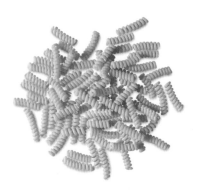

# PENNE WITH CHERRY TOMATOES AND PINE NUTS

*Serves: 4–6*

*Preparation: 15'*

*Cooking: 20'*

*Level of difficulty: 1*

- 6 tbsp extra-virgin olive oil
- 3 cloves garlic, whole but lightly crushed
- 1 lb/500 g cherry tomatoes, cut in half
- salt and freshly ground black pepper to taste
- $^1/_3$ cup/75 g pine nuts
- 1 lb/500 g penne
- 8 oz/250 g fresh small-leaf spinach

Heat the oil in a large frying pan and sauté the garlic until golden brown. Remove the garlic and discard. • Add the cherry tomatoes and cook over high heat for 5 minutes. Season with salt and pepper. Remove from the heat and set aside.

• Toast the pine nuts in a small frying pan over medium-high heat. Do not add any oil or fat to the pan. • In the meantime, cook the penne in a large pan of salted, boiling water for half the time indicated on the package. Add the spinach continue cooking until the pasta is al dente.

• Drain the penne and spinach and add to the frying pan with the cherry tomatoes. Toss over high heat for 2–3 minutes. • Add the pine nuts and a generous grinding of pepper and serve immediately.

# PENNE WITH SMOKED SALMON

P lace the celery, tomatoes, vinegar, oil, salt, and smoked salmon in a large bowl. • Pierce the garlic cloves with the tines (prongs) of a fork and use it to stir the ingredients in the bowl. The garlic will flavor the mixture (take care that the cloves do not come off). • Cook the penne in a large pot of salted, boiling water until al dente. • Drain and transfer to the bowl. Add the Parmesan and toss gently. • Serve hot or at room temperature.

*Serves: 4–6*

*Preparation: 10'*

*Cooking: 15'*

*Level of difficulty: 1*

- **2 stalks celery, 2 tomatoes, finely sliced**
- **4 tbsp vinegar**
- **$1/2$ cup/125 ml extra-virgin olive oil**
- **salt to taste**
- **4 oz/125 g smoked salmon, thinly sliced**
- **2 cloves garlic, whole**
- **1 lb/500 g penne**
- **6 tbsp freshly grated Parmesan cheese**

# PENNE WITH GORGONZOLA

Place the butter, Gorgonzola, and cream in a double boiler over barely simmering water until the cheese has melted. Season with salt. • Cook the pasta in a large pan of salted, boiling water until al dente. • Drain and transfer to a heated serving dish. • Pour the Gorgonzola sauce over the top, sprinkle with the Parmesan, and toss gently. • Serve hot.

206

Serves: 4–6

Preparation: 5'

Cooking: 15'

Level of difficulty: 1

- **2 tbsp butter**
- **12 oz/350 g creamy Gorgonzola cheese, crumbled**
- **$^3/_4$ cup/180 ml heavy/double cream**
- **salt to taste**
- **1 lb/500 g penne pasta**
- **8 tbsp freshly grated Parmesan cheese**

# PENNE WITH BELL PEPPER SAUCE

*Serves: 4–6*

*Preparation: 15'*

*Cooking: 45'*

*Level of difficulty: 1*

- 3 large yellow bell peppers/capsicums
- 6 tbsp extra-virgin olive oil
- ²/₃ cup/150 g pancetta, diced
- 1 large onion, finely chopped
- 2 cloves garlic, finely chopped
- 3 tbsp boiling water
- salt and freshly ground black pepper to taste
- 2 tbsp vinegar
- 1 lb/500 g penne
- 4–6 tbsp freshly grated Parmesan cheese

Cut the bell peppers in half, remove the stalks and seeds, and cut into thin strips. • Heat the oil in a large frying pan and sauté the bell peppers, pancetta, onion, and garlic for 8–10 minutes. • Add the tomatoes and boiling water. Season with salt and pepper. Simmer over medium heat for about 20 minutes, or until the bell peppers are tender. • Stir in the vinegar and cook over high heat for 2–3 minutes until the vinegar evaporates. Remove from heat. • Meanwhile, cook the pasta in a large pan of salted, boiling water until al dente. Drain well and place in a heated serving dish. • Pour the sauce over the top, sprinkle with the cheese, and toss well. • Serve hot.

# WHOLE-WHEAT RIGATONI WITH VEGETABLE SAUCE

Heat the oil in a large frying pan and sauté the onion, carrot, celery, parsley, and garlic over high heat for 5–7 minutes, or until the vegetables are wilted. • Pour in the wine and cook until evaporated. • Add the tomatoes, peas, capers, and olives. Taste the sauce—it may already be quite salty because of the capers and olives—then season with salt and pepper. Partially cover the pan and cook over low heat for 25–30 minutes. • About 15 minutes before the sauce is ready, cook the pasta in a large pan of salted, boiling water until al dente. • Drain the pasta and add to the sauce. Sprinkle with the Pecorino and toss gently over high heat for 1–2 minutes. • Serve hot.

Serves: 4–6

Preparation: 20'

Cooking: 45'

Level of difficulty: 1

- 6 tbsp extra-virgin olive oil
- 1 large onion, finely chopped
- 1 large carrot, finely chopped
- 1 stalk celery, finely chopped
- 1 tbsp finely chopped parsley
- 2 cloves garlic, finely chopped
- $^1/_2$ cup/125 ml dry white wine
- $1^1/_2$ lb/750 g peeled and chopped tomatoes
- 5 oz/150 g fresh or frozen peas
- 2 tbsp salted capers, rinsed
- 16 pitted black olives, sliced
- 1 lb/500 g whole-wheat/wholemeal rigatoni
- 1 cup/120 g freshly grated Pecorino cheese

# RIGATONI WITH SQUID

Heat 4 tablespoons of the oil in a large frying pan and sauté the garlic until pale golden brown. • Add the squid and sauté for 3–4 minutes over high heat. • Add the tomatoes and continue cooking over high heat., stirring often, for 10 minutes, or until the tomato juices have reduced and the squid is tender. • Season with salt and pepper and add the shredded basil, if liked. Cover the pan and turn off heat. • In the meantime, cook the pasta in a large pan of salted, boiling water until al dente. • Drain well and add to the pan with the sauce. • Toss over medium-high heat for 2 minutes. • Drizzle with the remaining oil and serve hot.

*Serves: 4–6*

*Preparation: 25'*

*Cooking: 20'*

*Level of difficulty: 1*

- **6 tbsp extra-virgin olive oil**
- **4 cloves garlic, cut in half**
- **12 oz/350 g small squid, cleaned**
- **1 lb/500 g firm, ripe tomatoes, peeled and coarsely chopped**
- **salt and freshly ground black pepper to taste**
- **16 leaves fresh basil, shredded (optional)**
- **1 lb/500 g rigatoni**

# MALLOREDDUS WITH SAUSAGE AND PECORINO

Heat the oil in a large frying pan then add the sausages, onion, garlic, and torn basil and sauté over medium heat until the onion turns pale gold. • Add the tomatoes and season with salt and pepper. Simmer for 15–20 minutes, or until the sauce thickens and reduces. • Cook the malloreddus in a large pan of salted, boiling water until al dente. • Drain well and add to the pan with the sauce. Sprinkle with the Pecorino and toss gently. • garnish with the extra basil and serve hot.

*Malloreddus pasta is a specialty of Sardinia. Substitute with another small, short pasta if preferred.*

212

Serves: 4–6

Preparation: 10'

Cooking: 45'

Level of difficulty: 1

- 4 tbsp extra-virgin olive oil
- 14 oz/400 g Italian pork sausages, skinned and crumbled
- 1 large onion, finely chopped
- 3 cloves garlic, finely chopped
- 8 basil leaves, torn + extra to garnish
- 1 1/2 lb/750 g fresh tomatoes, peeled and chopped
- salt and freshly ground black pepper to taste
- 1/3 cup/45 g freshly grated Pecorino cheese
- 1 lb/500 g malloreddus

# CONCHIGLIE WITH BEETROOT

*Serves: 4–6*

*Preparation: 15'*

*Cooking: 20'*

*Level of difficulty: 1*

- **4 tbsp extra-virgin olive oil**
- **2 tbsp butter**
- **1 large onion, finely chopped**
- **2 large beetroot, cooked, peeled and diced**
- **salt and freshly ground white pepper to taste**
- **juice of $1/2$ lemon**
- **$1/2$ cup/125 ml dry white wine**
- **1 lb/500 g conchiglie**
- **fresh basil leaves**
- **8 tbsp freshly grated Parmesan cheese**

Heat the oil and butter in a large frying pan and sauté the onion until translucent. • Add the beetroot and season with salt and pepper. Pour in the lemon juice and and wine and cook over high heat for 2–3 minutes, stirring all the time. • Lower heat and partially cover the pan. Cook over low heat for about 10 minutes. • In the meantime, cook the conchiglie in a large pan of salted, boiling water until al dente. • Drain well and add to the pan with the sauce. Add the cream and season again with salt and pepper. • Toss gently over medium heat and serve hot garnished with the basil and sprinkled with the Parmesan.

*The beetroot in this recipe tinges the pasta to a lovely pink color.*

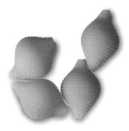

# SPICY FUSILLI WITH EGGPLANTS

Serves: 4–6
Preparation: 15'
Cooking: 15'
Level of difficulty: 1

Heat the oil in a large frying pan and sauté the garlic for 5 minutes. • Add the eggplant and chile pepper and cook for 10 minutes, stirring often. Season with salt and pepper. • Meanwhile, cook the pasta in a large pan of salted, boiling water until al dente. • Drain the pasta thoroughly and place in the pan with the eggplant. Add the capers, oregano, red pepper flakes, and pine nuts. Toss well. • Serve hot.

- 6 tbsp extra-virgin olive oil
- 2 cloves garlic, finely chopped
- 1 large eggplant/ aubergine, cut in small cubes
- 1 fresh chile pepper
- salt and freshly ground black pepper to taste
- 1 lb/500 g fusilli
- 2 tbsp salted capers, rinsed
- 2 tbsp finely chopped fresh oregano
- red pepper flakes, to taste
- 4 tbsp pine nuts

Serves: 4

Preparation: 20'

Cooking: 1 h

Level of difficulty: 1

- 2 tbsp extra-virgin olive oil
- 2 tbsp lard
- 1/2 cup/60 g diced pancetta
- 1 onion, finely chopped
- 7 oz/200 g shelled fava/broad beans
- 2 cups/500 ml cold water, + extra
- 8 oz/250 g ditali
- salt and freshly ground black pepper to taste
- 4 tbsp freshly grated Pecorino cheese

# DITALI WITH FAVA BEANS AND PANCETTA

Heat the oil and lard in an earthenware baking dish or large frying pan. Add the pancetta and sauté over low heat for 5 minutes. • Add the onion and cook for 10 minutes. • Stir in the fava beans and pour in the water. • Bring to a boil and simmer gently for about 40 minutes. • Add the pasta, season with salt, and cook until the pasta is just al dente. If, as you cook the pasta, there is not enough liquid, add more water. • Season with pepper and sprinkle with the Pecorino.

# PENNE WITH CRAB MEAT

Roughly chop the crab sticks. • Pour the oil into a large frying pan and sauté the garlic and parsley over medium-low heat for 1 minute. • Add the crab sticks and orange zest. Mix well and cook for 1 minute. Pour in the cognac and cook until it has evaporated. Add the orange juice. • Season

*The sweet flavor of the crab meat blends beautifully with the orange juice and parsley in this unusual dish.*

with salt and a generous grinding of pepper. Cook until the liquid has evaporated. • After about 10 minutes add the cream. • Meanwhile, cook the pasta in a large pot of salted, boiling water until al dente. Drain and transfer to the pan with the sauce. Toss gently for 1–2 minutes. • Serve immediately.

**218**

Serves: 4–6

Preparation: 25'

Cooking: 25'

Level of difficulty: 1

- **16 crab sticks, fresh or frozen**
- **6 tbsp extra-virgin olive oil**
- **2 cloves garlic, finely chopped**
- **2 tbsp finely chopped parsley**
- **1 tbsp orange zest, cut in julienne strips**
- **scant ¹/₂ cup/ 100 ml cognac**
- **¹/₂ cup/125 ml fresh orange juice**
- **salt and freshly ground black pepper to taste**
- **¹/₂ cup/125 ml heavy/double cream**
- **1 lb/500 g penne**

# MACCHERONI WITH MEATBALLS

220

P lace the milk in a small bowl and add the bread. • Place the beef, prosciutto, parsley, and garlic in a food processor and chop until smooth. • Transfer to a bowl and add the well-squeezed bread, egg yolk, lemon zest, and nutmeg. Season with salt and pepper and mix well. • Shape the mixture into balls about the size of a marble and roll them in the flour. Set aside. • Heat the oil in a large frying pan and sauté the onion until translucent. • Add the tomatoes and oregano and cook over medium heat for 10–15 minutes. Season with salt and pepper. • Cook the meatballs in a medium pan of simmering water for 3 minutes. Scoop out with a slotted spoon and drain on a clean cloth. • In the meantime, cook the pasta in a large pan of salted, boiling water until al dente. • Drain and add to the pan with the tomato sauce. • Add the meatballs and toss gently over medium heat for 1–2 minutes. • Sprinkle with the Parmesan and serve hot.

*Serves: 4–6*

*Preparation: 45'*

*Cooking: 30'*

*Level of difficulty: 2*

- 6 tbsp milk
- 2 thick slices of day-old bread, crusts removed and crumbled
- 14 oz/400 g ground beef
- 4 oz/125 g prosciutto
- small bunch of parsley, cleaned
- 1 clove garlic
- 1 egg yolk
- finely grated zest of 1 lemon
- pinch of nutmeg
- salt and freshly ground black pepper to taste
- $^1/_2$ cup/75 g all-purpose/plain flour
- 5 tbsp extra-virgin olive oil
- 1 small onion, finely chopped
- 1 lb/500 g peeled and chopped tomatoes
- 1 tsp dried oregano
- 1 lb/500 g maccheroni
- 6 tbsp freshly grated Parmesan cheese

# GARGANELLI WITH CRABMEAT

Serves: 4–6

Preparation: 30'

Cooking: 1 h 30'

Level of difficulty: 2

- 2 lb/1 kg crab, in shell
- 2 cups/500 ml cold water
- salt and freshly ground black pepper to taste
- 1 shallot
- 2 stalks celery
- 1 onion
- 1 carrot
- 1 lemon, cut in half
- 4 tbsp dry wine
- 4 tbsp butter
- 1 lb/500 g garganelli

Rinse the crab carefully, and remove the claws, legs, and shell. If preferred, ask your fish vendor to do this for you. • Prepare a bouillon: crush the shell and place it and the claws and legs in a saucepan with the water, carrot, onion, and lemon. Season with salt and pepper. Bring to a boil, cover, and cook over low heat for 1 hour. Strain and set aside. • Chop the crabmeat fairly finely with a sharp knife. • Peel the shallot and strip the filaments from the stalk of celery. Chop together the shallot and half of the stalk of celery. Cut the other half of the celery into very thin slices. • Melt the butter in a large frying pan and cook the mixture of shallot and celery until translucent. • Add the crabmeat and simmer for five minutes, stirring often with a wooden spoon. • Drizzle with the wine and allow to cook down over low heat, uncovered. • Drizzle with $^1/_2$ cup (125 ml) of the bouillon and cook for 15 minutes, or until it has cooked off. • In the meantime, cook the pasta in a large pan of salted, boiling water until al dente. • Drain and add to the pan with the sauce. Sprinkle with the remaining chopped celery and toss gently. • Serve hot.

# NEAPOLITAN-STYLE PENNE

Sauté the onion in 4 tablespoons of butter and the oil in a saucepan over low heat. • Add the tomatoes and basil and cook until the tomatoes have broken down. • Season with salt and pepper and add the remaining 2 tablespoons of butter. • Remove from heat and mix until the butter has melted. • Meanwhile, cook the pasta in a large pan of salted, boiling water until al dente. • Drain and transfer to the saucepan with the tomato sauce. Sprinkle with the cheese and serve hot.

*Serves: 4–6*

*Preparation: 20'*

*Cooking: 30'*

*Level of difficulty: 1*

- **1 red onion, finely chopped**
- **6 tbsp butter**
- **2 tbsp extra-virgin olive oil**
- **2¹/₂ lb/1,25 kg San Marzano (oval) tomatoes, peeled, seeded, and finely chopped**
- **8 leaves fresh basil, torn**
- **salt and freshly ground black pepper to taste**
- **1 lb/500 g penne**
- **³/₄ cup/90 g freshly grated Caciocavallo or Parmesan cheese**

# PENNE WITH SMOKED SALMON AND BLACK OLIVES

Cook the pasta in a large pan of salted, boiling water until al dente. • While the pasta is cooking, place the salmon, Parmesan, oil, and lemon juice in a large bowl. Season with salt and pepper and mix well. • Drain the pasta and add to the bowl. • Add the parsley and olives. Toss well and serve immediately.

226

*Serves: 4–6*

*Preparation: 10'*

*Cooking: 15'*

*Level of difficulty: 1*

- 1 lb/500 g penne
- 10 oz/300 g smoked salmon, cut in small pieces
- 1³/₄ cups/200 g freshly grated Parmesan cheese
- ¹/₂ cup/125 ml extra-virgin olive oil
- juice of 1 lemon
- salt and freshly ground black pepper to taste
- 1 tbsp finely chopped parsley
- 2 oz/60 g pitted black olives

# FARFALLE WITH SHRIMP AND ARUGULA PESTO

Preheat the oven to 400°F/200°C/gas 6. • Spread the pine nuts out in a large ovenproof dish or pan and toast in the oven until golden brown. • Rinse the arugula thoroughly under cold running water. Dry well and chop in a food processor with 3 tablespoons of the oil, the garlic, and Parmesan until smooth. Season with salt and pepper. • Heat the remaining oil in a large frying pan and sauté the shrimp for 3–4 minutes over high heat. Season with salt and pepper. • Meanwhile, cook the pasta in a large pan of salted, boiling water until al dente. • Drain the pasta and add to the frying pan with the shrimp. Add the arugula pesto and pine nuts and toss gently over medium-high heat for 1–2 minutes. • Sprinkle with extra Parmesan and serve hot.

Serves: 4–6

Preparation: 20'

Cooking: 20'

Level of difficulty: 1

- 3 oz/90 g pine nuts
- 8 oz/250 g arugula/rocket
- 6 tbsp extra-virgin olive oil
- 1 clove garlic, finely chopped
- $^1/_2$ cup/60 g freshly grated Parmesan cheese + extra to serve
- salt and freshly ground black pepper to taste
- 7 oz/200 g shrimp tails, shelled and chopped in short pieces
- 1 lb/500 g farfalle

228

# LUMACONI WITH VEGETABLES

*Serves: 4–6*

*Preparation: 10'*

*Cooking: 35'*

*Level of difficulty: 1*

- 1 large onion
- 1 large eggplant/ aubergine
- 2 large zucchini/ courgettes
- 1 green, 1 yellow, and 1 red bell pepper/capsicum
- 4 tbsp extra-virgin olive oil
- 1¹/₂ lb/750 g tomatoes, peeled and chopped
- ¹/₂ tsp red pepper flakes
- salt to taste
- 8 basil leaves, torn
- 6 tbsp freshly grated Parmesan cheese
- 1 lb/500 g lumaconi

Chop the onion coarsely. Peel the eggplant and dice it into bite-sized pieces. Slice the zucchini into rounds. Remove the seeds and cores from the bell peppers and chop into small pieces. • Put the onion in a large frying pan with the oil and cook over medium heat until it becomes transparent. Add the eggplant, bell peppers, and zucchini. Sauté the vegetables for 7–8 minutes. • Add the tomatoes, red pepper flakes, and salt to taste. Cook for 20 minutes. • Cook the lumaconi in a large pot of salted, boiling water until al dente. Drain and add to the skillet with the vegetables. Toss over high heat for 2–3 minutes until well mixed. Add the basil and Parmesan. • Transfer to a heated serving dish and serve hot.

# RIGATONI WITH RICOTTA BALLS

Preheat the oven to 400°F/200°C/gas 6. •
Place the Ricotta, Parmesan, flour, salt, egg
yolk, parsley, and lemon zest in a bowl and stir until
smooth. • Shape into marble-sized balls. Place in a
baking pan and drizzle with 2 tablespoons of oil.
Bake for 10 minutes, or until firm. • Chop the
celery leaves in a food processor with the stock, 3
tablespoons of oil, lemon juice, and salt. • Dice the
the celery stalks and sauté in a frying pan with 1
tablespoon of oil for 2–3 minutes. • Season with
salt and remove from heat. • Cook the pasta in a
large pan of salted, boiling water until al dente.
Drain well and transfer to a heated serving dish. •
Add the celery leaf purée, sautéed celery, and
Ricotta balls. • Toss gently
and serve.

| |
| --- |
| Serves: 4–6 |
| Preparation: 30' |
| Cooking: 30' |
| Level of difficulty: 1 |

- **10 oz/300 g fresh Ricotta cheese, drained**
- **4 tbsp freshly grated Parmesan cheese**
- **$^1/_2$ cup/75 g all purpose/plain flour**
- **1 egg yolk**
- **1 tbsp finely chopped parsley**
- **1 tbsp finely grated lemon zest**
- **6 tbsp extra-virgin olive oil**
- **1 celery heart with leaves**
- **4 tbsp vegetable stock**
- **1 tbsp lemon juice**
- **salt to taste**
- **1 lb/500 g rigatoni**

*Serves: 4–6*

*Preparation: 30'*

*Cooking: 1 h 15'*

*Level of difficulty: 1*

- 4 tbsp extra-virgin olive oil
- 1 bay leaf
- 2/3 cup/100 g all-purpose/plain flour
- 1 lb/500g g lean mutton, chopped into small pieces
- 4 tbsp port
- 8 shallots
- zest of 1 lemon
- 1/2 cup/125 ml Vegetable Stock (see page 956)
- salt and freshly ground white pepper to taste
- 1 lb/500 g penne
- celery leaves

# PENNE WITH LAMB AND ONION SAUCE

Heat the oil and bay leaf in a large frying pan. • Flour the lamb and sauté for 5–7 minutes, or until browned. • Drizzle with the port and add the shallots. Cover and cook over low heat until the shallots have caramelized, about 45 minutes.
• Add the lemon zest, salt, pepper, and stock and cook for 20 minutes over low heat. • Cook the pasta in a large pan of salted, boiling water with the celery leaves until al dente. Drain and add to the pan with the sauce. • Toss well and serve.

# WHOLE-WHEAT PENNE WITH AVOCADO AND FRESH HERBS

Clean the parsley, basil, and dill and place in a food processor with 4 tablespoons of oil and a pinch of salt. Chop until smooth. • Transfer to a large serving bowl. • Place the green onions and bell pepper in a separate bowl. • Peel the avocado. Cut in half and remove the pip. Slice thinly. Drizzle the slices with the lemon juice (to stop the avocado from turning black), and transfer to the bowl with the bell pepper. • Crumble the tuna and place in another bowl. • In the meantime, cook the pasta in a large pan of salted, boiling water until al dente. • Drain the pasta and place in the bowl with the creamed herbs. Add the green onions, bell peppers, avocado, and tuna. Toss quickly, drizzle with the remaining oil, and season with a little extra salt and pepper. • Serve immediately.

*Serves: 4–6*

*Preparation: 30'*

*Cooking: 15'*

*Level of difficulty: 1*

- **small bunch parsley**
- **small bunch basil**
- **small bunch dill**
- **6 tbsp extra-virgin olive oil**
- **2 green onions, thinly sliced**
- **1 large red bell pepper/capsicum, cleaned and cut in small dice**
- **1 avocado**
- **5 oz/150 g tuna, packed in oil, drained**
- **1 lb/500 g whole-wheat/wholemeal penne**

# RIGATONI WITH FRESH BASIL

Place the basil leaves, garlic, and a pinch of salt in a food processor and chop finely. • Melt the lard and oil in a large frying pan and add the chopped basil mixture. Sauté over low heat for 2 minutes and season with salt and pepper. • Cook the pasta in a large pan of salted, boiling water until al dente. • Drain and transfer to the pan with the basil mixture. Toss gently. • Sprinkle with Parmesan and Pecorino and serve.

236

*Serves: 4–6*

*Preparation: 10'*

*Cooking: 20'*

*Level of difficulty: 1*

- 3 bunches basil
- 2 cloves garlic
- salt and freshly ground white pepper to taste
- 3 tbsp lard
- 5 tbsp extra-virgin olive oil
- 1 lb/500 g rigatoni pasta
- 6 tbsp freshly grated Parmesan cheese
- 4 tbsp freshly grated Pecorino cheese

# PENNE WITH ARTICHOKES

*Serves: 4–6*

*Preparation: 30'*

*Cooking: 30'*

*Level of difficulty: 1'*

- 8 artichokes
- juice of 1 lemon
- 1/2 cup/125 ml extra-virgin olive oil
- 3 cloves garlic, finely chopped
- salt and freshly ground black pepper to taste
- 1 lb/500 g penne
- 4 tbsp finely chopped parsley
- 5 tbsp freshly grated Pecorino cheese

Wash the artichokes and remove all but the pale inner leaves by pulling the outer ones down and snapping them off. Cut off the stalk and the top third of the remaining leaves. Remove any tough pieces of leaves at the base with a sharp knife. • Cut the artichokes in half lengthwise and scrape the fuzzy choke away with the knife. Cut each artichoke half into thin slices lengthwise and place in a bowl of cold water with the lemon juice. Soak for 20 minutes. Remove and pat dry with paper towels. • Put the oil and garlic in a large frying pan and sauté until the garlic begins to change color. Add the artichokes and cook over medium-low heat for about 25 minutes, or until the artichokes are very tender. Add water if all the oil has been absorbed. Season with salt and pepper. • Cook the penne in a large pot of salted, boiling water until al dente. • Drain well and toss with the artichoke sauce over high heat for 2–3 minutes. Sprinkle with the parsley and Pecorino. Serve hot.

# FESTONATI WITH ITALIAN SAUSAGES AND BROCCOLI

Divide the broccoli into florets. Cut the stems into small cubes. • Plunge the florets and stems into a large pot of salted, boiling water and cook for about 5 minutes, or until tender but still crunchy. Drain well and set aside. • Place the oil in a large sauté pan with the garlic and parsley over medium heat. When the garlic begins to change color, add the sausages and tomato paste. Cook over medium heat for 5 minutes. • Add the broccoli, season with salt and pepper and cook for 10–15 minutes. • Meanwhile, cook the festonati in a large pot of salted, boiling water until al dente. • Drain and toss with the sauce. Sprinkle with the Pecorino and serve hot.

*Serves: 4–6*

*Preparation: 10'*

*Cooking: 30'*

*Level of difficulty: 1*

- **1 lb/500 g broccoli**
- **3 tbsp extra-virgin olive oil**
- **3 cloves garlic, finely chopped**
- **2 tbsp finely chopped parsley**
- **14 oz/400 g Italian pork sausages, skinned and crumbled**
- **2 tbsp tomato paste**
- **salt and freshly ground black pepper to taste**
- **6 tbsp freshly grated Pecorino cheese**
- **1 lb/500 g festonati**

# FUSILLI VESUVIAN-STYLE

Serves: 4–6

Preparation: 25'

Cooking: 35'

Level of difficulty: 1

- ¹/₂ cup/125 ml extra-virgin olive oil
- 1 lb/500 g peeled and chopped fresh tomatoes
- 2 tsp dried oregano
- salt and freshly ground black pepper to taste
- 6 oz/180 g diced fresh Mozzarella cheese
- 6 tbsp freshly grated Pecorino cheese
- 1 lb/500 g fusilli

Heat the oil in a large frying pan over medium heat. • Add the tomatoes, oregano, salt and pepper, and cook for about 15 minutes, stirring from time to time. When the tomatoes begin to separate from the oil, remove from the heat.
• Cook the fusilli in a large pot of salted, boiling water until al dente. Preheat the oven to 400°F/200°C/gas 6. • Drain the pasta well and place in an ovenproof dish. • Add the Mozzarella and Pecorino and toss well. • Bake in the oven for 15 minutes, or until the Mozzarella is slightly melted. • Serve hot.

*The volcano Vesuvius, near Naples, has given its name to this dish invented in its shadows.*

243

# RIGATONI WITH OCTOPUS, GARBANZO BEANS, AND SALAMI

Sauté the garlic, bell pepper, and rosemary in the oil in a heavy-bottomed pan over medium heat until soft. • Season with salt and pepper, then add the baby octopus. Cook over high heat for a few minutes, then pour in the wine. • When the wine has evaporated, add the garbanzo beans, salami, and tomatoes, and simmer for a few minutes more. • Meanwhile, cook the pasta in a large pan of salted, boiling water until al dente. • Drain the pasta and add to the pan with the sauce. • Toss over high heat for 2–3 minutes, then serve.

Serves: 4–6

Preparation: 15'

Cooking: 30'

Level of difficulty: 1

- 2 cloves garlic, finely chopped
- 1 bell pepper/ capsicum, cleaned and chopped
- 3 sprigs rosemary, finely chopped
- $1/2$ cup/125 ml extra-virgin olive oil
- salt and freshly ground black pepper to taste
- 12 oz/300 g baby octopus, cleaned
- $1/2$ cup/125 ml dry white wine
- 12 oz/300 g garbanzo beans/ chick-peas, cooked
- 5 oz/150 g salami, diced
- 2 ripe tomatoes, diced
- 1 lb/500 g rigatoni

# RIGATONI WITH BELL PEPPERS

*Serves: 4–6*

*Preparation: 10'*

*Cooking: 35'*

*Level of difficulty: 1*

- **3 medium bell peppers/ capsicums, mixed colors**
- **1 large onion, finely chopped**
- **2 cloves garlic, finely chopped**
- **$1/2$ cup/125 ml extra-virgin olive oil**
- **1 lb/500 g peeled and chopped fresh tomatoes**
- **10 basil leaves, torn**
- **3 tbsp boiling water**
- **salt and freshly ground black pepper to taste**
- **2 tbsp vinegar**
- **6 anchovy fillets**
- **1 lb/500 g rigatoni**

Cut the bell peppers in half, remove the stalks and seeds, and cut into thin strips. • Sauté the bell peppers, onion, and garlic in the oil in a large frying pan for 8–10 minutes. • Add the tomatoes, basil, and boiling water. Season with salt and pepper. Simmer over medium heat for about 20 minutes, or until the bell peppers are tender. • Stir in the vinegar and anchovies, and cook over high heat for 2–3 minutes until the vinegar evaporates. Remove from the heat. • Meanwhile, cook the pasta in a large pot of salted, boiling water until al dente. • Drain well and place in a heated serving dish. • Pour the sauce over the top and toss well. • Serve hot.

245

# FUSILLI WITH JUMBO SHRIMP

*Serves: 4–6*

*Preparation: 20'*

*Cooking: 25'*

*Level of difficulty: 1*

- **6 tbsp extra-virgin olive oil**
- **4 tbsp finely chopped parsley**
- **4 cloves garlic, finely chopped**
- **1 lb/500 g jumbo shrimp/tiger prawns) (5 oz/150 g left whole and 10 oz/ 350 g coarsely chopped**
- **1 lb/500 g fusilli**
- **2 tbsp butter**

Heat the oil in a large frying pan and sauté the parsley and garlic for 5 minutes. • Add the whole and chopped shrimp, season with salt, and sauté over high heat for 5 minutes. • Meanwhile, cook the fusilli in a large pan of salted, boiling water until al dente. Drain and add to the frying pan with the shrimp. • Cook for 2 minutes, add the butter, toss well, and serve immediately.

# FARFALLE WITH PEAS AND HAM

B oil the peas in salted water until half-cooked. •
Combine the peas, butter, and ham in a large
frying pan. Sauté over medium-low heat for
10 minutes. • Stir in half the cream and cook until
the sauce thickens. • Add the parsley, and season
with salt and pepper. • Meanwhile, cook the farfalle
in a large pot of salted, boiling water until al dente.
• Drain well and transfer to the pan with the sauce.
Add the remaining cream and the Parmesan. Toss
well and serve.

*Serves: 4–6*

*Preparation: 5'*

*Cooking: 25'*

*Level of difficulty: 1*

- **8 oz/250 g fresh or frozen peas**
- **4 tbsp butter**
- **10 oz/300 g prosciutto/Parma ham, diced**
- **4 tbsp heavy/ double cream**
- **2 tbsp finely chopped parsley**
- **salt and freshly ground black pepper to taste**
- **1 lb/500 g farfalle**
- **6 tbsp freshly grated Parmesan cheese**

# COOL
# PASTA

# FUSILLI SALAD WITH LEMON TUNA

Place the carrots in a bowl. Crumble the tuna and add to the bowl. • Add the garlic, parsley, basil, and the juice and zest of 1 lemon. • Drizzle with 5 tablespoons of oil and season with salt and pepper. Mix with a wooden spoon to blend the ingredients, cover with plastic wrap, and set aside to marinate for least 1 hour. • Cook the pasta in a large pan of salted, boiling water until al dente. • Drain well and run under cold running water. Drain again and dry on a clean cloth. • Add to the bowl with the carrot and tuna mixture. • Drizzle with the remaining oil, toss gently, and garnish with the mint. • Serve chilled or at room temperature.

*Serves: 4–6*

*Preparation: 25' + 1 h to marinate sauce*

*Cooking: 15'*

*Level of difficulty: 1*

- **4 carrots, grated**
- **12 oz/350 g drained tuna**
- **2 cloves garlic, finely chopped**
- **4 tbsp finely chopped parsley**
- **4 tbsp finely chopped basil**
- **juice of 2 lemons**
- **grated zest of 1 untreated lemon**
- **$^1/_2$ cup/125 ml extra-virgin olive oil**
- **salt and freshly ground black pepper to taste**
- **1 lb/500 g fusilli**
- **mint leaves, to garnish**

# PASTA SALAD

Grill the vegetables in a grill pan or under a broiler. • Place in a large serving bowl with the Mozzarella and sprinkle with the parsley, salt, and pepper. Drizzle with the oil. • Cook the pasta in a large pot of salted, boiling water until al dente. • Drain well and run under cold running water. Drain again and dry on a clean cloth. • Add to the serving bowl with the vegetables, toss well, and serve.

254

*Serves: 4–6*

*Preparation: 25'*

*Cooking: 45'*

*Level of difficulty: 2*

- **1 large eggplant/ aubergine**
- **2 bell peppers, cut in strips**
- **2 large zucchini/ courgettes, thinly sliced**
- **4 ripe tomatoes, sliced**
- **14 oz/400 g Mozzarella cheese, diced**
- **2 tbsp finely chopped parsley**
- **salt and freshly ground white pepper to taste**
- **6 tbsp extra- virgin olive oil**
- **1 lb/500 g fusilli**

# SUMMER PASTA SALAD

*Serves: 4–6*

*Preparation: 25'*

*Cooking: 15'*

*Level of difficulty: 1*

- **1 lb/500 g rigatoni**
- **6 tbsp extra-virgin olive oil**
- **8 oz/250 g Mozzarella cheese, in bite-sized pieces**
- **4 oz/125 g black olives**
- **2 tbsp capers**
- **2 cloves garlic, finely chopped**
- **4 medium salad tomatoes, diced**
- **8 leaves fresh basil,torn**

Cook the rigatoni in a large pot of salted, boiling water until al dente. • Drain well and run under cold running water. Drain again and dry on a clean cloth. • Place in a salad bowl large enough to hold all the ingredients. Toss with half the oil. • Add the Mozzarella, olives, capers, garlic, tomatoes, basil, and remaining oil. Toss well and serve.

*Serves: 4–6*

*Preparation: 30' + 1 h to drain tomatoes*

*Cooking: 15'*

*Level of difficulty: 1*

- 10 oz/300 g cherry tomatoes
- salt and freshly ground white pepper to taste
- 5 oz/150 g tuna packed in oil, drained
- 1 lb/500 g penne
- 10 black olives, pitted and finely chopped
- 10 green olives, pitted and finely chopped
- 2 scallions/spring onions, coarsely chopped
- 1 stalk celery, coarsely chopped
- 1 carrot, coarsely chopped
- 1 clove garlic, finely chopped
- 6 tbsp extra-virgin olive oil
- 2 tsp dried oregano
- 1 tbsp finely chopped fresh parsley
- 4–5 leaves fresh basil, torn

# PASTA SALAD WITH TUNA AND OLIVES

Cut the tomatoes into halves or quarters, season with salt, and place in a colander. Drain for 1 hour. • Use a fork to crumble the tuna. • Mix the tuna, tomatoes, olives, scallions, celery, carrot, and garlic. Drizzle with almost all the oil and season with salt, pepper, and oregano. • Cook the pasta in salted boiling water until al dente. • Drain well and run under cold running water. Drain again and dry on a clean cloth. • Transfer to a serving bowl and drizzle with the remaining oil. • Add the prepared ingredients and toss well • Garnish with the parsley and basil and serve.

# COOL SPIRAL PASTA WITH OLIVE SAUCE

Cook the pasta in a large pan of salted, boiling water until al dente. • Drain well and run under cold running water. Drain again and dry on a clean cloth. • Place the olives, chile pepper, parsley, and oil in a food processor and chop finely. • Rinse and dry the salad greens and arrange in the bottom of a large salad dish. • Pour the olive sauce over the cooled pasta and toss well. • Place the pasta on top of the salad greens and garnish with the beans, tomatoes, and bell pepper. • Serve at room temperature or, in summer, slightly chilled.

258

*Serves: 4–6*

*Preparation: 15'*

*Cooking: 10–15'*

*Level of difficulty: 1*

- 1 lb/500 g spiral pasta
- 36 large green olives, pitted
- 1 fresh red chile pepper
- 1 bunch fresh parsley
- 6 tbsp extra-virgin olive oil
- salt and freshly ground black pepper to taste
- mixed salad greens
- 6 oz/180 g green beans, boiled
- 4–6 small tomatoes, cut in halves or quarters
- $1/2$ yellow bell pepper/capsicum, chopped

# PASTA SALAD WITH HAM AND VEGETABLES

Cook the pasta in a large pan of salted, boiling water until al dente. About 3–4 minutes before the pasta is cooked, add the zucchini and carrots to the pot. • Drain well and run under cold running water. Drain again and dry on a clean cloth. • Place in a serving bowl with 2 tablespoons of oil. Toss gently to stop the pasta and vegetables from sticking together. • Place the remaining oil, vinegar, lemon juice, basil, salt, and pepper in a blender or food processor and pulse until well mixed. • Add the ham to the bowl with the pasta then drizzle with the dressing. • Toss well and serve chilled or at room temperature.

260

Serves: 4–6

Preparation: 15' + 1 h to chill

Cooking: 15'

Level of difficulty: 1

- 1 lb/500 g penne
- 14 oz/400 g zucchini/ courgettes, julienned
- 8 oz/250 g carrots, julienned
- $1/2$ cup/125 ml extra-virgin olive oil
- 3 tbsp red wine vinegar
- 2 tbsp lemon juice
- small bunch fresh basil
- salt to taste
- 1 tsp freshly ground white pepper
- 7 oz/200 g ham, diced

# MACCHERONI SALAD
# WITH BLACK OLIVE PESTO

*Serves: 4–6*

*Preparation: 15'*

*Cooking: 15'*

*Level of difficulty: 1*

- 1 lb/500 g
  maccheroni
- 6–8 tbsp extra-
  virgin olive oil
- 36 large black
  olives, pitted
- 10 anchovy fillets
- 16 basil leaves
- 1 fresh red chile
  pepper
- 1 tbsp finely
  chopped fresh
  oregano

Cook the pasta in a large pan of salted, boiling water until al dente. • Drain well and run under cold running water. Drain again and dry on a clean cloth. • Place in a serving bowl with 2 tablespoons of oil. Toss gently to stop it from sticking together. • Place the olives, anchovies, basil, chile pepper, and olive oil in a food processor or blender and chop until smooth. • Drizzle the pasta with the olive pesto and add the oregano and chile pepper. • Toss well and serve.

# FARFALLE SALAD WITH VEGETABLES

C ook the pasta in a large pan of salted, boiling water until al dente. Add the zucchini to the pan about 3 minutes before the pasta is cooked. • Drain well and run under cold running water. Drain again and dry on a clean cloth. • Place in a serving bowl with 2 tablespoons of oil. Toss gently to stop the pasta and zucchini from sticking together. • Rinse and pat dry the bell peppers; remove the seeds and filaments. Roast the bell peppers under the broiler (grill) until the skins are blackened. Place in a paper bag, shut tight, and leave for 10 minutes. Open the bag and peel away the skins. • Rinse under cold running water and dry carefully. Cut in thin strips. • Add the bell peppers to the bowl along with the Feta, capers, fennel seeds, salt, red pepper flakes, and remaining oil. Toss well. • Serve at chilled or at room temperature.

Serves: 4–6

Preparation: 35'

Cooking: 15'

Level of difficulty: 1

- 1 lb/500 g farfalle
- $^1/_2$ cup/125 ml extra-virgin olive oil
- 4 zucchini/ courgettes
- 1 small yellow bell pepper/capsicum
- 1 small yellow bell pepper/capsicum
- 5 oz/150 g Feta cheese, crumbled
- 1 tbsp capers packed in salt, rinsed
- 1 tsp fennel seeds
- salt to taste
- $^1/_2$ tsp red pepper flakes

# LUMACONI SALAD WITH MUSSELS

Serves: 4–6

Prep: 20' + 1 h to
   soak + 2 h to
   marinate

Cooking: 25'

Level of difficulty: 1

- 30 mussels, in shell
- 6 peeled and chopped tomatoes
- 1 tbsp finely chopped parsley
- 3 cloves garlic, finely chopped
- 1 red chile pepper, finely sliced
- 6 leaves basil
- 2 tbsp fresh lemon juice
- 6 tbsp extra-virgin olive oil
- salt and freshly ground black pepper to taste
- 1 lb/500 g giant lumaconi (snail-shaped)

Soak the mussels in a bowl of cold water for 1 hour. • Place the mussels in a large pan over high heat and cook until they open. Discard any that do not open. • Place the mussels in a bowl with the tomatoes, parsley, garlic, chile, basil, lemon juice, oil, salt and pepper and set aside to marinate for 2 hours • Cook the pasta in a large pan of salted, boiling water until al dente. • Drain well and run under cold running water. Drain again and dry on a clean cloth.
- Add to the bowl with the mussel sauce.
- Toss gently and serve.

# WHOLE-WHEAT PENNE WITH ZUCCHINI AND BELL PEPPERS

C ook the pasta in a large pan of salted, boiling water until al dente. • Drain well and run under cold running water. Drain again and dry on a clean cloth. • Place in a serving bowl with 2 tablespoons of oil. Toss gently to stop it from sticking together. • Sauté the zucchini in a frying pan with 3 tablespoons of oil. • Cut the bell peppers into small pieces. • Slice the Ricotta salata into small cubes. • Add the Ricotta salata, zucchini, and bell peppers to the bowl with the pasta. • Season with the remaining oil, the herbs, salt, pepper, and olives. Toss well and serve.

*Serves: 4–6*
*Preparation: 35*
*Cooking: 30'*
*Level of difficulty: 1*

- 1 lb/500 g whole-wheat/wholemeal penne
- $^1/_2$ cup/125 ml extra-virgin olive oil
- 1 lb/500 g mixed bell peppers/capsicums
- 10 oz/300 g zucchini/courgettes, diced
- 3 oz/90 g Ricotta salata
- 2–3 tbsp finely chopped mixed fresh herbs (parsley, basil, marjoram, thyme)
- salt and freshly ground white pepper to taste
- 3 oz/90 g pitted black olives

# FUSILLI SALAD

Serves: 4–6

Preparation: 25' + 1 h
for the eggplants

Cooking: 45'

Level of difficulty: 1

- **1 large eggplant/
  aubergine**
- **2 tbsp coarse
  sea salt**
- **2 bell peppers/
  capsicums, cut in
  strips**
- **2 large zucchini/
  courgettes, thinly
  sliced**
- **4 ripe tomatoes,
  chopped**
- **14 oz/400 g
  Mozzarella cheese,
  diced**
- **2 tbsp finely
  chopped parsley**
- **salt and freshly
  ground white
  pepper to taste**
- **1/2 cup/125 ml
  extra-virgin
  olive oil**
- **1 lb/500 g fusilli**

Cut the eggplants in slices about 1/4 inch (5 mm) thick. Place on a large flat dish and sprinkle with coarse salt. Place a plate on top with a weight on it and leave to drain for 1 hour. • Rinse well and dry with paper towels. • Grill the vegetables in a grill pan or under a broiler. • Place in a large serving bowl with the Mozzarella and sprinkle with the parsley, salt, and pepper. Drizzle with the oil. • Cook the pasta in a large pan of salted, boiling water until al dente. • Drain well and run under cold running water. Drain again and dry on a clean cloth. • Place in a serving bowl with the vegetables and cheese. • Toss well and serve.

# FUSILLI SALAD WITH BELL PEPPERS AND ARUGULA

Cook the pasta in a large pan of salted, boiling water until al dente. • Drain well and run under cold running water. Drain again and dry on a clean cloth. • Place in a serving bowl with 2 tablespoons of oil. Toss gently to stop it from sticking together. • Rinse and pat dry the bell peppers; remove the seeds and the filaments. Roast the bell peppers under the broiler (grill) until the skins are blackened. Place in a paper bag, shut tight, and leave for 10 minutes. Open the bag and peel away the skins. • Rinse under cold running water and dry carefully. • Cut in thin strips. • Add the bell peppers to the bowl along with the arugula, Pecorino, and basil. • Beat the remaining oil in a small bowl with the lemon juice, salt, and pepper. Drizzle over the salad.
• Toss well and serve.

*Serves: 4–6*

*Preparation: 35'*

*Cooking: 25'*

*Level of difficulty: 1*

- 1 lb/500 g fusilli
- $^1/_2$ cup/125 ml extra-virgin olive oil
- 1 red bell pepper/ capsicum
- 1 yellow bell pepper/capsicum
- 1 bunch rocket/arugula, rinsed and chopped
- 3 oz/90 g aged Pecorino cheese
- 10 basil leaves, torn
- 2 tbsp fresh lemon juice
- salt and freshly ground black pepper to taste

# NEAPOLITAN SALAD

Serves: 4–6

Preparation: 15'

Cooking: 15'

Level of difficulty: 1

- 1 lb/500 g fusilli
- 1/2 cup/125 ml extra virgin olive oil
- 1 small green bell pepper/capsicum, seeded and sliced into thin strips
- 1–2 spicy chile peppers, julienned
- 4 tomatoes, coarsely chopped
- 2 zucchini/ courgettes, julienned
- 5 oz/150 g Provolone cheese, diced
- 4 tbsp finely chopped parsley,
- 4 tbsp finely chopped onion
- 2 tbsp red wine vinegar
- 1 clove garlic, finely chopped
- 2 tbsp finely chopped basil leaves
- salt and freshly ground black pepper to taste

Cook the pasta in a large pan of salted, boiling water until al dente. • Drain well and run under cold running water. Drain again and dry on a clean cloth. • Place in a serving bowl with 2 tablespoons of oil. Toss gently to stop it from sticking together. • Add the bell pepper, chile, tomatoes, zucchini, cheese, parsley, and onion. • Place the remaining oil in a small bowl and add the vinegar, garlic, and basil. Season with salt and pepper and beat well. • Drizzle the dressing over the salad, toss well, and serve.

# RUOTE SALAD WITH VEGETABLES

C ook the pasta in a large pan of salted, boiling water until al dente. • Drain well and run under cold running water. Drain again and dry on a clean cloth. • Place in a serving bowl with 2 tablespoons of oil. Toss gently to stop it from sticking together. • Cut the stalk and hard base off the eggplant and peel. Cut crosswise into slices about $1/2$ inch (1 cm) thick. Place the slices under the broiler (grill) and cook for about 10 minutes, or until tender. Dice the cooked slices into small squares. • Quarter the bell peppers lengthwise and slice each quarter into thin strips. • Slice the white, bottom part of the scallions very finely. • Add the remaining oil, capers, oregano, parsley, eggplant, bell peppers, and Pecorino to the bowl with the pasta and toss well. Season with salt and pepper and serve.

Serves: 4–6

Preparation: 15'

Cooking: 15'

Level of difficulty: 1

- 1 lb/500 g plain, whole-wheat/wholemeal, or colored ruote
- 6 tbsp extra-virgin olive oil
- 1 large eggplant/ aubergine
- 1 yellow and 1 red bell pepper/ capsicum
- 2 scallions/spring onions
- 2 tbsp capers
- 1 tsp dried oregano
- 2 tbsp finely chopped parsley
- 4 tbsp freshly grated Pecorino cheese
- salt and freshly ground black pepper to taste

# FUSILLI SALAD WITH TOMATO, GARLIC, AND MOZZARELLA

C ook the pasta in a large pan of salted, boiling water until al dente. • Drain well and run under cold running water. Drain again and dry on a clean cloth. • Place in a serving bowl with 2 tablespoons of oil. Toss gently to stop it from sticking together. • Add the tomatoes to the pasta. Combine the garlic and parsley with the remainder of the oil and salt, and add to the salad bowl. Leave to cool completely. • Just before serving, dice the Mozzarella into small cubes on a cutting board. • Add to the salad with the torn basil leaves and freshly ground black pepper. • Toss well and serve.

*Serves: 4–6*

*Preparation: 15'*

*Cooking: 15'*

*Level of difficulty: 1*

- 1 lb/500 g plain or whole-wheat/ wholemeal fusilli
- salt and freshly ground black pepper to taste
- 6 tbsp extra-virgin olive oil
- 6 large ripe tomatoes, cut in bite-sized pieces
- 2 cloves garlic, finely chopped
- 2 tbsp parsley, finely chopped
- 14 oz/400 g Mozzarella cheese
- 6 fresh basil leaves

# PASTA SALAD WITH PICKLED VEGETABLES AND ARUGULA

Cook the pasta in a large pan of salted, boiling water until al dente. • Drain well and run under cold running water. Drain again and dry on a clean cloth. • Place in a serving bowl with 2 tablespoons of oil. Toss gently to stop it from sticking together. • Rinse the arugula thoroughly under cold running water and dry well. • Chop the arugula and add with the marjoram, capers, pickled vegetables, and mushrooms to the bowl with the pasta. • Drizzle with the remaining oil, toss well, and serve.

Serves: 4–6

Preparation: 25'

Cooking: 15'

Level of difficulty: 1

- 1 lb/500 g whole-wheat/wholemeal conchiglie
- 1/8 tsp saffron strands
- 4 tbsp extra-virgin olive oil
- 1 bunch arugula/ rocket
- 1 tbsp finely chopped marjoram
- 1 tbsp salted capers, rinsed
- 7 oz/200 g pickled vegetables, coarsely chopped
- 2 oz/60 g button mushrooms in oil

# COOL SUMMER PASTA

Serves: 4–6

Preparation: 15'

Cooking: 15'

Level of difficulty: 1

Cook the pasta in a large pan of salted, boiling water until al dente. • Drain well and run under cold running water. Drain again and dry on a clean cloth. • Place in a serving bowl with 2 tablespoons of oil. Toss gently to stop it from sticking together. • Add the tomatoes, spring onions, bell pepper, basil, and corn. • Drizzle with the oil and season with salt and pepper. • Toss well and serve.

- 1 lb/500 g farfalle
- 12 oz/350 g ripe, firm tomatoes, coarsely chopped
- 2 scallions/ spring onions, chopped
- 1 large yellow bell pepper/capsicum, diced
- 10 basil leaves, torn
- 5 oz/150 g canned corn
- 6 tbsp extra-virgin olive oil
- salt and freshly ground black pepper to taste

*Serves: 4–6*

*Preparation: 40' + 45'*
*to marinate & drain*

*Cooking: 15'*

*Level of difficulty: 1*

- **12 oz/350 g fresh tuna, in a single cut, skinned, boned, and coarsely chopped**
- **juice of 1 lemon**
- **1/2 cup/125 ml extra-virgin olive oil**
- **20 black olives, pitted and finely chopped**
- **2 cloves garlic, lightly crushed but whole**
- **1 lb/500 g firm-ripe tomatoes, peeled and seeded**
- **salt and freshly ground white pepper to taste**
- **1 lb/500 g g penne**
- **8 basil leaves, torn**

# PENNE WITH TUNA

Place the tuna in a large bowl. Drizzle with the lemon juice and 2 tablespoons of oil. Add the olives. Let marinate for 30 minutes. • Sauté the garlic in 4 tablespoons of the oil in a small frying pan over very low heat for a few seconds. Remove from the heat and let cool. Discard the garlic.
• Chop the tomatoes finely, salt them, and place in a colander. Let drain for 15 minutes. • Mix the tomatoes and the garlic-infused oil into the marinated tuna and season with salt and pepper.
• Cook the pasta in a large pan of salted, boiling water until al dente. • Drain well and run under cold running water. Drain again and dry on a clean cloth. Place in the bowl with the tuna. • Add the basil, toss well, and serve.

# PASTA SALAD WITH AVOCADO, BEANS, AND SHRIMP

Cook the pasta in a large pan of salted, boiling water until al dente. • Drain well and run under cold running water. Drain again and dry on a clean cloth. • Place in a serving bowl with 2 tablespoons of oil. Toss gently to stop it from sticking together. • Drain the beans and rinse thoroughly. Dry well and add to the bowl with the pasta. • Peel the avocado, remove the pit, and dice. Drizzle with the lemon juice and add to the bowl with the pasta. • Add the shrimp and parsley, if using, and season with salt and pepper.
• Toss well and serve.

*Serves: 4–6*

*Preparation: 20'*

*Cooking: 15'*

*Level of difficulty: 1*

- **1 lb/500 g penne**
- **6 tbsp extra-virgin olive oil**
- **1 (14-oz/400-g) can red kidney beans**
- **1 avocado**
- **juice of 1 lemon**
- **4 oz/125 g cooked shrimp/prawn tails**
- **1 tbsp finely chopped parsley, to garnish (optional)**
- **salt and freshly ground black pepper to taste**

# FRESH
# PASTA

# HOMEMADE PASTA

Making fresh pasta at home is a rewarding experience. It can be made by hand or using a machine.

| Plain Pasta | Spinach or Tomato Pasta |
| --- | --- |
| *Serves: 4* | *Serves: 4* |
| • 3 cups/450 g all-purpose/plain flour<br>• 4 large eggs | • 2$^1$/$_2$ cups/375 g all-purpose/plain flour<br>• 3 large eggs<br>• 2 oz/50 g spinach purée or tomato concentrate |

**1.** Sift the flour and salt into a mound on a clean work surface. Make a hollow in the center and break the eggs into it one by one. Using a fork, gradually mix the eggs into the flour. If making spinach pasta or tomato pasta, add the spinach purée or tomato concentrate now. Continue until all the flour has been incorporated. **2.** At a certain point the dough will be too thick to mix with a fork. Use your hands to shape it into a ball. It should be smooth and not too sticky. **3.** Knead the dough by pushing downward and forward on the ball of pasta with the heel of your palm. Fold the dough in half, give it a quarter-turn, and repeat the process. Knead for about 10 minutes. Set the kneaded dough aside for 15–20 minutes to rest. **4.** To roll the pasta by hand, flour a clean work surface and place a rolling pin on the top of the ball. Push outward from the center. When the dough is about $^1$/$_4$ in (6 mm) thick, curl the far edge of the dough around the pin and gently stretch it as you roll it onto the pin. Unroll and repeat until the dough is almost transparent.

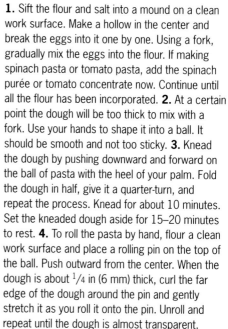

**5.** To cut the pasta by hand, fold the sheet of dough loosely into a flat roll. Use a sharp knife to cut the roll into $1/8$-in (3-mm) slices for tagliolini, $1/4$-in (6-mm) slices for fettuccine, $1/2$-in (1-cm) slices for tagliatelle, or $3/4$-in (2-cm) slices for pappardelle. Unravel the strips of pasta and lay them on a clean cloth. To make lasagna, cut the dough into 3 x 12-in (8 x 30-cm) sheets. To make maltagliati, roll the dough in strips about 2 in (5 cm) wide and cut into

diamond shapes. Paglia e fieno pasta for 4 servings is made with one half quantity each of plain fettuccine and spinach fettuccine.

## Using the pasta machine

**1.** To roll the dough using a pasta machine, divide it into several pieces and flatten by hand. Set the machine with its rollers at the widest, and run each piece through the machine. Reduce the width by one notch and repeat. Continue until all the pasta has gone through the machine at the thinnest setting.

**2.** Cut the pieces of rolled pasta into sheets about 12 in (30 cm) long. Attach the cutters to the pasta machine and set it at the widths given for the various types of pasta. Lay the cut pasta out on clean cloths to dry for 2 hours before use.

# TYPES OF FRESH PASTA

The fresh pasta types in this chapter are all simple ribbon shapes. Most are made from a basic mixture of flour and eggs, although sometimes they are flavored or colored with spinach, tomato, chestnut flour, or some other ingredient. If you do not have time to make pasta at home, most of the recipes will work just as well with store-bought fresh pasta or even the dried forms of the pasta suggested.

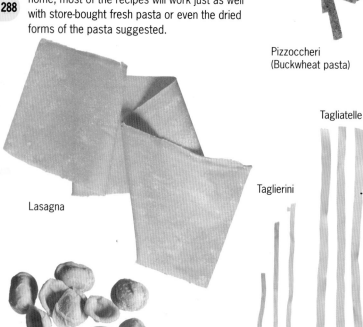

Pizzoccheri
(Buckwheat pasta)

Tagliatelle

Lasagna

Taglierini

Orecchiette

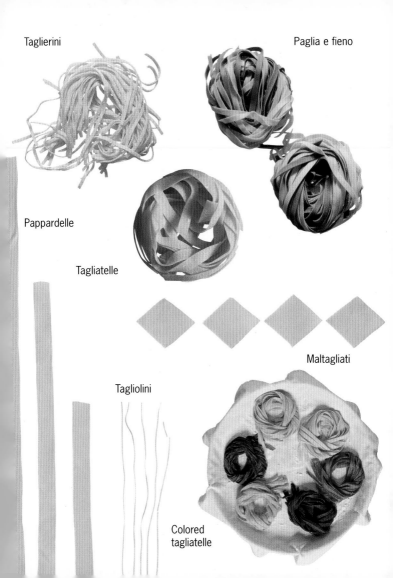

Taglierini

Paglia e fieno

Pappardelle

Tagliatelle

Maltagliati

Tagliolini

Colored
tagliatelle

# TAGLIATELLE WITH PROSCIUTTO

If making the pasta at home, prepare it several hours in advance. • Cut the fat away from the lean prosciutto meat and chop both, separately, into tiny dice. • Melt the butter in a large frying pan. Sauté the diced fat over low heat for 15 minutes. Adding the diced lean meat and sauté over medium heat for 5 minutes. • Season with salt and pepper. • Cook the pasta in a large pot of salted, boiling water until al dente. • Drain well, reserving 1 cup (250 ml) of the cooking water. • Add the pasta to the pan with the prosciutto. Return to a fairly high heat and cook for 1–2 minutes, adding a little of the reserved water to moisten, if necessary.

• Sprinkle with the Parmesan and serve at once.

*Serves: 4*

*Preparation: 15' + time to make pasta*

*Cooking: 20'*

*Level of difficulty: 1*

- **1 quantity tagliatelle (see pages 286–7) or 14 oz/400 g store-bought tagliatelle**
- **8 oz/250 g thickly sliced prosciutto/ Parma ham**
- **6 tbsp butter**
- **salt and freshly ground black pepper to taste**
- **1 cup/125 g freshly grated Parmesan cheese**

# PAPPARDELLE WITH MEAT SAUCE

If making the pasta at home, prepare it several hours in advance. • Sauté the meat in the oil over medium heat in a large saucepan until lightly browned, using a fork to break up any lumps. • Pour in the tomato paste and wine. Cook for 5 minutes. • Stir in the tomatoes and season with salt and pepper. Simmer over low heat for 40 minutes. • Cook the pasta in a large pot of salted, boiling water until al dente. • Mix the fresh ricotta with 2 tablespoons of the cooking water in a large serving dish. • Drain the pasta well. Add the pasta to the pan with the meat sauce. Toss with the fresh ricotta mixture. • Sprinkle with the ricotta salata and pecorino. Serve hot.

Serves: 4

Preparation: 10' + time to make pasta

Cooking: 50'

Level of difficulty: 2

- 1 quantity pappardelle (see pages 286–7) or 14 oz/400 g store-bought pappardelle
- 5 oz/150 g ground lean pork
- 5 oz/150 g ground lean veal
- 4 tbsp extra-virgin olive oil
- 1 tbsp tomato paste mixed with $^{1}/_{2}$ cup/ 125 ml white wine
- 1 cup/250 g canned tomatoes
- salt and freshly ground black pepper to taste
- $2^{1}/_{2}$ oz/75 g Ricotta salata cheese, crumbled
- $^{3}/_{4}$ cup/180 g Ricotta cheese
- $^{1}/_{2}$ cup/60 g freshly grated Pecorino

Serves: 4–6

Preparation: 55' + time to make pasta +12 h to soak beans

Cooking: 2 h 15'

Level of difficulty: 2

- 10 oz/300 g dried cranberry beans
- 1 quantity maltagliati (see pages 286–7) or 14 oz/400 g store-bought maltagliati
- 1¼ cups/150 g diced pancetta
- 1 onion, 1 clove garlic, 1 carrot, finely chopped
- 1 stalk celery, finely chopped
- 1 sprig rosemary, finely chopped
- 2 tbsp extra-virgin olive oil
- salt and freshly ground black pepper to taste

# MALTAGLIATI WITH BEANS

Soak the beans overnight in a large bowl of water. • If making the pasta at home, prepare it several hours in advance. • Drain the beans and transfer to a large saucepan with enough unsalted cold water to cover them. Boil gently for just under 2 hours, or until the beans are very tender. • Remove one-third of the cooked beans and their cooking liquid with a slotted spoon and whiz in a food processor or blender. • Return the purée to the pan and stir well. • Sauté the pancetta, onion, garlic, carrot, celery, and rosemary in the oil in a large frying pan until lightly browned. • Stir this mixture into the beans. Season with salt. Bring the beans back to a boil and add the pasta. Cook for 5 minutes, then remove from the heat. • Let the soup to stand for 20 minutes. • Quickly reheat and serve with a grinding of pepper and a light drizzling of oil.

# TAGLIATELLE WITH ARTICHOKES

*Serves: 4*

*Preparation: 15' +*
*time to make pasta*

*Cooking: 30'*

*Level of difficulty: 1*

- 1 quantity tagliatelle (see pages 286–7) or 14 oz/400 g store-bought tagliatelle
- 8 very fresh baby artichokes or 16 fresh or defrosted frozen artichoke hearts
- 1 small onion, finely chopped
- 5 tbsp extra-virgin olive oil
- salt and freshly ground black pepper to taste
- 1/2 cup/125 ml water
- 4 large eggs, lightly beaten
- 7 tbsp freshly grated Pecorino cheese

If making the pasta at home, prepare it several hours in advance. • Remove the tough outer leaves from the artichokes by snapping them off at the base. Cut off the top third of the remaining leaves. Cut the artichokes in half, remove any fuzzy choke with a sharp knife. Cut them lengthwise into thin slices. • Sauté the onion in the oil in a flameproof Dutch oven (casserole) over medium heat until transparent. • Add the artichokes and season with salt and pepper. Stir over medium heat for 3 minutes. • Pour in the water. Cover and cook for about 20 minutes, or until very tender but not mushy. • Cook the pasta in a large pot of salted, boiling water until al dente. • Drain the pasta and add to the pan with the artichokes. Mix in the beaten eggs and cook over low heat until the eggs are cooked. • Sprinkle with the Pecorino and serve at once.

# ROMAN-STYLE FETTUCCINE

If making the pasta at home, prepare it several hours in advance. • Soak the mushrooms in a small bowl of warm water. Soften for 15 minutes. • Melt the pork fat in a large frying pan over medium heat. Add the onion and garlic and sauté until the garlic turns pale gold. • Drain the mushrooms and add to the pan with the tomatoes. Season with salt and pepper. Cook over medium heat for about 15 minutes, or until the sauce reduces by half. • Clean the chicken livers, cutting off and discarding any stringy membranes. Chop coarsely. • Melt half the butter in a small frying pan and cook the chicken livers over medium heat for 5 minutes. • Pour in the wine and let it evaporate. • Pour in the stock. Cover and cook over low heat until the chicken livers are cooked through, about 15 minutes. • Add the chicken livers to the tomato sauce. • Cook the pasta in a large pot of salted, boiling water until al dente. • Drain the pasta and transfer to a heated serving bowl. Add the sauce and toss vigorously for 1–2 minutes. • Sprinkle with the Pecorino and serve at once.

Serves: 4

Preparation: 35' + time to make pasta

Cooking: 30'

Level of difficulty: 1

- **1 quantity fettuccine (see pages 286–7) or 14 oz/400 g store-bought fettuccine**
- **2 tbsp dried porcini mushrooms**
- **3 tbsp coarsely chopped pork fat**
- **1 small onion, finely chopped**
- **1 clove garlic, finely chopped**
- **1²/₃ cups/400 g canned chopped tomatoes**
- **salt and freshly ground black pepper to taste**
- **8 oz/250 g trimmed, diced chicken livers**
- **4 tbsp butter**
- **4 tbsp dry white wine**
- **¹/₂ cup/125 ml Chicken Stock (see page 955)**
- **4 tbsp freshly grated Pecorino cheese**

# TAGLIATELLE IN ROSEMARY AND BUTTER WITH TRUFFLES

*Serves: 4*

*Preparation: 30' +*
*time to make pasta*

*Cooking: 5'*

*Level of difficulty: 2*

- 1 quantity
  tagliatelle
  (see pages 286–7)
  or 14 oz/400 g
  store-bought
  tagliatelle
- 6 tbsp freshly
  grated Parmesan
  cheese
- 4 tbsp butter
- 1 sprig fresh
  rosemary (or
  1 sprig fresh sage)
- freshly grated
  white truffle

If making the pasta at home, prepare it several hours in advance. • Cook the pasta in a large pot of salted, boiling water until al dente. • Drain the pasta and transfer to a heated serving dish. Sprinkle with the Parmesan. • While the pasta is cooking, heat the butter and rosemary until the butter turns a pale, golden brown. • Drizzle the hot butter over the tagliatelle and toss gently. • Top with the fresh truffle and serve hot.

# TAGLIATELLE WITH LEEKS AND FONTINA CHEESE

If making the pasta at home, prepare it several hours in advance. • Heat the oil in a large frying pan. Add the leeks and just enough water to cover them. Cook over medium heat for about 10 minutes, or until the leeks are tender. • Season with salt and pepper. Add the Fontina and mustard, if using, and cook until the cheese has almost melted. • Cook the pasta in a large pot of salted, boiling water until al dente. • Drain the pasta and transfer to a heated serving dish. Add the leek sauce, toss gently, and serve at once.

Serves: 4

Preparation: 20' + time to make pasta

Cooking: 30'

Level of difficulty: 2

- 1 quantity tagliatelle (see pages 286–7) or 14 oz/400 g store-bought tagliatelle
- 4 tbsp extra-virgin olive oil
- 7 oz/200 g leeks, cleaned and thinly sliced
- 6 tbsp water
- salt and freshly ground black pepper to taste
- 5 oz/150 g Fontina cheese, diced
- 1 tbsp spicy mustard (optional)

# TAGLIATELLE WITH UNCOOKED TOMATO SAUCE

*Serves: 4*

*Preparation: 30' +*
*time to make pasta*

*Cooking: 5'*

*Level of difficulty: 2*

- **1 quantity tagliatelle (see pages 286–7) or 14 oz/400 g store-bought tagliatelle**
- **1¹/₂ lb/750 g cherry tomatoes**
- **2 cloves garlic, finely chopped**
- **1 small onion, finely chopped**
- **8 leaves fresh basil, torn**
- **¹/₂ red chile pepper, thinly sliced (optional)**
- **dash of salt**
- **4 tbsp extra-virgin olive oil**

If making the pasta at home, prepare it several hours in advance. • Cut the tomatoes in half and pass them through a food mill to eliminate seeds and skins. Place the garlic, onion, basil, chile pepper (if using), salt, and oil in a large bowl. Add the tomatoes and mix well. • Cook the pasta in a large pot of salted, boiling water until al dente. • Drain the pasta and transfer to the bowl with the sauce. Toss vigorously and serve at once.

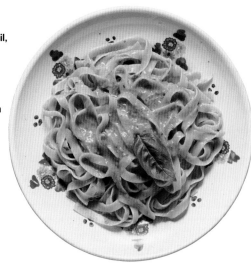

# PAPPARDELLE WITH HARE

Wash the pieces of hare pieces thoroughly, dry with paper towels and place in a large non-metallic bowl with the wine, onion, carrot, celery, bay leaves, rosemary, parsley, juniper berries, and peppercorns. • Leave for 6 hours, turning several times. • If making the pasta at home, prepare it several hours in advance. • Remove the hare from the marinade. Strain and reserve the liquid, discarding the vegetables and herbs. • Sauté the finely chopped onion and celery in the oil in a large saucepan over medium heat for 4 minutes. • Add the hare and cook over slightly higher heat for 5 minutes, turning the pieces to brown all over. • Ladle some of the reserved marinade over the hare and bring to a boil. Cover and simmer over low heat for $1^{1}/_{2}$ hours, or until the hare is tender, turning the pieces occasionally and adding more marinade as necessary. • Transfer the hare to a covered dish to keep warm. • Strain the cooking liquid, pressing the vegetables through a sieve (or use a food mill) and add to the liquid to add body. • Select three meaty pieces of hare from the center section or 'saddle,' remove the meat from the bones and chop finely. • Heat half the butter in a saucepan, add the cooking liquid and the chopped hare, stir and simmer for 10 minutes. • Cook the pasta in a large pot of salted, boiling water until al dente. • Drain the pasta and transfer to a heated serving dish. Stir in the remaining butter, the hare sauce and Parmesan. • Serve at once.

302

Serves: 4

Preparation: 30' + 5–6 h to marinate hare + time to make pasta

Cooking: 1 h 45'

Level of difficulty: 1

- 1 hare, well hung, cleaned and jointed
- 2 cups/500 ml dry red wine
- 1 onion, coarsely chopped
- 1 carrot, coarsely chopped
- 1 stalk celery, coarsely chopped
- 3 bay leaves
- 1 sprig rosemary
- 1 large sprig parsley
- 3 dried juniper berries
- 8 whole black peppercorns
- 1 quantity pappardelle (see pages 286–7) or 14 oz/400 g store-bought pappardelle
- 1 onion, finely chopped
- 1 stalk celery, finely chopped
- 6 tbsp extra-virgin olive oil
- 2–3 tbsp butter
- 1 cup/125 g freshly grated Parmesan cheese

# GARGANELLI WITH SPECK

S auté the onion in 2 tablespoons of butter in a large frying pan over medium heat for about 10 minutes, or until lightly browned. • In a separate frying pan, sauté the speck in the remaining butter until slightly crunchy. • Add the speck to the onion. • Cook the pasta in a large pot of salted boiling water until al dente. • Drain the pasta and add to the pan with the speck. Add 5 tablespoons of the cooking water from the pasta and cook for 2 minutes more. • Serve at once.

*Serves: 4–6*

*Preparation: 15'*

*Cooking: 15'*

*Level of difficulty: 2*

- **1 onion, finely chopped**
- **4 tbsp butter**
- **1 cup/120 g speck or prosciutto/ Parma ham, cut into thin strips**
- **1 lb/500 g fresh store-bought garganelli**

# TAGLIATELLE WITH SAUSAGE, BASIL, AND PECORINO

*Serves: 4*

*Preparation: 30' +
time to make pasta*

*Cooking: 45'*

*Level of difficulty: 1*

- **1 quantity
  tagliatelle
  (see pages 286–7)
  or 14 oz/400 g
  store-bought
  tagliatelle**
- **6 tbsp extra-virgin
  olive oil**
- **1 leek, thinly sliced**
- **1²/₃ cups/400 g
  chopped tomatoes**
- **20 leaves fresh
  basil, torn**
- **salt to taste**
- **12 oz/350 g fresh
  sausage meat**
- **7 oz/200 g freshly
  grated Pecorino
  cheese**

If making the pasta at home, prepare it several hours in advance. • Sauté the leek in the oil in a large frying pan over medium heat for about 5 minutes, or until softened. • Stir in the tomatoes and half the basil. Season with salt. Simmer over low heat for 30 minutes. • Remove from the heat and let cool slightly. • Process the sauce in a food processor or blender until smooth. • Return to the pan and stir in the remaining basil. • In a separate pan, cook the sausage meat with a little water until the meat crumbles with a fork. • Cook the pasta in a large pot of salted, boiling water until al dente. • Drain the pasta and add to the pan with the tomato sauce. Add the sausage and Pecorino. Serve hot.

# CHESTNUT TAGLIATELLE

Bring the milk and the first measure of salt to a boil in a large saucepan. • Cook the chestnuts for 1 hour, or until tender. • Use a fork or potato masher to mash the chestnuts in a large bowl, adding a little of the cooking liquid to form a purée. • Sift both flours and salt into a mound on a clean work surface and make a well in the center. Add enough water to make a smooth dough. Shape the dough into a ball, wrap in plastic wrap (cling film), and let rest for 30 minutes. • Roll out the dough into a sheet about 1/8-inch (2-mm) thick and cut into 3/4-inch (2-cm) wide strips. • Heat the cream in a frying pan over low heat. Mix in the Ricotta, nutmeg, and salt. • Cook the pasta in a large pot of salted boiling water until al dente. • Drain the pasta and add to the pan with the ricotta sauce. Add the Parmesan and the chestnut purée. Toss carefully and serve.

*Serves: 4*

*Preparation: 1 h 30' + time to make pasta*

*Cooking: 1 h 15'*

*Level of difficulty: 2*

- **2 cups/500 ml milk**
- **1/8 tsp salt**
- **15 chestnuts**
- **1 2/3 cups/250 g chestnut flour**
- **3/4 cup/125 g all-purpose/plain flour (or durum-wheat flour)**
- **3/4 tsp salt**
- **3/4 cup/180 ml warm water + more as needed**
- **4 tbsp heavy/ double cream**
- **generous 3/4 cup/ 200 g Ricotta cheese**
- **pinch of freshly grated nutmeg**
- **salt to taste**
- **4 tbsp freshly grated Parmesan cheese**

# MALTAGLIATI WITH BEANS AND POTATOES

Serves: 4

Preparation: 30' + time to soak beans + time to make pasta

Cooking: 1 h 40'

Level of difficulty: 2

If making the pasta at home, prepare it several hours in advance. • Cook the beans in a large pot of salted water with the bay leaf and sage for 1–2 hours, or until tender. • Remove the beans with a slotted spoon and set aside. • Cook the potatoes in the same water for 10–15 minutes, or until tender. • Purée half the beans in a food processor. • Sauté the carrot, celery, parsley, garlic, and pancetta in half the oil over medium heat for 5 minutes. • Season with salt and pepper. Add the whole beans and cook for 5 minutes. • Add the potatoes and rosemary and cook for 5 more minutes. • Cook the pasta in a large pot of salted boiling water until al dente. • Drain and add to the pan with sauce. Stir in the puréed beans and remaining oil. Toss gently and serve at once.

- 1 quantity maltagliati (see pages 286–7) or 14 oz/400 g store-bought maltagliati
- 3 cups/300 g dried borlotti beans, soaked overnight and drained
- 1 bay leaf
- 2 leaves fresh sage
- 4 potatoes, cubed
- 1 carrot, 1 stalk celery, finely chopped
- 1 tbsp finely chopped parsley
- 2 cloves garlic, finely chopped
- $1/2$ cup/60 g diced pancetta
- 5 tbsp extra-virgin olive oil
- salt and freshly ground black pepper to taste
- 1 tbsp chopped rosemary leaves

*Serves: 4*

*Preparation: 45' +
time to make pasta*

*Cooking: 1 h*

*Level of difficulty: 2*

- 1 quantity
  tagliatelle
  (see pages 286–7)
  or 14 oz/400 g
  store-bought
  tagliatelle
- 3 cloves garlic,
  finely chopped
- 1 sprig rosemary,
  finely chopped
- 6 tbsp extra-virgin
  olive oil
- 1 lb/500 g lamb,
  cut in small chunks
- 1/2 cup/125ml dry
  white wine
- 1 lb/500 g peeled
  and chopped ripe
  tomatoes
- salt and freshly
  ground black
  pepper to taste

# TAGLIATELLE WITH LAMB SAUCE

If making the pasta at home, prepare it several hours in advance. • Sauté the garlic and rosemary in the oil in a large frying pan over medium heat for 3 minutes. • Add the lamb and sauté until browned. • Pour in the wine and let it evaporate. • Stir in the tomatoes and season with salt and pepper. Cover and cook over low heat for about 45 minutes, or until the lamb is tender. • Cook the pasta in a large pot of salted boiling water until al dente. • Drain the pasta and add to the sauce. Toss gently and serve.

# MALTAGLIATI WITH LAMB SAUCE AND PECORINO

*Serves: 4*

*Preparation: 15' +
time to make pasta*

*Cooking: 1 h 15'*

*Level of difficulty: 2*

- 1 quantity
  maltagliati
  (see pages 286–7)
  or 14 oz/400 g
  store-bought
  maltagliati
- 4 cloves garlic,
  finely chopped
- 6 tbsp extra-virgin
  olive oil
- 1 lb/500 g ground
  lamb
- 5 oz/150 g ground
  lean pork
- 2 bay leaves
- 1¹/₂ lb/650 g
  peeled and
  chopped tomatoes
- 8 leaves fresh basil
- 1 tbsp finely
  chopped marjoram
- salt and freshly
  ground black
  pepper to taste
- ¹/₂ cup/60 g
  freshly grated
  Pecorino cheese

If making the pasta at home, prepare it several hours in advance. • Sauté the garlic in the oil in a large saucepan over medium heat until the garlic turns pale gold. • Add the lamb, pork, and bay leaves and sauté until the meat is browned all over. • Stir in the tomatoes, basil, and marjoram. Season with salt and pepper. Simmer over low heat for 1 hour. • Cook the pasta in a large pot of salted boiling water until al dente. • Drain the pasta and transfer to a heated serving dish. Toss carefully with the sauce. Discard the bay leaves before serving. • Sprinkle with the Pecorino and serve hot.

# PICI WITH SPICY TOMATO SAUCE

Sift the flour and salt into a large bowl and make a well in the center. Gradually add enough water to make a firm dough. Knead until smooth and elastic. • Roll out the dough to about ³/₄ in (2 cm) thick and cut into strips. • Roll each strip between your floured palms, slowly drawing it out until it is very thin and resembles rather untidy spaghetti. • Spread the pici out on a cloth. • Cook the pasta in a large pot of salted boiling water until al dente. • Drain the pasta and transfer to a heated serving dish. Add the sauce and toss carefully. Serve hot.

**312**

Serves: 4

Preparation: 45' + 2 h to dry pasta

Cooking: 10'

Level of difficulty: 2

- 2 cups/300 g durum wheat flour
- 1 cup/250 ml hot water
- dash of salt
- 1 quantity Tomato Sauce (see page 950), with 1–2 tsp red pepper flakes added

# BUCKWHEAT PASTA WITH POTATOES AND CHEESE

*Serves: 4–6*

*Preparation: 30'*

*Cooking: 45'*

*Level of difficulty: 2*

- 8 oz/250 g potatoes, in bite-sized pieces
- 6 oz/180 g Swiss chard, cut in strips
- 1 quantity buckwheat pasta (see page 392)
- 6 oz/180 g Fontina cheese, thinly sliced
- 2 cloves garlic, finely chopped
- 6 leaves fresh sage
- 6 tbsp butter
- 1 cup/125 g freshly grated Parmesan cheese

Preheat the oven to 350°F/180°C/gas 4. • Cook the potatoes in a large pot of salted boiling water for 5 minutes. • Add the Swiss chard and continue cooking for 10 minutes more. • Add the pasta and cook until al dente. • Drain the pasta and vegetables. • Sauté the garlic and sage in the butter in a small saucepan until pale gold. • Line a buttered ovenproof dish with a layer of pasta. Top with layers of potato, chard, and fontina. Drizzle with a little butter and sprinkle with pepper and Parmesan. • Bake for 25 minutes. • Serve hot.

# PAPPARDELLE WITH PHEASANT

If making the pasta at home, prepare it several hours in advance. • Place the pheasant in an earthenware dish and add the onion, carrot, shallots, rosemary, sage, cinnamon, juniper berries, bay leaf, cloves, and pepper corns. Pour in the wine, then cover and marinate in the refrigerator overnight. • Drain the pheasant, reserving the marinade, and pat dry with paper towels. • Sauté the pheasant in the oil in an earthenware casserole over high heat for 10 minutes, stirring often. • Add the wine from the marinade and cook over high heat for 30 minutes, uncovered. • Add the vegetables and spices from the marinade and season with salt. Cover and cook over low heat for 1 hour, or until the pheasant is tender. Add stock as needed to keep the sauce moist. • Purée the sauce in a food processor and return to the casserole. Add the dates and cook for another 15 minutes. • Cook the pasta in a large pot of salted, boiling water until al dente. • Drain the pasta and add to the casserole with the sauce. Toss gently and transfer to a heated serving dish. • Serve hot.

Serves: 4

Preparation: 1 h +
time to marinate +
time to make pasta

Cooking: 2 h

Level of difficulty: 2

- 1 quantity pappardelle (see pages 286–7) or 14 oz/400 g store-bought pappardelle
- 14 oz/400 g cleaned and boned pheasant, cut in small pieces
- 1 red onion, coarsely chopped
- 1 carrot, coarsely chopped
- 3 shallots, coarsely chopped
- 1 sprig rosemary
- 1 sprig sage
- 1 small stick cinnamon
- 3 juniper berries, crushed
- 1 bay leaf
- 2 cloves
- 1 tsp whole black peppercorns
- 2 cups/500 ml dry red wine
- 4 tbsp extra-virgin olive oil
- salt to taste
- 2 cups/500 ml Chicken Stock (see page 955)
- 7 oz/200 g pitted dates, chopped

# NETTLE TAGLIATELLE WITH GOAT'S CHEESE

Rinse the nettles under cold running water (be sure to wear gloves). Cook the nettles in a large pot of salted boiling water for 4 minutes. Drain well, let cool, then chop finely with a knife.
• Make the pasta dough following the instructions on pages 286–7, using the flour, eggs, and $3^1/2$ oz (100 g) of the chopped nettles to obtain a fairly firm dough. Knead for 15 minutes. Wrap in plastic wrap (cling film) and let rest for 30 minutes. • Divide the dough in 6 pieces and roll each one it through a pasta machine one notch at a time down to the second thinnest setting. • Dry the sheets of pasta on a lightly floured cloth for 30 minutes, then cut into tagliatelle. • Sauté the onion in the oil in a large frying pan over low heat for 15 minutes, adding a little water if they begin to brown. • Add the garlic and remaining cooked nettles and season with salt and pepper. Cook for 5 minutes.
• Mash the goat's cheese with the cream in a small bowl with a fork. • Cook the pasta in a large pot of salted boiling water until al dente. • Drain the pasta and add to the pan with the sauce. Toss gently for 1 minute, adding a little cooking water to make the sauce creamy. Spoon the goat's cheese over the top and turn off heat. • Serve immediately.

*Serves: 4–6*

*Preparation: 45'*

*Cooking: 30'*

*Level of difficulty: 2*

- $3^1/2$ oz/100 g cooked nettles (about 10 oz/ 300 g uncooked weight)
- 3 cups/450 g all-purpose/plain flour
- 4 large eggs
- 3 tbsp extra-virgin olive oil
- 1 small onion, finely chopped
- 1 clove garlic, finely chopped
- 14 oz/400 g nettles (tender, young part only)
- salt and freshly ground white pepper to taste
- $1/2$ cup/125 g fresh creamy goat's cheese
- 4 tbsp heavy/ double cream

316

# TAGLIOLINI WITH MULLET

If making the pasta at home, prepare it several hours in advance. • Sauté the garlic and parsley in the oil in a large frying pan over medium heat until the garlic turns pale gold. • Pour in the wine and let it evaporate. • Add the fish and tomatoes. Season with salt and red pepper flakes. Cook for 10 minutes. • Cook the pasta in a large pot of salted, boiling water until al dente. • Drain the pasta and add to the pan with the sauce, adding 2 tablespoons of cooking water, if needed. • Toss gently and serve hot.

*Serves: 4*

*Preparation: 30' + time to make pasta*

*Cooking: 15'*

*Level of difficulty: 2*

- 1 quantity tagliolini (see pages 286–7) or 14 oz/400 g store-bought tagliolini
- 2 cloves garlic, finely chopped
- 1 tbsp finely chopped parsley
- 4 tbsp extra-virgin olive oil
- $^1/_2$ cup/125 ml dry white wine
- 1 lb/500 g mullet, cleaned, filleted, and cut into small chunks
- 16 cherry tomatoes, sliced
- salt to taste
- $^1/_8$ tsp red pepper flakes

# HOMEMADE SPAGHETTI WITH GARLIC SAUCE

*Serves: 4–6*

*Preparation: 1 h + 30'*
*to rest the pasta*

*Cooking: 1 h*

*Level of difficulty: 3*

- 3¹/₃ cups/500 g all purpose/plain flour
- 1 small egg, lightly beaten
- 1 tbsp water + more if needed
- 8–10 cloves garlic, lightly crushed but whole
- 5 tbsp extra-virgin olive oil
- 2 lb/1 kg tomatoes, peeled, seeded, and finely chopped
- ¹/₄ tsp red pepper flakes
- salt to taste

Sift the flour onto a work surface and make a well in the center. Stir in the egg and enough water to make a fairly sticky dough. • Roll out the dough on a lightly floured surface to ¹/₂-in (1-cm) thick. Cover with a damp cloth and let rest for 30 minutes. • Tear off strips of dough, pulling them into lengths about the diameter of large spaghetti. Wrap into nests and let dry on a floured cloth until ready to cook. • Sauté the garlic in the oil in a small saucepan over low heat until it turns pale gold. • Stir in the tomatoes, red pepper flakes, and salt. Cook over low heat for 40 minutes. Season with salt. • Cook the pasta in a large pot of salted boiling water for 4–5 minutes, depending on the thickness. • Drain the pasta and add to the pan with the sauce. • Toss gently and serve hot.

# SPINACH TAGLIATELLE WITH YOGURT AND VEGETABLES

*Serves: 4*

*Preparation: 30' +
time to make pasta*

*Cooking: 30'*

*Level of difficulty: 2*

- **1 quantity spinach tagliatelle (see pages 286–7) or 14 oz/400 g store-bought spinach tagliatelle**
- **2 cloves garlic, finely chopped**
- **1 small red bell pepper/capsicum, cut in small pieces**
- **1 small yellow bell pepper/capsicum, cut in small pieces**
- **4 medium zucchini/ courgettes, cut in small pieces**
- **12 pitted green olives, sliced**
- **6 tbsp extra-virgin olive oil**
- **salt to taste**
- **$^1/_2$ cup/125 ml heavy/double cream**
- **$^1/_2$ cup/125 ml plain yogurt**
- **$^1/_2$ cup/60 g freshly grated Parmesan cheese (optional)**
- **paprika to taste**

If making the pasta at home, prepare it several hours in advance. • Sauté the garlic, bell peppers, zucchini, and olives in the oil in a large frying pan over medium-high heat for 15 minutes. Season with salt. • Cook the pasta in a large pot of salted boiling water until al dente. • Drain and add to the pan with the vegetables with the cream. Toss gently over medium heat for 1–2 minutes, or until the cream has been absorbed by the pasta. • Remove from heat and spoon the yogurt and Parmesan, if using, over the top. Sprinkle with the paprika. Serve hot.

# TAGLIOLINI WITH TREVISO RADICCHIO

If making the pasta at home, prepare it several hours in advance. • Sauté the onion in the butter in a large frying pan for about 10 minutes, or until softened. • Add the pancetta and cook for 5 minutes. • Add the radicchio and season with salt and pepper. Pour in the wine and let it evaporate. • Cook the pasta in a large pot of salted boiling water until *al dente*. Drain and add to the pan with the sauce. Toss gently and serve hot.

*Serves: 4*

*Preparation: 15' + time to make pasta*

*Cooking: 20'*

*Level of difficulty: 2*

- **1 quantity tagliolini (see pages 286–7) or 14 oz/400 g store-bought tagliolini**
- **1 red onion, finely chopped**
- **generous $1/3$ cup/ 100 g butter**
- **3 oz/100 g diced pancetta**
- **salt and freshly ground black pepper to taste**
- **14 oz/400 g red Treviso radicchio, finely shredded**
- **1 cup/250 ml dry red wine**

Serves: 4

Preparation: 10' +
time to make pasta

Cooking: 10'

Level of difficulty: 2

- ½ quantity plain
  tagliatelle and
  ½ quantity
  spinach tagliatelle
  (see pages 286–7)
  or 14 oz/400 g
  store-bought plain
  and spinach
  tagliatelle
- 4 tbsp butter
- 8 oz/250 g
  Gorgonzola
  cheese, cut into
  small cubes
- ⅔ cup/150 ml
  heavy/double
  cream (or milk)
- salt and freshly
  ground white
  pepper to taste
- 6 tbsp freshly
  grated Parmesan
  cheese (optional)

# PAGLIA E FIENO
# WITH GORGONZOLA

If making the pasta at home, prepare it several
hours in advance. • Melt the butter in a saucepan
and add the Gorgonzola and cream. Season with
salt and pepper. Cook over low heat, stirring
constantly, until the cheese has melted. • Cook
both types of pasta together in a large pot of
salted boiling water until al dente. • Drain the pasta
and transfer to heated individual serving bowls.
Add the Gorgonzola sauce and toss carefully using
two forks. • Sprinkle with the Parmesan, if liked.

# SPRINGTIME PAPPARDELLE

If making the pasta at home, prepare it several hours in advance. • Cook the asparagus in lightly salted, boiling water for 5 minutes. • Drain well and chop the stalks into short pieces. Leave the tips whole. • Sauté the asparagus in the butter in a large frying pan over medium-low heat for 4 minutes. • Stir in the Mascarpone and cook for 2 minutes, stirring constantly. Season with salt and pepper. • Cook the pasta in a large pot of salted boiling water until al dente. • Drain the pasta and transfer to a heated serving dish. Pour the sauce over the top and toss gently. Sprinkle with the Parmesan and parsley, if using. • Serve hot.

Serves: 4

Preparation: 30' +
  time to make pasta

Cooking: 5'

Level of difficulty: 2

- 1 quantity pappardelle (see pages 286–7) or 14 oz/400 g store-bought pappardelle
- 1 lb/500 g tender asparagus stalks
- 4 tbsp butter
- $1^2/_3$ cups/400 g Mascarpone cheese
- salt and freshly ground black pepper to taste
- $1/_2$ cup/60 g freshly grated Parmesan cheese
- 1 tbsp finely chopped parsley (optional)

# WHOLE-WHEAT SPAGHETTI WITH WALNUT SAUCE

**M**elt the butter in a frying pan and add the bread crumbs. • Finely chop the walnuts, garlic, sugar, cinnamon, and nutmeg together in a food processor. • Transfer to a bowl and stir in the bread crumbs, butter, and oil. Season with salt and pepper and mix well. • Cook the pasta in a large pot of salted boiling water until al dente. • Drain the pasta and place in a heated serving dish. Add the walnut mixture, toss carefully, and serve.

*Serves: 4–6*

*Preparation: 30'*

*Cooking: 5'*

*Level of difficulty: 2*

- 3 tbsp butter
- 4 tbsp fine dry bread crumbs
- 1 lb/500 g shelled walnuts
- 3 cloves garlic
- 1 tsp sugar
- ½ tsp each ground cinnamon and nutmeg
- ½ cup/125 ml extra-virgin olive oil
- salt and freshly ground black pepper to taste
- 1 quantity pici (see page 312), made with whole-wheat (wholemeal) flour

# SPINACH FETTUCCINE WITH BUTTER AND PARMESAN

*Serves: 4*

*Preparation: 10' +
time to make pasta*

*Cooking: 5'*

*Level of difficulty: 2*

- **1 quantity spinach
  fettuccine
  (see pages 286–7)
  or 14 oz/400 g
  store-bought
  spinach fettuccine**
- **¹/₂ cup/125 g
  butter**
- **1 cup/125 g
  freshly grated
  Parmesan cheese**

If making the pasta at home, prepare it several hours in advance. • Cook the pasta in a large pot of salted boiling water until al dente. • Drain the pasta and transfer to a heated serving dish. • Melt the butter in a small saucepan. Sprinkle the pasta with the Parmesan and drizzle the butter over the top. Toss carefully but well and serve.

# ORECCHIETTE WITH PUGLIA-STYLE MEAT SAUCE

*Serves: 4*

*Preparation: 30'*

*Cooking: 1 h 50'*

*Level of difficulty: 2*

- 4 tbsp extra-virgin olive oil
- 1 onion, finely chopped
- 2 cloves garlic, finely chopped
- 1 lb/500 g mixed meats (lamb, lean pork, beef), cut in small chunks
- salt and freshly ground black pepper to taste
- $^1/_2$ cup/125 ml dry white wine
- 1 quantity Tomato Sauce (see page 950)
- 1–2 cups/250–500 ml cold water
- 14 oz/400 g fresh store-bought orecchiette pasta
- 8 tbsp freshly grated Pecorino cheese

Sauté the onion and garlic in the oil in a large frying pan over medium heat until pale golden brown. • Add the meat and season with salt and pepper. Sauté over high heat for 5 minutes, or until the meat is nicely browned. • Pour in the wine and let it evaporate. • Stir in the tomato sauce. Cover and cook over low heat for about 1 hour and 30 minutes, adding water as needed if the sauce dries out. • Cook the pasta in a large pot of salted boiling water until al dente. • Drain the pasta and add to the pan with the sauce. Toss gently for 2–3 minutes over medium heat until the pasta has absorbed the flavors of the sauce. • Sprinkle with the Pecorino, toss again, and serve hot.

# TAGLIATELLE WITH MUSHROOMS

If making the pasta at home, prepare it several hours in advance. • Sauté the garlic and parsley in the oil in a large frying pan over medium heat until the garlic turns pale gold. • Add the mushrooms and cook until the liquid they produce has evaporated. • Stir in the olives, mint, salt, pepper, and boiling water. Simmer for 5 minutes. • Cook the pasta in a large pot of salted boiling water until al dente. • Drain the pasta and transfer to a heated serving dish. Toss gently with the sauce and serve.

- 1 quantity tagliatelle (see pages 286–7) or 14 oz/400 g store-bought tagliatelle
- 2 cloves garlic, finely chopped
- 3 tbsp finely chopped parsley
- 1/2 cup/125 ml extra-virgin olive oil
- 12 oz/300 g mushrooms, chopped
- 1 cup/100 g black olives
- 8 leaves fresh mint, torn
- salt and freshly ground black pepper to taste
- 6 tbsp boiling water

330

Serves: 4

Preparation: 30' +
time to make pasta

Cooking: 30'

Level of difficulty: 1

- **1 quantity tagliatelle (see pages 286–7) or 14 oz/400 g store-bought tagliatelle**
- **1 lb/500 g asparagus**
- **2 cups/500 ml Béchamel Sauce (see page 946)**
- **$^1/_2$ cup/60 g freshly grated Parmesan cheese**
- **pinch of nutmeg**
- **salt to taste**
- **1 tbsp minced ginger root**
- **6 tbsp extra-virgin olive oil**
- **6 slices smoked salmon, chopped**
- **3 tbsp brandy**

# ORIENTAL TAGLIATELLE

If making the pasta at home, prepare it several hours in advance. • Cook the asparagus in salted boiling water for 10 minutes, or until tender. • Separate the tips from the stalks and chop the stalks in a food processor until smooth. • Prepare the Béchamel. • Stir the Parmesan, asparagus purée, and nutmeg into the Béchamel. Season with salt. • Sauté the ginger and asparagus tips in 4 tablespoons of oil in a small frying pan over high heat for 3–4 minutes. • Cook the pasta in a large pot of salted boiling water until al dente. • Drain the pasta and place in a heated serving dish. Add the Béchamel and asparagus and ginger mixture. Toss gently. • Sear the salmon in a small frying pan with the remaining oil and brandy for 1 minute. Add to the dish. Serve hot.

# ORECCHIETTE WITH CAULIFLOWER AND ANCHOVY

Rinse the cauliflower and cut the stalks into small cubes. Divide the tops into small florets. • Cook the cauliflower in a large pot of salted boiling water for 7 minutes. • Add the pasta to the pan with the cauliflower and cook until al dente. • Sauté the garlic and anchovies in the oil in a small saucepan for 3 minutes. • Add the bread and sauté until nicely browned. • Season with salt—not too much salt as the anchovies are already quite salty —and pepper. • Drain the pasta and cauliflower and transfer to a heated serving bowl. • Pour the sauce over the top and toss gently. • Serve hot.

*Serves: 4*

*Preparation: 25'*

*Cooking: 15'*

*Level of difficulty: 2*

- 1 lb/500 g cauliflower
- 14 oz/400 g fresh store-bought orecchiette pasta
- 2 cloves garlic, finely chopped
- 6–8 anchovy fillets
- $^1/_2$ cup/125 ml extra-virgin olive oil
- salt and freshly ground white pepper to taste
- 2 thick slices day-old bread, cut in tiny cubes

# PAGLIA E FIENO WITH PEAS AND HAM

If making the pasta at home, prepare it several hours in advance. • Boil the peas in a small pan of lightly salted water until just cooked. • Sauté the onion and ham in the butter in a large frying pan over medium heat for 5 minutes. • Add the peas and season with salt and pepper. Cook for 5 minutes. • Cook the pasta in a large pot of salted boiling water until al dente. • Drain the pasta and place in a heated serving dish. Pour the sauce over the top and toss carefully. Sprinkle with the Parmesan and serve hot.

Serves: 4

Preparation: 15' + time to make pasta

Cooking: 15'

Level of difficulty: 2

- $^{1}/_{2}$ quantity plain tagliatelle and $^{1}/_{2}$ quantity spinach tagliatelle (see pages 286–7) or 14 oz/400 g store-bought plain and spinach tagliatelle
- $2^{1}/_{2}$ cups/300 g fresh or frozen peas
- 1 small onion, finely chopped
- $1^{1}/_{4}$ cups/150 g diced ham
- 4 tbsp butter
- salt and freshly ground black pepper to taste
- $^{1}/_{2}$ cup/125 ml heavy/double cream
- 1 cup/125 g freshly grated Parmesan cheese

Serves: 4

Preparation: 25' + time to make pasta

Cooking: 1 h 30'

Level of difficulty: 2

- 1 quantity pappardelle (see pages 286–7) or 14 oz/400 g store-bought pappardelle
- 1 carrot, 1 small onion, 1 stalk celery, finely chopped
- 1 tsp fennel seeds
- 4 leaves fresh sage, torn
- 1 cup/120 g prosciutto/Parma ham
- zest and juice of 1 orange
- 4 tbsp extra-virgin olive oil
- 1 small duck, weighing about 2 lb/1 kg, cut in pieces
- $1/2$ cup/125 ml dry white wine
- 2 lb/1 kg tomatoes, chopped
- salt and freshly ground black pepper to taste
- 4 tbsp butter
- 6 tbsp freshly grated Parmesan cheese

# PAPPARDELLE WITH DUCK SAUCE

If making the pasta at home, prepare it several hours in advance. • Sauté the carrot, onion, celery, fennel seeds, sage, prosciutto, and orange zest in the oil in a large frying pan for 5 minutes. • Add the duck and fry for 5 minutes. • Pour in the wine and orange juice and cook until reduced by half. • Stir in the tomatoes, season with salt and pepper, and simmer over low heat for $1^1/2$ hours. • Remove the pieces of duck from the sauce. Chop the sauce in a food processor until smooth and return to the pan. • Cook the pasta in a large pot of salted boiling water until al dente. Drain. • Stir the butter into the sauce and add the pasta. Sprinkle with the cheese and toss. Arrange the duck on top and serve.

# ORECCHIETTE WITH ARUGULA

*Serves: 4*

*Preparation: 25'*

*Cooking: 15'*

*Level of difficulty: 2*

- **14 oz/400 g fresh store-bought orecchiette pasta**
- **1 large bunch arugula/rocket, coarsely chopped**
- **3 cloves garlic, finely chopped**
- **$1/2$ cup/125 ml extra-virgin olive oil**
- **2 thick slices day-old bread, cut in tiny cubes**
- **salt and freshly ground black pepper to taste**
- **8 tbsp freshly grated Pecorino cheese**

Cook the pasta and arugula in a large pot of salted boiling water until the pasta is al dente.
• Sauté the garlic in the oil in a small saucepan until pale gold. • Add the bread and sauté until nicely browned. Season with salt and pepper.
• Drain the pasta and arugula and transfer to a heated serving bowl. • Sprinkle with the Pecorino and pour the sauce over the top. Toss gently. Serve hot.

*Another southern Italian dish. Try adding 4 tablespoons of toasted pine nuts.*

337

# TAGLIATELLE WITH EGG AND MOZZARELLA SAUCE

*Serves: 4*

*Preparation: 20' + time to make pasta*

*Cooking: 20'*

*Level of difficulty: 2*

- 1 quantity tagliatelle (see pages 286–7) or 14 oz/400 g store-bought tagliatelle
- 3 large egg yolks
- 6 anchovy fillets
- 5 oz/150 g Mozzarella cheese, cut in small cubes
- 5 tbsp butter
- salt and freshly ground white pepper to taste
- 6–8 tbsp freshly grated Parmesan cheese (optional)

If making the pasta at home, prepare it several hours in advance. • Beat the egg yolks in a small bowl. Add the anchovies and Mozzarella and mix well. • Cook the pasta in a large pot of salted, boiling water until al dente. • While the pasta is cooking, melt the butter in a large frying pan. • Drain the pasta and add to the pan with the butter. Add 5 tablespoons of cooking water from the pasta pan and the egg mixture and toss gently until the sauce is creamy (the egg should not cook into hard pieces). • Season with salt and pepper and sprinkle with the Parmesan. • Serve hot.

# TAGLIERINI WITH SHRIMP AND GARLIC SAUCE

*Serves: 4*

*Preparation: 45' + time to make pasta*

*Cooking: 40'*

*Level of difficulty: 2*

- 1 quantity taglierini (see pages 286–7) or 14 oz/400 g store-bought taglierini
- 7 oz/200 g garlic, peeled
- 3/4 cup/200 ml milk
- 1/2 cup/125 ml extra-virgin olive oil
- 8 oz/250 g peeled, cleaned shrimp, cut in half if large
- 12 anchovy fillets
- salt to taste
- 8 leaves fresh basil, torn
- 1 tbsp finely chopped parsley (optional)

If making the pasta at home, prepare it several hours in advance. • Place the garlic in a small saucepan with 4 tablespoons of milk. Bring to a boil and then strain, discarding the milk. Repeat twice more with the remaining milk and the same garlic. Discard the milk. • Place the garlic in a food processor with 6 tablespoons of oil and chop until smooth. • Place 1 tablespoon of water in a small saucepan over low heat and dissolve the anchovy fillets. Add 3 tablespoons of oil, then chop in a food processor until smooth. • Sauté the shrimp in 1 tablespoon of oil in a large frying pan over high heat for 2–3 minutes until they turn pink. • Season with salt and keep warm. • Cook the pasta in a large pot of salted boiling water until al dente. • Drain the pasta and add to the pan with the shrimp and the garlic sauce. Toss gently then place in 4 individual serving bowls. Spoon the anchovy sauce over the top and garnish with the basil and parsley, if using. • Serve immediately.

# PICI WITH MEAT SAUCE

S oak the porcini mushrooms in warm water for 20 minutes. • Drain and chop coarsely.
• Sauté the onion, carrot, celery and parsley in the oil in a large saucepan over medium heat for 5 minutes. • Add the beef and sausage meat and cook for 5 minutes. • Stir in the mushrooms and wine and cook over high heat for 5 minutes. • Add the tomatoes and season with salt and pepper.
• Cover and simmer over low heat for 45 minutes, adding a little stock to moisten. • Cook the pasta in a large pot of salted boiling water until al dente.
• Drain the pasta and transfer to a heated serving dish. Add the meat sauce and toss quickly
• Sprinkle with the Parmesan and serve hot.

*Serves: 4*

*Preparation: 50'*

*Cooking: 1 h*

*Level of difficulty: 2*

- **1 quantity pici (see page 312)**
- **1 oz/30 g dried porcini mushrooms**
- **1 onion, 1 carrot, 1 stick celery, finely chopped**
- **2 tbsp finely chopped parsley**
- **10 oz/300 g ground lean beef**
- **1 sausage, skinned**
- **$1/2$ cup/125 ml dry red wine**
- **$1^2/3$ cups/400 g chopped tomatoes**
- **1 cup/250 ml water**
- **6 tbsp extra-virgin olive oil**
- **salt and freshly ground black pepper to taste**
- **1 cup/125 g freshly grated Parmesan cheese**

Serves: 4

Preparation: 5' + time to make pasta

Cooking: 10'

Level of difficulty: 2

- $^{1}/_{2}$ **quantity plain tagliatelle and $^{1}/_{2}$ quantity spinach tagliatelle (see pages 286–7) or 14 oz/400 g store-bought plain and spinach tagliatelle**
- **4 tbsp butter**
- **1 white truffle, in shavings**
- **1 cup/250 ml light/single cream**
- **salt and freshly ground black pepper to taste**
- **6 tbsp freshly grated Parmesan cheese**

# PAGLIA E FIENO WITH TRUFFLES

I f making the pasta at home, prepare it several hours in advance. • Melt the butter in a small saucepan and cook the truffle over low heat for 1 minute. • Increase the heat and add the cream. Season with salt and pepper. Simmer for 4–5 minutes, or until the cream reduces. • Cook the pasta in a large pot of salted boiling water until al dente. • Drain the pasta and add to the pan with the truffle sauce. • Sprinkle with the Parmesan and toss carefully over medium heat for 1–2 minutes. • Serve hot.

# WHORTLEBERRY TAGLIERINI WITH TOMATO AND MOZZARELLA

*Serves: 4*

*Preparation: 25' +
time to make pasta
and chill the sauce*

*Cooking: 5'*

*Level of difficulty: 3*

### PASTA

- 2²/₃ cups/400 g
  durum wheat flour

- 10 oz/300 g
  whortleberries,
  chopped in a food
  processor and
  strained

### SAUCE

- 1¹/₄ lb/625 g ripe
  tomatoes, peeled,
  seeded, and cut in
  small cubes

- 4 tbsp extra-virgin
  olive oil

- salt and freshly
  ground black
  pepper to taste

- 1 tbsp fresh lemon
  juice

- 1 tbsp sugar

- 8 fresh mint leaves,
  torn

- 7 oz/200 g
  Mozzarella cheese,
  cut in small cubes

P asta: Prepare the dough using the flour and whortleberry juice following the instructions on pages 286–7, to obtain a fairly firm dough.
• Place the tomatoes in a large bowl with the oil, salt, pepper, lemon, sugar, and mint. • Refrigerate for 2 hours, stirring often. • Divide the dough in 4 pieces and roll each one through a pasta machine one notch at a time down to the second thinnest setting. Cut the pasta into taglierini and shape into nests. Dry the pasta on a lightly floured cloth for 30 minutes. • Cook the pasta in a large pot of salted boiling water until al dente, about 4–5 minutes. • Drain the pasta and add to the bowl with the sauce. Toss gently and serve in individual serving bowls. Garnish each bowl with the Mozzarella. • Serve immediately.

# TAGLIATELLE WITH SALAMI

If making the pasta at home, prepare it several hours in advance. • Sauté the onion in the oil in a large frying pan over medium heat for 10 minutes. • Add the salami and cook over high heat for 30 seconds. Pour in the wine and let it evaporate. • Add the tomatoes and season with salt. Partially cover and cook over low heat for 20 minutes. • Cook the pasta in a large pot of salted boiling water until al dente. • While the pasta is cooking, add the Provolone to the frying pan so that it melts a little. • Drain the pasta and add to the pan with the salami. Toss gently for 1 minute. Add the Parmesan and parsley, if using. Serve immediately.

*Serves: 4*

*Preparation: 30' + time to make pasta*

*Cooking: 40'*

*Level of difficulty: 2*

- 1 quantity tagliatelle (see pages 286–7) or 14 oz/400 g store-bought tagliatelle
- 1 large white onion, cut in thin rings
- 4 tbsp extra-virgin olive oil
- 5 oz/150 g salami, thickly sliced and cut in strips
- 4 tbsp dry white wine
- 1 lb/500 g tomatoes, peeled, seeded, and chopped
- salt to taste
- 3$^1$/$_2$ oz/100 g Provolone dolce cheese, cut in strips
- 4 tbsp freshly grated Parmesan cheese
- 1 tbsp finely chopped parsley (optional)

# FETTUCCINE WITH BORAGE

Rinse the borage leaves thoroughly under cold running water. Bring 1 quart (1 liter) of water to a boil in a saucepan with a generous pinch of salt and cook the borage for about 20 minutes. Drain and let cool. • Chop the borage in a food processor to very fine, then strain it. Place in a clean cloth and squeeze well to eliminate excess moisture. Beat the eggs in a bowl and stir the borage into the eggs. • Prepare the pasta dough following the instructions on pages 286–7, using the flour and borage-flavored eggs to obtain a fairly firm dough. Knead for 20 minutes. Wrap in plastic wrap (cling film) and let rest for 30 minutes. • Divide the dough in 4 pieces and roll each one through a pasta machine one notch at a time down to the thinnest setting. Cut the pasta into noodles about $1/2$ x 10 inches (1 x 25 cm). Dry the pasta on a lightly floured cloth for 30 minutes. • Cook the pasta in a large pot of salted boiling water until al dente. • While the pasta is cooking, melt the butter over medium heat until browned. • Drain the pasta and transfer to a heated serving dish. Pour in the butter, sprinkle with the Parmesan, and toss gently. • Serve hot.

Serves: 4

Preparation: 15' +
time to make pasta

Cooking: 15'

Level of difficulty: 2

- **10 oz/300 g borage leaves**
- **salt to taste**
- **2 cups/300 g all-purpose/plain flour**
- **3 large eggs**
- **6 tbsp butter**
- **8 tbsp freshly grated Parmesan cheese**

# MALTAGLIATI WITH VEGETABLES AND BEANS

If making the pasta at home, prepare it several hours in advance. • Melt the lard in a large frying pan and sauté the garlic and parsley until the garlic turns pale gold. • Discard the garlic. Add the onion, celery, potatoes, and carrot and sauté for 5 minutes. • Add the beans, tomatoes, and enough cold water to cover. Cook for about 1 hour, or until the beans are almost tender. • Season with salt. Add the pasta and cook until al dente. • Serve at once.

*Serves: 4*

*Preparation: 30' + time to make pasta*

*Cooking: 1 h 20'*

*Level of difficulty: 2*

- 1 quantity maltagliati (see pages 286–7) or 14 oz/400 g store-bought maltagliati
- 4 tbsp lard
- 1 clove garlic, peeled but whole
- 2 tbsp finely chopped parsley
- 1 onion, 1 stalk celery, finely chopped
- 3 potatoes, coarsely chopped
- 1 carrot, coarsely chopped
- 4 cups/400 g fresh cannellini beans
- 14 oz/400 g peeled and chopped tomatoes
- 1 quart/1 liter water
- salt to taste

# ORECCHIETTE WITH BROCCOLI

*Serves: 4–6*

*Preparation: 30'*

*Cooking: 25'*

*Level of difficulty: 2*

- **1 lb/500 g broccoli**
- **2 cloves garlic, finely chopped**
- **4 tbsp extra-virgin olive oil**
- **1–2 spicy red chile peppers, seeded and thinly sliced**
- **salt to taste**
- **1 lb/500 g store-bought fresh orecchiette pasta**
- **1 cup/120 g freshly grated Pecorino cheese**

Trim the broccoli stem and dice it into small cubes. Divide the broccoli heads into small florets. Boil the stem and florets in a large pot of salted water for about 8 minutes, or until tender. • Drain the broccoli, reserving the water to cook the pasta. • Sauté the garlic in the oil in a large frying pan until pale gold. • Add the broccoli and chile pepper. Season with salt. Cook over low heat for 5 minutes. • Bring the water used to cook the broccoli back to a boil, add the pasta, and cook until al dente. • Drain the pasta and add to the pan with the broccoli. Toss over high heat for 1–2 minutes. • Sprinkle with the Pecorino and serve.

# TAGLIOLINI WITH CURRY SAUCE

If making the pasta at home, prepare it several hours in advance. • Melt the butter in a large frying pan and add the onion and a pinch of salt. Cover and cook over low heat for 20 minutes. • Add the garlic and ham and cook over medium heat for 4 minutes. • Add the curry and stir for 1 minute. • Stir in the almonds and cook for 3 minutes. • Add the cream. Bring to a boil and season with salt. • Cook the pasta in a large pot of salted boiling water until al dente. • Drain the pasta and add to the pan with the sauce. Toss gently for 1 minute, adding a little cooking water if needed. • Serve at once.

*Serves: 4*

*Preparation: 30' + time to make pasta*

*Cooking: 30'*

*Level of difficulty: 2*

- 1 quantity tagliolini (see pages 286–7) or 14 oz/400 g store-bought tagliolini
- 2 tbsp butter
- 2 medium white onions, finely chopped
- salt to taste
- 1 clove garlic, finely chopped
- 1 cup/120 g diced ham
- 2 tbsp hot curry powder
- 15 almonds, peeled and chopped
- $^3/_4$ cup/180 ml light/single cream

# TAGLIOLINI WITH ALMONDS, BASIL, AND TOMATOES

*Serves: 4*

*Preparation: 15' +*
*time to make pasta*

*Cooking: 5'*

*Level of difficulty: 2*

- **1 quantity tagliolini (see pages 286–7) or 14 oz/400 g store-bought tagliolini**
- **4 oz/125 g peeled almonds, finely chopped**
- **1 clove garlic, finely chopped**
- **salt to taste**
- **1 small bunch fresh basil**
- **2 large tomatoes, peeled, seeds removed and chopped**
- **$^1/_2$ tsp red pepper flakes**
- **3 tbsp extra-virgin olive oil**
- **4 tbsp almond slivers, to garnish**

If making the pasta at home, prepare it several hours in advance. • Chop the almonds, garlic, and a pinch of salt in a food processor until almost smooth. • Add the basil and 1 tomato and chop until smooth. Season with salt and red pepper flakes. Drizzle with the oil. Transfer to a serving dish. • Cook the pasta in a large pot of salted boiling water until al dente. • Drain the pasta and place in the serving dish with the sauce, adding a little of the pasta water if the sauce is too dry. • Garnish with the remaining tomato, cut in very small pieces, and sprinkle with the almond slivers. • Serve at once.

*Serves: 4*

*Preparation: 30' +
time to make pasta*

*Cooking: 45'*

*Level of difficulty: 2*

### PASTA

- 1¹/₃ cups/200 g all-purpose/plain flour
- 1¹/₃ cups/200 g durum wheat flour
- 1 tbsp extra-virgin olive oil
- about ³/₄ cup/ 180 ml warm milk

### SAUCE

- 1¹/₂ lb/750 g cherry tomatoes
- 4 tbsp fine dry bread crumbs
- 3 cloves garlic, finely chopped
- 2 tbsp finely chopped parsley
- 1 tbsp finely chopped oregano
- 8 leaves fresh basil, torn
- pinch of sugar
- 6 tbsp extra-virgin olive oil
- salt and freshly ground black pepper to taste

# MILK PASTA WITH CHERRY TOMATOES

Pasta: Prepare the pasta dough following the instructions on pages 286–7, using both flours and oil and enough milk to obtain a fairly firm dough. Knead for 15 minutes. Wrap in plastic wrap (cling film) and let rest for 30 minutes. • Divide the dough in 4 pieces and roll each one through a pasta machine one notch at a time down to the second thinnest setting. • Cut into 1-in (2.5-cm) squares. Dry the squares of pasta on a lightly floured cloth for 30 minutes. • Preheat the oven to 350°F/180°C/gas 4. • Cut the cherry tomatoes in half. • Mix the bread crumbs, garlic, parsley, oregano, and half the basil in a small bowl. Add the sugar and half the oil. • Place the tomatoes in a large shallow baking dish, cut side up. Season with salt and the herb mixture. • Bake for 40 minutes.
• Cook the pasta in a large pot of salted boiling water until al dente, about 4–5 minutes. • Drain the pasta and place in a heated serving dish. Spoon the tomatoes and their cooking liquid over the top. Drizzle with the remaining oil and sprinkle with the remaining basil and a generous grinding of pepper. Toss gently. Serve hot.

Serves: 4

Preparation: 30' +
time to make pasta

Cooking: 45'

Level of difficulty: 2

- 1 quantity
  tagliatelle
  (see pages 286–7)
  or 14 oz/400 g
  store-bought
  tagliatelle
- 2 small carrots,
  1 leek, cut in
  julienne strips
- 2 stalks celery, cut
  in julienne strips
- 2 onions, sliced
- 4 tbsp extra-virgin
  olive oil
- 1 shallot, chopped
- 1-inch/2.5-cm
  piece fresh ginger
  root, peeled and
  finely chopped
- $^1$/$_2$ cup/125 ml
  sherry
- 6 champignon
  mushrooms, sliced
- 1 bunch Swiss chard,
  cut in thin strips
- 2 cups/500 ml
  Chicken Stock
  (see page 955)
- 1 duck's breast, cut
  in thin strips
- 2 tbsp all-purpose/
  plain flour
- 3 tbsp butter
- salt and freshly
  ground black
  pepper to taste
- 1 tbsp cornstarch/
  cornflour

# PASTA WITH DUCK AND VEGETABLES

If making the pasta at home, prepare it several hours in advance. • Bring a large pot of salted water to a boil and blanch the carrots for 2 minutes. • Drain and cool in a bowl of cold water and ice. Separately blanch and cool the leek, celery, and onions in the same way. • Sauté the shallot in the oil in a large frying pan over medium heat for 3 minutes. • Add the ginger and half the sherry. Cook until the alcohol has evaporated, about 4 minutes. • Gradually add the mushrooms and cook over high heat for 3 minutes. Stir in the blanched vegetables. Cook for 4 minutes more. • Add the Swiss chard and half the stock. Cook over high heat for 2 minutes. • Coat the pieces of duck in the flour, shaking off any excess. • Heat the butter in a large frying pan over high heat and sauté the duck for 1 minute. • Season with salt and pepper. Pour in the remaining sherry and let it evaporate. • Add the duck to the vegetables. • Stir the cornstarch into the remaining stock in a small bowl and pour into the pan. Bring the sauce to a boil. • Cook the pasta in a large pot of salted boiling water until al dente. • Drain the pasta and add to the pan with the sauce. Toss gently for 1 minute, adding a little cooking water if needed. • Serve at once.

# SAFFRON PAPPARDELLE WITH LAMB SAUCE

Prepare the pasta dough following the instructions on pages 286–7, adding the saffron and water mixture to the eggs. Wrap the dough in plastic wrap (cling film) and let rest for 30 minutes. • Divide the dough into 6 pieces. Roll it through a pasta machine one notch at a time down to the thinnest setting. Use a knife to cut into pappardelle about 5 x $^3/_4$-inches (12 x 2-cm). Let dry on a lightly floured cloth for 30 minutes. • Heat the oil and butter in a large saucepan and sauté the lamb over high heat until browned all over. • Pour in the sherry and let it evaporate. Season with salt and pepper. Cook over low heat for 1 hour, or until very tender, moistening with enough stock to keep the sauce moist. • Take the lamb out of the pan and remove the meat from the bone. Cut the meat into small strips. • Add 3 tablespoons of stock to the pan with the cooking juices. Add the onion and cook for 5 minutes. • Add the lamb and cook for 3–5 minutes more. Stir in the flour and 2 cups (500 ml) of stock. Add the lettuce, marjoram, and saffron and season with salt and pepper. Cook over low heat until the sauce has thickened, about 5 minutes. • Cook the pasta in a large pot of salted boiling water until al dente. • Drain the pasta and transfer to a heated serving dish. Spoon the sauce over the top and toss gently. • Serve immediately.

Serves: 4–6

Preparation: 40' + time to make pasta

Cooking: 1 h 30'

Level of difficulty: 3

**PASTA**

- 3$^1/_3$ cups/500 g all-purpose/plain flour
- 1 tsp saffron powder, dissolved in 1 tbsp warm water + pinch of saffron (for the cooking water)
- 4 large whole eggs + 2 large egg yolks

**SAUCE**

- 4 tbsp extra-virgin olive oil
- 3 tbsp butter
- 1 leg of lamb, weighing about 2$^1/_2$ lb/1.2 kg
- $^1/_2$ cup/125 ml sherry
- salt and freshly ground white pepper to taste
- 1 quart/1 liter Beef Stock (see page 955)
- 1 small onion, finely chopped
- 1 lettuce heart, cut in strips
- 1 tbsp finely chopped marjoram
- 2 tbsp all-purpose/ plain flour
- 6–8 threads saffron, crumbled

# PICI WITH ANCHOVIES

*Serves: 4–6*

*Preparation: 20' +*
*time to make pasta*

*Cooking: 15'*

*Level of difficulty: 2*

- 3 slices day-old firm-textured bread
- generous ⅓ cup/ 100 ml extra-virgin olive oil
- 6 anchovy fillets
- freshly ground black pepper to taste
- 1 quantity pici (see page 312)

Preheat the oven to 300°F/150°C/gas 4. • Crumble the slices of bread and toast them lightly. • Heat the oil in a large frying pan over medium heat. Add the anchovies and stir with a fork until they have dissolved in the oil. • Add the bread crumbs and mix for 2 minutes. Season with pepper. • Cook the pasta in a large pot of salted boiling water until al dente. • Drain the pasta and add to the pan with the sauce. Add 1–2 tablespoons of cooking water if the sauce is too dry. • Toss gently until the pasta has absorbed the flavors of the sauce. • Serve hot.

# TAGLIATELLE WITH BEEF AND CLOVES

If making the pasta at home, prepare it several hours in advance. • Sprinkle the salt, pepper, 1 tablespoon of the parsley, and half the garlic on a chopping board. Roll the lard in this mixture. Cut holes in the direction of the grain with a long, thin knife and insert strips of the seasoned lard. Tie up the meat with kitchen string so it keeps its shape. • Heat the oil in an Dutch oven (casserole) over medium heat. Add the remaining garlic, parsley, onion, and celery and sauté until the garlic turns pale gold. • Add the beef and sear all over. Season with salt, pepper, nutmeg, and the cloves. • When the vegetables begin to brown, pour in the wine. Cook for 30 minutes more, adding water if the mixture starts to dry. • Stir in the tomatoes and enough water or stock to cover the meat. • Cook over very low heat for about 2 hours, or until the sauce has thickened. • Cook the pasta in a large pot of salted boiling water until al dente. • Drain the pasta and place in a heated serving dish. • Remove the meat from the sauce and pour it over the pasta. Toss gently and serve hot. • The beef should be sliced and served as a second course.

Serves: 4

Preparation: 45' + time to make pasta

Cooking: 3 h

Level of difficulty: 2

- 1 quantity tagliatelle (see pages 286–7) or 14 oz/400 g store-bought tagliatelle
- salt and freshly ground black pepper to taste
- 2 tbsp finely chopped parsley
- 3 cloves garlic, finely chopped
- generous 1/3 cup/ 100 g lard or fatty cooked ham, cut into strips
- 2 lb/1 kg beef rump
- 3 tbsp extra-virgin olive oil
- 2 tbsp lard
- 1 red onion, finely chopped
- 1 stalk celery, finely chopped
- 1/8 tsp freshly grated nutmeg
- 3 cloves, crushed
- generous 3/4 cup/ 200 ml dry red wine
- 1 cup/250 g peeled and chopped tomatoes

# FRESH PASTA WITH WALNUT AND CHOCOLATE SAUCE

*Serves: 4*

*Preparation: 45' + overnight to rest*

*Cooking: 20'*

*Level of difficulty: 2*

**PASTA**

- 1$^1/_3$ cups/200 g all purpose/plain flour
- 1$^1/_3$ cups/200 g durum wheat flour
- $^2/_3$ cup/150 ml warm water + more as needed

**SAUCE**

- $^3/_4$ cup/100 g shelled walnuts
- $^1/_2$ cup/100 g sugar
- 4 tbsp Alchermes liqueur or dark rum
- 1$^1/_2$ oz/45 g semisweet/dark chocolate, coarsely chopped
- 1 tbsp fine dry bread crumbs
- grated zest of $^1/_2$ lemon
- $^1/_4$ tsp ground cinnamon

Pasta: Sift both flours onto a work surface and make a well in the center. Add enough water and knead to make a smooth dough. Shape the dough into a ball, wrap in plastic wrap (cling film), and let rest for 30 minutes. • Roll out the dough on a lightly floured surface to a thickness of $^1/_8$ in (3 mm) and cut into 1-in (3-cm) squares.

*If you use the Alchermes liqueur you will get a striking dark red sauce like the one shown here.*

Lay out to dry on a lightly floured clean cloth. • Sauce: Blanch the walnuts in boiling water for 1 minute. Transfer to a large clean cloth. Fold the cloth over the nuts and rub them to remove the thin inner skins. Pick out the nuts. • Process the nuts with the sugar, liqueur, chocolate, bread crumbs, lemon zest, and cinnamon until a smooth paste has formed. • Let stand overnight in a cool place. • Cook the pasta in a large pot of salted boiling water until al dente. • Drain the pasta and place a layer in the bottom of a serving dish. Cover with a layer of sauce, repeating until all the ingredients are in the dish. • Serve warm or at room temperature.

# CAVATELLI WITH SPICY TOMATO SAUCE

Sift the flour onto a clean work surface and make a well in the center. Use a wooden spoon to stir in enough water to make a smooth dough. Knead for 20 minutes. • Shape the dough into a ball, wrap in plastic wrap (cling film), and let rest for 10 minutes. • Roll out the dough into logs about 2/3 in (1.5 cm) in diameter. • Cut into 3/4-in (2-cm) sections and use two fingertips to push down and turn, hollowing them out into a curved shell. • Sauté the garlic, chile peppers, and bell peppers in the oil in a large frying pan until the garlic turns pale gold. • Stir in the tomatoes and cook over high heat for 5 minutes, or until the tomatoes have broken down. Season with salt. • Cook the pasta in a large pot of salted boiling water until al dente, about 3–4 minutes. • Drain and add to the pan with the sauce. Toss gently over high heat until the pasta has absorbed the flavors of the sauce. • Sprinkle with parsley and Parmesan and serve.

*Serves: 4–6*

*Preparation: 45' + time to make pasta*

*Cooking: 30'*

*Level of difficulty: 2*

**PASTA**
- 2²/₃ cups/400 g all-purpose/plain flour
- about ²/₃ cup/ 150 ml water, boiling

**SAUCE**
- 2 cloves garlic, finely chopped
- 1 fresh chile pepper, finely chopped
- 10 oz/300 g green bell peppers/ capsicums coarsely chopped
- 6 tbsp extra-virgin olive oil
- 2 lb/1 kg firm-ripe tomatoes, peeled and coarsely chopped
- salt to taste
- 1 tbsp finely chopped fresh parsley
- ³/₄ cup/90 g freshly grated Parmesan cheese

# MALTAGLIATI WITH MASCARPONE CHEESE

If making the pasta at home, prepare it several hours in advance. • Mix the Mascarpone and egg yolks in a large bowl. • Add the Parmesan and season with salt and nutmeg. • Cook the pasta in a large pot of salted, boiling water until al dente. • Drain the pasta and transfer to a heated serving dish. • Spoon the Mascarpone mixture over the top, adding a few tablespoons of cooking water, and toss gently. • Serve hot.

370

Serves: 4

Preparation: 20' + time to make pasta

Cooking: 10'

Level of difficulty: 2

- 1 quantity maltagliati (see pages 286–7) or 14 oz/400 g store-bought maltagliati
- $^3/_4$ cup/180 g Mascarpone cheese
- 2 egg yolks
- 6 tbsp freshly grated Parmesan cheese
- salt to taste
- $^1/_2$ tsp freshly grated nutmeg

# TAGLIATELLE WITH HAZELNUTS

Serves: 4

Preparation: 20' +
    time to make pasta

Cooking: 10'

Level of difficulty: 2

1 quantity
tagliatelle
(see pages 286–7)
or 14 oz/400 g
store-bought
tagliatelle

1 cup/60 g fresh
bread crumbs

1 cup/250 ml milk

2 cups/300 g
hazelnuts

3 cloves garlic,
finely chopped

salt and freshly
ground white
pepper to taste

4 tbsp butter,
chopped

If making the pasta at home, prepare it several hours in advance. • Place the bread crumbs in a medium bowl and add the milk. • Shell the hazelnuts. Coarsely chop about $1/2$ cup (75 g). • Place the rest in a food processor and chop with the bread crumb mixture and garlic until smooth. Season with salt and pepper. • Cook the pasta in a large pot of salted, boiling water until al dente. • Drain the pasta and transfer to a heated serving dish. Spoon the sauce over the top and toss gently with the sauce and butter. • Serve immediately.

# MALTAGLIATI WITH SCALLIONS, TOMATOES, AND YOGURT

*Serves: 4*

*Preparation: 20' +*
*time to make pasta*

*Cooking: 30'*

*Level of difficulty: 2*

- 1 quantity maltagliati (see pages 286–7) or 14 oz/400 g store-bought maltagliati
- 12 oz/300 g cherry tomatoes, cut in half
- 1/2 cup/75 g freshly grated Parmesan cheese
- salt and freshly ground black pepper to taste
- 2 tbsp chopped thyme
- 6 tbsp extra-virgin olive oil
- 14 oz/400 g scallions/spring onions, cleaned and sliced in thin wheels
- 1 cup/250 ml plain yogurt

If making the pasta at home, prepare it several hours in advance. • Preheat the oven to 400°F/200°C/gas 6. • Place the cherry tomatoes cut side up in an ovenproof baking dish. Sprinkle with half the Parmesan, salt, pepper, and thyme. Drizzle with half the oil. • Bake for 15–20 minutes, or until the cheese is browned. • Sauté the scallions in the remaining oil in a large frying pan over low heat for about 7 minutes. • Stir in the yogurt and remaining Parmesan. Season with salt and pepper and keep the sauce warm over very low heat. • Cook the pasta in a large pot of salted boiling water until al dente. • Drain the pasta and add to the pan with the yogurt sauce. Toss gently. • Transfer to a heated serving dish, add the baked cherry tomatoes and toss again. • Top with a grinding of pepper and serve hot.

# TAGLIATELLE WITH CHICKEN SAUCE

If making the pasta at home, prepare it several hours in advance. • Finely chop the onion, carrot, parsley, and garlic together. • Heat the oil in a large frying pan over medium heat and sauté the mixture for 7 minutes. • Add the chicken and sauté until browned. Season with salt and pepper. • Pour in the wine and let it evaporate. • Remove the chicken from the pan and stir in the tomatoes. Cook for 10 minutes. • Chop the chicken into small pieces and return to the pan. Cook for 20 minutes more. • Cook the pasta in a large pot of salted boiling water until al dente. • Drain the pasta and add to the pan with the sauce. Add the ham and Parmesan. • Toss gently and serve hot.

374

Serves: 4

Preparation: 20' + time to make pasta

Cooking: 30'

Level of difficulty: 2

- 1 quantity tagliatelle (see pages 286–7) or 14 oz/400 g store-bought tagliatelle
- 1 onion
- 1 carrot
- 1 sprig parsley
- 1 clove garlic
- 6 tbsp extra-virgin olive oil
- 5 oz/150 g chicken breasts
- salt and freshly ground black pepper to taste
- $^{1}/_{2}$ cup/125 ml dry white wine
- $1^{2}/_{3}$ cups/ 400 g chopped tomatoes
- $1^{1}/_{4}$ cups/ 150 g diced ham
- 8 tbsp freshly grated Parmesan

| | |
|---|---|
| *Serves: 4* | |
| *Preparation: 45'* | |
| *Cooking: 30'* | |
| *Level of difficulty: 2* | |

# CARROT TAGLIATELLE WITH RICOTTA

- 8 oz/250 g carrots
- 1 tbsp tomato concentrate
- 2¹/₃ cups/350 g all-purpose/plain flour
- 3 eggs
- salt and freshly ground black pepper to taste
- ²/₃ cup/150 g Ricotta cheese, drained
- 8 tbsp freshly grated Parmesan cheese
- 16 walnuts, finely chopped
- 3 tbsp butter

Steam the carrots until tender then purée in a food processor. • Place in a saucepan over low heat and stir in the tomato concentrate. Let cool. • Sift the flour onto a clean work surface. Make a well in the center and mix in the eggs, carrot purée, and 2 pinches of salt. Mix until a smooth dough is formed. Add more flour if needed. Knead the dough, let rest, and cut into tagliatelle (see pages 286–7). • Cook the pasta in a large pot of salted boiling water until al dente. • Drain the pasta and transfer to a heated serving dish. • Add the Ricotta, Parmesan, walnuts, and butter. Season with salt and pepper. Toss gently and serve hot.

# TAGLIATELLE WITH PESTO, PINE NUTS, AND TOMATOES

If making the pasta at home, prepare it several hours in advance. • Toast the pine nuts in a small, nonstick frying pan until golden brown. • Sauté the onion in the oil in a saucepan over medium heat for 10 minutes, or until softened. • Stir in the tomatoes and pine nuts and cook over high heat for 5 minutes. • Cook the pasta in a large pot of salted boiling water until al dente. • Drain the pasta and add to the pan with the sauce, adding a little of the cooking water from the pasta. • Add the pesto, toss gently, and serve.

*Serves: 4*

*Preparation: 30' + time to make pasta*

*Cooking: 20'*

*Level of difficulty: 2*

- **1 quantity tagliatelle (see pages 286–7) or 14 oz/400 g store-bought tagliatelle**
- **4 tbsp pine nuts**
- **1 onion, finely chopped**
- **6 tbsp extra-virgin olive oil**
- **1 lb/500 g tomatoes, peeled and coarsely chopped**
- **6 tbsp Pesto (see page 948)**

# TAGLIATELLE WITH FISH AND GRAPEFRUIT SAUCE

If making the pasta at home, prepare it several hours in advance. • Sauté the celery, carrot, onion, and garlic in the oil in a large frying pan over high heat for 5 minutes, or until tender. • Cut two long spirals of zest from each grapefruit. Squeeze the juice and set aside. • Add the zest to the pan with the tomato paste. Stir for 2 minutes, then add the mullet. • Season with salt and pepper and drizzle with the grapefruit juice and cook over low heat for 5 minutes. • Remove the grapefruit zest and add the olives. Simmer, stirring often. • Cook the pasta in a large pot of salted boiling water until al dente. • Drain the pasta and add to the pan with the sauce. Sprinkle with the fennel and serve hot.

*Serves: 4*

*Preparation: 20' + time to make pasta*

*Cooking: 20'*

*Level of difficulty: 2*

- 1 quantity tagliatelle (see pages 286–7) or 14 oz/400 g store-bought tagliatelle
- 1 stalk celery, finely chopped
- 1 carrot, finely chopped
- 1 small red onion, finely chopped
- 1 clove garlic, finely chopped
- 4 tbsp extra-virgin olive oil
- 1 pink grapefruit
- 1 yellow grapefruit
- 1 tbsp tomato paste
- 1 lb/500 g mullet fillets, coarsely chopped
- salt and freshly ground black pepper to taste
- 15 pitted black olives
- 1 sprig wild fennel, finely chopped

# TAGLIATELLE WITH SCALLOPS AND ARUGULA

If making the pasta at home, prepare it several hours in advance. • Slice the larger scallops with a very sharp knife. Leave the smaller ones whole. • Melt the butter in a large frying pan and sweat the shallots over low heat for 10–15 minutes, or until softened. Do not brown them. • Turn the heat up to high and add the scallops. Sauté for 3 minutes. • Season with salt and pepper. Turn off heat and toss with half the arugula. • Cook the pasta in a large pot of salted boiling water until al dente. • Drain the pasta and add to the pan with the scallops. • Add the remaining arugula and toss gently over medium heat for 2 minutes. • Serve hot.

*Serves: 4*

*Preparation: 20' + time to make pasta*

*Cooking: 25'*

*Level of difficulty: 1*

- **1 quantity tagliatelle (see pages 286–7) or 14 oz/400 g store-bought tagliatelle**
- **12 oz/350 g scallops, shucked**
- **4 tbsp butter**
- **4 shallots, finely chopped**
- **1 small bunch arugula/rocket, cut in thin strips**
- **salt and freshly ground black pepper to taste**

# FETTUCCINE WITH SALMON

Serves: 4

Preparation: 15' + time to make pasta

Cooking: 20'

Level of difficulty: 1

If making the pasta at home, prepare it several hours in advance. • Sauté the garlic and chile pepper in 2 tablespoons of oil in a large frying pan over medium heat for 2 minutes. • Add the broccoli and cook over low heat for 10 minutes, stirring often. • Season with salt and discard the garlic. • Beat the egg yolks and cream in a medium bowl. • Sauté the salmon in the remaining oil in a medium frying pan over medium-high heat for 1 minute. • Cook the pasta in a large pot of salted boiling water until al dente. • Drain the pasta and transfer to the pan with the broccoli. Toss gently. • Add the egg and cream sauce and a generous grinding of pepper. Toss gently until the egg is creamy. Add the salmon. • Serve at once.

- **1 quantity fettuccine (see pages 286–7) or 14 oz/400 g store-bought fettuccine**
- **1 clove garlic**
- **1 dried chile pepper, crumbled**
- **3 tbsp extra-virgin olive oil**
- **1 lb/500 g broccoli, in florets**
- **salt and freshly ground black pepper to taste**
- **4 egg yolks**
- **6 tbsp heavy/ double cream**
- **7 oz/200 g salmon fillets, chopped**

Serves: 4

Preparation: 20' +
time to make pasta

Cooking: 40'

Level of difficulty: 1

- 1 quantity
  pappardelle
  (see pages 286–7)
  or 14 oz/400 g
  store-bought
  pappardelle
- 14 oz/400 g
  roasted meat
- 1 egg
- 6 tbsp freshly
  grated Parmesan
  cheese
- ¾ cup/45 g fresh
  bread crumbs
- 2 tbsp milk
- zest of ½ lemon
- salt to taste
- 4 tbsp extra-virgin
  olive oil
- 1 small onion,
  finely chopped
- 1 carrot, finely
  chopped
- 1 stalk celery,
  finely chopped
- 6 tbsp tomato paste
- 1²/₃ cups/400 ml
  Beef Stock
  (see page 955)
- 2 sprigs thyme,
  finely chopped
- 6 tbsp freshly
  grated Pecorino
  romano cheese

# PAPPARDELLE WITH MEATBALLS

If making the pasta at home, prepare it several hours in advance. • Chop the meat, egg, Parmesan, bread crumbs, milk, lemon zest, and salt in a food processor until smooth. • Shape into marble-sized meatballs. • Sauté the onion, carrot, and celery in the oil in a large frying pan over medium heat for 3 minutes. • Dissolve the tomato paste in the stock with the thyme. Pour into the pan, partially cover, and cook for 15 minutes. • Add the meatballs and cook for 20 minutes. • Cook the pasta in a large pot of salted boiling water until al dente. • Drain the pasta and add to the pan with the meatballs. Toss gently. • Sprinkle with the Pecorino and serve hot.

# ORECCHIETTE WITH SWISS CHARD

C ook the chard in a large pot of salted boiling water (3–4 minutes for frozen, 8–10 minutes for fresh). Drain well, squeezing out any extra moisture. Chop finely. • Sauté the garlic and anchovies in the oil in a large frying pan over medium heat until the garlic turns pale gold. • Add the chard. Season with salt and pepper. • Cook the orecchiette in a large pot of salted boiling water until al dente. • Drain the pasta and transfer to the pan with the sauce. Toss for 1–2 minutes over medium-high heat. Sprinkle with the pecorino and serve hot.

Serves: 4–6

Preparation: 10'

Cooking: 15'

Level of difficulty: 1

- 1 lb/500 g fresh, or 12 oz/350 g frozen, Swiss chard
- 3 cloves garlic, finely chopped
- 2 anchovy fillets, crumbled
- $^{1}/_{2}$ cup/125 ml extra-virgin olive oil
- 1 tsp crushed chile pepper
- salt and freshly ground black pepper to taste
- 1 lb/500 g fresh store-bought orecchiette pasta
- 4 tbsp freshly grated pecorino cheese

# TUSCAN-STYLE PAGLIA E FIENO

If making the pasta at home, prepare it several hours in advance. • Sauté the pancetta, prosciutto, onion, celery, and carrot in half the butter in a large frying pan over medium heat for 5 minutes. • Add the tomatoes, mushrooms, and nutmeg. Season with salt and pepper. Cook over medium heat for 15 minutes. • Add the wine and let it evaporate. • Stir in the peas. Simmer over medium-low heat until the peas and mushrooms are tender, adding the stock as needed to keep the sauce liquid. • Cook the pasta in a large pot of salted boiling water until al dente. • Drain the pasta and transfer to a heated serving dish. Toss vigorously with the remaining butter. • Place the pasta, sauce, and Parmesan separately on the table so that your guests can help themselves.

*Serves: 4*

*Preparation: 30' + time to make pasta*

*Cooking: 50'*

*Level of difficulty: 2*

- $1/2$ **quantity plain tagliatelle and $1/2$ quantity spinach tagliatelle (see pages 286–7) or 14 oz/400 g store-bought plain and spinach tagliatelle**
- 1 cup/120 g diced **pancetta**
- $1/2$ cup/60 g diced **prosciutto**
- 1 large onion, 1 stalk celery, 1 large carrot, **finely chopped**
- 4 tbsp butter
- $1^1/4$ lb/575 g **tomatoes, peeled and chopped**
- 12 oz/350 g **mushrooms**
- dash of nutmeg
- salt and freshly **ground black pepper to taste**
- $3/4$ cup/180 ml dry **white wine**
- 3 cups/400 g peas
- scant 1 cup/200 ml **Beef Stock (see page 955)**
- $3/4$ cup/90 g **freshly grated Parmesan cheese**

# SPINACH TAGLIATELLE WITH GORGONZOLA AND PEAS

*Serves: 4*

*Preparation: 10' + time to make pasta*

*Cooking: 15'*

*Level of difficulty: 2*

- 1 quantity spinach tagliatelle (see pages 286–7) or 14 oz/400 g store-bought spinach tagliatelle
- 1³/₄ cups/200 g peas
- 3 oz/90 g Gorgonzola cheese, cut into small cubes
- 1¹/₄ cups/310 ml light/single cream
- salt and freshly ground black pepper to taste
- 2 tbsp finely chopped fresh parsley
- ¹/₂ cup/60 g freshly grated Parmesan cheese

If making the pasta at home, prepare it several hours in advance. • Cook the peas in a pot of salted boiling water until tender. • Drain and set aside. • Stir the Gorgonzola in a large saucepan over low heat until it melts. • Stir in the cream. Add the peas and season with salt and pepper to taste. • Cook the pasta in a large pot of salted boiling water until al dente. • Drain the pasta and add to the pan with the sauce. • Add the parsley and Parmesan. Toss well and serve.

# MALTAGLIATI WITH RADICCHIO

If making the pasta at home, prepare it several hours in advance. • Sauté the garlic in the oil in a large frying pan over medium heat until pale gold. • Discard the garlic. Add the sausages to the oil and sauté until well browned. • Add the onion and cook for 10 minutes, or until softened. • Stir in the radicchio and cook for 3 minutes. • Cook the pasta in a large pot of salted boiling water until al dente. • Drain the pasta and add to the sauce. Sprinkle with the Parmesan and toss gently. • Serve hot.

Serves: 4–6

Preparation: 15' + time to make pasta

Cooking: 30'

Level of difficulty: 2

- 1 quantity maltagliati (see pages 286–7) or 14 oz/400 g store-bought maltagliati
- 1 clove garlic, lightly crushed but whole
- 4 tbsp extra-virgin olive oil
- 2 Italian sausages, peeled and crumbled
- $1/2$ onion, finely chopped
- 1 lb/500 g Treviso radicchio or red chicory, shredded
- 6 tbsp freshly grated Parmesan cheese

# PASTA WITH BEANS AND SAUSAGES

Serves: 4–6

Preparation: 40' +
  time to soak beans
  + make pasta

Cooking: 1 h 30'

Level of difficulty: 2

- 1 cup/100 g dried cannellini or borlotti beans, soaked overnight
- 2 quarts/2 liters cold water
- 1 cup/150 g all-purpose/plain flour
- 1 cup/150 g finely ground cornmeal
- $^2/_3$ cup/150 ml water + more as needed
- $^1/_2$ carrot, finely chopped
- $^1/_2$ stalk celery, finely chopped
- $^1/_2$ onion, finely chopped
- $^3/_4$ cup/90 g diced pancetta
- 2 tbsp extra-virgin olive oil
- 1 Italian sausage, crumbled
- salt and freshly ground black pepper to taste
- 1 tbsp tomato paste

Cook the beans in the water over low heat for 1 hour. • Drain, reserving the liquid. • Sift the flour and cornmeal onto a work surface and make a well in the center. Stir in enough water to make a smooth dough. Shape into a ball, wrap in plastic wrap (cling film), and let rest for 30 minutes. • Roll out the dough to a thickness of $^1/_8$ inch (3 mm). Cut into $^3/_4$-inch (2-cm) squares. • Sauté the carrot, celery, onion, and pancetta in the oil in a small frying pan for 5 minutes. • Add the sausage and brown all over. • Season with salt and pepper. Cook over low heat for 10 minutes. • Add the tomato concentrate, beans, and cooking liquid. • Cook the pasta in a large pot of salted boiling water until al dente. • Drain and add to the pan with the sauce. Serve hot.

# BUCKWHEAT TAGLIATELLE WITH POTATOES AND ONIONS

Sift the buckwheat flour and salt onto a work surface and make a well in the center. Use a wooden spoon to stir in the eggs and enough water to make a smooth dough. Shape the dough into a ball, wrap in plastic wrap (cling film), and let rest for 30 minutes. • Roll out the dough on a lightly floured work surface until paper-thin. Cut into $^1/_2$-inch (1-cm) wide strips. • Cook the potatoes in salted boiling water for 10 minutes. • Sauté the onion and garlic in the butter in a large frying pan until the onion has softened. • Cook the pasta in the pot with the potatoes until al dente. • Drain and serve with the sautéed onions and garlic. • Sprinkle with the Parmesan and serve piping hot.

Serves: 4–6

Preparation: 30' + 30' to rest the dough

Cooking: 25'

Level of difficulty: 2

PASTA

- 3$^1/_3$ cups/500 g buckwheat flour
- $^1/_8$ tsp salt
- 3 eggs
- scant $^1/_2$ cup/ 100 ml warm water + more as needed

SAUCE

- 4 potatoes, cut into small cubes
- 1 large onion, finely chopped
- 3 cloves garlic, finely chopped
- 4 tbsp butter
- 6 tbsp freshly grated Parmesan cheese

# PAPPARDELLE WITH BELL PEPPERS

If making the pasta at home, prepare it several hours in advance. • Sauté the onion, celery, and carrot in the oil in a medium saucepan over low heat for 15 minutes. • Add the pancetta and cook until crisp. • Add the bell peppers. Cover and cook over medium heat for 10 minutes, or until the bell peppers have softened. Season with salt and pepper. • Cook the pasta in a large pot of salted boiling water until al dente. • Drain the pasta and transfer to heated individual serving plates. Top with the bell pepper sauce. Melt the butter over the top and sprinkle with the Parmesan and parsley. • Serve at once.

Serves: 4

Preparation: 30' + time to make pasta

Cooking: 35'

Level of difficulty: 2

- 1 quantity pappardelle (see pages 286–7) or 14 oz/400 g store-bought pappardelle
- 1 onion, finely chopped
- 1 stalk celery, finely chopped
- 1 carrot, finely chopped
- 4 tbsp extra-virgin olive oil
- $^1/_2$ cup/100 g finely chopped pancetta
- 1 lb/500 g yellow bell peppers/ capsicums, seeded, cored, and cut into thin strips
- salt and freshly ground black pepper to taste
- 2 tbsp butter
- 1 cup/125 g freshly grated Parmesan cheese
- 1 small bunch parsley, finely chopped

# ORECCHIETTE WITH ARUGULA AND POTATOES

C ook the potatoes in salted boiling water for
15 minutes. • Add 2 cloves garlic and the
arugula. Cook for 10 minutes more. • Add the
pasta and cook until al dente. • Sauté the
remaining garlic and red pepper flakes in the oil in
a large frying pan until aromatic. • Drain the pasta
with the arugula and potatoes and transfer to the
pan. • Discard the garlic and serve at once.

*Serves: 4*

*Preparation: 10'*

*Cooking: 20'*

*Level of difficulty: 1*

- **14 oz/400 g potatoes, peeled and thinly sliced**
- **4 cloves garlic, lightly crushed but whole**
- **12 oz/350 g arugula/rocket, shredded**
- **14 oz/400 g fresh store-bought orecchiette pasta**
- **¹/₂ tsp red pepper flakes**
- **5 tbsp extra-virgin olive oil**

# PICI WITH MUSHROOM SAUCE

*Serves: 4*

*Preparation: 1 h + 30'*
*to rest the pasta*

*Cooking: 30'*

*Level of difficulty: 2*

- 1 lb/500 g
  mushrooms
- 5 tbsp extra-virgin
  olive oil
- salt to taste
- 2 cloves garlic,
  finely chopped
- 1 red chile pepper,
  finely chopped
- 2 tbsp finely
  chopped fresh
  parsley
- 1 quantity pici
  (see page 312)

Rinse the mushrooms and pat dry with paper towels. Separate the stalks from the caps and chop the stalks coarsely. Slice the caps thinly.
• Sauté the stalks in half the oil in a large frying pan over high heat for 2 minutes. • Add the sliced crowns and cook for about 10 minutes, or until tender. • Season with salt. Sauté the garlic, chile, and 1 tablespoon of oil in a saucepan over medium heat until the garlic is pale gold. • Add the mushrooms and cook for 5 minutes. • Stir in the remaining parsley. • Cook the pasta in a large pot of salted boiling water until al dente. • Drain the pasta and add to the pan with the sauce. • Toss gently and serve hot.

# PAPPARDELLE WITH WILD GAME SAUCE

If making the pasta at home, prepare it several hours in advance. • Place the hare (without the giblets) in a bowl with the carrot, celery, onion, 2 cloves garlic, and 4 tablespoons of vinegar. Pour in enough wine to cover and marinate for 12 hours. • Remove the hare and pat dry on paper towels. • Chop the vegetables finely and reserve the marinade liquid. • Sauté the vegetables in the oil in a Dutch oven (casserole) over medium heat for 10 minutes, or until lightly golden. • Add the sage, rosemary, and hare and cook over high heat for 15 minutes, or until browned all over. • Pour in 4 tablespoons of the reserved marinade liquid from the marinade. Add $1/2$ cup (125 ml) of stock, the giblets, and 2 tablespoons of capers. Season with salt and pepper. Cook, partially covered, for about 1 hour, adding more stock if the mixture starts to dry. • Remove the larger pieces of hare, place on a chopping board, and bone them. Transfer the boned meat to a food processor or blender and add the drippings, giblets, the remaining clove of garlic, and the remaining capers. Process until finely chopped. • Return the processed mixture to a saucepan still containing the small pieces of hare. Pour in the remaining vinegar and thicken with some stock if needed. • Stir in the olives and cook for 5 minutes more. • Cook the pasta in a large pot of salted boiling water until al dente.
• Drain the pasta and add to the sauce.
• Toss gently and serve hot.

Serves: 4–6

Preparation: 1 h +
12 h to marinate +
time to make pasta

Cooking: 1 h 45'

Level of difficulty: 3

- 1 quantity pappardelle (see pages 286–7) or 14 oz/400 g store-bought pappardelle
- 1 hare or rabbit, cleaned and cut into 6 + liver, heart, and spleen
- 1 carrot, coarsely chopped
- 1 stalk celery, coarsely chopped
- 1 onion, coarsely chopped
- 3 cloves garlic, crushed but whole
- $1/3$ cup/ 90 ml white wine vinegar
- 1 quart/1 liter dry white wine + more as needed
- 5 tbsp extra-virgin olive oil
- 1 bunch fresh sage
- 1 twig rosemary
- 2 cups/500 ml Beef Stock (see page 955)
- 3 tbsp capers
- salt and freshly ground black pepper to taste
- 1 cup/100 g black olives, pitted

# FRESH PASTA SQUARES WITH FAVA BEANS

S ift the flour onto a work surface and make a well in the center. Add enough of the beaten eggs to make a smooth dough. Knead for 10 minutes. Shape into a ball, wrap in plastic wrap (cling film), and let rest for 30 minutes. • Roll out the dough very thinly and cut into 1-inch (2.5-cm) squares. Place on a lightly flour clean cloth until ready to cook. • Finely chop the prosciutto with the mint, onion, and a pinch of salt. • Sauté the chopped mixture in the oil in a saucepan over medium heat until aromatic. • Add the tomatoes and fava beans. • After a few minutes, pour in the hot stock. Cover and cook over low heat for about 1 hour, adding more stock if needed. • Season with salt and pepper. • Cook the pasta in a large pot of salted boiling water until al dente. • Drain and add to the pan with the fava beans. • Toss gently and serve hot.

Serves: 4

Preparation: 1 h

Cooking: 30'

Level of difficulty: 2

- 1$^{1}/_{3}$ cups/200 g all purpose/plain flour
- 2 eggs, lightly beaten
- 2 oz/60 g prosciutto/Parma ham
- 1 tbsp finely chopped fresh mint
- $^{1}/_{2}$ red onion, finely chopped
- salt and freshly ground black pepper to taste
- 4 tbsp extra-virgin olive oil
- 4 firm-ripe tomatoes, peeled and coarsely chopped
- 3 cups/300 g fresh fava/broad beans
- generous $^{3}/_{4}$ cup/ 200 ml Beef Stock (see page 955)

# FILLED
# PASTA

# TYPES OF FILLED PASTA

F illed pasta is made using fresh pasta dough (see pages 286–7) and delicious combinations of meat, vegetable, cheese, and herb fillings. The recipes in this chapter explain how to make filled pasta from scratch. If you are short of time, buy ready-made filled pasta and serve with the sauces suggested here.

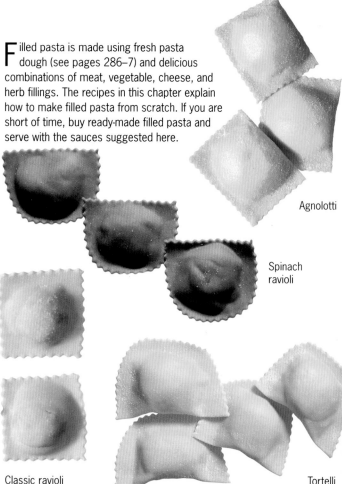

Agnolotti

Spinach
ravioli

Classic ravioli

Tortelli

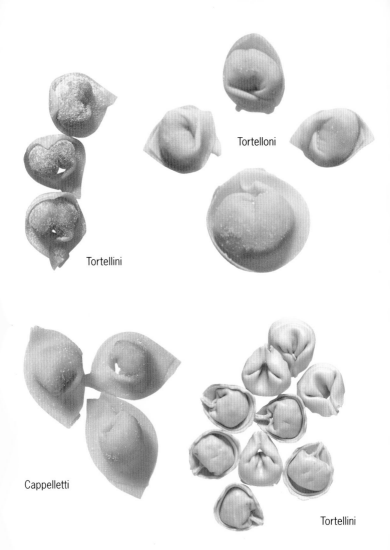

Tortellini

Tortelloni

Tortellini

Cappelletti

Tortellini

# HOMEMADE FILLED PASTA

## To make agnolotti, ravioli, and tortelli

**1.** Cut the rolled dough into sheets about 4 in (10 cm) wide. Place teaspoonfuls of filling at intervals of about 2 in (5 cm) down the center.

**2.** Moisten the edges of the dough with a little water and fold it over to seal. Press down lightly between the mounds of filling.

**3.** Use a sharp knife or wheel cutter to cut between the mounds. If using a wheel cutter, roll it around the other sides so that they are all attractively fluted. Lay the pasta out on cloths for 2 hours before use.

Making filled pasta at home is time-consuming but fun. Getting it right may take a little time, but it is well worth the effort. Throughout this chapter we have suggested that you make one full quantity of plain pasta dough (see page 286); this will be more than sufficient for the fillings in most recipes. However, if you are a novice filled-pasta-maker, you will need a little extra to make up for errors and wastage.

## To make tortellini

**1.** Cut the rolled dough into sheets about 2 in (5 cm) wide. Cut them in squares.

**2.** Place teaspoonfuls of the filling mixture at the center of each. Moisten the edges of the pasta with a little water and fold over into a triangular shape.

**3.** Fold the top of the triangle over and pull the edges around to meet. Pinch the edges together and seal them. Lay the stuffed pasta out on clean cloths for 2 hours before use.

# SPINACH, SAUSAGE, AND BEEF AGNOLOTTI

Pasta: Cook the potatoes in salted boiling water for 15–20 minutes, or until tender. • Drain and peel them. Use a fork or potato masher to mash the potatoes until smooth. • Spread the potatoes out on a work surface and let cool. • Add the beaten egg, flour, and salt. Knead the mixture into a smooth dough. Shape into a ball, wrap in plastic wrap (cling film), and let rest for 30 minutes. • Filling: Sauté the onion in the butter in a large frying pan over medium heat for 10 minutes, or until softened. • Stir in the spinach, sausage, and beef. Cook over low heat for 15 minutes. • Season with salt and let cool. • Roll out the dough into a fairly thin sheet. Cut into 2$^1$/$_2$-in (6-cm) strips and then into squares. • Drop a heaped teaspoon of the filling onto the center of half of the dough squares. Cover with the remaining squares, pressing down lightly on the edges to seal. If liked, cut around the edges of the agnolotti with a fluted pastry cutter to give them decorative edges.• Cook the pasta in two or three batches in a large pot of salted boiling water for 2–3 minutes. • Drain and drizzle with the melted butter. Sprinkle with the Parmesan and serve hot.

Serves: 4–6

Preparation: 45' + 30' to rest

Cooking: 10'

Level of difficulty: 3

**PASTA DOUGH**
- **2 lb/1 kg boiling potatoes**
- **1 egg, lightly beaten**
- **2 cups/300 g all-purpose/plain flour**
- **$^1$/$_8$ tsp salt**
- **$^1$/$_2$ onion, finely chopped**

**FILLING**
- **3 tbsp butter**
- **8 oz/250 g spinach, cooked, squeezed dry, and finely chopped**
- **4 oz/125 g sausage meat, crumbled**
- **4 oz/125 g lean ground beef**

**SAUCE**
- **$^1$/$_2$ cup/125 g butter, melted**
- **$^1$/$_2$ cup/60 g freshly grated Parmesan cheese**

# ROMAGNOL STUFFED PASTA

Prepare the pasta dough. Shape into a ball, wrap in plastic wrap (cling film), and let rest for 1 hour. • Mix the cheeses, eggs, nutmeg, and salt in a large bowl. • Roll the pasta out into a thin sheet. Fill and assemble the pasta following the instructions for tortellini on page 407. Let rest for 2 hours. • Add the pasta to the boiling stock and simmer for 2–3 minutes. • Ladle into soup bowls and serve hot.

Serves: 4–6

Preparation: 1 h + 3 h to rest

Cooking: 3'

Level of difficulty: 3

- **1 quantity Plain Pasta Dough (see page 286)**
- **1 cup/250 g fresh, white soft cheese**
- **1 cup/250 g Ricotta cheese, drained**
- **$^3$/4 cup/90 g freshly grated Parmesan cheese**
- **2 eggs**
- **$^1$/4 tsp freshly grated nutmeg**
- **salt to taste**
- **1$^1$/2 quarts/ 1.5 liters boiling Beef Stock (see page 955)**

# TORTELLI WITH SQUASH FILLING

*Serves: 4–6*

*Preparation: 1 h + 2 h to rest*

*Cooking: 40'*

*Level of difficulty: 3*

- 2³⁄₄ lb/1.3 kg squash/pumpkin
- 1³⁄₄ cups/200 g freshly grated Parmesan cheese
- 1 egg
- ¹⁄₄ tsp freshly grated nutmeg
- ¹⁄₂ cup/60 g fine dry bread crumbs
- salt to taste
- 7 tbsp butter, melted
- 1 quantity Plain Pasta Dough (see page 286)

Preheat the oven to 400°F/200°C/gas 6. • Without peeling the squash, scrape away the seeds and fibers and cut into 1¹⁄₂-in (4-cm) thick slices. • Bake until tender. • Remove the flesh from the peel. Press through a sieve into a bowl while still hot. • Mix with three-quarters of the Parmesan, the egg, nutmeg, bread crumbs, and salt. • Cover the bowl with plastic wrap (cling film) and let stand for 2 hours. • Prepare the pasta dough. Shape into a ball, wrap in plastic wrap (cling film), and let rest for 1 hour. • Roll out the dough to a thin, almost transparent sheet. • Fill and assemble the pasta following the instructions for tortelli on page 406. • Cook in a large pan of salted, boiling water for 2–3 minutes. • Drizzle with the butter and sprinkle with the remaining Parmesan. • Serve hot.

# TORTELLINI IN MEAT STOCK

*Serves: 4–6*

*Preparation: 1 h + 1 h to rest*

*Cooking: 2 h*

*Level of difficulty: 3*

- 1 quantity Plain Pasta Dough (see page 286)
- 2 tbsp butter
- 4 oz/125 g lean pork (tenderloin), chopped into small pieces
- 4 oz/125 g mortadella
- 3 oz/90 g prosciutto/Parma ham
- 1 egg
- 1³/₄ cups/215 g freshly grated Parmesan cheese
- dash of freshly grated nutmeg
- salt and freshly ground black pepper to taste
- 1¹/₂ quarts/1.5 liters boiling Beef Stock (see page 955)

Prepare the pasta dough. Shape into a ball, wrap in plastic wrap (cling film), and let rest for 1 hour. • Melt the butter in a large frying pan and gently sauté the pork until cooked through. • Transfer to a food processor, add the prosciutto and mortadella and chop finely. • Transfer the meat mixture to a bowl and mix in the egg, Parmesan, nutmeg, salt, and pepper. (The filling can be prepared a day in advance). • Roll out the dough to a thin, almost transparent sheet. • Fill and assemble the pasta following the instructions for tortelli on page 407. • Add the tortellini to the stock and simmer for 2–3 minutes (if boiled fast, they tend to come apart). • Ladle into soup bowls and serve hot.

# STUFFED PASTA WITH CHEESE FILLING

Prepare the pasta dough. Shape into a ball, wrap in plastic wrap (cling film), and let rest for 1 hour. • Mix the fresh white cheese, Parmesan, eggs, and salt in a large bowl.
• Roll out the dough to a thin, almost transparent sheet. • Fill and assemble the pasta following the instructions for tortelli on page 406. • Add the pasta to the stock and simmer for 2–3 minutes (if boiled fast, they tend to come apart).
• Ladle into soup bowls and serve hot.

*Serves: 4–6*

*Preparation: 1 h + 1 h to rest*

*Cooking: 3'*

*Level of difficulty: 3*

- 1 quantity Plain Pasta Dough (see page 286)
- 1 cup/250 g mild, soft white cheese
- 1 cup/125 g freshly grated Parmesan cheese
- 2 eggs
- salt to taste
- 1¹/₂ quarts/1.5 liters boiling Beef Stock (see page 955)

# SPINACH AND RICOTTA RAVIOLI

*Serves: 4–6*

*Preparation: 30' + 1 h
to rest*

*Cooking: 25'*

*Level of difficulty: 3*

- **1 quantity Plain
  Pasta Dough
  (see page 286)**
- **14 oz/400 g fresh
  spinach leaves**
- **1¼ cups/310 g
  Ricotta cheese**
- **1 egg**
- **1¾ cups/215 g
  freshly grated
  Parmesan cheese**
- **salt to taste**
- **¼ tsp freshly
  grated nutmeg**
- **7 tbsp melted,
  butter**

**P**repare the pasta dough. Shape into a ball, wrap in plastic wrap (cling film), and let rest for 1 hour. • Cook the spinach in a little salted water until tender. Drain well, squeezing out excess moisture. Chop finely. • Mix the spinach, Ricotta, egg, half the Parmesan, salt, and nutmeg in a large bowl. • Roll out the dough to a thin, almost transparent sheet. • Fill and assemble the pasta following the instructions for ravioli on page 406. • Cook in batches in a large pot of salted, boiling water for 4–5 minutes. • Use a slotted spoon to transfer the pasta to serving plates. • Drizzle with the butter and sprinkle with the remaining Parmesan. • Serve hot.

# TORTELLI WITH BEET STUFFING

S ift the flour onto a clean work surface. Make a well in the center and break the eggs into it. Add the water and salt and stir with your fingertips or a fork so that the flour is gradually incorporated. Knead until smooth and elastic. Cover with a damp cloth and let rest for about 30 minutes. • Chop the beets and sauté over high heat in 6 tablespoons of butter and a dash of salt. • Remove from the heat, stir in the Ricotta, adding some bread crumbs if the filling is too moist. • Roll out the pasta dough to a thin, almost transparent sheet. • Use the rim of a 3-in (8-cm) diameter glass or round cookie cutter to cut out disks. • Place a little of the filling in the center of each disk and fold it in half, enclosing the filling. Pinch the edges firmly together with the tips of your fingers to seal well. • Cook the pasta in batches in a large pot of salted, boiling water for about 5 minutes. • Use a slotted spoon to transfer them to serving dishes. Dot with the remaining butter and sprinkle with the poppy seeds.
• Serve hot.

*Serves: 6*

*Preparation: 1 h + 30' to rest*

*Cooking: 20'*

*Level of difficulty: 3*

**PASTA DOUGH**
- 3⅓ cups/500 g unbleached all-purpose/strong plain flour
- 5 eggs
- 2 tbsp warm water
- salt to taste

**FILLING**
- 2 lb/1 kg boiled beets/beetroot
- ¾ cup/180 g butter
- salt to taste
- ½ cup/125 g Ricotta cheese
- fine bread crumbs (to be used if needed)
- 4 tbsp poppy seeds

Serves: 4–6

Preparation: 1 h 15′ +
3 h to rest

Cooking: 15′

Level of difficulty: 3

- 1 quantity Plain
  Pasta Dough
  (see page 286)
- 2 tbsp butter
- 3 tbsp cooking
  juices from roasted
  meat (optional)
- 3 oz/90 g very
  finely chopped
  Savoy cabbage
- white part of
  1 small leek, finely
  chopped
- 2 oz/60 g fresh
  Italian sausage
  meat (optional)
- 6 oz/180 g each,
  lean roasted beef
  and pork
- 1 egg
- 2 tbsp freshly
  grated Parmesan
  cheese
- 1/8 tsp freshly
  grated nutmeg
- salt and freshly
  ground white
  pepper to taste

SAUCE
- 4 tbsp butter
- 6 fresh sage leaves
- 4 tbsp freshly
  grated Parmesan
  cheese

# RAVIOLI WITH SAGE AND BUTTER SAUCE

Prepare the pasta dough. Shape into a ball, wrap in plastic wrap (cling film), and let rest for 1 hour. • Melt the butter in a large saucepan over medium heat. Add the meat juices, cabbage, leek, and the crumbled sausage meat (if using). Cook for 5–6 minutes, stirring often and moistening, if necessary, with a little stock or water. • Let cool before chopping finely in a food processor with the roast meat. • Transfer the mixture to a large bowl. Mix in the egg, Parmesan, nutmeg, salt, and pepper. Mix very thoroughly, then set aside. • Roll out the dough to a thin, almost transparent sheet. • Fill and assemble the pasta following the instructions for ravioli on page 406. • Let dry in a cool place for at least 2 hours. • Cook in batches in a large pot of salted, boiling water for 3–5 minutes. • Use a slotted spoon to transfer them to serving dishes. • Heat the butter and sage until golden and drizzle over the pasta. Sprinkle with the Parmesan and serve hot.

# POTATO TORTELLI

Prepare the pasta dough. Shape into a ball, wrap in plastic wrap (cling film), and let rest for 1 hour. • Boil the potatoes until tender but firm. Drain well and mash in a large bowl. • Mix in the egg, half the Parmesan, the first measure of butter, nutmeg, and salt. • Roll out the pasta dough to a thin, almost transparent sheet. • Fill and assemble the pasta following the instructions for tortelli on page 406. • Set aside in a single layer on a lightly floured cloth for 2 hours. • Cook the pasta in batches in a large pot of salted, boiling water for 3–4 minutes. • Use a slotted spoon to transfer to serving plates. Drizzle with the butter and sprinkle with the remaining Parmesan. • Season with pepper and serve hot.

*Serves: 4–6*

*Preparation: 40' + 3 h to rest*

*Cooking: 40'*

*Level of difficulty: 3*

- **1 quantity Plain Pasta Dough (see page 286)**
- **1³/₄ lb/800 g boiling potatoes**
- **1 egg**
- **³/₄ cup/90 g freshly grated Parmesan cheese**
- **2 tbsp butter**
- **¹/₄ tsp freshly grated nutmeg**
- **salt and freshly ground black pepper to taste**
- **4 tbsp butter, melted**

# RAVIOLI WITH SPINACH FILLING IN TOMATO SAUCE

Serves: 4–6

Preparation: 30' + 3 h
to rest pasta

Cooking: 30'

Level of difficulty: 3

- 1 quantity Plain
  Pasta Dough
  (see page 286)
- 2 lb/1 kg spinach
  leaves, washed
- 2 cups/500 g fresh
  Ricotta
- 2 large eggs +
  1 egg yolk
- 1¼ cups/150 g
  freshly grated
  Parmesan cheese
- pinch of freshly
  grated nutmeg
- salt and freshly
  ground black
  pepper to taste
- 1 quantity
  Tomato Sauce
  (see page 950)

Prepare the pasta dough. Shape into a ball, wrap in plastic wrap (cling film), and let rest for 1 hour. • Cook the spinach in salted water for 8–10 minutes. • Drain, squeeze out excess moisture, and chop finely. • Mix the spinach, Ricotta, 2 eggs and 1 egg yolk, Parmesan, nutmeg, salt, and pepper in a large bowl. • Roll out each piece of dough until very thin. • Roll out the pasta dough to a thin, almost transparent sheet. • Fill and assemble the pasta following the instructions for ravioli on page 406. • Let rest in a single layer on a floured cloth for 2 hours. • Cook in batches in a large pot of salted, boiling water for 4–5 minutes. • Use a slotted spoon to transfer to serving dishes. Serve hot with the sauce.

# SEAFOOD RAVIOLI

Prepare the pasta dough. Shape into a ball, wrap in plastic wrap (cling film), and let rest for 1 hour. • Fill a medium saucepan with cold water and add the onion, pepper, bay leaf, and parsley. Season with salt, bring to a boil, and cook for 20 minutes. • Add the hake and cook over low heat for 5 minutes. • Drain the hake, remove the skin and bones, and chop finely • Heat 1 tablespoon of garlic-flavored oil in a large frying pan. Add the gurnard and cook over high heat for 2 minutes. Pour in the sherry and let it evaporate. Remove from heat and finely chop. • Lightly flour the scallops. Melt the butter in a small frying pan and cook the scallops for 3–4 minutes. Season with salt and chop finely. • Mix the hake, gurnard, and scallops in a medium bowl. Season with salt and pepper and add 1 tablespoon of garlic-flavored oil. Stir in the egg and parsley. • Roll out the pasta dough to a thin, almost transparent sheet. • Fill and assemble the pasta following the instructions for tortelli on page 406. • Heat the remaining garlic-flavored oil in a large frying pan and add the mullet. Cook, using a fork to break it up. Add the shrimp and cook for 2 minutes over high heat. Add the vermouth and let it evaporate. • Add the tomato. Season with salt and pepper. Cook for 5 minutes. • Cook the pasta in batches in a large pot of salted, boiling water for 3 minutes. • Use a slotted spoon to transfer to the pan with the sauce. Add the butter. • Serve hot.

Serves: 4–6

Preparation: 2 h + 30' to rest

Cooking: 1 h

Level of difficulty: 3

- 1 quantity Plain Pasta Dough (see page 286)
- 1/2 white onion
- 1 bay leaf
- 3 grains pepper
- 2 sprigs parsley
- salt and freshly ground black pepper
- 8 oz/250 g hake, chopped
- 2 cloves garlic, soaked in 4 tbsp extra-virgin olive oil
- 10 oz/300 g gurnard fillets, chopped
- 2 tbsp sherry
- 4 tbsp flour
- 7 oz/200 g shelled scallops, diced
- 2 tbsp butter
- 1 egg
- 1 tbsp finely chopped parsley
- 7 oz/200 g shelled shrimp, chopped
- 7 oz/200 g mullet fillets
- 10 oz/350 g peeled and chopped tomatoes
- 2 tbsp vermouth
- 2 tbsp butter

# RAVIOLI WITH ARUGULA AND RICOTTA

Prepare the pasta dough. Shape into a ball, wrap in plastic wrap (cling film), and let rest for 1 hour. • Boil the Swiss chard and arugula in salted water for about 10 minutes. • Drain well, squeeze out excess moisture, and chop finely. • Place in a bowl and stir in the Ricotta, Parmesan, and egg yolks. Season with salt and pepper and refrigerate until ready to use. • Roll out the pasta dough to a thin, almost transparent sheet. • Use a glass or cookie cutter to cut the pasta into 2-in (5-cm) disks. • Place 1 teaspoon of filling at the center of half of the disks and cover each one with a disk of pasta. Press down on the edges to seal. • Cook the pasta in batches in a large pot of salted boiling water for 3 minutes. • Mix the pesto with the oil and 2 tablespoons of cooking water. • Use a slotted spoon to transfer the pasta to a heated serving dish. Spoon the pesto over the top.
• Serve at once.

*Serves: 4–6*

*Preparation: 1 h + 1 h to rest*

*Cooking: 30'*

*Level of difficulty: 3*

- **1 quantity Plain Pasta Dough (see page 286)**
- **1 1/4/625 g Swiss chard leaves, stalks removed**
- **10 oz/300 g arugula/rocket**
- **1/2 cup/125 g Ricotta cheese, drained**
- **6 tbsp freshly grated Parmesan cheese**
- **2 egg yolks**
- **salt and freshly ground white pepper to taste**
- **1 quantity Pesto (see page 948)**
- **4 tbsp extra-virgin olive oil**

424

Serves: 4–6

Preparation: 1 h 30' + 1 h to rest

Cooking: 1 h

Level of difficulty: 3

## PASTA

- 2 cups/300 g all-purpose/plain flour
- ½ cup/125 ml warm water
- pinch of salt

## FILLING

- 4 tbsp butter
- 1 small red onion, finely chopped
- 14 oz/400 g boiled potatoes, mashed
- 1 tsp ground cinnamon
- 4 tbsp golden raisins/sultanas, soaked in cold water for 2 hours
- 6 tbsp finely chopped walnuts
- finely grated zest of ½ lemon
- 1 tsp dried mint
- 1 tbsp sugar
- salt and freshly ground black pepper to taste
- 1 egg, lightly beaten

## TO SERVE

- 3 oz/90 g freshly grated smoked Ricotta cheese
- 6 tbsp melted butter

# SWEET RAVIOLI FRIULI-STYLE

Prepare the pasta dough using the flour, water, and salt as explained on page 286. Shape into a ball, wrap in plastic wrap (cling film), and let rest for 1 hour. • Heat the butter in a medium saucepan. Add the onion and a pinch of salt and sweat over low heat for 10 minutes. • Place the mashed potatoes in a medium bowl and stir in the onion, cinnamon, the drained sultanas, walnuts, lemon zest, mint, and sugar. Season with salt and pepper and refrigerate until ready to use.• Roll out the pasta dough to a thin, almost transparent sheet. • Use a fluted round pastry or cookie cutter to cut into 3-in (8-cm) disks. • Shape pieces of filling into balls the size of a walnut and place one at the center of each disk. Brush with beaten egg and fold over into a half moon shape, pressing down around the edges to seal. Fold the edges back on themselves to make a decorative border. Place on a floured cloth until ready to cook. • Cook the pasta in batches in a large pot of salted, boiling water for 3–4 minutes. • Use a slotted spoon to transfer to a heated serving dish. Sprinkle with the Ricotta and drizzle with the butter. • Serve at once.

# CLASSIC AGNOLOTTI

Prepare the pasta dough. Shape into a ball, wrap in plastic wrap (cling film), and rest for 1 hour. • Sauté the onion and garlic in the oil in a large frying pan. • Add the sausage, pancetta, cloves, and bay leaf and sauté for 5 minutes. • Chop in a food processor with the beef. • Return half the mixture to the pan, season with salt and pepper, add the mushrooms, and simmer for 1–2 hours. Gradually add the mushroom water and wine. • Filling: Cook the spinach in a little salted water. Drain, squeeze out excess moisture, and chop finely. • Place the remaining meat mixture in a large bowl and add the egg, Parmesan, and spinach. Mix well. • Prepare the agnolotti following the instructions on page 406. • Cook in batches in a large pot of salted, boiling water for 4–5 minutes. • Serve hot with the sauce.

Serves: 4

Preparation: 30' + 1 h to rest

Cooking: 2 h

Level of difficulty: 3

- 1 quantity Plain Pasta Dough (see page 286)
- 2 tbsp extra-virgin olive oil
- 1 onion, finely chopped
- 2 cloves garlic, finely chopped
- 6 oz/180 g Italian sausage
- 2 oz/60 g pancetta
- 2 cloves, 1 bay leaf
- 14 oz/450 g roasted beef
- salt and and freshly ground black pepper to taste
- 1 oz/30 g dried porcini mushrooms, soaked in 1/2 cup/125 ml warm water
- 1/2 cup/125 ml dry red wine
- 10 oz/300 g spinach
- 1 egg
- 6 tbsp freshly grated Parmesan cheese

# RAVIOLI WITH SWEET RICOTTA FILLING AND MEAT SAUCE

*Serves: 4–6*

*Preparation: 30' + 1 h to rest*

*Cooking: 15'*

*Level of difficulty: 3*

- **1 quantity Plain Pasta Dough (see page 286)**
- **3 cups/750 g Ricotta cheese**
- **2 tbsp sugar**
- **2 eggs, lightly beaten**
- **½ tsp ground cinnamon**
- **1 quantity Tomato Sauce (see page 950)**
- **6 tbsp freshly grated Parmesan cheese**

Prepare the pasta dough. Shape into a ball, wrap in plastic wrap (cling film), and rest for 1 hour. • Wrap the ricotta in muslin (cheesecloth) and hang over a bowl for 30 minutes to drain. It should be as dry as possible. • Mix the Ricotta, sugar, eggs, and cinnamon in a large bowl. • Roll out the pasta dough to a thin, almost transparent sheet.
• Prepare the ravioli following the instructions on page 406. • Cook the pasta in batches in a large pot of salted, boiling water for 4–5 minutes. • Use a slotted spoon to transfer to serving dishes.
• Pour the sauce over the top and toss gently. Sprinkle with the Parmesan. • Serve hot.

Serves: 4–6

Preparation: 1 h 30' +
1 h to rest

Cooking: 45'

Level of difficulty: 3

- 1¹/₃ cups/200 g all-purpose/plain flour
- 1 egg
- 4 tbsp cold water
- 10 oz/300 g lean pork, diced
- 1½ tbsp butter
- 2 tbsp Marsala
- 3¹/₂ oz/100 g sliced prosciutto/Parma ham
- ¹/₂ cup/30 g fresh bread crumbs
- 1 egg
- 2 tbsp freshly grated Parmesan cheese
- salt and freshly ground black pepper to taste

SAUCE
- 3¹/₂ oz/100 g apples, peeled, cored, thinly sliced
- 4 tbsp Marsala
- 1½ tbsp butter
- 1 scallion/spring onion, finely chopped
- ¹/₂ cup/125 ml Beef Stock (see page 955)
- salt and freshly ground black pepper to taste

# PORK RAVIOLI

Prepare the pasta dough using the flour, egg, and water as explained on page 286. Shape into a ball, wrap in plastic wrap (cling film), and rest for 1 hour. • Sauté the pork in the butter in a large frying pan over medium heat for 4–5 minutes, or until browned all over. • Add the Marsala and let it evaporate. • Remove from heat and let cool. Drain off the cooking juices and reserve. • Place the drained filling in a food processor with the prosciutto and bread crumbs and chop finely. • Transfer to a medium bowl and add the egg, Parmesan, salt, and pepper. Refrigerate until ready to use. • Roll out the pasta dough to a thin, almost transparent sheet.
• Fill and assemble the pasta following the instructions for ravioli on page 406. • Place on a floured cloth until ready to cook. • Sauce: Heat the cooking juices reserved from the filling with the butter in a small saucepan. Add the apples and scallion and cook over low heat for 5 minutes.
• Add the Marsala and let it evaporate. Pour in the stock. Season with salt and pepper. Cook over low heat for 5 more minutes. • Chop in a food processor then return to the pan over low heat. • Cook the pasta in batches in a large pot of salted boiling water for 2–3 minutes. • Use a slotted spoon to transfer to the pan. • Serve hot.

# ARNO VALLEY RAVIOLI

Prepare the pasta dough. Shape into a ball, wrap in plastic wrap (cling film), and rest for 1 hour. • Sauce: Heat the oil in an earthenware casserole and add the onion, celery, carrot, and salt. Cover and cook for 10 minutes. • Add the goose meat and garlic and sauté over medium heat for 15 minutes. • Add the wine and let it evaporate. Cook for 15 minutes. • Add the tomatoes, scant 1 cup (100 ml) stock, parsley, salt, and pepper. Cover and cook over low heat for 1 hour, or until the meat is tender and the sauce has reduced. Add more stock if the pan dries out. • Filling: Strain the Ricotta into a large bowl and stir in the egg and parsley. Season with salt and pepper. Place in a piping bag and refrigerate until ready to use. • Roll out the pasta dough to a thin, almost transparent sheet. • Fill and assemble the pasta following the instructions for ravioli on page 406. • Place on a floured cloth until ready to cook. • Cook the pasta in batches in a large pot of salted, boiling water for 4 minutes. • Use a slotted spoon to transfer to serving dishes. Toss gently with the sauce. • Serve at once.

Serves: 4–6

Preparation: 1 h 30' + 30' to rest

Cooking: 2 h 30'

Level of difficulty: 3

- **1 quantity Plain Pasta Dough (see page 286)**

**SAUCE**
- **5 tbsp extra-virgin olive oil**
- **1 red onion, finely chopped**
- **2 oz/60 g finely chopped celery**
- **3½ oz/100 g finely chopped carrot**
- **salt to taste**
- **1½ lb/750 g goose meat, cubed**
- **2 cloves garlic**
- **³/₄ cup/180 ml dry red wine**
- **1¼ cups/310 g canned tomatoes**
- **2 cups/500 ml Beef Stock (see page 955)**
- **1 tbsp finely chopped parsley**

**FILLING**
- **2 cups/500 g Ricotta cheese**
- **1 egg**
- **2 tbsp finely chopped parsley**

# RICOTTA RAVIOLI WITH ZUCCHINI

Prepare the pasta dough. Shape into a ball, wrap in plastic wrap (cling film), and rest for 1 hour.
• Filling: Strain the Ricotta into a bowl and mix in the Pecorino, egg, and mint. Season with salt and pepper. • Place the mixture in a piping bag and refrigerate until ready to use. • Sauce: Sauté the garlic in the oil in a large frying pan for 2–3 minutes. • Add the zucchini and sauté over high heat for 10 minutes. • Add the tomatoes and parsley and cook for 10 minutes. Season with salt and pepper and turn off heat. Stir in the basil.
• Roll out the pasta dough to a thin, almost transparent sheet. Cut into four sheets. • Place two sheets of pasta on a floured work surface and pipe small blobs of filling all over, spacing them about 2 inches (5 cm) apart. Cover with the remaining sheets of pasta, pressing down gently with your fingertips between the blobs of pasta to seal. • Cut out disks about $1/2$ in (4 cm) in diameter. • Cook the pasta in batches in a large pot of salted, boiling water for 2 minutes. • Use a slotted spoon to transfer to serving dishes.
• Spoon the zucchini sauce over the top.
• Serve at once.

*Serves: 4–6*

*Preparation: 45' + 1 h to rest*

*Cooking: 45'*

*Level of difficulty: 3*

- **1 quantity Plain Pasta Dough (see page 286)**

### Filling

- **3 1/3 cups/500 g very fresh Ricotta cheese**
- **3/4 cup/90 g freshly grated Pecorino cheese**
- **1 egg**
- **2 tbsp finely chopped mint**
- **salt and freshly ground white pepper to taste**

### Sauce

- **1 lb/500 g zucchini/courgettes, cut in matchsticks**
- **3 ripe tomatoes, peeled and chopped**
- **2 cloves garlic, finely chopped**
- **5 leaves basil, torn**
- **1 tbsp finely chopped parsley**
- **4 tbsp extra-virgin olive oil**
- **salt and freshly ground black pepper to taste**

# RAVIOLI WITH MEAT FILLING IN TOMATO MEAT SAUCE

Prepare the pasta dough. Shape into a ball, wrap in plastic wrap (cling film), and rest for 1 hour. • Sauté the onion in the butter in a large frying pan until softened. • Add the parsley, chicken, beef, ham, and bread crumbs. Season with salt and pepper. Sauté for 10 minutes. Remove from heat. • Place in a large bowl and mix in the egg. • Roll out the pasta dough to a thin, almost transparent sheet. • Fill and assemble the pasta following the instructions for ravioli on page 406. • Cook in batches in a large pot of salted, boiling water for 4–5 minutes. • Use a slotted spoon to transfer to serving dishes. Toss with the sauce and serve hot.

**436**

Serves: 4–6

Preparation: 30' + 1 h to rest

Cooking: 30'

Level of difficulty: 3

- 1 quantity Plain Pasta Dough (see page 286)
- 1 onion, finely chopped
- 2 tbsp butter
- 2 tbsp finely chopped parsley
- 7 oz/200 g ground chicken
- 5 oz/150 g ground roast beef or veal
- 5 oz/150 g finely chopped ham or salami
- $^3/_4$ cup/90 g fine dry bread crumbs
- salt and freshly ground black pepper to taste
- 1 egg, lightly beaten
- 1 quantity Meat Sauce (see page 952)

# POTATO TORTELLI WITH BUTTER AND SAGE

*Serves: 4–6*

*Preparation: 30' + 1 h to rest*

*Cooking: 45'*

*Level of difficulty: 3*

- 1 quantity Plain Pasta Dough (see page 286)
- 1³/₄ lb/750 g potatoes
- 1 large egg
- ³/₄ cup/90 g freshly grated Parmesan cheese
- dash of freshly grated nutmeg
- salt and freshly ground black pepper to taste
- 6 tbsp butter
- 8 leaves sage

Prepare the pasta dough. Shape into a ball, wrap in plastic wrap (cling film), and rest for 1 hour. • Boil the potatoes in their skins until tender. Slip off the skins and mash. • Place in a large bowl and mix in half the Parmesan, egg, nutmeg, salt, and pepper. • Roll out the pasta dough to a thin, almost transparent sheet. • Fill and assemble the pasta following the instructions for tortelli page 406. • Cook the pasta in batches in a large pot of salted, boiling water for 4–5 minutes. • Use a slotted spoon to transfer to serving dishes. • Melt the butter with the sage and drizzle over the tortelli. Sprinkle with the Parmesan and serve at once.

# INDIVIDUAL LASAGNA WITH VEGETABLES

P repare the pasta dough. Shape into a ball, wrap in plastic wrap (cling film), and rest for 1 hour. • Roll out thinly and cut into pieces 6 in (15 cm) square. You will need 16 pieces. • Sauce: Place the water in a large saucepan with the onion, celery, carrot, parsley, and garlic. Add the salt and simmer for 40 minutes. • Remove from heat and strain, reserving the stock. • Melt the butter in a saucepan and add the flour. Stir over medium heat for 2 minutes, then add 1 quart (1 liter) of the stock and beat with a wire whisk. Bring to a boil, stirring constantly. Season with nutmeg, salt, and pepper. Simmer, stirring often, for 15 minutes. • Filling: Heat 3 tablespoons of oil in a saucepan. Add the shallot, lard, fava beans, peas, parsley, sugar, and 2 cups (500 ml) of stock. Cover and cook for 30 minutes. Season with salt and pepper. • Clean the artichokes and slice thinly. • Heat 4 tablespoons of oil in a frying pan and add 2 cloves of garlic, mint, artichokes, and 1 cup (250 ml) of stock. Season with salt and pepper. Cook for 25 minutes. • Chop the asparagus. • Heat 3 tablespoons of oil with 1 clove of garlic in a frying pan. Add the asparagus and sauté for 10 minutes. Place 2 tablespoons of sauce in 4 serving plates. Cook 4 pieces of pasta, drain, and place one on each plate. Cover with asparagus and a layer of sauce. Top with pasta and cover with peas and a layer of sauce and Pecorino. Cover with pasta, artichokes, sauce, and Pecorino. Top with the last layer of pasta, sauce, and Pecorino. • Serve hot.

---

*Serves: 4*

*Preparation: 2 h 30'*

*Cooking: 1 h 30'*

*Level of difficulty: 3*

- **1 quantity Plain Pasta Dough (see page 286)**

**SAUCE**

- **3 quarts/3 liters cold water**
- **1 onion, sliced**
- **1 stalk celery + 1 carrot, sliced**
- **3 sprigs parsley**
- **1 clove garlic**
- **1 tbsp sea salt**
- **4 tbsp butter**
- **½ cup/75 g flour**
- **8 tbsp freshly grated Pecorino**
- **pinch of nutmeg**
- **salt and freshly ground white pepper**

**FILLING**

- **½ cup/125 ml extra-virgin olive oil**
- **1 shallot, sliced**
- **2½ oz/75 g lard**
- **8 oz/250 g fresh fava/broad beans**
- **7 oz/200 g peas**
- **2 tbsp parsley**
- **1 tbsp sugar**
- **4 artichokes**
- **3 cloves garlic**
- **1¼ lb/625 g asparagus**
- **1 tbsp finely chopped mint**

# BROCCOLI RAVIOLI WITH ANCHOVIES

Prepare the pasta dough. Shape into a ball, wrap in plastic wrap (cling film), and rest for 1 hour.
• Filling: Chop the broccoli stalks into small dice. Divide the heads into florets. Place the stalks in a steamer and season with salt. Cook for 10 minutes.
• Add the florets and cook for 10 more minutes. Chop in a food processor until smooth. • Place the mixture in a large frying pan and cook, stirring often, over medium-low heat for 4 minutes to remove any extra moisture. • Place the potatoes in a large bowl and mix in the broccoli, garlic, oil, parsley, red pepper flakes, and salt. • Transfer the mixture to a piping bag and refrigerate until ready to use. • Sauce: Heat the oil in a medium frying pan and add the onion and salt. Cover and cook over low heat for 10 minutes.
• Add the anchovies and garlic and stir until dissolved in the oil. • Roll out the pasta dough to a thin, almost transparent sheet. • Fill and assemble the pasta following the instructions for ravioli on page 406.
• Place on a lightly floured cloth until ready to cook.
• Cook the pasta in batches in a large pot of salted, boiling water for 2–3 minutes. Use a slotted spoon to transfer to serving dishes. • Pour the anchovy sauce over the top and sprinkle with the toasted bread crumbs. • Serve hot.

Serves: 4

Preparation: 45' + 1 h to rest

Cooking: 45'

Level of difficulty: 3

• 1 quantity Plain Pasta Dough (see page 286)

FILLING
• 2 1/2 lb/1.25 kg broccoli
• 10 oz/300 g boiled potatoes, mashed
• 2 cloves garlic, finely chopped
• 2 tbsp extra-virgin olive oil
• 1 tbsp finely chopped parsley
• 1/2 tsp red pepper flakes
• salt to taste

SAUCE
• 4 tbsp extra-virgin olive oil
• 1/2 white onion, finely chopped
• salt to taste
• 8 anchovy fillets
• 3 cloves garlic, finely chopped
• 4 tbsp toasted dry bread crumbs

440

# TORTELLI WITH SWEET SQUASH FILLING

Prepare the pasta dough. Shape into a ball, wrap in plastic wrap (cling film), and rest for 1 hour. • Without peeling the pumpkin, scrape away the seeds and fibers and slice about 2 in (5 cm) thick. Bake until tender. • Remove the flesh from the skin. Mash the flesh in a large bowl while still hot. • Mix with almost all the Parmesan, the egg, amaretti, and salt. Let stand for 2 hours. • Roll out the pasta dough to a thin, almost transparent sheet. • Fill and assemble the pasta following the instructions on page 406. • Cook in batches in a large pot of salted, boiling water for 3–4 minutes. • Use a slotted spoon to transfer to serving dishes. Drizzle with the butter and remaining Parmesan. Serve hot.

*Serves: 4–6*

*Preparation: 45' + 3 h to rest*

*Cooking: 15'*

*Level of difficulty: 3*

- **1 quantity Plain Pasta Dough (see page 286)**
- **2¹/₂ lb/1.2 kg squash/pumpkin**
- **1³/₄ cups/215 g freshly grated Parmesan cheese**
- **1 egg, lightly beaten**
- **12 amaretti cookies, crushed**
- **salt to taste**
- **6 tbsp butter, melted**

# TORTELLINI IN BOILING BEEF STOCK

*Serves: 4–6*

*Preparation: 1 h + 3 h to rest*

*Cooking: 10'*

*Level of difficulty: 3*

- 1 quantity Plain Pasta Dough (see page 286)
- 2 tbsp butter
- 4 oz/125 g lean pork, coarsely chopped
- 3 oz/90 g mortadella
- 3 oz/90 g prosciutto/Parma ham
- 1 egg
- 2 cups/250 g freshly grated Parmesan cheese
- dash of nutmeg
- salt and freshly ground black pepper to taste
- 2 quarts/2 liters Beef Stock (see page 955)

Prepare the pasta dough. Shape into a ball, wrap in plastic wrap (cling film), and rest for 1 hour. • Melt the butter in a large frying pan and sauté the pork until cooked through. • Transfer to a food processor with the mortadella and prosciutto and chop finely. • Transfer to a large bowl and mix in the egg, Parmesan, nutmeg, salt, and pepper. • Fill and assemble the pasta following the instructions for tortellini on page 407. • Spread out on a clean cloth to dry for about 2 hours. • Bring the stock to a boil in a large pot and add the tortellini. Simmer gently for 4–5 minutes. • Ladle into individual soup bowls and serve hot.

# RAVIOLI THAI-STYLE

To reduce the volume of the cabbage, place it in a large bowl and rub in 2–3 pinches of salt. Set aside for 1 hour. • Prepare the pasta dough using both flours, oil, and enough water to obtain a firm dough as explained on page 286. Let rest for 30 minutes. • Filling: Squeeze the cabbage to remove excess water. Return to the bowl and mix in the pork, lemon grass, carrot, scallions, soy sauce, sherry, cornstarch, ginger, and sugar. Refrigerate until ready to use. • Roll out the pasta dough to a thin, almost transparent sheet. • Use a large glass or pastry cutter to cut out disks about 3 in (8 cm) in diameter. • Place a heaped tablespoon of filling in the center of each disk of pasta. Pull the pasta over the top to form half-moon shapes and pinch the edges to seal. If the pasta is too dry, brush it with a little warm water. • Place a large pot of water over high heat. Cover and bring to a boil. • Place the ravioli well spaced in an oriental steamer over the boiling water and cook for 10 minutes. • Serve hot with soy sauce.

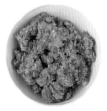

Serves: 4

Preparation: 1 h + 1 h 30' to rest

Cooking: 10'

Level of difficulty: 3

- **7 oz/200 g cabbage, thinly sliced**
- **salt to taste**

**PASTA DOUGH**
- **1 cup/150 g all-purpose/plain flour**
- **1/3 cup/50 g durum wheat flour**
- **1 tbsp peanut oil**
- **scant 1 cup/100 ml warm water**

**FILLING**
- **7 oz/200 g ground pork**
- **2 tbsp finely chopped lemon grass**
- **1 small carrot, finely chopped**
- **3 scallions/green onions, finely chopped**
- **1 tbsp soy sauce**
- **2 tbsp sherry**
- **1 tbsp cornstarch/ cornflour**
- **1 tsp fresh ginger root, finely chopped**
- **pinch of sugar**

# RAVIOLONI WITH CHEESE FILLING

Prepare the pasta dough. Shape into a ball, wrap in plastic wrap (cling film), and rest for 1 hour.
• Place the soft white cheese in a medium bowl and mix in the Ricotta, Parmesan, eggs, salt, and pepper to make a smooth cream. Refrigerate until ready to use. • Roll out the pasta dough to a thin, almost transparent sheet. • Cut the dough into disks about 3 in (8 cm) in diameter. • Place a heaped tablespoon of filling in the center of half of the disks of pasta. Cover each filled disk with a disk of pasta, pressing down on the edges to seal.
• If liked, cut around the edges of the ravioli with a fluted pastry cutter. • Cook the pasta in batches in a large pot of salted, boiling water for 3–4 minutes.
• Use a slotted spoon to transfer to serving dishes.
• Melt the butter in a small saucepan and sauté the peppercorns for 3 minutes. • Drizzle the butter and peppercorns over the ravioli and serve hot.

*Serves: 4–6*

*Preparation: 30' + 1 h to rest*

*Cooking: 15'*

*Level of difficulty: 3*

• 1 quantity Plain Pasta Dough (see page 286)
• 7 oz/200 g soft mild white cheese
• 2/3 cup/150 g Ricotta cheese
• 1 cup/125 g freshly grated Parmesan cheese
• 2 eggs
• salt and freshly ground white pepper to taste
• 6 tbsp butter
• 4 tbsp green peppercorns, pickled in vinegar

# RAVIOLI WITH VEGETABLE SAUCE

Prepare the pasta dough. Shape into a ball, wrap in plastic wrap (cling film), and rest for 1 hour.
• Place the Ricotta in a large bowl. Stir in the oil, basil , salt, and pepper. • Mix the tomatoes with the garlic and 1 tablespoon of oil in a small bowl.
• Heat the remaining oil with the thyme and fry the eggplant until crisp. Drain on paper towels, sprinkling with salt. • Roll out the pasta dough to a thin, almost transparent sheet. • Roll out the pasta dough to a thin, almost transparent sheet. • Fill and assemble the pasta following the instructions on page 406. • Cook the pasta in batches in a large pot of salted, boiling water for 3–4 minutes. • Use a slotted spoon to transfer to a frying pan with the tomato sauce and fried eggplant. Toss gently over high heat for 3 minutes. • Serve hot.

Serves: 4–6

Preparation: 45' + 1 h to rest

Cooking: 45'

Level of difficulty: 3

- **1 quantity Plain Pasta Dough (see page 286)**
- **1²/₃ cups/400 g fresh Ricotta cheese**
- **2 tbsp extra-virgin olive oil**
- **2 tbsp finely chopped basil**
- **salt and freshly ground black pepper to taste**
- **1 lb/500 g tomatoes, peeled and chopped**
- **1 clove garlic, finely chopped**
- **¹/₂ cup/125 ml extra-virgin olive oil**
- **1 sprig fresh thyme**
- **1 eggplant/ aubergine, cut in small cubes**

| | |
|---|---|
| Serves: 4–6 | |
| Preparation: 30' + 1 h to rest | |
| Cooking: 15' | |
| Level of difficulty: 3 | |

- 1 quantity Plain Pasta Dough (see page 286)
- 2 lb/1 kg spinach
- 8 oz/250 g Italian pork sausage meat
- 1 cup/250 g fresh Ricotta cheese
- 2 eggs
- $^1/_2$ cup/60 g freshly grated Parmesan cheese
- 1 tbsp finely chopped marjoram
- salt and freshly ground black pepper to taste
- 6 tbsp butter
- 6 leaves sage

# RICOTTA RAVIOLI IN TOMATO SAUCE

Prepare the pasta dough. Shape into a ball, wrap in plastic wrap (cling film), and rest for 1 hour.
• Cook the spinach in salted, boiling water for 8–10 minutes. Drain well, squeeze out excess moisture, and chop finely. • Mix the spinach, sausage meat, Ricotta, eggs, half the Parmesan, and the marjoram in a large bowl. Season with salt and pepper. • Roll out the pasta dough to a thin, almost transparent sheet. • Fill and assemble the pasta following the instructions on page 406.
• Cook the pasta in batches in a large pot of salted, boiling water for 3–4 minutes. • Use a slotted spoon to transfer to serving dishes.
• Melt the butter and sage and pour over the top. Sprinkle with the remaining Parmesan. • Serve hot.

# ZUCCHINI RAVIOLI WITH BUTTER AND ROSEMARY SAUCE

Prepare the pasta dough. Shape into a ball, wrap in plastic wrap (cling film), and rest for 1 hour.
• Place the Ricotta in a bowl. Add the parsley, basil, eggs, nutmeg, and salt. Mix well. • Roll out the pasta dough to a thin, almost transparent sheet.
• Fill and assemble the pasta following the instructions for ravioli on page 406. • Cook the pasta in batches in a large pot of salted, boiling water for 4–5 minutes. • Use a slotted spoon to transfer to serving dishes. • Pour the tomato sauce over the top and sprinkle with the Parmesan. • Serve hot.

Serves: 4–6

Preparation: 30' + 1 h to rest

Cooking: 10'

Level of difficulty: 3

- 1 quantity Spinach Pasta Dough (see page 286)
- 1 cup/180 g fresh Ricotta cheese
- 4 cups/90 g parsley, finely chopped
- 4 cups/90 g basil, finely chopped
- 2 eggs
- $1/4$ tsp nutmeg
- salt to taste
- 1 quantity Tomato Sauce (see page 950)
- 6 tbsp freshly grated Parmesan cheese

# RICOTTA RAVIOLI WITH TOMATO SAUCE

Prepare the pasta dough using the flour, eggs, and enough water to obtain a firm dough as explained on page 286. Let rest for 30 minutes.
• Filling: Mix the Ricotta, eggs, sugar, parsley, lemon zest, nutmeg, cinnamon, salt, and pepper in a large bowl. • Roll out the pasta dough to a thin, almost transparent sheet. • Fill and assemble the pasta following the instructions for ravioli on page 406. • Cook the pasta in batches in a large pot of salted, boiling water for 2–3 minutes. • Use a slotted spoon to transfer to serving dishes. Spoon the sauce over the top and sprinkle with the Parmesan. Garnish with the basil. Serve at once.

452

*Serves: 4*

*Preparation: 30' + 30' to rest*

*Cooking: 30'*

*Level of difficulty: 3*

**PASTA DOUGH**

- 2²/₃ cups/400 g all-purpose/plain flour
- 2 eggs
- 6 tbsp water + more as needed

**FILLING**

- 1²/₃ cups/400 g Ricotta cheese
- 2 eggs
- 4 tbsp sugar
- 1 tbsp finely chopped parsley
- grated zest of ¹/₂ lemon
- ¹/₈ tsp freshly grated nutmeg
- ¹/₄ tsp ground cinnamon
- salt and freshly ground white pepper to taste

**TO SERVE**

- 1 quantity Tomato Sauce (see page 950)
- 1 cup/125 g freshly grated Parmesan cheese
- fresh basil, to garnish

# PUMPKIN AND NUT RAVIOLI IN RAISIN AND SHERRY SAUCE

Serves: 4

Preparation: 30' + 1 h to rest

Cooking: 1 h

Level of difficulty: 3

- 1 quantity Plain Pasta Dough (see page 286)
- 1 cup/250 ml water
- 1 lb/500 g pumpkin/winter squash, peeled and thickly sliced
- $^1/_2$ white onion, finely chopped
- $^1/_2$ cup/60 g finely chopped walnuts
- 1 tbsp finely chopped sage
- 2 tbsp butter
- 1 shallot, finely chopped
- 2 tbsp all-purpose/ plain flour
- 1 cup/250 ml Beef Stock (see page 955)
- 4 tbsp sweet sherry
- $^1/_2$ cup/100 g raisins/currants
- salt and freshly ground white pepper to taste

Prepare the pasta dough. Shape into a ball, wrap in plastic wrap (cling film), and rest for 1 hour. • Preheat the oven to 350°F/180°C/gas 4. • Bake the pumpkin for about 45 minutes, or until tender. • Place the pumpkin in a large bowl and mash with a fork. • Add the onion, walnuts, and sage and season with salt and pepper. • Roll out the pasta dough to a thin, almost transparent sheet. • Fill and assemble the pasta following the instructions for ravioli on page 406. • Melt the butter in a small frying pan. Add the shallot and sauté for 3 minutes. • Sprinkle with the flour. Stir in the stock and sherry and cook for 1 minute. • Add the raisins and cook for 3 more minutes. Season with salt and pepper. • Cook the pasta in batches in a large pot of salted, boiling water for 3–4 minutes. • Use a slotted spoon to transfer to serving dishes.
• Drizzle with the sherry and add the raisin sauce. Serve hot.

# RAVIOLI WITH ORANGE AND WALNUT

Serves: 4

Preparation: 45' + 30' to rest

Cooking: 15'

Level of difficulty: 3

Prepare the pasta dough using the flour, cornmeal, eggs, egg yolks, oil, and salt as explained on page 286. Shape into a ball, wrap in plastic wrap (cling film), and rest for 30 minutes.
• Cook the potatoes in their skins in salted, boiling water until tender. Drain, slip off the skins, and mash in a medium bowl. • Mix in the Fontina, walnuts, parsley, and sage. Season with salt and pepper. • Roll out the pasta dough to a thin, almost transparent sheet. • Fill and assemble the pasta following the instructions for ravioli on page 406.
• Sauce: Thinly peel the orange, using just the bright orange outer layer of zest. Chop into small pieces. • Melt the butter in a frying pan and sauté the orange zest, saffron, and nuts for 3–4 minutes.
• Cook the pasta in batches in a large pot of salted, boiling water for 3–4 minutes. • Use a slotted spoon to transfer to serving dishes.
• Drizzle with the orange and walnut sauce. Sprinkle with the Parmesan. • Serve hot.

## PASTA DOUGH

- 1 2/3 cups/250 g all-purpose/plain flour
- 2/3 cup/100 g cornmeal
- 2 eggs + 2 egg yolks
- 1 tbsp olive oil
- pinch of salt

## FILLING

- 14 oz/400 g potatoes
- 1 3/4 cups/215 g freshly grated Fontina cheese
- 1 tbsp finely chopped parsley
- 1 tbsp finely chopped sage
- salt and freshly ground white pepper to taste

## SAUCE

- 1 orange
- 1/2 cup/125 g butter
- pinch of saffron strands
- 1 cup/100 g chopped walnuts
- 4 tbsp freshly grated Parmesan cheese

# CHINESE TORTELLINI

*Serves: 4*

*Preparation: 45' + 30'*
 *to rest*

*Cooking: 15'*

*Level of difficulty: 3*

### Pasta Dough
- 1 cup/150 g all purpose/plain flour
- $3^1/2$ tbsp boiling water

### Filling
- 6 tbsp extra-virgin olive oil
- 6 scallions/spring onions, 2 whole and 4 finely chopped
- 1 clove garlic, finely chopped
- 5 oz/150 g ground pork
- 4 tbsp white wine
- 6 oz/180 g cooked shrimp tails
- 1 large egg white
- $1^3/4$ cups/215 g ham
- $1^3/4$ cups/200 g boiled peas
- salt to taste
- 1 tsp soy sauce

Place the flour in a medium bowl and make a well in the center. Pour in the water and knead until the dough is soft, smooth, and elastic. Wrap in plastic wrap (cling film) and let rest for 30 minutes. • Sauté the finely chopped scallions and garlic in 2 tablespoons of oil in a large frying pan over high heat for 3–4 minutes. • Add the pork and sauté for 5 minutes until nicely browned all over. • Pour in the wine and let it evaporate.• Add the shrimp and cook over medium-low heat for 5 minutes. • Remove from heat and season with salt. Add the egg white, ham, and almost all the peas (reserve about 40 to decorate the tortellini). Season with salt. • Chop the filling in a food processor until smooth. • Roll out the dough in small batches into very thin sheets. Dust lightly with flour. Use a $2^1/2$-in (6-cm) cookie cutter or glass to cut out about 30 small disks of dough. • Place a teaspoon of filling at the center of each disk and shape into tortellini following the instructions on page 407. • Place the remaining scallions in a large pot of salted, boiling water and cover with a bamboo steamer. • Brush the grillwork of the steamer with the soy sauce and place the tortellini in it. Brush with oil, cover and cook for 10–12 minutes. • Place the tortellini on serving dishes and fill each one with a pea. • Serve hot.

# ASPARAGUS TORTELLI

Prepare the pasta dough. Shape into a ball, wrap in plastic wrap (cling film), and rest for 1 hour.
• Filling: Cook the asparagus in salted boiling water until tender. • Set aside a few tips for garnish. Transfer the remaining asparagus to a food processor or blender and process until smooth.
• Cook the potatoes in their skins in salted, boiling water for 15–20 minutes, or until tender. • Drain and slip off the skins. Mash while still hot. • Add the garlic, butter, asparagus cream, and onion seeds. Season with salt and pepper. • Roll out the pasta dough to a thin, almost transparent sheet. • Fill and assemble the pasta following the instructions for tortelli on page 406. • Sauce: Heat the oil in a medium saucepan with the bay leaves, basil, garlic, thyme, and orange zest. • Add the tomatoes and season with salt. Cook over high heat for 10 minutes. • Add the orange juice and cook for 1 minute. Remove the herbs and orange zest and press through a strainer. • Cook the pasta in batches in a large pot of salted, boiling water for 2–3 minutes. • Use a slotted spoon to transfer to serving dishes. • Serve hot with the sauce, garnished with the reserved asparagus.

Serves: 4–6

Preparation: 45' + 1 h to rest

Cooking: 1 h

Level of difficulty: 3

• **1 quantity Plain Pasta Dough (see page 286)**

**FILLING**
• **10 oz/300 g asparagus, cut into short lengths**
• **10 oz/300 g boiling potatoes**
• **1 clove garlic, finely chopped**
• **4 tbsp butter**
• **1 tbsp onion seeds**
• **salt and freshly ground white pepper to taste**

**SAUCE**
• **4 tbsp extra-virgin olive oil**
• **2 bay leaves**
• **4 leaves basil, torn**
• **2 cloves garlic, chopped**
• **1 sprig thyme**
• **zest and juice of 1 orange**
• **1 1/2 lb/750 g firm-ripe tomatoes, peeled, seeded, and chopped**
• **salt to taste**

# RAVIOLI BRINDISI-STYLE

Prepare the pasta dough. Shape into a ball, wrap in plastic wrap (cling film), and rest for 1 hour. • Mix the Ricotta, eggs, and ³/₄ cup (90 g) of Pecorino in a large bowl until smooth. Season with salt and pepper. • Roll out the pasta dough to a thin, almost transparent sheet. • Use a glass or cookie cutter to cut the dough into disks. • Place heaped teaspoons of filling in the center of each disk and fold the pasta over to form half-moon shapes, pressing down on the edges to seal. • Cook the pasta in batches in a large pot of salted, boiling water for 4–5 minutes. • Use a slotted spoon to transfer to serving dishes. • Pour the tomato sauce over the top and sprinkle with the remaining Pecorino.

*Serves: 4–6*

*Preparation: 45' + 1 h to rest*

*Cooking: 15'*

*Level of difficulty: 3*

- **1 quantity Plain Pasta Dough (see page 286)**
- **2 cups/500 g Ricotta cheese, drained**
- **3 eggs**
- **1 cup/125 g freshly grated Pecorino cheese**
- **salt and freshly ground black pepper to taste**
- **1 quantity Tomato Sauce (see page 950)**

# RAVIOLI WITH YOGURT

*Serves: 4–6*

*Preparation: 45' + 1 h to rest*

*Cooking: 35'*

*Level of difficulty: 3*

- **1 quantity Plain Pasta Dough (see page 286)**
- **1 onion, finely chopped**
- **3 tbsp extra-virgin olive oil**
- **25 walnuts, shelled and coarsely chopped**
- **4 oz/125 g lean lamb**
- **$^1/_2$ tsp ground cinnamon**
- **$^1/_2$ tsp dried red pepper flakes**
- **salt and freshly ground black pepper to taste**
- **2 cups/500 ml plain yogurt**
- **2 tbsp finely chopped mint**
- **2 cloves garlic, finely chopped**

Prepare the pasta dough. Shape into a ball, wrap in plastic wrap (cling film), and rest for 1 hour.
• Sauté the onion in the oil in a large frying pan for 5 minutes. • Add the walnuts, lamb, cinnamon, red pepper flakes, salt, and pepper. Sauté for 10 more minutes. • Roll out the pasta dough to a thin, almost transparent sheet. • Use a glass or cookie·cutter to cut the pasta dough into disks. • Place heaped teaspoons of filling in the center of half of the disks. Cover with the remaining disks of pasta, pressing down on the edges to seal. • Cook the pasta in batches in a large pot of salted, boiling water for 4–5 minutes. • Use a slotted spoon to transfer to a serving dish. • Mix the mint and garlic with the yogurt and spoon over the top.
• Serve immediately.

# SCALLOP AND GINGER PARCELS

Sauté the scallions and ginger in the oil in a large frying pan over medium heat for 2 minutes. • Add the scallops and sauté over high heat for 30 seconds. • Whisk the Marsala, sesame oil, cornstarch, salt, and pepper in a small bowl until dense. • Pour over the scallops in the pan. Cook over high heat for 30 seconds, or until the sauce has thickened. Let cool. • Cut the sheets of won-ton dough into quarters and cook them, a few at a time, in plenty of boiling water. Keep the won-ton dough you are not using covered with a damp cloth so that it doesn't dry out. • Scoop out the sheets of pasta and lay them on a clean kitchen cloth. • Brush the edges of each square with beaten egg, place a piece of scallop and a little of the cooking juices in the center of each one. Pull the pasta up around the scallop and press the edges together to seal. You should get small sack-shaped parcels. Repeat until all the ingredients are used up. • Fry the parcels in small batches in the oil for 4–5 minutes. • Drain on paper towels and garnish by tying a chive around the neck of each sack-like parcel.

Serves: 4

Preparation: 1 h

Cooking: 35'

Level of difficulty: 3

- 4 scallions/spring onions, finely chopped
- 2 in/5 cm piece fresh ginger root, finely chopped
- 2 tbsp extra-virgin olive oil
- 12 oz/350 g scallops, coarsely chopped
- 1 tbsp Marsala
- 2 tsp sesame oil
- 1 tsp cornstarch/ cornflour
- salt and freshly ground black pepper to taste
- 25 sheets won-ton dough
- 1 egg, beaten
- oil for frying
- 1 small bunch chives, snipped

# ORIENTAL RAVIOLI

Serves: 4

Preparation: 1 h +30' to rest

Cooking: 35'

Level of difficulty: 3

Mix the flour and water in a large bowl and knead until smooth. Shape into a ball and let rest for 30 minutes. • Sprinkle the bok choy with salt and let drain for 10 minutes. Pat dry with paper towels. • Sauté the pork, bok choy, ginger, scallion, soy sauce, and rice wine in a frying pan over medium heat for 5 minutes, or until the meat is cooked. Season with salt. • Roll the dough into a cylinder 1 in (2.5 cm) in diameter. Cut into 50 pieces. Flatten into rounds. • Place 1 teaspoon of filling on each piece of pasta. Fold into a half moon, pressing down on the edges. • Cook the pasta in a large pot of salted, boiling water for 5 minutes. • Use a slotted spoon to transfer to serving plates. Drizzle with the sesame oil and vinegar. Serve at once.

- 3¹/₃ cups/500 g all-purpose/plain flour
- 1 cup/250 ml water
- 8 oz/250 g bok choy, chopped
- salt to taste
- 10 oz/300 g pork, finely chopped
- 1 tbsp finely chopped ginger
- 1 scallion/spring onion, finely chopped
- 1 tbsp soy sauce
- 1 tbsp rice wine
- 4 tbsp sesame oil
- 4 tbsp red rice vinegar

Serves: 4

Preparation: 1 h + 30'
to rest

Cooking: 35'

Level of difficulty: 3

- 2²/₃ cups/400 g
  all-purpose/plain
  flour
- ³/₄ cup/180 ml
  water
- 10 oz/300 g pork
- ¹/₂ bok choy
- 1 small onion
- 2 tbsp soy sauce
- 2 tbsp sesame oil
- 1 dried chile
  pepper, crumbled
- 1 tsp vinegar
- salt to taste

# CHINESE RAVIOLI

Mix the flour and water and knead until smooth. Shape into a ball and let rest for 30 minutes. • Finely chop the pork, bok choy, and onion together in a large bowl. Mix in 1 tablespoon of soy sauce and 1 tablespoon of sesame oil. • Roll out the dough into disks 3 in (8 cm) across. Place a teaspoon of filling at the center of each one. Fold the disks over into half moon shapes and decorate with the a fork. • Cook in a large pot of salted, boiling water for 5 minutes. • Use a slotted spoon to transfer to serving dishes. • Sprinkle with the chile pepper and drizzle with vinegar and the remaining soy sauce and sesame oil. Serve hot.

# ARTICHOKE RAVIOLI

Prepare the pasta dough. Shape into a ball, wrap in plastic wrap (cling film), and rest for 1 hour.
• Clean the artichokes and chop coarsely. Place in a bowl of cold water with the lemon juice. • Melt the butter in a medium saucepan and sweat the scallion with a pinch of salt over low heat for 10 minutes. • Drain the artichokes and add to the pan along with the walnuts. Season with salt and pepper. Cover and cook over low heat for 40 minutes, adding the milk gradually. Let cool. • Chop the filling in a food processor. Transfer to a bowl and mix in the Parmesan, egg, and enough of the bread crumbs to obtain a firm mixture. • Divide the pasta dough into 4 pieces. • Roll out the pasta dough to a thin, almost transparent sheet. • Fill and assemble the pasta following the instructions for ravioli on page 406. • Place the ravioli on a lightly floured cloth until ready to cook. • Cook the pasta in a large pot of salted, boiling water for 2–3 minutes. • Use a slotted spoon to transfer to serving dishes. • Drizzle with the butter and sprinkle with the Parmesan. • Serve at once.

*Serves: 4*

*Preparation: 1 h 30' + 1 h to rest*

*Cooking: 1 h*

*Level of difficulty: 3*

- 1 quantity Plain Pasta Dough (see page 286)
- 4 artichokes
- juice of 1 lemon
- 2 tbsp butter
- 1 scallion/spring onion, finely chopped
- salt and freshly ground white pepper to taste
- 8 walnuts, shelled and coarsely chopped
- 4 tbsp milk
- 6 tbsp freshly grated parmesan cheese
- 1 egg
- 1/2 cup/75 g dry bread crumbs
- 5 tbsp melted butter
- 4 tbsp freshly grated Parmesan cheese

# RAVIOLINI WITH CANDIED CITRON PEEL

**P**repare the pasta dough. Shape into a ball, wrap in plastic wrap (cling film), and rest for 1 hour. • Filling: Mix the citron peel, almonds, lemon zest, Ricotta, and egg in a medium bowl. Season with salt and pepper and mix well. • Divide the pasta dough into 4 pieces. • Roll out each piece to a thin, almost transparent sheet. • Cut the dough into small disks about 1 in (2.5 cm) across. • Place tiny balls of filling in the center of half the disks. Cover with filling with the remaining disks, pressing down along the edges to seal. • Cook the pasta in a large pan of salted, boiling water for 2–3 minutes. • Use a slotted spoon to transfer to a large heated serving dish. • Drizzle with the butter, sprinkle with the sugar, and dust with the nutmeg. • Serve at once.

*Serves: 4*

*Preparation: 45' + 1 h to rest*

*Cooking: 20'*

*Level of difficulty: 3*

- **1 quantity Plain Pasta Dough (see page 286)**
- **3 oz/90 g candied citron peel, very finely chopped**
- **3¹/₂ oz/100 g ground almonds**
- **finely grated zest of ¹/₂ lemon**
- **3¹/₂ oz/100 g Ricotta cheese, drained**
- **1 small egg**
- **salt and freshly ground white pepper to taste**
- **6 tbsp butter, melted**
- **1 tbsp sugar**
- **¹/₂ tsp freshly grated nutmeg**

# RED AND WHITE TORTELLINI

P repare the pasta doughs. Shape into balls, wrap in plastic wrap (cling film), and rest for 1 hour. • Mix the Parmesan, bread crumbs, egg, butter, nutmeg, salt, and pepper in a small bowl. Transfer to a piping bag and refrigerate until ready to use. • Divide each piece of pasta into 2 pieces. • Roll each piece out into a thin, almost transparent sheet. • Cut the dough into 1-in (2.5-cm) squares. • Pipe marble-sized blobs of filling onto the center of each square and shape into tortellini following the instructions on page 407. Place on a floured cloth until ready to cook. • Sauce: Heat the butter in a medium saucepan and add the spinach. Cook for 2–3 minutes. • Add the flour and cook for 2–3 minutes. Add the stock, salt, and pepper. Bring to a boil and cook over low heat for 15 minutes, stirring often. • Remove from heat and chop finely in a food processor. Reheat then spoon most of it into individual serving dishes. • Cook the pasta in a large pot of salted, boiling water for 2 minutes. • Use a slotted spoon to transfer to the serving dishes on top of the sauce. Spoon the remaining sauce over the top. • Serve at once.

Serves: 4

Preparation: 1 h + 1 h to rest

Cooking: 30'

Level of difficulty: 3

- $1/4$ quantity Plain Pasta Dough (see page 286)
- $1/4$ quantity Tomato Pasta Dough (see page 286)

FILLING

- 8 tbsp freshly grated Parmesan cheese
- 6 tbsp dry bread crumbs
- 1 egg
- $1^1/2$ tbsp butter
- pinch of freshly grated nutmeg
- salt and freshly ground white pepper to taste

SAUCE

- 2 tbsp butter
- 7 oz/200 g cooked spinach, finely chopped
- 4 tbsp all-purpose/ plain flour
- $2^1/2$ cups/625 ml Chicken Stock (see page 955)
- salt and freshly ground white pepper to taste

# FRIED SQUASH TORTELLI

**P**repare the pasta dough using the flour, oil, and water following the instructions on page 286. Let rest for 30 minutes. • Mix the pumpkin and sausage meat in a medium bowl. Stir in the truffles, Parmesan, and nutmeg. Season with salt and pepper. • Divide the pasta dough into 4 pieces. • Roll each piece out into a thin, almost transparent sheet. • Cut the dough into 3 x 12-in (8 x 30-cm) strips. • Place a scant tablespoon of filling at one end of a strip and fold a corner of pasta over the top to form a triangle. Fold the triangle four more times down the strip and seal the edges. Continue until all the pasta and filling have been used. • Heat the oil in a deep-fryer and fry the tortelli in batches until golden brown. • Drain on paper towels and serve hot.

476

Serves: 4

Preparation: 45' + 30' to rest

Cooking: 30'

Level of difficulty: 3

**PASTA DOUGH**
- 1¹/₃ cups/200 g all-purpose/plain flour
- 2 tbsp extra-virgin olive oil
- 4–5 tbsp water

**FILLING**
- 5 oz/150 g squash/pumpkin, baked in the oven, and mashed
- 5 oz/150 g Italian sausage meat
- 2 oz/60 g black truffles, finely chopped
- 4 tbsp freshly grated Parmesan cheese
- pinch of freshly grated nutmeg
- salt and freshly ground black pepper to taste
- 1–2 cups/ 250–500 ml olive oil, for frying

# RAVIOLI WITH ITALIAN SAUSAGE FILLING

Serves: 4–6

Preparation: 20' + 1 h
to rest

Cooking: 25'

Level of difficulty: 2

- 1 quantity Plain
  Pasta Dough
  (see page 286)
- 8 oz/250 g spinach
- 1¹/₄ lb/575 g Swiss
  chard
- 8 oz/250 g Italian
  pork sausages,
  skinned and
  crumbled
- 1 cup/250 g fresh
  Ricotta cheese
- 2 eggs
- 6 tbsp freshly
  grated Parmesan
  cheese
- 1 tsp finely
  chopped marjoram
- salt to taste
- 6 tbsp butter
- 2 sprigs fresh sage

Prepare the pasta dough. Shape into a ball, wrap in plastic wrap (cling film), and rest for 1 hour.
• Cook the spinach and chard in salted boiling water until tender. Squeeze out excess moisture and chop finely. • Mix the spinach, Swiss chard, sausages, Ricotta, eggs, half the Parmesan, and marjoram in a large bowl. Season with salt.
• Roll out the pasta dough to a thin, almost transparent sheet. • Prepare the ravioli as explained on page 406. • Cook the pasta in batches in a large pot of salted, boiling water for 4–5 minutes.
• Use a slotted spoon to transfer to serving dishes. Melt the butter with the sage in a small saucepan.
• Drizzle the butter over the ravioli and sprinkle with the remaining Parmesan. • Serve at once.

# RAVIOLI WITH SWISS CHARD AND BUTTER

Prepare the pasta dough. Shape into a ball, wrap in plastic wrap (cling film), and rest for 1 hour.
• Cook the chard in a pot of salted, boiling water until tender. • Drain well and squeeze out any extra moisture. Chop finely and place in a large bowl.
• Mix in the Ricotta, Mascarpone, 3/4 cup (90 g) of Parmesan, eggs, and nutmeg. Season with salt.
• Roll out the pasta dough to a thin, almost transparent sheet. • Prepare the ravioli as explained on page 406. • Cook the ravioli in a large pot of salted boiling water for 4–5 minutes. • Use a slotted spoon to transfer to serving dishes. • Melt the butter in a small saucepan and drizzle over the ravioli. Sprinkle with the Parmesan. • Serve hot.

*Serves: 4–6*

*Preparation: 45' + 1 h to rest*

*Cooking: 15'*

*Level of difficulty: 3*

- 1 quantity Plain Pasta Dough (see page 286)
- 1 lb/500 g fresh Swiss chard
- 1 cup/250 g fresh Ricotta cheese
- 2/3 cup/150 g Mascarpone cheese
- 3/4 cup/90 g freshly grated Parmesan cheese
- 2 eggs
- 1/8 tsp freshly grated nutmeg
- salt to taste
- 6 tbsp butter

# STUFFED PASTA ROLL

P repare the pasta dough. Shape into a ball, wrap in plastic wrap (cling film), and rest for 1 hour.
• Roll it out to a thin, rectangular sheet measuring 12 x 16-in (30 x 40-cm). Cover with a clean cloth.
• Wash the spinach leaves and cook until tender. Squeeze out excess moisture and chop coarsely.
• Sauté the spinach in 2 tablespoons of butter and stir in 1 tablespoon of Parmesan. • Sauté the mushrooms in 2 tablespoons of butter for 5 minutes. • Poach the chicken livers in a little water. Drain and chop finely. • Melt 1 tablespoon of butter in a saucepan and fry the sausage meat over a low heat with the chopped chicken livers and ground veal. Season with salt and cook for 10 minutes, moistening with a little water if necessary. • Spread the mixture over the sheet of pasta dough, stopping just short of the edges. Cover with with an even layer of spinach. • Roll up lengthwise to form a long sausage. • Wrap tightly in a piece of cheesecloth (muslin) and tie the gathered ends of the cloth with string. • Place the roll in boiling water in an oval casserole dish and simmer for 50 minutes. • Remove from the water and set aside to cool a little, before untying and removing the cloth. • Slice and sprinkle with the remaining Parmesan. Drizzle with the remaining butter and serve hot.

*Serves: 4*

*Preparation: 1 h + 1 h to rest*

*Cooking: 1 h 30'*

*Level of difficulty: 3*

• **1 quantity Plain Pasta Dough (see page 286)**
• **2 lb/1 kg spinach leaves**
• **generous ¾ cup/ 200 g butter**
• **¾ cup/90 g freshly grated Parmesan cheese**
• **7 oz/200 g fresh mushrooms, thinly sliced**
• **7 oz/200 g trimmed chicken livers**
• **3½ oz/100 g fresh Italian sausage meat**
• **7 oz/200 g ground lean veal**
• **salt to taste**

# TORTELLINI WITH CREAM

P repare the pasta dough. Shape into a ball, wrap in plastic wrap (cling film), and rest for 1 hour. • Sauté the pork and chicken in the butter in a large frying pan over medium heat for about 5 minutes, or until cooked through. • Remove from the pan and chop finely in a food processor. • Sauté the prosciutto and mortadella in the same pan over medium heat for 2–3 minutes. • Mix the pork, chicken, prosciutto, and mortadella in a large bowl. Add the eggs, parmesan, and nutmeg. Season with salt and pepper to taste. Set aside. • Roll out the pasta dough to a thin, almost transparent sheet. • Prepare the tortellini as explained on page 407. • Cook the pasta in batches in a large pot of salted, boiling water for 4–5 minutes. • Melt the butter in a large saucepan over low heat. Stir in the cream and cook for 3 minutes. • Use a slotted spoon to transfer the pasta to the pan with the cream. Add the parmesan and shavings of truffle. Toss gently over medium-low heat for 2–3 minutes. • Serve hot.

Serves: 4–6

Preparation: 25' + 1 h to rest

Cooking: 25'

Level of difficulty: 3

- 1 quantity Plain Pasta Dough (see page 286)

**FILLING**

- 2 oz/60 g boneless lean pork, coarsely chopped
- 2 oz/60 g chicken breast, coarsely chopped
- 4 tbsp butter
- 2 oz/60 g prosciutto/Parma ham
- 4 oz/125 g mortadella, finely chopped
- 2 eggs
- 6 tbsp freshly grated Parmesan cheese
- 1/4 tsp freshly grated nutmeg
- salt and freshly ground black pepper to taste

**SAUCE**

- 6 tbsp butter
- 1 cup/250 g heavy/double cream
- 1 truffle, white or black
- 8 tbsp freshly grated Parmesan cheese

484

# TORTELLINI WITH PEA AND MUSHROOM SAUCE

C ook the peas in boiling water until tender. • Drain and set aside. • Cook the mushrooms, garlic, and parsley in the oil in a large frying pan for 5 minutes, or until the water produced by the mushrooms has evaporated. • Add the tomatoes and simmer for about 20 minutes. Stir in the peas and season with salt and pepper. Cook for 3–4 minutes more. • Cook the pasta in batches in a large pot of salted, boiling water for 4–5 minutes. • Use a slotted spoon to transfer to the pan with the sauce. Toss gently and garnish with the parsley. Serve at once.

Serves: 4–6

Preparation: 25'

Cooking: 35'

Level of difficulty: 3

- 2¹/₂ cups/300 g fresh or frozen peas
- 14 oz/450 g mushrooms, coarsely chopped
- 2 cloves garlic, finely chopped
- 3 tbsp finely chopped parsley
- 4 tbsp extra-virgin olive oil
- 1¹/₂ lb/750 g tomatoes, peeled and chopped
- salt and freshly ground black pepper to taste
- 1 quantity Tortellini (see page 484)
- 1 sprig fresh flat-leaf parsley

# TORTELLONI WITH VEAL, SPINACH, AND ROSEMARY

*Serves: 4–6*

*Preparation: 1 h + 1 h 30' to rest*

*Cooking: 8'*

*Level of difficulty: 3*

- 1 quantity Plain Pasta Dough (see page 286)

**FILLING**

- 1 tbsp fresh rosemary, finely chopped
- 4 tbsp butter
- 10 oz/300 g lean veal
- 2 tbsp dry white wine
- 8 oz/250 g fresh, or 5 oz/150 g frozen spinach
- 1 egg and 1 egg yolk
- 4 tbsp freshly grated Parmesan cheese
- dash of nutmeg
- salt and freshly ground black pepper to taste

**SAUCE**

- 7 oz/200 g Fontina cheese
- 4 tbsp butter
- dash of nutmeg

Prepare the pasta dough. Shape into a ball, wrap in plastic wrap (cling film), and rest for 1 hour. • Melt the butter with the rosemary in a large frying pan. Add the veal and white wine and simmer over medium-low heat until the veal is tender. • Chop finely in a food processor. • Cook the spinach in salted, boiling water until tender. • Squeeze out excess moisture and chop finely. • Mix the veal and spinach in a bowl and add the eggs, Parmesan, and nutmeg. Season with salt and pepper. Set aside for 1 hour. • Roll out the pasta dough to a thin, almost transparent sheet. • Prepare the pasta, following the instructions for tortellini on page 407. Make them slightly larger. • Cook the pasta in batches in a large pot of salted boiling water for 4–5 minutes. • Use a slotted spoon to transfer to serving dishes. • Mix the Fontina, butter, and nutmeg in a small saucepan over very low heat until the cheese has melted. Drizzle over the tortelloni and serve hot.

# RAVIOLI WITH RICOTTA FILLING IN BUTTER AND SAGE SAUCE

Prepare the pasta dough. Shape into a ball, wrap in plastic wrap (cling film), and rest for 1 hour.
• Mix the Ricotta, eggs, Parmesan, nutmeg, and salt in a large bowl. • Roll out the pasta dough to a thin, almost transparent sheet. • Prepare the ravioli as explained on page 406. • Cook the pasta in a large pot of salted boiling water for 4–5 minutes.
• Use a slotted spoon to transfer to serving dishes.
• Melt the butter with the sage in a small saucepan over low heat. Drizzle over the ravioli. Toss gently and serve hot.

Serves: 4

Preparation: 40' + 1 h to rest

Cooking: 15'

Level of difficulty: 2

- **1 quantity Plain Pasta Dough (see page 286)**
- **3 cups/450 g fresh Ricotta cheese**
- **2 eggs**
- **4 tbsp freshly grated Parmesan cheese**
- **$1/8$ tsp freshly grated nutmeg**
- **salt to taste**
- **6 tbsp butter, melted**
- **1 sprig fresh sage**

# SPINACH RAVIOLI WITH RICOTTA CHEESE FILLING

P repare the pasta dough. Shape into a ball, wrap in plastic wrap (cling film), and rest for 1 hour.
• Mix the Ricotta, parsley, basil, eggs, nutmeg, and salt in a large bowl. • Roll out the pasta dough to a thin, almost transparent sheet. • Prepare the ravioli as explained on page 406. • Cook the pasta in batches in a large pot of salted boiling water for 4–5 minutes. • Use a slotted spoon to transfer to serving dishes. • Pour the tomato sauce over the ravioli and toss gently. Sprinkle with the Parmesan and serve hot.

*Serves: 4*

*Preparation: 45' + 1 h to rest*

*Cooking: 5'*

*Level of difficulty: 2*

- 1 quantity Spinach Pasta Dough (see page 286)
- 1 cup/250 g fresh Ricotta cheese
- 4 cups/125 g parsley, finely chopped
- 5 cups/150 g fresh basil, torn
- 2 eggs
- $1/8$ tsp freshly grated nutmeg
- dash of salt
- 1 quantity Tomato Sauce (see page 950)
- 4 tbsp freshly grated Parmesan cheese

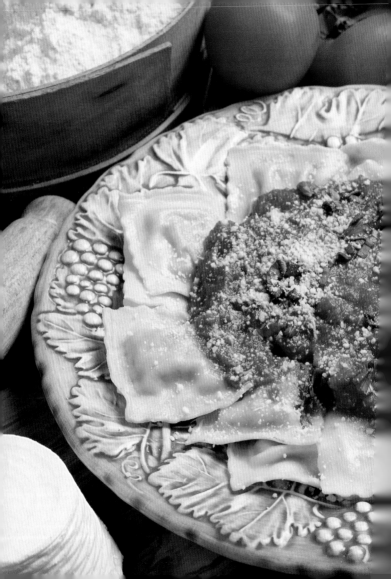

| | |
|---|---|
| Serves: 4–6 | |
| Preparation: 1 h | |
| Cooking: 30' | |
| Level of difficulty: 3 | |

# RAVIOLI SARDINIAN-STYLE

**PASTA DOUGH**
- 3 cups/450 g all-purpose/plain flour
- 2 large eggs
- 6 tbsp water

**FILLING**
- 1²/₃ cups/400 g Ricotta cheese
- 2 large eggs, beaten
- ¹/₃ cup/70 g sugar
- 1 tbsp finely chopped parsley
- zest of ¹/₂ lemon
- ¹/₂ cup/60 g fine dry bread crumbs
- ¹/₈ tsp nutmeg
- ¹/₄ tsp cinnamon
- salt and freshly ground white pepper to taste

**SAUCE**
- 3 tbsp extra-virgin olive oil
- 2 lb/1 kg tomatoes, peeled and chopped
- 1 clove garlic, peeled
- 1 tbsp finely chopped parsley
- 2 tbsp butter
- 2 tbsp freshly grated Parmesan cheese
- 4 leaves basil, torn

Sift the flour onto a work surface and make a well in the center. Add the eggs and enough water to make a smooth dough. Roll out the dough using a pasta machine or by hand. Cut into long sheets about 4-in (10-cm) wide. • Filling: Mix the Ricotta, eggs, sugar, parsley, lemon zest, bread crumbs, nutmeg, cinnamon, salt, and pepper until well blended. • Place heaped teaspoons of the filling down the center of the sheets of pasta at intervals of about 2 in (5 cm). Moisten the edges of the dough and fold over to seal, pressing down gently between the mounds of filling. Use a sharp knife or a wheel cutter (for fluted edges) to cut between the mounds. • Sauce: Heat the oil in a large frying pan over medium heat. Stir in the tomatoes and garlic. Season with salt and pepper. Cook for 8–10 minutes, or until the sauce has reduced. Remove the garlic and add the parsley and butter. • Cook the pasta in small batches in a large pot of salted boiling water for 5–7 minutes. • Use a slotted spoon to transfer to serving plates. Spoon the sauce over the top and sprinkle with the Parmesan and basil. • Serve hot.

# RAVIOLI WITH BEER

Serves: 4–6

Preparation: 30' +
12 h to marinate +
30' to rest

Cooking: 20'

Level of difficulty: 3

M arinate the beef in a bowl with the onions, celeriac, carrot, garlic, cinnamon, juniper berries, pepper, and beer in the refrigerator for 12 hours. • Prepare the pasta dough. Shape into a ball, wrap in plastic wrap (cling film), and rest for 1 hour. • Remove the meat from the marinade and pat dry with paper towels. Sauté the meat in the oil in a large frying pan until browned all over. • Bring the marinade to a boil in a saucepan and add the meat. Stir in the tomato paste and season with salt. Simmer over low heat for 2 hours, or until the meat is tender. • Remove the meat from the cooking liquids and let cool. • Chop the meat in a food processor and transfer to a large bowl. Add the eggs and Parmesan and season with salt and pepper. Refrigerate until ready to use. • Divide the pasta dough into 4 pieces. • Roll it out to a thin, almost transparent sheet. • Cut the dough into $2^1/_2$-in (6-cm) disks with a smooth pastry cutter. • Place teaspoons of filling in the center of each disk and cover with another disk of pasta, sealing the edges well. Cut with a fluted pastry cutter, if liked. Place on a floured cloth until ready to cook. • Cook the pasta in batches in a large pot of salted boiling water for 3 minutes. • Use a slotted spoon to transfer to serving dishes. Spoon the reheated cooking liquids over the top. Sprinkle with the Parmesan and serve at once.

- **14 oz/400 g stewing beef**
- **2 onions, finely chopped**
- **$3^1/_2$ oz/100 g celeriac, cut in cubes**
- **1 carrot, cut in cubes**
- **2 cloves garlic, cut in half**
- **1 in/2.5 cm cinnamon stick**
- **2 juniper berries**
- **salt and freshly ground black pepper to taste**
- **$1^1/_4$ cups/310 ml dark beer**
- **1 quantity Plain Pasta Dough (see page 286)**
- **2 tbsp extra-virgin olive oil**
- **1 tsp tomato paste**
- **2 eggs**
- **8 tbsp freshly grated Parmesan cheese**

Serves: 4–6

Preparation: 40' + 1 h
to rest

Cooking: 45'

Level of difficulty: 3

- **1 quantity Plain Pasta Dough (see page 286)**

**FIRST FILLING**

- 7 oz/200 g Ricotta cheese, drained
- 3$\frac{1}{2}$ oz/100 g cooked spinach
- 2 tbsp chives
- 1 egg yolk
- salt and freshly ground white pepper to taste

**SECOND FILLING**

- 8 oz/250 g asparagus, sliced
- 3 tbsp butter
- 2 hard-boiled egg yolks, crumbled

**THIRD FILLING**

- 1 scallion/spring onion, chopped
- 3 tbsp butter
- 5 oz/150 g carrots, cut in small cubes
- pinch of sugar
- 1 tbsp finely chopped parsley
- 1 tbsp balsamic vinegar
- 2 tbsp freshly grated Parmesan cheese
- 6 tbsp melted butter
- 4 tbsp freshly grated Parmesan cheese

# MIXED RAVIOLI WITH VEGETABLES

Prepare the pasta dough. Shape into a ball, wrap in plastic wrap (cling film), and rest for 1 hour. • First Filling: Mix the Ricotta, spinach, chives, and egg yolk in a large bowl. Season with salt and pepper. Refrigerate until ready to use. • Second Filling: Cook the asparagus in salted boiling water for 2–3 minutes. • Drain and sauté in a frying pan with the butter for 5 minutes. • Transfer the asparagus to a food processor and chop until smooth. Add the egg yolks and season with salt and pepper. Refrigerate until ready to use. • Third Filling: Sauté the scallion in the butter in a large frying pan for 8 minutes. • Add the carrots and sugar. Cook over high heat for 5 minutes, stirring often. • Add the parsley and balsamic vinegar. Remove from heat and let cool. • Stir in the Parmesan. Refrigerate until ready to use. • Divide the pasta dough in 4 and roll out until very thin using a pasta machine or by hand. • Cut the pasta into 1$\frac{3}{4}$ x 2-in (4 x 6 cm) rectangles. Place a tablespoon of filling in the center of half of the pieces of pasta. Cover with the remaining pasta, pressing down around the edges. If liked, cut around the edges with a fluted pastry cutter. • Cook the pasta in small batches in a large pot of salted boiling water for 3–4 minutes. • Use a slotted spoon to transfer to serving dishes. Drizzle with the melted butter, sprinkle with the Parmesan, and serve at once.

# RAVIOLI WITH WALNUT PESTO

C hop the walnuts, garlic, marjoram, coarse salt, and Parmesan in a food processor. Add the oil, water, and bread crumbs and chop until smooth. • Transfer to a large bowl, cover with plastic wrap (cling film), and refrigerate for 30 minutes. • Cook the pasta in small batches in a large pot of salted boiling water for 4–5 minutes. • Use a slotted spoon to transfer to serving dishes. • Cut the tomatoes in half and add to the sauce in the bowl. • Pour the sauce over the pasta and toss gently. • Season generously with black pepper and serve at once.

Serves: 4–6

Preparation: 30' + 30' to chill the sauce

Cooking: 15'

Level of difficulty: 3

- 1 cup/150 g shelled walnuts
- 2 cloves garlic
- 1 small bunch fresh marjoram
- 1 tsp coarse sea salt
- $^2/_3$ cup/75 g freshly grated Parmesan cheese
- 6 tbsp extra-virgin olive oil
- 1 tbsp warm water
- $1^1/_2$ cups/90 g fresh bread crumbs soaked in 4 tbsp milk
- 1 quantity Ravioli (see page 490)
- 16 cherry tomatoes
- freshly ground black pepper to taste

# ANOLINI IN BEEF STOCK

**F**illing: Place the lard on top of the piece of beef and tie with kitchen string. Season with salt, pepper, and nutmeg. • Heat the butter in a large saucepan and sauté the meat over high heat until browned all over. • Add the onion and sauté for 4 minutes more. • Pour in a scant cup (200 ml) of stock. Cover and cook over low heat for 3 hours, or until the meat is falling apart. • Let cool. • Chop the meat and its cooking juices in a food processor. • Transfer to a large bowl and mix in the bread crumbs, Parmesan, and egg. Season with salt and pepper and refrigerate until ready to use.
• Prepare the pasta dough. Shape into a ball, wrap in plastic wrap (cling film), and rest for 1 hour.
• Divide the dough into 4 pieces. Roll it through the machine one notch at a time down to the thinnest setting. Use a fluted round pastry or cookie cutter to cut into 1-inch (2.5-cm) disks. • Place small blobs of filling in the center of half of the disks and cover with other disks of pasta, pressing down around the edges to seal. Place on a floured cloth until ready to cook. • Bring the stock to a boil in a large saucepan. Cook the pasta in small batches in the boiling stock for 3 minutes. • Ladle the pasta and stock into individual bowls. • Serve at once.

*Serves: 4*

*Preparation: 1 h 30' + 1 h to rest*

*Cooking: 3 h 30'*

*Level of difficulty: 3*

- 1 oz/30 g lard, in a strip $^1/_2$ x $2^1/_2$-in (1 x 6-cm)
- 14 oz/400 g lean beef, in a single piece
- salt and freshly ground black pepper to taste
- pinch of freshly grated nutmeg
- 4 tbsp butter
- 1 onion, finely chopped
- $^1/_2$ cup/75 g fine dry bread crumbs
- $^1/_2$ cup/60 g freshly grated Parmesan cheese
- 1 egg
- $1^1/_4$ quarts/1.25 liters Beef Stock (see page 955)
- $1^1/_3$ cups/200 g all-purpose/plain flour
- 2 eggs
- 1 tbsp water

Serves: 4

Preparation: 45' + 1 h
to rest

Cooking: 15'

Level of difficulty: 3

## PASTA DOUGH

- 2 cups/300 g all-purpose/plain flour
- 2 tbsp extra-virgin olive oil
- 2 tbsp white wine
- 1 tbsp water

## FILLING AND SAUCE

- 10 oz/300 g mixed wild greens (dandelion greens, common brighteyes, borage, burnet, cress)
- scant 1 cup/200 g Ricotta cheese
- 1 egg, beaten
- 4 tbsp freshly grated Parmesan cheese
- 1 tbsp finely chopped marjoram
- salt and freshly ground black pepper to taste
- 6 tbsp coarsely chopped walnuts
- 4 tbsp fresh bread crumbs, soaked in 2 tbsp milk and squeezed dry
- 2 cloves garlic
- pinch of coarse salt
- 4 tbsp plain yogurt

# FILLED PASTA WITH WILD GREENS

Prepare the pasta dough. Shape into a ball, wrap in plastic wrap (cling film), and rest for 1 hour.
• Filling and Sauce: Blanch the mixed wild greens in salted boiling water for 5 minutes. • Drain, squeezing out the excess moisture, and chop finely. • Mix in the Ricotta, egg, Parmesan, and marjoram. Season with salt and pepper. • Roll out the dough until paper-thin using a pasta machine or by hand. Cut into 3-in (8-cm) squares. • Drop heaped teaspoons of the filling onto the center of each square and fold over into a triangle. Fold two edges of the triangle around and press together to seal. • Chop the walnuts, bread crumbs, garlic, and salt in a food processor until smooth. Stir in the yogurt until well blended. • Cook the pasta in small batches in a large pot of salted boiling water for 3–4 minutes. • Use a slotted spoon to transfer to serving dishes. • Pour the walnut sauce over the top, toss gently, and serve at once.

# SPINACH AND SAUSAGE PASTA ROLL

Prepare the pasta dough. Shape into a ball, wrap in plastic wrap (cling film), and rest for 1 hour. • Filling: Sauté the veal and sausage in the oil in a large frying pan over medium heat for 5 minutes. • Add the tomato sauce and wine and season with salt and pepper. Cover and cook over low heat for about 30 minutes, stirring occasionally and adding a little water if the sauce begins to dry out. • Cook the spinach with just the water clinging to the leaves over high heat for 4 minutes until wilted. • Remove from the heat, squeeze dry, and chop finely. • Sauté the spinach in the butter in a large frying pan over high heat for 3 minutes. • Let cool and sprinkle with the Parmesan. • Roll out the dough until very thin using a pasta machine or by hand. • Cut into a rectangle about 8 x 15 in (20 x 38 cm). • Spread with the spinach and meat sauce, leaving a border about $^1/_2$ in (1 cm) wide. • Roll up the dough fairly tightly from the shorter side. • Lay the roll on a long piece of cheesecloth and tie the two ends with kitchen string. • Place in a fish poacher (oblong pan with a basket) of salted simmering water and cook for about 40 minutes. • Remove the basket and drain the roll. Remove the cloth and set the roll on a cutting board. Let rest for 5 minutes. • Cut into slices. Drizzle with the butter and sprinkle with the Parmesan. Serve at once.

506

*Serves: 4–6*

*Preparation: 45' + 1 h to rest*

*Cooking: 1 h 20'*

*Level of difficulty: 3*

- $^1/_2$ **quantity Plain Pasta Dough (see page 286)**

**FILLING**

- **10 oz/300 g lean ground/minced veal**
- **3 oz/90 g sausage meat**
- **2 tbsp extra-virgin olive oil**
- **4 tbsp tomato paste**
- **$^1/_2$ cup/125 ml dry white wine**
- **salt and freshly ground black pepper to taste**
- **14 oz/400 g spinach leaves**
- **$^1/_2$ cup/60 g freshly grated Parmesan cheese**
- **2 tbsp butter**
- **6 tbsp melted butter, to serve**

# BAKED PASTA

# MACARONI PIE FERRARA-STYLE

Short-crust Pastry: Sift the flour and salt into a large bowl. Stir in the sugar. • Use a pastry blender to cut in the butter until the mixture resembles coarse crumbs. • Mix in the egg yolks to form a smooth dough. Shape the dough into a ball, wrap in plastic wrap (cling film), and refrigerate for 30 minutes. • Preheat the oven to 350°F/180°C/gas 4. • Butter a 9$^1$/$_2$-in (23-cm) springform pan and sprinkle it with the bread crumbs. • Roll out two-thirds of the pastry dough into a round large enough to line the bottom and sides of the springform pan. Use it to line the pan. • Cook the pasta in a large pan of salted, boiling water until very *al dente*. • Drain and mix with half the meat sauce. • Spoon a layer of the macaroni mixture into the pastry. Cover with a layer of the remaining meat sauce, followed by a layer of Béchamel. Sprinkle with Parmesan. Repeat until you have used up all the ingredients, finishing with Parmesan. • Roll out the remaining third of the pastry into a round to form a lid for the pie. Pinch the edges to seal tightly. • Bake for 35–40 minutes, or until the pastry is golden brown. • Remove from the oven and let stand for 10 minutes before serving.

*Serves: 4–6*

*Preparation: 1 h + 30' to chill the pastry*

*Cooking: 1 h*

*Level of difficulty: 3*

SHORT-CRUST PASTRY
- 2 cups/300 g all-purpose/plain flour
- $^1$/$_8$ tsp salt
- $^1$/$_4$ cup/50 g sugar
- $^2$/$_3$ cup/150 g butter, cut up
- 3 egg yolks
- $^1$/$_2$ cup/60 g fine dry bread crumbs
- 14 oz/400 g macaroni
- 1 quantity Meat Sauce (see page 952)
- 1 quantity Béchamel Sauce (see page 946)
- $^3$/$_4$ cup/90 g freshly grated Parmesan cheese

# PENNE WITH OLIVES AND CHEESE

**P**reheat the oven to 350°F/180°C/gas 4. • Butter a baking dish and sprinkle it with half the bread crumbs. • Cook the pasta in a large pan of salted, boiling water until *al dente*. • Drain and mix with the Béchamel sauce, Parmesan, and olives. Transfer to the prepared baking dish. Sprinkle with the remaining bread crumbs and dot with the butter. • Bake for 15–20 minutes, or until golden brown. Serve hot.

512

*Serves: 4*

*Preparation: 15'*

*Cooking: 30'*

*Level of difficulty: 1*

- 4 tbsp fine dry bread crumbs
- 1 lb/500 g penne pasta
- 1 quantity Béchamel Sauce (see page 946)
- 2¹/₂ cups/300 g freshly grated Parmesan cheese
- 1 cup/100 g pitted and coarsely chopped black olives
- 4 tbsp butter, cut into flakes

# SPINACH CANNELLONI

*Serves: 4*

*Preparation: 30'*

*Cooking: 35'*

*Level of difficulty: 2*

- **1¹/₂ lb/750 g young spinach leaves**
- **16 store-bought dried cannelloni tubes**
- **1¹/₄ cups/310 g Ricotta cheese**
- **1 cup/250 g Mascarpone cheese**
- **2 cups/250 g freshly grated Parmesan cheese**
- **1 egg**
- **dash of nutmeg**
- **salt and freshly ground black pepper to taste**
- **1 cup/250 ml Béchamel Sauce (see page 946)**
- **1 tbsp butter, cut into flakes**

Preheat the oven to 350°F/180°C/gas 4. • Butter a baking dish large enough to hold the cannelloni in a single layer. • Rinse the spinach and cook it in just the water left clinging to the leaves. Drain, squeezing it dry, and chop finely. Place in a large bowl. • Cook the cannelloni in a large pan of salted, boiling water following the instructions on the package. • Drain and set aside. • Mix the Ricotta, Mascarpone, half the Parmesan, the egg, nutmeg, and salt and pepper into the spinach. • Fill the cannelloni with this mixture and arrange them in the dish. • Spoon the Béchamel over the top and sprinkle with the remaining Parmesan. Dot with the butter. • Bake for 25–30 minutes, or until golden brown on top. • Serve hot.

# BAKED LASAGNE BOLOGNA-STYLE

*Serves: 4–6*

*Preparation: 30' + 1 h to rest the pasta*

*Cooking: 1¹/₂ h*

*Level of difficulty: 2*

- 1 quantity **Spinach Pasta Dough (see page 286)**
- 1 tbsp extra-virgin olive oil
- 1 quantity **Meat Sauce (see page 952)**
- 1 quantity **Béchamel sauce (see page 946)**
- 2 cups/250 g freshly grated Parmesan cheese
- 4 tbsp butter, cut into flakes

Roll the pasta dough out to ¹/₄-in (3-mm) thick. Cut into 6 x 4-in (15 x 10-cm) rectangles.
• Bring a very large saucepan of salted water to a boil. Add the oil to prevent the sheets of lasagne from sticking to one another. • Blanch the sheets of lasagne one at a time for 1–2 minutes each in the water. • Drain each sheet, squeezing it gently to remove as much moisture as possible. Lay the sheets out on clean kitchen towels to dry. • Preheat the oven to 375°F/190°C/gas 5. • Spread a thin layer of the meat sauce over the bottom of a fairly deep, rectangular baking dish and cover with a layer of lasagne. Top with a layer of Béchamel and sprinkle with Parmesan. Repeat until all the ingredients are used up, finishing with a sprinkling of Parmesan. Dot with the butter. • Bake for 25–30 minutes, or until golden brown on top. • Let stand for 10 minutes before serving.

# TORTELLINI SOUFFLÉ

Preheat the oven to 400°F/200°C/gas 6. •
Butter a large soufflé mold. • Prepare the
béchamel. • Stir the egg yolks into the béchamel.
Season with nutmeg. • Cook the tortellini in a
large pot of salted, boiling water until the pasta
around the edges is cooked al dente. • Drain well
and add to the béchamel. • Beat the egg whites
until stiff. • Stir the cream and Parmesan into
the tortellini mixture, then fold in the egg whites.
• Spoon the mixture into the prepared mold.
• Bake for 20–25 minutes, or until golden brown
on top. Serve hot.

Serves: 4–6

Preparation: 30'

Cooking: 40'

Level of difficulty: 2

- 1 tbsp butter
- 1 quantity
  Béchamel Sauce
  (see page 946)
- 1 lb/500 g store-
  bought tortellini
- 4 eggs, separated
- dash of nutmeg
- 5 tbsp heavy/
  double cream
- $^3/_4$ cup/90 g
  freshly grated
  Parmesan cheese

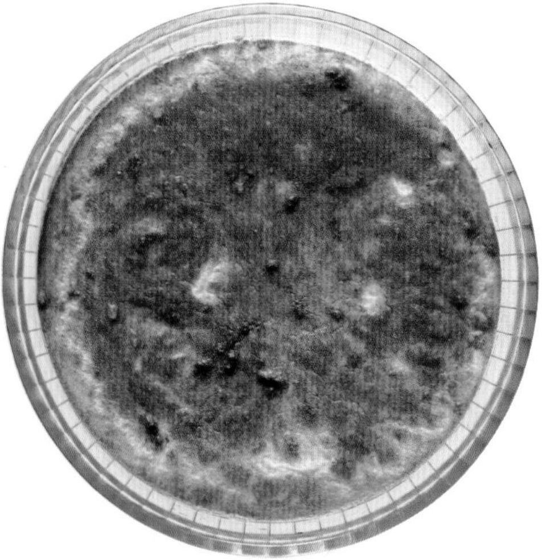

# BAKED MACARONI IN PASTRY

*Serves: 4–6*

*Preparation: 1 h*

*Cooking: 50'*

*Level of difficulty: 3*

- **1 lb/500 g macaroni pasta**
- **1 quantity Short-Crust Pastry (see page 510)**
- **2 cups/500 ml Meat Sauce (see page 952)**
- **1 quantity Béchamel sauce (see page 946)**
- **1 cup/125 g freshly grated Pecorino cheese**

Preheat the oven to 350°F/180°C/gas 4. •
Cook the pasta in a large pan of salted, boiling water for half the time indicated on the package.
• Roll the pastry dough out and use two-thirds of it to line a deep-sided 12-in (30-cm) baking dish.
• Drain the pasta and mix with the meat sauce.
• Spoon a layer of macaroni into the pastry. Cover with a layer of Béchamel and sprinkle with Pecorino. Repeat until you have used up all the ingredients, finishing with a sprinkling of Parmesan.
• Roll out the pastry into a round to form a lid for the pie. Pinch the edges to seal tightly. • Bake for 35–40 minutes, or until golden brown. • Serve hot.

# BAKED SEAFOOD SPAGHETTI

Serves: 4–6

Preparation: 1 h + 1 h
to purge shellfish

Cooking: 45'

Level of difficulty: 2

- 1¹/₂ lb/750 g
  clams, in shell
- 1¹/₂ lb/750 g
  mussels, in shell
- 14 oz/400 g squid,
  cleaned
- 6 tbsp extra-virgin
  olive oil
- 2 cloves garlic,
  finely chopped
- 1 dried red chile
  pepper, crumbled
- 2 tbsp finely
  chopped fresh
  parsley
- scant ¹/₂ cup/
  100 ml dry
  white wine
- 1 lb/500 g firm-
  ripe tomatoes,
  peeled, seeded,
  and thinly sliced
- 12 oz/350 g
  shrimp
- 1 lb/500 g
  spaghetti

Soak the clams and mussels in separate large bowls of warm salted water for 1 hour. • Drain and set aside. Scrub the beards off the mussels. • Cook the clams and mussels separately (or one at a time) in a large frying pan over high heat, shaking the pan often, until they have all opened. Discard any that have not opened. • Remove most of the mollusks from their shells, leaving just a few to garnish the dish. • Cut the squid's bodies into rounds and the tentacles in pieces. • Preheat the oven to 350°F/180°C/gas 4. • Heat the oil in a large frying pan and sauté the garlic, chile, and parsley until the garlic is pale gold. • Pour in the wine and cook until it evaporates. • Stir in the tomatoes and cook for 5 minutes. • Add the squid, clams, mussels, and shrimp. Cover and cook over medium heat for 10 minutes. • Cook the spaghetti in salted, boiling water for half the time indicated on the package. Reserve the cooking water. • Drain and add to the pan with the sauce. • Cut four to six large pieces of aluminum foil and fold each in half to double the thickness. • Divide the pasta into four to six portions and place in the center of the pieces of foil, adding 3 tablespoons of the cooking water from the pasta to each portion. Close, sealing the foil well. There should be an air pocket in each of the packages. • Transfer to a large baking sheet. • Bake for 12–15 minutes, or until the parcels have puffed up slightly. • Serve the parcels, still closed, on individual plates.

# BAKED FUSILLI WITH TOMATO AND MOZZARELLA CHEESE

Preheat the oven to 375°F/190°C/gas 5. •
Blanch the tomatoes in a large pan of salted,
boiling water for 1 minute. Remove with a slotted
spoon and let cool under cold running water. • Add
the pasta to the boiling water and cook until *al
dente*. • Peel the tomatoes and chop them
coarsely. • Heat the oil in a medium saucepan and
add the tomatoes, oregano, and salt and pepper.
• Drain the pasta and toss with the tomato sauce,
basil, Mozzarella, and Pecorino. • Transfer to an
ovenproof baking dish. • Bake for 10–15 minutes,
or until the cheeses have melted. Serve hot.

520

*Serves: 4–6*

*Preparation: 20'*

*Cooking: 25'*

*Level of difficulty: 1*

- 1¹/₂ lb/750 g firm-
  ripe tomatoes
- 1 lb/500 g fusilli
- 4 tbsp extra-virgin
  olive oil
- 1 tsp dried oregano
- salt and freshly
  ground black
  pepper to taste
- 10 leaves fresh
  basil, torn
- 8 oz/250 g
  Mozzarella cheese
- 8 tbsp freshly
  grated Pecorino
  cheese

# BAKED LASAGNE, FERRARA-STYLE

*Serves: 4–6*

*Preparation: 30' +*
*time to make pasta*

*Cooking: 45'*

*Level of difficulty: 2*

- 1 tbsp extra-virgin olive oil
- 1 lb/500 g fresh lasagne sheets, store-bought or home-made (see pages 286–7)
- 2 cups/500 ml Meat sauce (see page 952)
- 1 quantity Béchamel sauce (see page 946)
- 1¹/₄ cups/150 g freshly grated Parmesan cheese
- 5 tbsp butter

Preheat the oven to 400°F/200°C/gas 6. • Butter a large baking dish. • Bring a large pan of salted water to a boil. Add the oil to prevent the sheets of lasagne from sticking to one another. • Blanch the sheets of lasagne one at a time for 1–2 minutes each in the water. • Drain each sheet, squeezing it gently to remove as much moisture as possible. Lay the sheets on clean kitchen towels to dry. • Place a layer of lasagne in the prepared dish. Cover with a layer of meat sauce, 2 tablespoons of Béchamel, and sprinkle with Parmesan. Repeat until you have used up all the ingredients, finishing with Parmesan. Dot with the butter. • Bake for 20–25 minutes, or until golden brown. • Let stand for 10 minutes before serving.

521

# BAKED SPAGHETTI PACKAGES WITH TOMATOES AND OLIVES

P reheat the oven to 400°F/200°C/gas 6 • Cook the spaghetti in a large pan of salted, boiling water for half the time indicated on the package. • Drain and place in a large bowl. Toss with the oil then add the tomatoes, olives, parsley, and garlic, if using. Season with salt and pepper and toss again. • Set out two large sheets of waxed paper or aluminum foil. Divide the spaghetti mixture between the two. Seal the packages loosely, leaving plenty of air. • Bake in the oven for 10 minutes. • Place the packages in a heated serving dish and bring to the table. • Serve immediately, opening the packages as you serve.

522

*Serves: 4–6*

*Preparation: 20'*

*Cooking: 20'*

*Level of difficulty: 1*

- 1 lb/500 g spaghetti
- 6 tbsp extra-virgin olive oil
- 30 cherry tomatoes, cut in half
- 30 pitted and chopped black olives
- 1–2 tbsp finely chopped parsley
- 1–2 cloves garlic, finely chopped (optional)
- salt and freshly ground black pepper to taste

# RADICCHIO AND PASTA PIE

*Serves: 4–6*

*Preparation: 10'*

*Cooking: 35'*

*Level of difficulty: 3*

- **6 heads Treviso radicchio or red chicory**
- **salt and freshly ground black pepper to taste**
- **1 cup/250 ml heavy/double cream**
- **1 lb/500 g fresh maltagliati or tagliatelle**
- **1 quantity Béchamel Sauce (see page 946)**
- **³/₄ cup/90 g freshly grated Parmesan cheese**

Preheat the oven to 350°F/180°C/gas 4. • Rinse the radicchio. • Slice each head lengthwise into four and place in a baking dish. Season with salt and pepper and pour the cream over the top. • Bake for 15 minutes. • Remove from the oven and set aside. • Raise the oven temperature to 400°F/200°C/gas 6. • Butter a large baking dish. • Cook the pasta in a large pan of salted, boiling water until very al dente • Drain and mix with the baked radicchio mixture and Béchamel. Place in the baking dish and sprinkle with the Parmesan. • Bake for 20–25 minutes, or until golden brown. • Serve hot.

525

# BAKED PASTA ROLL WITH TOMATO SAUCE

C ook the spinach in a large pan of salted, boiling water until tender. Squeeze well and chop finely.
• Transfer to a large bowl and mix in the Ricotta, 4 tablespoons of Parmesan, and nutmeg. Season with salt and pepper. • Roll the pasta dough out very thin and cut into a 12 x 16-in (30 x 40-cm) rectangle. • Spread with the spinach mixture and roll up into a long sausage. Squeeze the ends together to seal. Wrap tightly in muslin and tie the ends with string. • Simmer gently in a large pan of boiling water (or fish poacher) for 20 minutes. • Preheat the oven to 350°F/180°C/gas 4. • Butter a baking dish. • Drain the roll and unwrap it. Slice and arrange in the dish. Spoon the tomato sauce over the top and sprinkle with the remaining Parmesan. • Bake for 15–20 minutes, or until golden brown. Serve hot.

*Serves: 4–6*

*Preparation: 30' + time to prepare the pasta dough*

*Cooking: 45'*

*Level of difficulty: 3*

- 1 1/2 lb/750 g fresh spinach leaves
- 1 2/3 cups/400 g Ricotta cheese
- 2 cups/250 g freshly grated Parmesan cheese
- 1/2 tsp freshly grated nutmeg
- salt and freshly ground black pepper to taste
- 1 quantity Fresh Pasta Dough (see pages 286–7)
- 1–2 cups/250–500 ml Tomato Sauce (see page 950)

Serves: 4–6

Preparation: 20'

Cooking: 1 h

Level of difficulty: 1

- 1/2 cup/125 ml extra-virgin olive oil
- 3 lb/1.5 kg firm-ripe tomatoes
- 10 leaves fresh basil, torn
- salt and freshly ground black pepper to taste
- 1 lb/500 g potatoes
- 1 lb/500 g pasta shells
- 12 oz/300 g black olives, pitted and thinly sliced
- 1 large red onion, thinly sliced
- 1 cup/125 g freshly grated Pecorino cheese
- 1 tbsp finely chopped fresh oregano
- 1/2 cup/60 g fine dry bread crumbs

# CALABRIAN BAKED PASTA

Preheat the oven to 350°F/180°C/gas 4. • Grease a deep ovenproof dish with a little of the oil. • Blanch the tomatoes in a large pan of salted, boiling water for 1 minute. Remove with a slotted spoon and run under cold water. Peel and chop finely. • Transfer to a large bowl with the basil and season with salt and pepper. • Peel the potatoes and slice 1/4-inch (3-mm) thick. • Place a layer of tomatoes on the bottom of the prepared dish. Cover with a layer of raw pasta, followed by layers of potatoes, olives, and onion. Drizzle each layer with the oil and sprinkle with Pecorino and oregano. • Sprinkle with the bread crumbs and drizzle with the remaining oil. • Bake for 1 hour, or until the pasta is cooked and the potatoes are tender. • Serve hot.

# BAKED RAVIOLI WITH CRESCENZA CHEESE AND NUTS

Preheat the oven to 425°F/220°C/gas 7. •
Butter a baking dish. • Cook the ravioli in a
large pan of salted, boiling water for 4–5 minutes,
or until *al dente*. • Drain and set aside. • Rinse the
watercress and blanch it for a few seconds in
salted, boiling water. Drain, run under cold water,
squeeze well, and chop finely. • Mix the Crescenza,
Parmesan, milk, salt, and pepper in a large bowl.
• Stir in the walnuts, cress, and ravioli and mix
gently. • Roll the pasta dough out to very thin and
lay half of it on the bottom of the prepared dish.
• Spoon the ravioli mixture over the pasta. • Cover
with the remaining sheet of pasta, making sure that
it adheres snugly along the edges. Brush with the
egg yolk and make parallel cuts in the surface.
• Bake for about 20 minutes, or until the pasta is
crispy. • Let stand for 5 minutes before serving.

*Serves: 4–6*

*Preparation: 20'*

*Cooking: 35'*

*Level of difficulty: 2*

- 1 lb/500 g store-bought ravioli with beef filling
- 14 oz/400 g watercress
- 10 oz/300 g Crescenza or Stracchino (or other fresh, creamy cheese)
- 1/2 cup/60 g freshly grated Parmesan cheese
- 3/4 cup/180 ml milk
- salt and freshly ground black pepper to taste
- 1/2 cup/50 g finely chopped shelled walnuts
- 1 quantity Fresh Pasta Dough (see pages 286–7)
- 1 egg yolk

# SOUTHERN TIMBALE

Place the eggplant slices in a colander. Sprinkle generously with the coarse sea salt and let drain for 1 hour. • Heat 3 tablespoons of oil in a large frying pan and sauté the garlic until pale gold. Discard the garlic. • Stir in the tomatoes. Season with salt and add the basil. Cook over high heat for 15 minutes, stirring often. Remove from heat and let cool. • Rinse the eggplant slices and dry carefully on paper towels. Lay them on a baking sheet and broil (grill) until golden brown all over, turning often. • Cook the pasta in a large pan of salted, boiling water until just *al dente*. • Drain and add to the pan with the tomato sauce. Sprinkle with Ricotta salata and set aside. • Preheat the oven to 375°F/190°C/gas 5. • Line a deep 8-inch (20-cm) round mold or baking pan with parchment paper. Line with slices of eggplant, allowing them to overlap at the top. Spoon in the pasta and fold the overlapping eggplants back over the pasta. Cover with the remaining eggplant slices, pressing down firmly with your fingers to level the timbale. • Drizzle with the remaining oil and bake for 20 minutes. • Turn onto a serving plate and slice to serve.

*Serves: 4–6*

*Preparation: 30' + 1 h to drain eggplants*

*Cooking: 30'*

*Level of difficulty: 3*

- **2 large eggplants/ aubergines, thinly sliced**
- **coarse sea salt**
- **6 tbsp extra-virgin olive oil**
- **2 cloves garlic, lightly crushed but whole**
- **1 lb/500 g chopped tomatoes**
- **1 small bunch fresh basil, torn**
- **salt to taste**
- **1 lb/500 g spaghetti**
- **5 oz/150 g Ricotta salata, in flakes**

# BAKED MACARONI WITH HAM AND MUSHROOMS

Preheat the oven to 400°F/200°C/gas 6. • Butter a baking dish. • Mix half the Parmesan into the Béchamel. • Sauté the mushrooms in half the butter in a frying pan over high heat for 8–10 minutes. • Add the ham and prosciutto and cook for 5 minutes. • Cook the pasta in a large pan of salted, boiling water until just *al dente*. • Drain and arrange half the pasta in the prepared dish. Top with half the mushrooms and ham. Cover with half of the Béchamel. Make a second layer with the pasta, mushrooms, ham, and Béchamel. Sprinkle with the remaining Parmesan and dot with the remaining butter. • Bake for 12–15 minutes, or until golden brown. • Serve hot.

*Serves: 4–6*

*Preparation: 30'*

*Cooking: 45'*

*Level of difficulty: 2*

- $^1/_2$ cup/60 g freshly grated Parmesan cheese
- 1 quantity Béchamel Sauce (see page 946)
- 5 oz/150 g mushrooms, thinly sliced
- 4 tbsp butter
- 3 oz/100 g ham, cut into thin strips
- 5 oz/150 g prosciutto/Parma ham, cut into thin strips
- 1 lb/500 g macaroni

532

# LASAGNE WITH PROSCIUTTO AND PEAS

Serves: 4–6

Preparation: 30'

Cooking: 45'

Level of difficulty:2

- 5 tbsp butter
- 3 oz/90 g prosciutto/Parma ham, but in strips
- 1 small onion, finely chopped
- 2 1/2 cups/350 g cooked peas
- 1 cup/250 ml heavy/double cream
- salt and freshly ground black pepper to taste
- 1 small bunch fresh basil, torn
- 8 oz/250 g fresh lasagne sheets, store-bought or homemade (see pages 286–7)
- 1 cup/125 g freshly grated Parmesan cheese

Preheat the oven to 350°F/180°C/gas 4. • Butter an ovenproof baking dish. • Melt 3 tablespoons of butter in a large frying pan and sauté the prosciutto and onion for 5 minutes. • Stir in the peas and cook for 3 minutes. Pour in the cream and season with salt and pepper. Cook over medium heat for 5 minutes. • Remove from heat and add the basil. • Blanch the lasagne sheets in boiling water. Dip in cold water, drain, and squeeze gently. Place on a clean cloth. • Arrange a layer of lasagne in the prepared dish. Top with peas and prosciutto and sprinkle with Parmesan. Repeat until all the ingredients are in the dish, finishing with Parmesan. • Bake for 10–15 minutes, or until golden brown. • Serve hot.

533

# BAKED MUSHROOM RIGATONI WITH CREAM OF ZUCCHINI

Serves: 4–6

Preparation: 30'

Cooking: 50'

Level of difficulty: 2

- 1 1/4 lb/600 g mixed mushrooms
- 6 shallots, finely chopped
- 4 tbsp butter
- 2 tbsp water
- salt and freshly ground black pepper to taste
- 1 tbsp finely chopped fresh tarragon
- 3/4 cup/90 g freshly grated Parmesan cheese
- 1 tbsp fine dry bread crumbs
- 1 lb/500 g rigatoni
- 2 tbsp extra-virgin olive oil
- 1 lb/500 g zucchini/courgettes, cut into wheels
- 1 egg yolk
- 3/4 cup/180 ml heavy/double cream

C lean the mushrooms and chop coarsely. • Sauté the shallots in a large frying pan with 2 tablespoons of butter and the water until softened. • Add the mushrooms and season with salt and pepper. Cover and cook for 10 minutes, or until the mushrooms are tender. • Add the tarragon and cook over high heat for 1 minute. • Remove from the heat and stir in 3 tablespoons of Parmesan and the bread crumbs. Let cool.

• Cook the pasta in a large pan of salted, boiling water until just *al dente*. • Drain and cool under cold running water. • Transfer to a large bowl and drizzle with 2 tablespoons of oil. Toss gently. This will prevent it from sticking together. • Stuff the rigatoni with the mushroom mixture. • Preheat the oven to 425°F/220°C/gas 7. • Steam the zucchini for 5–6 minutes, or until cooked but still firm.

• Transfer the zucchini to a food processor with the egg yolk and cream. Season with salt and pepper. Process until smooth. • Spread the zucchini cream on the bottom of a large baking dish. Lay the stuffed rigatoni on top and sprinkle with the remaining Parmesan. Dot with the butter.

• Bake for 10–15 minutes, or until golden brown. • Serve hot.

# BAKED ZUCCHINI ROLLS

Serves: 4

Preparation: 1 h

Cooking: 20'

Level of difficulty: 3

Melt 2 tablespoons of butter in a large frying pan and sauté the zucchini until golden. • Add the flowers, sauté for 1 minute, then remove from heat. • Mix the Robiola, zucchini, flowers, half the Parmesan, salt, and pepper in a large bowl. • Blanch the lasagne sheets. Drain and lay on a cloth to dry. • Preheat the oven to 350°F/180°C/gas 4. • Transfer each lasagna sheet to a piece of buttered waxed paper. Spread the cheese and zucchini mixture over the pasta and roll up. Wrap in the paper and tie the ends with string. Bake for 10 minutes. • Heat the oil in a large frying pan and sauté the garlic until pale gold. Remove from heat and add the basil. Discard the garlic. • Slice the baked rolls and sprinkle with the remaining Parmesan. Top with the pine nuts and drizzle with the basil sauce. • bake for 5 more minutes.

- 4 tbsp butter, cut up
- 10 oz/300 g zucchini/ courgettes, cut in thin strips
- 8 zucchini/ courgette flowers, chopped
- 7 oz/200 g Robiola cheese
- 1/2 cup/60 g freshly grated Parmesan cheese
- salt and freshly ground black pepper to taste
- 3 large fresh lasagne sheets, store-bought or homemade (see pages 286–7)
- 5 tbsp extra-virgin olive oil
- 1 clove garlic, crushed but whole
- 8 leaves basil, torn
- 2 tbsp pine nuts, toasted

Serves: 4

Preparation: 40'

Cooking: 35'

Level of difficulty: 2

- 1 1/2 lb/750 g
  asparagus, woody
  stalks removed
- 4 tbsp extra-virgin
  olive oil
- 1 clove garlic,
  crushed but whole
- 7 oz/200 g carrots,
  finely chopped
- 2 cups/250 g peas
- 4 tbsp hot water
- 4 tbsp freshly
  grated Parmesan
  cheese
- 1 quantity
  Béchamel Sauce
  (see page 946)
- 8 oz/250 g rigatoni
  or penne pasta
- 3 oz/90 g Fontina
  cheese, cut into
  cubes

# PASTA AND VEGETABLE TIMBALES

Cut the asparagus tips into short lengths and blanch in salted, boiling water for 3 minutes. Drain and let cool. • Heat the oil in a large frying pan and sauté the garlic until pale gold. • Discard the garlic. Add the carrots and peas and cook for 5 minutes. • Add the asparagus and water. Cook for 10 minutes more. • Mix half the vegetables and Parmesan into the Béchamel. • Cook the pasta in a large pan of salted, boiling water until just *al dente*. Drain and mix with the Béchamel and Fontina. • Preheat the oven to 350°F/180°C/gas 4. • Line four 4-in (10-cm) soufflé molds with parchment paper. Slice the asparagus tips lengthwise and use them to line the sides of the molds. Spoon in the pasta, smoothing the tops. • Bake for 15 minutes. • Let cool for 15 minutes then invert onto serving plates. • Garnish with the remaining vegetables.

# SICILIAN PASTA TIMBALE

*Serves: 4–6*

*Preparation: 30'*

*Cooking: 1 h*

*Level of difficulty: 2*

- 1 onion, finely chopped
- 8 firm-ripe tomatoes, peeled and coarsely chopped
- salt and freshly ground black pepper to taste
- 2 tbsp extra-virgin olive oil
- 1 lb/500 g anellini (small pasta rings)
- 2 tbsp butter
- 5 oz/150 g Caciocavallo cheese, sliced
- toasted bread crumbs
- 14 oz/400 g Ricotta cheese, drained

C ook the onion and tomatoes in a large frying pan until the tomatoes have broken down. Season with salt and pepper. • Transfer to a food processor with the oil and chop until smooth. • Return to the heat for 5 minutes. • Preheat the oven to 375°F/190°C/gas 5. • Cook the pasta in a large pan of salted, boiling water until just *al dente*. • Dot with the butter, letting it melt into the pasta. • Sprinkle with half of the Caciocavallo. • Butter a 9-in (23-cm) springform pan and sprinkle with the bread crumbs. Spoon in a layer of pasta and cover with Ricotta, tomato sauce, and Caciocavallo. Repeat until you have used up all the ingredients. • Bake for 20–25 minutes, or until golden brown on top. • Turn out of the pan, slice, and serve hot.

# BAKED PASTA WITH PEAS AND MEAT SAUCE

Heat 4 tablespoons of oil in a large frying pan and sauté half the onion until softened. • Add the beef and pork and cook until browned all over. • Pour in the wine and let it evaporate. • Stir in the tomatoes and water. Season with salt. Cover and cook over low heat for 1 hour. • Heat the remaining oil in a large frying pan and sauté the remaining onion until softened. Stir in the peas. Cover and cook for 15 minutes. • Cook the pasta in a large pan of salted, boiling water until just *al dente*. • Drain and add to the meat sauce. Sprinkle with Pecorino. • Preheat the oven to 425°F/ 220°C/gas 7. • Butter a 10-in (25-cm) springform pan and sprinkle it with half the bread crumbs. Spoon in half the pasta and top with the Ricotta salata and cooked peas. Cover with the remaining pasta, smoothing the top. Sprinkle with the remaining bread crumbs and drizzle with the remaining oil. • Bake for 20 minutes. • Let cool for 15 minutes and invert the mold onto a serving platter. Serve hot.

Serves: 4–6

Preparation: 40'

Cooking: 1 h 30'

Level of difficulty: 3

- 5 tbsp extra-virgin olive oil
- 1 onion, finely chopped
- 8 oz/250 g beef, cut into small cubes
- 7 oz/200 g pork, cut into small cubes
- 1 cup/250 g dry red wine
- 14 oz/400 g peeled and chopped tomatoes
- 2 cups/500 ml hot water
- salt to taste
- 2$^1$/$_2$ cups/300 g frozen peas, thawed
- 1 lb/500 g anellini (small pasta rings)
- 10 oz/300 g freshly grated Pecorino cheese
- $^3$/$_4$ cup/100 g dry bread crumbs
- $^2$/$_3$ cup/150 g Ricotta salata cheese, cut into cubes

# BAKED TAGLIATELLE MOLD WITH PEAS

*Serves: 4–6*

*Preparation: 40' +*
*time to make pasta*

*Cooking: 55'*

*Level of difficulty: 2*

- 4 tbsp butter
- 4 scallions/spring onions, finely chopped
- 2 tbsp all-purpose/ plain flour
- 1²/₃ cups/400 ml milk, warmed
- salt to taste
- ¹/₂ cup/60 g freshly grated Parmesan cheese
- 4 eggs, separated
- 1 lb/500 g tagliatelle, store-bought or homemade (see pages 286–7)
- 2 cups/300 g fresh or frozen peas, thawed if frozen
- ³/₄ cup/90 g diced prosciutto/Parma ham

Melt 2 tablespoons of butter in a large frying pan and sauté the scallions until softened. • Stir in the flour and pour in the milk. Cook over low heat for 5 minutes, stirring constantly. • Season with salt, stir in the Parmesan, and let cool. • Use a wooden spoon to mix in the egg yolks. • Beat the egg whites until stiff and fold them into the scallion mixture. • Preheat the oven to 400°F/200°C/gas 6. • Butter an 8-in (20-cm) ring mold and sprinkle it with the bread crumbs. • Cook the pasta in a large pan of salted, boiling water until just *al dente*. • Drain and add to the pan with the sauce. Spoon the pasta into the prepared pan. • Bake for 25 minutes. • Cook the peas in salted, boiling water for 10 minutes. • Drain and set aside. Melt the remaining butter in a large frying pan and sauté the peas and prosciutto for 3 minutes. • Invert the mold onto a serving platter and serve with the peas.

# BAKED MACARONI

Serves: 4–6

Preparation: 30'

Cooking: 1 h 20'

Level of difficulty: 3

Mix the beef, parsley, salt, and pepper in a bowl. Shape into balls and set aside. • Heat the oil in a large frying pan and sauté the sausage until browned. • Add the ham and mushrooms and cook for 5 minutes. • Bring the stock to a boil. Add the meatballs and cook for 10 minutes. Drain, reserving the stock. • Cook the pasta in a large pan of salted, boiling water until *al dente*. • Preheat the oven to 350°F/180°C/gas 4. • Butter an ovenproof dish and line with two-thirds of the pastry. • Spoon in half the pasta, then the sauce and remaining pasta. • Thicken the reserved stock with the flour over medium heat. Drizzle over the pie. • Cover with the remaining pastry. • Make a few holes into the top and brush with the egg yolk. • Bake for 45 minutes, or until golden brown. • Serve hot.

- **12 oz/350 g ground beef**
- **2 tbsp finely chopped parsley**
- **salt and freshly ground black pepper to taste**
- **4 tbsp extra-virgin olive oil**
- **8 oz/250 g Italian sausage, crumbled**
- **7 oz/200 g diced ham**
- **3¹/₂ oz/100 g dried mushrooms, soaked and chopped**
- **2 cups/500 ml Beef Stock (see page 955)**
- **14 oz/400 g macaroni**
- **14 oz/400 g frozen short crust pastry, thawed and rolled**
- **2 tbsp all purpose/ plain flour**
- **1 egg yolk, beaten**

# BAKED TAGLIATELLE FRITTATA

- 2 tbsp extra-virgin olive oil
- 2 shallots, finely chopped
- 1 lb/500 g dried tagliatelle
- 4 eggs
- 1 cup/120 g freshly grated Parmesan cheese
- 1 tbsp finely chopped parsley
- freshly grated nutmeg to taste
- salt to taste

Preheat the oven to 400°F/200°C/gas 6 •
Heat the oil in a small frying pan and sauté the
shallots over low heat for 10 minutes. • Cook the
pasta in a large pan of salted, boiling water for half
the time indicated on the package. • Meanwhile,
beat the eggs in a large bowl with the Parmesan,
parsley, salt, and nutmeg. • Drain the pasta well
and add to the bowl with the eggs. • Add the
shallots and transfer the mixture to an oiled 9-inch
(24-cm) springform pan. • Bake for 20 minutes,
or until golden brown. • Serve hot or at room
temperature.

545

# BAKED PASTA WITH RICOTTA

M ix the beef, bread crumbs, Parmesan, parsley, garlic, nutmeg, and salt in a large bowl. Shape into meatballs. • Heat the oil in a large frying pan and fry the meatballs until browned and cooked through. • Drain the oil from frying pan, leaving the meatballs in it, and pour in the tomato sauce. Cook for 2 minutes, then remove the meatballs with a slotted spoon and set aside. • Smear a thin layer of the sauce over the bottom of a large baking dish. • Preheat the oven to 350°F/180°C/gas 4.
• Mix the Ricotta with the water and season with salt. • Cook the lasagne sheets a few at a time in a large pan of salted, boiling water until *al dente*. (Add a few drops of oil to the water to prevent the sheets from sticking together during cooking).
• Drain well and place a layer in the baking dish.
• Spread with a layer of Ricotta, tomato sauce, Mozzarella, and eggs. Cover with pasta and a layer of meatballs and ham. Cover with pasta and repeat the Ricotta, tomato, Mozzarella, and egg layer.
• Repeat until all the ingredients are in the dish, finishing with a layer of Ricotta. • Bake for 30 minutes, or until golden brown. • Serve hot.

*Serves: 4*

*Preparation: 1 h*

*Cooking: 1 h*

*Level of difficulty: 3*

- **12 oz/350 g ground beef**
- **1 cup/60 g fresh bread crumbs**
- **$^1/_2$ cup/60 g freshly grated Parmesan cheese**
- **2 tbsp finely chopped parsley**
- **1 clove garlic, finely chopped**
- **$^1/_8$ tsp nutmeg**
- **$^1/_8$ tsp salt**
- **1 cup/250 ml olive oil, for frying**
- **2 cups/500 g Tomato Sauce (see page 950)**
- **$^3/_4$ cup/180 g Ricotta cheese**
- **salt to taste**
- **1 tbsp hot water**
- **8 oz/250 g fresh lasagne sheets**
- **8 oz/250 g Mozzarella cheese, thinly sliced**
- **$^3/_4$ cup/90 g diced ham**
- **2 hard-cooked eggs, thinly sliced**

# BAKED PASTA WITH EGGPLANT

*Serves: 4–6*

*Preparation: 40' + 1 h to drain*

*Cooking: 1 h*

*Level of difficulty: 2*

- 2 eggplants/ aubergines, thinly sliced
- coarse sea salt
- 2 eggs
- 2 tbsp cold water
- $1/3$ cup/50 g all-purpose/plain flour
- 1 cup/250 ml olive oil, for frying
- 4 tbsp extra-virgin olive oil
- 1 onion, finely chopped
- $2^1/3$ cups/580 g chopped tomatoes
- 1 bunch fresh parsley, finely chopped
- salt to taste
- 10 oz/300 g rigatoni
- 1 cup/125 g freshly grated Pecorino cheese

549

Place the eggplants in a colander. Sprinkle with the sea salt and let drain for 1 hour. • Beat the eggs and water in a small bowl. Use a balloon whisk to beat in the flour until smooth. • Rinse the eggplant well and dry with paper towels. • Dip the slices of eggplant into the egg mixture. • Heat the frying oil in a large frying pan and fry the eggplant in batches until golden brown on both sides. • Drain well on paper towels. • Heat the extra-virgin olive oil in a frying pan and sauté the onion until softened. • Stir in the tomatoes and parsley and season with salt. • Cook the pasta in a large pan of salted, boiling water until just *al dente*. • Drain and add to the pan with the sauce. • Sprinkle some of the Pecorino cheese into a baking dish and top with a little tomato sauce. Spoon in a layer of the pasta, followed by layers of fried eggplants, Pecorino, and tomato sauce. Repeat until all the ingredients are in the pan, finishing with a layer of tomato sauce. • Bake for 30 minutes. • Serve hot.

# LASAGNE WITH SPRING VEGETABLES

**B**lanch the lasagne sheets a few at a time in a large pan of salted, boiling water with the oil. Drain well and lay on a clean cloth. • Preheat the oven to 350°F/180°C/gas 4. • Butter a large ovenproof baking dish. • Filling: Stir the pesto into the Béchamel. • Mix the tomatoes, potatoes, green beans, and Mozzarella in a large bowl. • Spread the bottom of the baking dish with a layer of the Béchamel mixture. Cover with a layer of pasta, followed by a layer of vegetables and Mozzarella. Season with salt and pepper and sprinkle with Parmesan. Repeat until all the ingredients are in the dish, finishing with a layer of Béchamel. Sprinkle with the Parmesan. • Bake for 45 minutes, or until golden brown on top. • Let stand for 15 minutes before serving.

*Serves: 4–6*

*Preparation: 45' + time to make pasta*

*Cooking: 1 h 30'*

*Level of difficulty: 2*

- 12 oz/350 g fresh lasagne sheets, store-bought or homemade (see pages 286–7)
- 1 tbsp extra-virgin olive oil
- 1/2 quantity Pesto (see page 948)
- 1 quantity Béchamel Sauce (see page 946)
- 2 lb/1 kg firm-ripe tomatoes, peeled, seeded, and coarsely chopped
- 1 lb/500 g cooked potatoes, cut in cubes
- 14 oz/400 g green beans, cooked and cut into pieces
- 10 oz/300 g Mozzarella cheese, thinly sliced
- salt and freshly ground white pepper to taste
- 3/4 cup/90 g freshly grated Parmesan cheese

*Serves: 4–6*

*Preparation: 1 h*
*+ 1 h to rest pasta*

*Cooking: 1 h*

*Level of difficulty: 2*

**PASTA**

- 1 cup/150 g garbanzo bean/chickpea flour
- 1 cup/150 g all-purpose/plain flour
- 3 eggs, beaten

**FILLING**

- 7 tbsp extra-virgin olive oil
- 4 oz/125 g green beans, cut into short lengths
- 1 onion, chopped
- 1 lb/500 g zucchini/courgettes, diced
- 10 oz/300 g carrots, diced
- 1 red bell pepper/capsicum, diced
- salt and freshly ground white pepper to taste
- ³/₄ cup/ 180 ml heavy/double cream
- 2 cups/500 g Ricotta cheese
- 1 cup/125 g freshly grated Parmesan cheese

# GARBANZO LASAGNE WITH VEGETABLES

Pasta: Sift both flours into a bowl and make a well in the center. Use a wooden spoon to stir in the eggs to form a smooth dough. Knead for 20 minutes, Wrap in plastic wrap (cling film), and let rest for 30 minutes. • Divide the dough into 5.pieces. Roll them through a pasta machine down to the thinnest setting. Cut into 4 x 6-inch (10 x 15-cm) rectangles and let dry on a lightly floured cloth for 30 minutes. • Blanch the pasta in small batches in a large pan of salted, boiling water with 1 tablespoon of oil. • Preheat the oven to 350°F/180°C/gas 4. • Butter a large baking dish. • Blanch the green beans in salted, boiling water for 3 minutes. Drain. • Heat the remaining oil in a large frying pan and sauté the onion until softened. • Add the zucchini, carrots, bell pepper, and green beans. Season with salt and sauté over high heat for 10 minutes. • Pour in the cream and bring to a boil. Cook for 2 minutes, then remove from the heat. • Place the Ricotta in a large bowl and season with salt and pepper. • Arrange a layer of pasta in the bottom of the prepared dish. Spread with a layer of Ricotta and top with a layer of vegetables. Sprinkle with Parmesan. Repeat until all the ingredients are in the dish, finishing with a layer of vegetables and Parmesan. • Bake for 30 minutes, or until golden brown on top. • Let stand for 15 minutes before serving.

# SEAFOOD LASAGNE

B lanch the lasagne sheets in small batches in a large pan of salted, boiling water with 1 tablespoon of oil. Scoop out with a slotted spoon, squeeze gently, and let dry on a clean cloth. • Heat the remaining oil in a large frying pan and sauté the garlic and half the parsley until the garlic is pale gold. • Pour in the wine and let it evaporate. • Add the shrimps, shellfish, fish, and squid. Season with salt and pepper and cook over medium heat for 10 minutes. Add the remaining parsley just before removing from heat. • Preheat the oven to 350°F/180°C/gas 4. • Butter a large ovenproof baking dish. • Melt the butter in a medium saucepan and stir in the flour until well mixed. Pour in the stock and simmer for 10 minutes, stirring often. • Arrange a layer of pasta in the bottom of the prepared dish. Spread with a layer of fish sauce and cover with a layer of fish cream. Repeat until all the ingredients are in the dish. • Bake for 20 minutes, or until golden brown on top. • Let stand for 10 minutes before serving.

Serves: 4–6

Preparation: 45' + time to make pasta

Cooking: 1 h

Level of difficulty: 2

- 12 oz/350 g lasagne sheets, store-bought or homemade (see pages 286–7)
- 5 tbsp extra-virgin olive oil
- 2 cloves garlic, finely chopped
- 2 tbsp finely chopped parsley
- $1/2$ cup/125 ml dry white wine
- 10 oz/300 g shrimps/prawns
- 12 oz/350 g mixed clams and mussels
- 1 firm-textured fish (about 14 oz/ 400 g), fillets, chopped
- 10 oz/300 g squid, cleaned and chopped
- salt and freshly ground white pepper to taste
- 6 tbsp butter
- $1/2$ cup/75 g all-purpose/plain flour
- 1 quart/1 liter Fish Stock (see page 958)

# PASTA ROLLS
# WITH CHEESE AND HAM

*Serves: 6*

*Preparation: 1 h 30'
+ 30' to rest pasta*

*Cooking: 40'*

*Level of difficulty: 3*

- 1 quantity Fresh
  Pasta Dough
  (see pages 286–7)
- 1 tbsp extra-virgin
  olive oil
- 1 quantity
  Béchamel Sauce
  (see page 946)
- 12 oz/350 g thinly
  sliced Edam or
  Emmental
- 6 oz/180 g thinly
  sliced mortadella
- 6 oz/180 g thinly
  sliced prosciutto/
  Parma ham
- 1$^1$/$_2$ cups/180 g
  freshly grated
  Parmesan cheese

Divide the pasta dough into 5 pieces. Roll it
through the machine one notch at a time down
to the thinnest setting. Let dry on a lightly floured
cloth for 30 minutes. • Cut the pasta into 4 x 6-
inch (10 x 14-cm) rectangles. • Blanch the pasta in
small batches in a large pan of salted, boiling water
with the oil. Scoop out with a slotted spoon and
squeeze gently. Drain and place on a damp cloth,
sticking the sheets of pasta together in pairs along
the short sides. • Preheat the oven to 350°F/
180°C/gas 4. • Butter a large ovenproof baking
dish and spread a little of the Béchamel on the
bottom. • Cover half the pasta with the Edam and
mortadella and the remaining pasta with the
prosciutto. • Sprinkle with Parmesan and roll the
pasta up into loose rolls, about 4 inches (10 cm)
long. Cut each roll in half and arrange in the
dish. Spoon the Béchamel over the top. • Bake for
20 minutes, or until nicely browned. • Serve hot.

# SPINACH CANNELLONI WITH VEGETABLES

D ivide the pasta dough into 5 pieces. Roll it through a machine one notch at a time down to the second thinnest setting, or roll out thinly with a rolling pin. Let dry on a lightly floured cloth for 30 minutes. • Cut the pasta into 4-inch (10-cm) squares. • Blanch the pasta in small batches in a large pan of salted, boiling water with the oil.
• Drain and place on a damp cloth, sticking the sheets together in pairs along the short sides.
• Filling: Cook the artichokes in salted, boiling water with the lemon juice until just tender. Drain and set aside. • Cook the carrots and zucchini in salted, boiling water with the sugar until just tender. Drain and set aside. • Heat the butter and oil in a large frying pan and sauté the leek with a little salt for 15 minutes. • Add the carrots and cook for 2 minutes. • Add the artichokes, cook for 2 more minutes, then add the zucchini. Season with salt and cook over low heat for 5 minutes more. •
Remove from the heat. • Preheat the oven to 350°F/180°C/gas 4. • Butter a large ovenproof baking dish. Spread with most of the Béchamel.
• Mix the Stracchino, Parmesan, and lemon zest in a medium bowl. Stir in the artichokes, leek, and carrots and season with salt and pepper. • Spread each piece of pasta with vegetable mixture and roll them up to form cannelloni. • Arrange the cannelloni in the dish, top with the zucchini, and cover with the remaining Béchamel. • Bake for 15 minutes, or until golden brown. • Serve hot.

---

Serves: 4–6

Preparation: 1 h +
time to make pasta

Cooking: 1 h

Level of difficulty: 2

---

- 1 quantity Spinach Pasta Dough (see pages 286–7)
- 2 tbsp extra-virgin olive oil
- 1 quantity Béchamel Sauce (see page 946)
- salt and freshly ground white pepper to taste

FILLING

- 3 artichoke hearts, sliced and soaked in lemon juice
- 2 carrots, thinly sliced
- 2 zucchini/ courgettes, thinly sliced
- ¹/₂ tsp sugar
- 3 tbsp butter
- 2 tbsp extra-virgin olive oil
- 1 leek, white part only, thinly sliced
- salt and freshly ground white pepper to taste
- 7 oz/200 g Stracchino cheese
- 1 cup/125 g freshly grated Parmesan cheese
- grated zest and juice of ¹/₂ lemon

*Serves: 6*

*Preparation: 50' +*
*time to make pasta*

*Cooking: 1 h 30'*

*Level of difficulty: 2*

- 12 oz/350 g
  lasagne,
  store-bought
  or homemade
  (see pages 286–7)
- $^1/_2$ cup/125 ml
  extra-virgin olive oil
- 7 oz/200 g nettles
- 10 oz/300 g Swiss
  chard, cleaned
- 10 oz/300 g
  watercress
- salt and freshly
  ground white
  pepper to taste
- generous $^1/_3$ cup/
  100 ml water
- 3 scallions/spring
  onions, chopped
- 10 oz/300 g
  zucchini/
  courgettes, sliced
- 1 egg
- 14 oz/400 g
  Stracchino cheese
- $1^2/_3$ cups/400 ml
  milk
- 15 zucchini flowers,
  cut in strips
- 1 tbsp finely
  chopped parsley
- 1 tbsp finely
  chopped marjoram
- 5 tbsp freshly
  grated Parmesan
  cheese
- 2 tbsp butter

# LASAGNE WITH ZUCCHINI FLOWERS

Blanch the pasta in small batches in a large pan of salted, boiling water with 1 tablespoon of the oil. • Drain, squeeze gently, and set aside on a clean cloth. • Preheat the oven to 400°F/200°C/gas 6. • Butter a large ovenproof baking dish. • Cook the nettles, Swiss chard, and watercress in a large pan with a pinch of salt and the water for 10 minutes, or until the greens are tender. Drain well and chop coarsely. • Heat 4 tablespoons of oil in a large frying pan and sauté the scallions for 3 minutes. Add the zucchini and cook for 4 minutes more. • Beat the egg in a medium bowl and stir in the cheese. Add the milk and season with salt and pepper. • Line the ovenproof dish with a layer of pasta. Cover with one-third of the greens, one-third of the zucchini flowers, and one-third of the zucchini. Cover with a layer of pasta and spread this with one-fourth of the cheese sauce and sprinkle with parsley, marjoram, and Parmesan. Repeat until all the ingredients are in the dish, finishing with a layer of cheese sauce and Parmesan. Dot with the butter. • Bake for 20 minutes, or until pale golden brown. • Let stand for 15 minutes before serving.

# MARSALA AND CHICKEN LASAGNE

Use the flour, eggs, first measure of wine, and oil to make a smooth pasta dough as explained on pages 286–7. Shape into a ball, wrap in plastic wrap (cling film), and let rest for 30 minutes. • Divide the dough into 5 pieces. Roll it through a pasta machine one notch at a time down to the second thinnest setting (or roll out thinly with a rolling pin). Let dry on a lightly floured cloth for 30 minutes. • Cut the pasta into 4-inch (10-cm) squares. • Blanch the pasta in small batches in a large pan of salted, boiling water with the oil. Drain, squeeze gently, and place on a damp cloth. • Heat 4 tablespoons of butter and sauté the onion in a small saucepan until softened. • Add the mushrooms and cook for 2 minutes. • Add the ham and a little stock. Stir in the chicken and cook until browned all over. • Add the chicken livers. Increase the heat and pour in the Marsala. Add enough hot water or stock to cover and season with salt and pepper. • Add the truffle and cook over low heat for about 20 minutes. • Butter a baking dish. • Line the dish with pasta. Top with a layer of Béchamel and a layer of meat sauce. Sprinkle with Parmesan. Repeat until all the ingredients are in the dish, finishing with a little meat sauce. Dot with the remaining butter and let rest at room temperature for at least 1 hour.
• Preheat the oven to 350°F/180°C/gas 5.
• Bake for 25–35 minutes, or until golden brown on top. • Let rest for 10 minutes before serving.

Serves: 4–6

Preparation: 1 h
+ 1 h 30' to rest

Cooking: 1 h 15'

Level of difficulty: 3

**PASTA**
- 2 cups/300 g all-purpose/plain flour
- 2 eggs
- 3 tbsp Marsala wine

**SAUCE**
- 1 tbsp extra-virgin olive oil
- $^1/_2$ cup/125 g butter
- 1 onion, finely chopped
- 1 oz/30 g dried mushrooms, soaked and finely chopped
- 2 oz/60 g cooked ham, diced
- generous $^1/_3$ cup/ 100 ml chicken stock
- 1 chicken breast, cut into strips
- 10 oz/300 g chicken livers, diced
- 7 tbsp Marsala wine
- salt and freshly ground black pepper to taste
- 1 black truffle, finely chopped
- 1 quantity Béchamel Sauce (see page 496)
- 8 tbsp freshly grated Parmesan cheese

# LASAGNE WITH MEATBALLS AND EGGS

Serves: 4–6

Preparation: 1 h + 30'
to rest the dough

Cooking: 2 h

Level of difficulty: 2

- 1 quantity Fresh
  Pasta Dough
  (see pages 286–7)
- 2 tbsp extra-virgin
  olive oil

**MEATBALLS**
- 10 oz/300 g
  ground beef
- 2 eggs
- 2 tbsp freshly
  grated Pecorino
  cheese
- salt and freshly
  ground black
  pepper to taste
- 1 quantity
  Meat Sauce
  (see page 952)
- 10 oz/300 g
  Mozzarella cheese,
  sliced
- 3 hard-cooked
  eggs, chopped
- ³/₄ cup/90 g
  freshly grated
  Pecorino cheese
- 2 tbsp butter, cut
  into flakes

Divide the pasta dough into 5 pieces. Roll it through a machine one notch at a time down to the second thinnest setting, or roll out thinly with a rolling pin. Let dry on a lightly floured cloth for 30 minutes. • Cut into 6 x 4-inch (15 x 10-cm) rectangles. • Blanch the sheets of lasagne in small batches in a large pan of salted, boiling water with the oil. Drain and squeeze gently. Lay on a damp cloth. • Preheat the oven to 400°F/ 200°C/gas 6. • Grease a baking dish with oil. • Meatballs: Mix the beef, eggs, and Pecorino in a large bowl. Season with salt and pepper and shape into small balls the size of marbles. • Add the meatballs to the meat sauce and cook for 10 minutes. • Line the baking dish with a layer of pasta, leaving enough overlapping the top of the dish to fold back over the filling. Cover with a layer of the meat sauce, Mozzarella, eggs, and Pecorino. Repeat until all the ingredients are in the dish, reserving a little Pecorino for the top. Fold the overlapping pasta over the top of the filling. Dot with the butter and sprinkle with the remaining Pecorino. • Bake for 35–40 minutes, or until golden brown. • Let rest for 20 minutes before serving.

# BAKED MACARONI WITH MEAT SAUCE

Heat the oil in a large frying pan and sauté the onion until softened. • Pierce the sausages all over and blanch them in boiling water for 3 minutes. Drain, remove the casings, and crumble the meat. • Add the sausage meat, salami, and beef to the onion and cook until browned all over. Cook over medium heat for about 30 minutes, adding some stock if the mixture starts to dry out. • Stir in the eggs and season with salt and pepper. • Cook the pasta in a large pan of salted, boiling water for half the time indicated on the package. • Drain and let cool. • Preheat the oven to 350°F/180°C/gas 4. • Butter a baking dish and sprinkle with bread crumbs. • Fill each piece of pasta with the meat sauce. • Arrange the filled pasta in the baking dish in layers, alternating with the sauce and Pecorino. • Cover with the remaining sauce and Pecorino. • Bake for 40–45 minutes, or until the top is golden brown. • Serve hot.

*Serves: 6–8*

*Preparation: 1 h*

*Cooking: 1 h 20'*

*Level of difficulty: 2*

- **4 tbsp extra-virgin olive oil**
- **1 large onion, finely chopped**
- **2 Italian sausages, weighing about 7 oz/200 g**
- **1 cup/150 g diced salami**
- **1 lb/500 g ground beef**
- **1 cup/250 ml meat stock or water**
- **3 hard-boiled eggs, crumbled**
- **salt and freshly ground black pepper to taste**
- **1 lb/500 g large macaroni pasta**
- **1 quantity Tomato Sauce (see page 950)**
- **1 cup/125 g freshly grated Pecorino cheese**

# BAKED PANCAKES WITH MEAT BALLS

**M**ix the beef, eggs, and Pecorino in a large bowl. Season with salt and pepper and shape into small balls. • Place in the meat sauce and cook for 10 minutes. • Sift the flour and salt into a medium bowl. Add the eggs, milk, and parsley. Beat until smooth. Let rest for at least 1 hour. • Preheat the oven to 400°F/200°C/gas 6. • Heat a small amount of oil in a small frying pan. Pour in one-twelfth of the batter, tilting so that it covers the pan. Cook until pale gold, flip, and cook the other side. Repeat with remaining batter. • Grease a baking dish and lay 2 pancakes on the bottom. Cover with meat sauce, Mozzarella, eggs, peas, and Pecorino. Repeat until all the ingredients are in the dish. Dot with the butter.
• Bake for 35–40 minutes, or until golden brown.
• Let rest for 20 minutes before serving.

*Serves: 4–6*

*Preparation: 45'*
*+ 1 h to rest*

*Cooking: 1 h*

*Level of difficulty: 2*

- **10 oz/300 g lean ground beef**
- **2 eggs**
- **salt and freshly ground black pepper to taste**
- **1 quantity Meat Sauce (see page 952)**
- **1¹/₃ cups/200 g all-purpose/plain flour**
- **¹/₈ tsp salt**
- **4 eggs**
- **1 cup/250 ml milk**
- **4 tbsp extra-virgin olive oil**
- **5 oz/150 g Mozzarella, sliced**
- **3 hard-boiled eggs, sliced**
- **4 oz/125 g cooked peas**
- **4 tbsp freshly grated Pecorino cheese**

# CANNELLONI WITH MEAT SAUCE

*Serves: 4–6*

*Preparation: 45'*

*Cooking: 35'*

*Level of difficulty: 2*

- **12 oz/350 g dried cannelloni**
- **14 oz/400 g roast beef**
- **3 oz/100 g cooked, drained spinach**
- **5 oz/150 g prosciutto/ Parma ham**
- **2 eggs**
- **8 tbsp freshly grated Parmesan cheese**
- **salt and freshly ground black pepper to taste**
- **$^1/_4$ tsp freshly grated nutmeg**
- **1 quantity Meat Sauce (see page 952)**
- **1 quantity Béchamel Sauce (see page 946)**
- **1 tbsp butter, cut into flakes**

Preheat the oven to 400°F/200°C/gas 6. • Butter a large baking dish. • Cook the cannelloni in a large pan of salted, boiling water for half the time indicated on the package. Drain and lay on a clean cloth. • Finely chop the veal, spinach, and prosciutto and transfer to large bowl. Mix in the eggs and half the Parmesan. Season with salt, pepper, and nutmeg. • Fill the cannelloni with the filling and arrange them in layers in the baking dish. Cover each layer with meat sauce. Top with Béchamel sauce. Dot with the butter and sprinkle with Parmesan. • Bake for 15–20 minutes, or until golden brown. • Let stand for 15 minutes before serving.

569

# GIANT CONCHIGLIE STUFFED WITH VEGETABLES AND CHEESE

*Serves: 6–8*

*Preparation: 1 h*

*Cooking: 1 h 20'*

*Level of difficulty: 2*

- 2 tbsp butter
- 2 tbsp extra-virgin olive oil
- about 24 giant conchiglie
- 3 zucchinis/ courgettes, diced
- 2 carrots, diced
- 1 lb/500 g broccoletti
- 10 oz/300 g French beans/ green beans, diced
- ¹/₂ cup/125 ml water
- 1 small onion, diced
- 8 oz/250 g Gruyère/Swiss cheese, chopped
- 4 oz/125 g chopped tomatoes
- salt and freshly ground black pepper to taste
- 1 quantity Béchamel Sauce (see page 946)
- nutmeg
- 1 cup/125 g freshly grated Parmesan cheese

Heat the butter and oil in a large frying pan and sauté the onion for 3–4 minutes. • Add the zucchini, carrots, broccoli, and green beans and sauté for 7–8 minutes. • Add the water and season with salt and pepper. Cover and cook over low heat for about 20 minutes. • Prepare the Béchamel. Stir in a generous grating of nutmeg. • When the vegetables are almost ready, uncover the pan so that all the liquid cooks off. • Remove from the heat and stir in the Gruyère and a ladleful of Béchamel sauce. • Preheat the oven to 350°F/ 180°C/gas 4. • Butter a large baking dish. • Cook the giant conchiglie in a large pan of salted, boiling water for half the time indicated on the package. • Drain well and let cool a little. • Fill the conchiglie with the vegetables and arrange in the baking dish. Cover with the remaining Béchamel and the tomatoes. Sprinkle with the Parmesan. • Bake for about 20 minutes, or until golden brown. • Serve hot.

571

# POPPY-SEED LASAGNE

Sift the both flours into a large bowl and make a well in the center. Use a wooden spoon to stir in the eggs, oil, and enough water to make a smooth dough. Knead for 10 minutes. • Shape the dough into a ball, wrap in plastic wrap (cling film), and let rest for 30 minutes. • Chop one apple into small cubes and cut the other into thin slices. Place the apple cubes and slices in separate bowls of water and lemon juice. Let stand for 15 minutes. Drain well. • Mix the apple cubes, figs, raisins, and walnuts in a large bowl. • Preheat the oven to 325°F/170°C/gas 3. • Butter a baking dish. • Roll the dough through a pasta machine down to the thinnest setting, or roll out thinly with a rolling pin. Cut into 3/4 x 3-inch (2 x 8-cm) rectangles. • Cook the pasta in small batches in a large pan of salted, boiling water until al dente. • Drain and place a layer in the baking dish. Drizzle with butter and spread with the apple and fig mixture. Continue until all the pasta and apple and fig mixture are in the dish. • Drain the apple slices and arrange on top of the pasta. • Drizzle with the remaining melted butter and sprinkle with the poppy seeds and cinnamon. • Bake for 25–30 minutes, or until the apple has softened but not burnt. • Let rest for 15 minutes before serving.

*Serves: 4–6*

*Preparation: 1 h 30'*

*Cooking: 40'*

*Level of difficulty: 2*

- 1 1/3 cups/200 g durum wheat semolina flour
- 1 1/3 cups/200 g all purpose/plain flour
- 2 eggs + 1 egg yolk
- 1 tbsp extra-virgin olive oil
- 1 tbsp water, + more if needed
- 2 tart apples, such as Granny Smiths
- juice of 1/2 lemon
- 2 oz/50 g dried figs, coarsely chopped
- 2 tbsp raisins, plumped in warm water for 1 hour
- 1 cup/100 g coarsely chopped walnuts
- 2/3 cup/150 g butter, melted
- 1/2 tsp ground cinnamon
- 2 oz/50 g poppy seeds
- salt to taste

# SOUTHERN ITALIAN STUFFED ZITI

Serves: 4–6

Preparation: 25'

Cooking: 45–50'

Level of difficulty: 2

- 6 tbsp extra-virgin olive oil
- 1 onion, finely chopped
- 14 oz/400 g finely chopped lean pork
- 4 oz/125 g salami, finely chopped
- 1 lb/500 g very thick ziti
- 2 eggs
- salt and freshly ground black pepper to taste
- nutmeg
- 1 clove garlic, finely chopped
- 8 oz/250 g peeled and chopped tomatoes
- $1/3$ cup/50 g bread crumbs
- 6 oz/180 g Caciocavallo or Mozzarella cheese, grated or finely chopped

Heat half the oil in a large frying pan and sauté the onion for 3–4 minutes. • Add the pork and salami and sauté for about 8 minutes. • Remove from the heat and place in a food processor. Chop until smooth and let cool. • Break the ziti into thirds. Cook them in a large pan of salted, boiling water for half the time indicated on the package. • Drain well and run under cold running water. Set aside. • Stir the eggs, salt, pepper, and nutmeg into the chopped pork mixture. Mix well and place in a piping bag. • Place the nozzle of the piping bag at the end of each ziti and fill with the meat mixture. • Preheat the oven to 400°F/200°C/gas mark 6. • Grease a large baking dish. • Sauté the garlic in a large frying pan with the remaining oil, for 2–3 minutes. • Add the tomatoes, season with salt and pepper, and cook over medium heat for 10 minutes. • Spread the bottom of the baking dish with a little of the tomato sauce. Cover with a layer of stuffed ziti. Sprinkle with more tomato sauce, bread crumbs, and Caciocavallo cheese. Repeat until all the ingredients are in the dish.
• Bake for 15–20 minutes, or until the cheese is melted and the top is golden brown. • Serve hot, straight from the oven.

# BAKED PASTA, SICILIAN-STYLE

Heat 4 tablespoons of oil in a large frying pan and sauté half the onion for 5 minutes. • Add the beef and pork and sauté for 5 minutes, or until nicely browned. • Pour in the wine and cook until it has evaporated. • Add the tomatoes and water and season with salt and pepper. Partially cover and cook over low heat for about 1 hour.

*Primosale is a young Sicilian Pecorino cheese. Substitute with another mild young cheese.*

• Heat 2 tablespoons of oil in a small frying pan and sauté the remaining onion for 2–3 minutes.
• Add the peas and season with salt and pepper. Cover and cook over low heat for 15 minutes.
• Cook the pasta in a large pan of salted, boiling water for half the time indicated on the package.
• Drain well and place in a bowl with half the meat sauce and the aged Pecorino. • Preheat the oven to 425°F/ 220°C/gas 7. • Grease a large baking dish and sprinkle with half the bread crumbs.
• Spoon half the pasta and meat sauce mixture into the dish and smooth into an even layer. • Sprinkle with the primosale (or young Pecorino) and cover with the peas. Top with the remaining meat sauce and cover with the remaining pasta. Spread evenly with the back of a spoon. • Sprinkle with the remaining bread crumbs and drizzle with the remaining oil. • Bake for 20 minutes, or until browned on top. • Serve hot.

*Serves: 4–6*

*Preparation: 30'*

*Cooking: 1 h 30'*

*Level of difficulty: 1*

- 6 tbsp extra-virgin olive oil
- 1 large onion, finely chopped
- 8 oz/250 g ground beef
- 8 oz/250 g ground pork
- 1 cup/250 ml dry red wine
- 14 oz/400 g canned tomatoes
- 2 cups/500 ml boiling water
- salt and freshly ground black pepper to taste
- 10 oz/300 g fresh or frozen spring peas
- 1 lb/500 g small pasta, such as anellini
- 10 oz/300 g aged Pecorino cheese, diced
- 1 cup/100 g dry bread crumbs
- 5 oz/150 g Primosale (or other young Pecorino)

# BAKED SPINACH TAGLIATELLE

Preheat the oven to 375°F/190°C/gas 5. •
Butter a baking dish. • Cook the tagliatelle for
half the time indicated on the package. • Sauté the
prosciutto in the butter in a large frying pan for
5 minutes. • Drain the mushrooms, reserving the
water. Chop coarsely and add to the prosciutto.
• Cook over medium heat for 6–7 minutes, or until
the mushrooms are tender, adding the reserved
water. Season with salt and pepper. • Add the
pasta and mix in almost all the Béchamel and 3
tablespoons of Parmesan. • Place in the baking
dish and spread with the remaining Béchamel.
Sprinkle with the remaining Parmesan. • Bake for
30–35 minutes, or until golden brown. • Serve hot.

*Serves: 4–6*

*Preparation: 20'*

*Cooking: 45'*

*Level of difficulty: 1*

- **14 oz/400 g dried spinach tagliatelle**
- **¹/₂ cup/60 g prosciutto/Parma ham, finely chopped**
- **4 tbsp butter**
- **2 oz/60 g dried mushrooms, soaked in warm water for 15 minutes**
- **salt and freshly ground white pepper to taste**
- **1 quantity Béchamel Sauce (see page 946)**
- **4 tbsp freshly grated Parmesan cheese**

# BAKED PASTA WITH CHEESE

*Serves: 4–6*

*Preparation: 30'*

*Cooking: 45'*

*Level of difficulty: 1*

- 1 lb/500 g short hollow dried pasta, such as macaroni or penne
- 2 tbsp extra-virgin olive oil
- 1 quantity Béchamel Sauce (see page 946)
- $1/8$ tsp freshly grated nutmeg
- $1^1/4$ cups/150 g freshly grated Pecorino cheese
- 5 oz/150 g Parmesan cheese, thinly sliced

Preheat the oven to 400°F/200°C/gas 6. • Butter a large baking dish. • Cook the pasta in a large pot of salted boiling water with a drop of the oil for half the time indicated on the package. • Drain, running it under cold water to stop the cooking process, and transfer to a serving bowl. Drizzle with the remaining oil to prevent sticking. • Prepare the Béchamel and let cool to lukewarm. • Mix the pasta into the Béchamel sauce with nearly all of the Pecorino. • Arrange a layer of pasta in the baking dish and cover with the Parmesan. Top with the remaining pasta and sprinkle with Pecorino. Top with the remaining 2 tablespoons of butter. • Bake for 40–45 minutes, or until the top is golden brown.

# BAKED RAVIOLI

Serves: 4–6

Preparation: 1 h +
time to make pasta

Cooking: 45'

Level of difficulty: 3

**P**repare the pasta dough and set aside to rest.
• Preheat the oven to 400°F/ 200°C/gas 6.
• Butter a baking dish. • Sauté the spinach in the
butter in a medium frying pan over medium heat
for 2 minutes. Season with salt, pepper, and
nutmeg and sprinkle with flour. • Pour in the milk
and let it reduce. • Remove from the heat and let
cool. • Mix in the egg yolk and Parmesan. • Roll
out the dough on a lightly floured work surface until
paper-thin. Cut into 2$^1$/$_2$-inch (6-cm) wide strips and
arrange marble-sized balls of filling, about $^3$/$_4$ in
(2 cm) apart down the center of each strip. Cover
with another strip of pasta, pressing down between
the blobs of filling with your fingertips. Seal, after
making sure no air pockets remain, then cut into
squares with a serrated pastry cutter. • Lay the
ravioli on a kitchen cloth dusted with flour. • Cook
the pasta in small batches in a large pan of salted,
boiling water for 2–3 minutes. • Drain and transfer
in layers to the prepared baking dish. Dot each
layer with the melted butter, tomato sauce, and the
Parmesan. • Bake for 12–15 minutes, or until
heated through. • Serve hot.

- **1 quantity Fresh Pasta Dough (see pages 286–7)**
- **1$^1$/$_4$ lb/600 g spinach leaves, cooked, squeezed dry, and finely chopped**
- **4 tbsp butter**
- **salt and freshly ground white pepper**
- **$^1$/$_8$ tsp freshly grated nutmeg**
- **1 tbsp all-purpose/ plain flour**
- **4 tbsp milk**
- **1 egg yolk**
- **$^1$/$_2$ cup/60 g freshly grated Parmesan cheese**
- **6 tbsp butter, melted**
- **1 quantity Tomato Sauce (see page 950)**
- **1 cup/125 g freshly grated Parmesan cheese**

# BAKED SPAGHETTI WITH TOMATO SAUCE

C ook the spaghetti in a large pan of salted, boiling water for just over half the time indicated on the package. • Preheat the oven to 350°F/180°C/gas 4. • Butter a large baking dish. • Drain the spaghetti and placed in the prepared dish. • Spoon the tomato sauce over the top. • Sprinkle with the Parmesan and oregano. • Bake for about 25 minutes, or until the cheese is nicely browned. • Serve hot.

*For extra flavor, add 1 tablespoon of capers and 4 tablespoons of chopped black olives to the sauce.*

582

*Serves: 4–6*

*Preparation: 15' + time to make sauce*

*Cooking: 35'*

*Level of difficulty: 1*

- 1 lb/500 g spaghetti
- 1 quantity **Tomato Sauce** (see page 950)
- 1 cup/125 g freshly grated Parmesan cheese
- 1 tsp dried oregano

# BAKED TAGLIATELLE

Prepare the Béchamel. • Let cool slightly then stir in the eggs and half the Parmesan. • Preheat the oven to 350°F/180°C/gas 4. • Butter a large ovenproof dish. • Bring the vegetable stock to a boil and cook the tagliatelle in it for 1 minute. Drain well and add to the baking dish. • Spoon the Béchamel sauce over the top. Sprinkle the remaining Parmesan and dot with the butter. • Bake for 15–20 minutes, or until golden brown on top. • Let rest for 15 minutes before serving.

*Serves: 4–6*

*Preparation: 30'*

*Cooking: 20'*

*Level of difficulty: 1*

- **1 quantity Béchamel Sauce (see page 946)**
- **3 eggs, lightly beaten**
- **1 cup/125 g freshly grated Parmesan cheese**
- **2 tbsp butter**
- **3 quarts/3 liters Vegetable Stock (see page 956)**
- **1 lb/500 g store-bought tagliatelle**

# RIGATONI BAKED IN A PASTRY CRUST

Pastry: Sift the flour into a large bowl. Add the eggs, lemon zest, salt, and butter (reserving 4 tablespoons), and mix well. • Roll the dough into a ball, cover with plastic wrap (cling film), and refrigerate for 1 hour. • Preheat the oven to 400°F/200°C/ gas 6. • Roll the dough out to $1/2$ in (1 cm) thick. • Butter a 9-in (23-cm) springform pan and line with the dough. Prick well with a fork. • Bake for 20 minutes, or until golden brown. • Cook the rigatoni in a large pan of salted, boiling water for half the time indicated on the package. Drain well. • Stir the rigatoni into the Béchamel and tomato sauce. • Spoon into the pastry. Sprinkle with the cheese. Bake for 10 minutes more. • Remove the sides from the pan and serve hot.

*Serves: 4–6*

*Preparation: 45' + 1 h to chill pastry*

*Cooking: 40'*

*Level of difficulty: 2*

**PASTRY**
- 2 cups/300 g all-purpose flour
- 2 egg yolks
- zest of 1 lemon, finely grated
- dash of salt
- 1 cup/250 g butter

- 1 lb/500 g rigatoni
- $1/2$ quantity Béchamel Sauce (see page 946)
- 1 quantity Tomato Sauce (see page 950)
- $1/2$ cup/60 g freshly grated Parmesan cheese

# BAKED TAGLIATELLE WITH MOZZARELLA

- **1 onion, 1 small stick celery, both finely chopped**
- **2 tbsp finely chopped parsley**
- **6 tbsp extra-virgin olive oil**
- **1 lb/500 g peeled and chopped tomatoes**
- **salt and freshly ground black pepper to taste**
- **1 lb/500 g tagliatelle**
- **14 oz/400 g Mozzarella cheese, sliced**
- **1 cup/120 g freshly grated Parmesan cheese**

Sauté the onion, celery, and parsley in the oil in a large frying pan for 5 minutes. • Add the tomatoes and season with salt and pepper. • Reduce the heat, partially cover, and simmer for 30 minutes. • Preheat the oven to 400°F/200°C/gas 6. • Butter a large baking dish. • Place a layer of sauce in the bottom of the dish. Cover with the tagliatelle. Top with the remaining sauce, followed by the Mozzarella. Sprinkle with the Parmesan. • Bake for about 25 minutes, or until golden brown on top. • Serve hot.

587

# NOODLES

# CHINESE VERMICELLI WITH CHICKEN AND VEGETABLES

Cook the noodles as indicated on the package. Drain and set aside in a large heated bowl.
• Heat the oil in a large frying pan and add the chicken, ginger, and Tabasco. Sauté until the chicken is white, then transfer to a plate. • Discard the ginger. • Add the vegetables and sauté for 3 minutes. • Return the chicken to the pan and cover and cook over low heat for 3 minutes more.
• Add the scallions and sauté for 1–2 minutes, or until slightly softened. • Drizzle with the soy sauce, Marsala, and cornstarch. Add the water chestnuts, stirring continuously, and cook until the mixture comes to a boil. • Spoon the sauce over the vermicelli. Toss well and serve hot.

Serves: 4

Preparation: 20'

Cooking: 25'

Level of difficulty: 1

- **12 oz/350 g Chinese egg vermicelli**
- **3 tbsp extra-virgin olive oil**
- **1 lb/500 g chicken breasts, skinned, boned, and cut into small strips**
- **3 thin slices fresh ginger root**
- **1 tbsp Tabasco sauce**
- **1 lb/500 g fresh vegetables (carrots, tomatoes, broccoli, peas, or cabbage)**
- **1 cup/250 ml chicken stock**
- **4 scallions, sliced**
- **2 tbsp soy sauce**
- **2 tbsp Marsala wine**
- **2 tbsp cornstarch/ cornflour**
  - **1 can (8 oz/250 g) water chestnuts, drained**

# CHINESE VERMICELLI WITH CHICKEN AND CABBAGE

*Serves: 4*

*Preparation: 20'*

*Cooking: 20'*

*Level of difficulty: 1*

- **12 oz/350 g Chinese egg vermicelli**
- **3 tbsp extra-virgin olive oil**
- **3 onions, thinly sliced**
- **3 cloves garlic, finely chopped**
- **2 chicken breasts, skinned, boned, and cut into thin strips**
- **2 tbsp soy sauce**
- **1 stalk celery, thinly sliced**
- **7 oz/200 g white Chinese cabbage, finely chopped**
- **1 lb/500 g shrimp/ prawns, shelled**
- **salt and freshly ground black pepper to taste**

Cook the noodles as indicated on the package. Drain and set aside in a large heated bowl.
• Heat the oil in a frying pan and sauté the onions and garlic until softened and pale gold. • Add the chicken and sauté until white. Drizzle with the soy sauce. Cover and cook over low heat until the chicken is tender. • Add the celery and cabbage and cook for 3–4 minutes. • Add the shrimp, season with salt and pepper, and cook for 2 minutes. • Remove from the frying pan and keep warm. • Add the vermicelli to the pan and sauté over medium-high heat for 2 minutes. Return to the heated dish and spoon the sauce over the top.
• Toss well and serve hot.

# BALI NOODLES WITH SHRIMP AND ONIONS

Cook the noodles as indicated on the package. Drain and set aside in a large heated bowl.
• Heat half the oil in a large frying pan and sauté 2 onions, the celery, bell peppers, and chile peppers over high heat until tender. • Drizzle with the soy sauce and Marsala. • Add the noodles to the pan. Sauté for 1 minute, stirring constantly, until well mixed. • Fry the remaining onions in the remaining oil until crisp and golden brown. Add the shrimp and cook for 2 minutes. • Spoon the noodles onto serving plates and garnish with the shrimp and onions.

*Serves: 4*

*Preparation: 20'*

*Cooking: 15'*

*Level of difficulty: 1*

- **14 oz/400 g Oriental egg angel-hair noodles**
- **6 tbsp extra-virgin olive oil**
- **4 large onions, thinly sliced**
- **2 stalks celery, thinly sliced**
- **1 green bell pepper/capsicum, seeded and cut into thin strips**
- **1 red bell pepper/capsicum, seeded and cut into thin strips**
- **1–2 fresh spicy chile peppers, finely chopped**
- **3 tbsp soy sauce**
- **3 tbsp Marsala wine**
- **12 oz/350 g cooked shrimp, shelled**

# CHINESE NOODLES WITH CHICKEN

**R**ub the chicken with salt, pepper, and saffron. Place in a large pan and pour in the water. Bring to a boil and simmer for 1 hour. • Remove the chicken from the stock (which you will continue to cook down to reduce) and cut the flesh into small pieces, removing the bones and skin. Transfer the chicken to a large bowl and mix in the garlic, onions, ginger, and red pepper flakes. Let marinate for 15 minutes. • Heat the oil in a frying pan and sauté the chicken, turning often, until browned all over. Pour in the reduced stock, coconut, and milk mixture. Cook over low heat until the sauce thickens, stirring often. • Cook the noodles as indicated on the package. Drain and add to the pan. Toss well and serve hot, accompanied with the egg, cucumber, and leek.

*Serves: 4*

*Preparation: 30' + 15' to marinate*

*Cooking: 1 h 30'*

*Level of difficulty: 2*

- $^1/_2$ oven-ready chicken, cut in 4–6 pieces
- salt and freshly ground black pepper to taste
- 4 strands saffron, crumbled
- 1 quart/1 liter water
- 4 cloves garlic, finely chopped
- 2 onions, finely chopped
- 1 thin piece ginger root, grated
- $^1/_2$ tsp red pepper flakes
- 4 tbsp extra-virgin olive oil
- 12 oz/350 g Chinese egg tagliatelle
- 7 oz/200 g coconut flesh
- 2 tbsp all-purpose/ plain flour dissolved in 2 cups/500 ml milk
- 4 hard-boiled eggs, sliced
- 1 cucumber, sliced
- 2 leeks, white part only, thinly sliced

# NOODLES WITH VEGETABLES

Serves: 4

Preparation: 15'

Cooking: 15'

Level of difficulty: 1

- 3 scallions/spring onions, trimmed
- 2 zucchinis/ courgettes, trimmed
- 2 carrots, trimmed
- 12 oz/350 g Chinese egg noodles
- 5 tbsp extra-virgin olive oil
- 1 tbsp dark soy sauce

Slice the scallions, zucchini, and carrots into very thin strips, using either a paring knife or use a grater with large holes. • Bring a large pan of salted water to a boil. Add the noodles and cook for 3 minutes. • Heat the oil in a large frying pan (or, if you prefer, a wok) and sauté the vegetables over high heat for 3 minutes. • Drain the noodles and add to the pan. Sauté for 2 minutes. Drizzle with the soy sauce and serve.

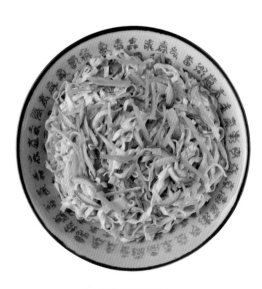

# BAHMI GORENG

Bring a large pan of salted water to a boil. Add the vermicelli and cook for 3 minutes. Drain thoroughly. • Beat the eggs with a pinch of salt and pepper in a small bowl until frothy. • Grease a small frying pan with oil and heat until hot but not smoking. Spoon in 1 tablespoon of the batter, tilting the pan and cook on both sides for 2 minutes. Continue until all the batter is used. Roll up the crêpes and cut them into slices. • Heat 2 tablespoons of oil in a large frying pan and sauté the pork until browned all over. Remove from the pan and set aside. • Sauté the onions and garlic in the same oil until the garlic is pale gold. Add the ginger. Set aside with the meat. • Add the remaining oil to the pan and sauté the bok choy until softened. • Stir in the bean sprouts and shrimp. Season with salt and return the meat and onions to the pan. Drizzle with the soy sauce and season with pepper. Cover and cook over low heat for 5 minutes. • Sauté the vermicelli in a separate frying pan until golden brown. Spoon onto serving plates and top with the meat and cabbage mixture. Arrange the egg strips on top and serve hot.

Serves: 4

Preparation: 30'

Cooking: 30'

Level of difficulty: 2

- 7 oz/200 g Chinese vermicelli or ordinary egg tagliatelle
- 2 eggs
- salt and freshly ground black pepper to taste
- 4 tbsp extra-virgin olive oil
- 8 oz/250 g lean pork, cut into short lengths
- 2 onions, finely chopped
- 2 cloves garlic, finely chopped
- 1/2 tsp finely grated fresh ginger root
- 1 heart of bok choy or cabbage, trimmed and finely shredded
- 2 oz/60 g soy bean sprouts
- 3 1/2 oz/100 g shelled shrimp
- 1 tbsp soy sauce

596

# RICE VERMICELLI
# WITH SPICY COCONUT MILK

*Serves: 4*

*Preparation: 30'*

*Cooking: 40'*

*Level of difficulty: 2*

- 1 tbsp shrimp paste
- 1 tbsp ground red chile pepper
- 2 tsp ground turmeric
- 3 cloves garlic, finely chopped
- 1 scallion/spring onion, finely chopped
- 8 oz/250 g rice vermicelli
- 3 tbsp extra-virgin olive oil
- salt to taste
- 2 tbsp sugar
- 1 quart/1 liter coconut milk
- 8 shrimp/prawns, shelled
- 5 oz/150 g chicken breast

Mix the shrimp paste, chile pepper, turmeric, garlic, and scallion in a small bowl until smooth. • Cook the vermicelli according to the instructions on the package. Drain well and set aside. Add 1 tablespoon of oil and toss to prevent the vermicelli from sticking together. • Heat the remaining oil in a large frying pan and sauté the shrimp paste mixture for 2 minutes. Season with salt and add the sugar. Mix in the coconut milk and bring to a boil. Simmer over low heat until the coconut milk reduces. • Boil the chicken and shrimp in a large pan of water until tender. Drain and cut the chicken into small pieces. • Arrange the vermicelli in serving bowls and top with chicken and prawns. Cover with the spicy coconut milk.

# CHINESE NOODLES WITH BEEF AND MUSHROOMS

C ook the noodles as indicated on the package. Drain and set aside in a large heated bowl. Stir in 1 tablespoon of oil to prevent the vermicelli from sticking together. • Dredge the beef in the flour until well coated. Shake off the excess. • Heat 2 tablespoons of oil in a large frying pan or wok. Add the beef and ginger and cook over high heat until browned all over. • Drizzle with the rice wine and 1 tablespoon of soy sauce. Remove the meat and set aside. • Heat the remaining oil and sauté the scallions, mushrooms, bok choy, and bamboo sprouts for 1–2 minutes, or until the vegetables are crunchy-tender. • Add the noodles and pour in the stock. • Drizzle with the remaining soy sauce and season with salt and pepper. • Add the meat and cook for 1 minute. • Serve hot.

Serves: 4–6

Preparation: 20'

Cooking: 25'

Level of difficulty: 1

- **15 oz/450 g Chinese egg noodles**
- **6 tbsp extra-virgin olive oil**
- **10 oz/300 g fillet of beef, cut into thin strips**
- **$1/2$ cup/75 g all-purpose/plain flour**
- **3 thin slices ginger root, grated**
- **2 tsp rice wine**
- **6 tbsp light soy sauce**
- **4 scallions/spring onions, finely chopped**
- **2 oz/60 g fresh mushrooms, finely chopped**
- **10 oz/300 g bok choy or spinach, finely shredded**
- **1 oz/30 g bamboo sprouts**
- **$2/3$ cup/150 ml Beef Stock (see page 955)**
- **salt and freshly ground white pepper to taste**

# ANGEL-HAIR NOODLES IN GARLIC AND GINGER SAUCE

**M**ix the pork and half the rice wine in a medium bowl. • Heat the oil in a frying pan or wok until very hot. Add the noodles to the hot oil in 4 batches, frying each batch for 2–3 minutes, or until the noodles break up. • Remove the noodles with a slotted spoon and set aside. • Discard the oil, leaving 2 tablespoons in the pan. • Add the pork and cook until browned all over. • Add the leek, garlic, and ginger and sauté for 2 more minutes. • Drizzle with the remaining rice wine and soy sauce and pour in the water. • Return the noodles to the pan and cook over high heat for 2 minutes, stirring constantly, until the liquid has evaporated. • Serve hot.

*Serves: 4*

*Preparation: 10'*

*Cooking: 15'*

*Level of difficulty: 1*

- **12 oz/350 g ground pork**
- **2 tbsp rice wine**
- **2 cups/500 ml vegetable oil, for frying**
- **10 oz/300 g Chinese angel-hair noodles**
- **1 leek, white part only, cut into thin strips**
- **1 clove garlic, finely chopped**
- **4 thin slices of ginger root, finely chopped**
- **1 cup/250 ml water**

RICE

# TYPES OF RICE

Rice is the most consumed grain in the world. It is easy to digest, extremely versatile, and free of gluten (to which many people are allergic). In its less processed form (brown rice) it is an excellent source of B vitamins and fiber, most of which are lost when the bran and part of the germ are removed to produce white rice. Brown rice is quite chewy and has a delicious nutty flavor. It takes about 40 minutes to cook. White rice has a more delicate flavor and takes about half as long to cook. Long-grain rice has less starch and is most widely used in oriental cuisines. Short-grain rices, such as Italian arborio, are high in starch and are ideal for making risotto or other starchy dishes, including sweets and puddings.

Cooked long-grain rice

Long-grain rice

Italian soup rice

Brown rice

Italian Arborio rice
(ideal for risotto)

# RICE AND POTATOES

Heat the oil in a large frying pan and sauté the onion and celery until softened. • Stir in the tomatoes and cook until they have broken down. • Add the potatoes and pour in the water. Bring to a boil and add the rice. Season with salt. Cook until the rice and potatoes are tender, 15–20 minutes. • Sprinkle with the cheese and serve hot.

Serves: 4

Preparation: 10'

Cooking: 35'

Level of difficulty: 1

- **4 tbsp extra-virgin olive oil**
- **1 onion, finely chopped**
- **1 stalk celery, finely chopped**
- **5 firm-ripe tomatoes, peeled, seeded, and coarsely chopped**
- **1 lb/500 g potatoes, peeled and cut into small chunks**
- **3 cups/750 ml water**
- **$^3/_4$ cup/150 g long-grain rice**
- **salt to taste**
- **freshly grated cheese, to serve**

# RICE WITH TOMATO, ANCHOVY, AND OLIVE SAUCE

*Serves: 4*

*Preparation: 15'*

*Cooking: 25'*

*Level of difficulty: 1*

- 1³/₄ cups/350 g short-grain rice
- 4 tbsp extra-virgin olive oil
- 1 onion, thinly sliced
- 2 anchovy fillets
- scant ¹/₂ cup/100 ml dry white wine
- 1 tbsp Italian red or white wine vinegar
- 6 large tomatoes, peeled and coarsely chopped
- juice of 2 lemons
- ¹/₂ fresh red chile pepper, crumbled
- 1 tsp finely chopped marjoram
- 3–4 leaves fresh basil, torn
- 8 large black olives, pitted and chopped

Cook the rice in 2 quarts (2 liters) of salted, boiling water for 13–15 minutes, or until tender. • Heat the oil in a medium saucepan and sauté the onion until softened. • Add the anchovies, crushing them with a fork, until completely dissolved. • Pour in the wine and vinegar and cook until they evaporate. • Stir in the tomatoes, lemon juice, chile, marjoram, basil, and olives and cook over medium heat for 8 minutes, stirring occasionally. • Drain the rice and transfer to a heated serving dish. Pour the sauce over the top and serve hot.

# RICE WITH PEAS AND ARTICHOKES

C ook the rice in 2 quarts (2 liters) of salted, boiling water for 13–15 minutes, or until tender. • Strip off the outer leaves from the artichokes and cut off the top third of the leaves. Cut in half and remove any fuzzy choke. Rub all the cut surfaces with lemon juice to prevent discoloration. Cut into quarters lengthwise. • If using defrosted artichoke hearts, cut them in halves or quarters. • Heat the oil in a large frying pan and sauté the onion until softened. • Add the garlic and cook for 1 minute. • Add the anchovies, crushing them with a fork until completely dissolved. • Add the artichokes and peas. Season with salt and pepper and add 4 tablespoons of water. Cover and cook for 10 minutes. • Drain the rice and place in a serving bowl. • Spoon the sauce over the top. Sprinkle with Pecorino and serve hot.

*Serves: 4*

*Preparation: 10'*

*Cooking: 30'*

*Level of difficulty: 1*

- **1³/₄ cups/350 g short-grain rice**
- **4 baby artichokes or 12–16 frozen artichoke hearts, thawed**
- juice of 1 lemon
- **4 tbsp extra-virgin olive oil**
- **1 onion, thinly sliced**
- **1–2 cloves garlic, finely chopped**
- **4 anchovy fillets**
- **1 cup/125 g fresh or frozen peas, thawed if frozen**
- **salt and freshly ground black pepper to taste**
- **¹/₂ cup/125 ml water**
- **¹/₂ cup/60 g freshly grated Pecorino cheese**

Serves: 6

Preparation: 30'

Cooking: 50'

Level of difficulty: 1

# RICE AND PEAS

- 2¹/₃ lb/1.3 kg very fresh, young peas in the pod
- 2 cups/500 ml Vegetable Stock (see page 956)
- 6 tbsp butter
- ¹/₂ cup/60 g diced pancetta or thick sliced bacon
- 1 onion, finely chopped
- 2¹/₂ cups/500 g Italian Arborio rice
- ¹/₂ cup/125 ml dry white wine
- scant 1 cup/100 g freshly grated Parmesan cheese
- 2 tbsp finely chopped parsley
- salt and freshly ground black pepper to taste

Hull (shell) the peas. Set the peas aside and rinse the pods well. Cook the pods for 20–30 minutes in salted, boiling water until tender. Drain and chop in a food processor. • Stir the pea pod purée into the stock in a large saucepan and keep hot. • Melt 2 tablespoons of butter in a large frying pan and sauté the pancetta and onion for 5 minutes. • Add the rice and cook for 1 minute, stirring constantly. • Pour in the wine and let it evaporate. • Add the peas and cook for 3 minutes. • Stir in half the stock. Cook, stirring often, until the stock is absorbed. Add the remaining stock and stir until the rice is tender. • Remove from the heat and dot with the butter, letting it melt into the rice. Sprinkle with Parmesan and the parsley. Season with salt and pepper and serve.

# MEXICAN RICE

H eat the oil in a large frying pan over medium heat and sauté the onion and bell pepper until softened. • Add the rice and stir over high heat for 2 minutes. • Add the tomatoes and cook for 5 minutes. Season with salt and pepper. • Pour in the stock, cover, and cook over medium-low heat until the rice is tender, about 12–15 minutes. • Serve hot.

*Serves: 4–6*

*Preparation: 15'*

*Cooking: 25'*

*Level of difficulty: 1*

- **2 tbsp extra-virgin olive oil**
- **1 green bell pepper/capsicum, coarsely chopped**
- **1 onion, coarsely chopped**
- **2 cups/400 g long-grain rice**
- **2 tomatoes, coarsely chopped**
- **salt and freshly ground black pepper to taste**
- **2 cups/500 ml Vegetable Stock (see page 956)**

# FRIED RICE WITH HAM

Serves: 4–6

Preparation: 10'

Cooking: 25'

Level of difficulty: 1

- 2 cups/400 g long-grain rice
- 2 tbsp extra-virgin olive oil
- 2 cloves garlic, finely chopped
- 8 oz/250 g ham
- salt and freshly ground black pepper to taste
- 2 eggs, lightly beaten
- 1 tbsp light soy sauce

Cook the rice in 1 quart (1 liter) of salted, boiling water for 13–15 minutes, or until tender. • Drain and set aside. • Heat 1 tablespoon of oil in a wok and sauté the garlic until pale gold. • Add the ham and sauté for 1 minute. • Add the rice and stir until all the ingredients are well mixed. Season with salt and pepper. Transfer to a heated serving bowl. • Heat the remaining oil in the wok and add the eggs. Stir with a fork to scramble. • When the eggs are cooked, add them to the rice mixture then return it to the wok. Drizzle with the soy sauce and stir until well mixed. • Serve hot.

# RICE TIMBALES WITH VEAL AND MARSALA SAUCE

*Serves: 4*

*Preparation: 30'*

*Cooking: 30'*

*Level of difficulty: 2*

- **6 tbsp butter**
- **2 tbsp all purpose/ plain flour**
- **8 oz/250 g sliced veal or beef**
- **4 tbsp dry Marsala wine**
- **1 small bunch fresh mint, finely chopped**
- **4 tbsp coarsely chopped almonds, toasted**
- **salt and freshly ground black pepper to taste**
- **1 cup/250 ml Beef Stock (see page 955)**
- **2 cups/400 g short-grain rice**
- **4 tbsp freshly grated Parmesan cheese**

Melt the butter in a large frying pan. Add the flour and cook for 3–4 minutes, stirring constantly. • Add the veal and Marsala. Stir in the mint and almonds. Season with salt and pepper and pour in the stock. Cook over low heat until the meat is tender. • Cook the rice in 2 quarts (2 liters) of salted, boiling water for 13–15 minutes, or until tender. • Drain well and place in a bowl. Add the Parmesan. • Butter four individual bombe molds or small bowls. Spoon in the rice, pressing it in firmly with the back of the spoon. Let stand for 15 minutes. • Turn the molds out onto serving plates and spoon the sauce over the top and around the sides.

# BROWN RICE WITH VEGETABLES

Cook the green beans in salted, boiling water until crunchy-tender. Drain and cut into short lengths. • Use a fork to crush the tomatoes. • Heat the oil in a large frying pan and sauté the leeks until pale gold. • Add the pancetta, onion, carrots, and green beans and cook for 5 minutes, stirring often. • Add the rice and cook for 3 minutes, stirring constantly. • Pour in the wine and let it evaporate. • Dilute the saffron in 4 tablespoons of the stock and add it to the rice. • Pour in enough stock to cover the rice. Add the peas and stir well. Cover and cook over low heat for about 20 minutes, or until the rice is tender, adding more stock if the rice becomes too dry. • Season with salt and pepper, sprinkle with the parsley, and serve.

*Serves: 4*

*Preparation: 20'*

*Cooking: 35'*

*Level of difficulty: 1*

- **4 oz/125 g green beans**
- **2 tomatoes, peeled, seeded, and coarsely chopped**
- **3 tbsp extra-virgin olive oil**
- **2 leeks, cut into wheels**
- **1/2 cup/60 g diced pancetta**
- **1 onion, finely chopped**
- **2 carrots, finely chopped**
- **2 cups/400 g brown rice**
- **1 cup/250 ml dry white wine**
- **4 strands saffron, crumbled**
- **1 quart/1 liter Vegetable Stock (see page 956)**
- **3 oz/90 g frozen peas, thawed**
- **salt and freshly ground white pepper to taste**
- **2–3 tbsp finely chopped parsley**

6 tbsp butter

1 onion, finely chopped

1 bay leaf

$1/2$ tsp cumin seeds

pinch of ground cinnamon

1 small piece fresh ginger root

1 chile pepper, finely chopped

2 oz/60 g peanuts

2 oz/60 g raisins

$1 3/4$ cup/350 g Patna rice

1 cup/250 ml water

salt to taste

4 tbsp extra-virgin olive oil

5 oz/150 g apples, peeled, cored, and coarsely chopped

1 tsp curry powder

1 cup/250 ml heavy/double cream

1 carrot, finely chopped

5 oz/150 g green beans, chopped

1 tbsp balsamic vinegar

# ORIENTAL RICE WITH VEGETABLES

Preheat the oven to 350°F/180°C/gas 4. • Melt 2 tablespoons of butter in a Dutch oven (earthenware casserole) and sauté half the onion until softened. Add the bay leaf, cumin, cinnamon, ginger, chile pepper, raisins, and peanuts. • Add the rice and cook for 3 minutes, stirring constantly. • Pour in the water and season with salt. Cover and bake in the oven for 20 minutes. • Heat 2 tablespoons of butter and 2 tablespoons of oil in a pan and sauté the remaining onion until softened. Add the apple and curry. Season with salt and cook for about 7 minutes, or until the apple is tender. Transfer to a food processor, add the cream, and chop until smooth. • Heat the remaining oil and butter in a frying pan and sauté the carrot and green beans until lightly browned. Season with salt and drizzle with the balsamic vinegar. Toss the vegetables with the rice and spoon the sauce over the top.

617

# BAKED RICE WITH VEGETABLES AND TOFU

*Serves: 4–6*

*Preparation: 30'*

*Cooking: 40'*

*Level of difficulty: 1*

- 6 scallions/spring onions
- 6 tbsp extra-virgin olive oil
- 2 cloves garlic, finely chopped
- 2 cups/400 g Patna rice
- 4 tbsp tomato concentrate/purée
- 2 cups/200 g fava/broad beans
- 1 cup/125 g shelled peas
- 5 oz/150 g green beans, cut in half
- 1 small Swiss chard, shredded
- 4 strands saffron, crumbled
- 1 quart/1 liter Vegetable Stock (see page 956)
- 2 oz/60 g diced tofu
- 2 tbsp finely chopped parsley
- 2 tbsp finely chopped basil
- 3 tbsp butter
- salt and freshly ground black pepper to taste

Preheat the oven to 350°F/180°C/gas 4. • Cut the green part of the scallions into sections and cut the bulbs in half. • Heat 3 tablespoons of oil in a large frying pan and sauté the garlic until pale gold. • Add the rice and cook for 2 minutes, stirring constantly. • Stir in the tomato concentrate and three-quarters of the vegetables. Dilute the saffron in 1 cup (250 ml) of stock and mix into the rice. • Transfer to a baking dish and pour in the remaining stock. Cover with a sheet of aluminum foil and bake for 20 minutes. • Remove from the oven and sprinkle with half the tofu and the parsley and basil. Dot with the butter and season with salt and pepper. Mix well, cover, and let rest for 5 minutes. • Arrange the rice on serving plates. Garnish with the remaining vegetables and tofu. Drizzle with the remaining oil and serve.

# BROILED RICE WITH POTATOES AND ASPARAGUS

Melt 1 tablespoon of butter in a large frying pan and sauté the onion until softened. • Add the potatoes and asparagus and sauté over high heat for 5 minutes. • Add the rice and cook for 3 minutes, stirring constantly. Season with salt and pepper. • Pour in the wine and almost all the stock. Cover and cook for 15 minutes, or until the rice is tender. • Transfer to a large baking dish and sprinkle with the Parmesan. Dot with the remaining butter and broil (grill) until the surface is golden brown. • Serve hot.

*Serves: 4*

*Preparation: 20'*

*Cooking: 30'*

*Level of difficulty:*

- **4 tbsp butter**
- **2 tbsp finely chopped onion**
- **3 potatoes, peeled and cut into small cubes**
- **8 stalks asparagus, thinly sliced lengthwise**
- **1³/₄ cups/350 g short-grain rice**
- **salt and freshly ground black pepper to taste**
- **¹/₂ cup/125 ml dry white wine**
- **1 quart/1 liter Vegetable Stock (see page 956)**
- **¹/₂ cup/60 g freshly grated Parmesan cheese**

# CABBAGE AND RICE BOMBE WITH BROCCOLI SAUCE

Heat 1 tablespoon of oil in a large frying pan and sauté the cabbage and onion for 5 minutes. • Add 4 tablespoons of stock and cook for 5 minutes. Season with salt. • Heat 2 tablespoons of oil in a frying pan and sauté the shallot until softened. • Add the rice and cook for 3 minutes, stirring constantly. • Pour in the wine and let it evaporate. • Add the stock, cover, and cook over low heat for 15 minutes, or until the rice is tender. • Add the Fontina and spoon half the mixture into a buttered mold. • Spoon the cabbage into the mold and cover with the remaining rice. • Process the broccoli (reserving a few florets to garnish) with the remaining oil, salt, and pepper. • Turn the rice out onto a serving plate and spoon the broccoli sauce around the sides. Garnish with the florets and serve.

*Serves: 6*

*Preparation: 30'*

*Cooking: 40'*

*Level of difficulty: 2*

- 4 tbsp extra-virgin olive oil
- 3¹/₂ oz/100 g thinly sliced red cabbage
- 1 red onion, finely chopped
- 1 quart/1 liter Vegetable Stock (see page 956)
- salt and freshly ground black pepper to taste
- 1 shallot, finely chopped
- 2 cups/400 g short-grain rice
- 1 cup/250 ml dry white wine
- 7 oz/200 g Fontina cheese
- 1 lb/500 g broccoli florets, boiled in salted water

# BAKED RICE MOLD WITH SQUAB

Serves: 4–6

Preparation: 40'

Cooking: 1 h 20'

Level of difficulty: 2

- 1 young squab/pigeon, weighing about 1 lb/500 g
- 6 tbsp butter
- 1 onion, finely chopped
- 2 leaves fresh sage
- $^1/_2$ cup/125 ml dry white wine
- 1 tbsp tomato purée dissolved in $^1/_2$ cup/125 ml water
- $2^1/_2$ cups/500 g short-grain rice
- 2 eggs
- $^1/_2$ cup/60 g freshly grated Parmesan cheese
- 4 tbsp fine dry bread crumbs

Wash the squab and pat dry with paper towels. Cut into 6 pieces. • Heat half the butter in a large frying pan and sauté the onion until softened. • Add the sage and squab and cook until browned. • Pour in the wine and let it evaporate. • Stir in the tomato mixture. Cover and simmer over low heat for 20 minutes. • Cook the rice in a large pan of salted, boiling water for 8 minutes. Drain and transfer to a large bowl. • Preheat the oven to 350°F/180°C/gas 4. • Butter a bombe mold and sprinkle with the bread crumbs. • Stir the cooking juices from the squab, eggs, Parmesan, and remaining butter into the rice. • Use two-thirds of the rice to line the mold. Arrange the squab in the center. Cover with the remaining rice and sprinkle with the remaining bread crumbs. • Bake for 40 minutes. • Let stand for 10 minutes. Invert carefully onto a heated plate and serve.

# RICE WITH CURRY AND SHRIMPS

C ook the rice in 2 quarts (2 liters) of salted, boiling water for 13–15 minutes, or until tender. • Drain and toss with 1 tablespoon of oil, the scallions, and the chile peppers. • Beat the eggs, cream, salt, and pepper in a small bowl. • Heat the remaining oil in a small frying pan and cook the beaten egg mixture, stirring constantly. • Add the curry, mix well, and remove from the heat. • Toss the shrimp and eggs with the rice and serve.

| | |
|---|---|
| Serves: | 4 |
| Preparation: | 25' |
| Cooking: | 30' |
| Level of difficulty: | 1 |

- **2 cups/400 g Basmati rice**
- **3 tbsp extra-virgin olive oil**
- **2 scallions/spring onions, finely chopped**
- **7 oz/200 g small sweet green chile peppers**
- **2 fresh spicy red chile peppers, seeded and finely chopped**
- **3 eggs**
- **1 tbsp heavy/ double cream**
- **salt to taste**
- **1 tbsp curry powder**
- **7 oz/200 g cooked shrimp/prawn tails, shelled**

# BAKED RICE WITH MUSHROOMS AND POTATOES

*Serves: 6*

*Preparation: 20'*

*Cooking: 1 h*

*Level of difficulty: 1*

- 1 lb/500 g potatoes, peeled and finely sliced
- 2 cups/400 g short-grain rice
- 14 oz/400 g mushrooms, finely sliced
- salt to taste
- 3 cloves garlic, finely chopped
- 1 bunch fresh parsley, finely chopped
- 6 tbsp freshly grated Pecorino cheese
- 4 tbsp fine dry bread crumbs
- 6 tbsp extra-virgin olive oil
- 3 cups/750 ml water

Preheat the oven to 350°F/180°C/gas 4. •
Grease a large ovenproof baking dish with oil.
• Arrange the potatoes in a layer in the bottom of
the dish. Cover with a layer of rice and, finally, a
layer of mushrooms. As you work, season each
layer with salt, garlic, parsley, Pecorino, and bread
crumbs. Drizzle with the oil. • Pour in the water
and cover the dish with aluminum foil. Bake for
about 1 hour, or until the rice and potatoes are
tender. • Serve hot.

# RICE WITH CRABMEAT

Serves: 4

Preparation: 40'

Cooking: 25'

Level of difficulty: 1

Heat the oil in a large frying pan and sauté the onion and garlic until pale gold. • Add the rice and cook for 3 minutes, stirring constantly.
• Stir in the mint and add enough water to cover the rice. Season with salt and pepper. Cook over medium heat, stirring occasionally, until the rice is tender, adding more water if it begins to dry.
• Mix in the crabmeat and let rest for 20 minutes.
• Season with salt and pepper and serve.

628

- **2 tbsp extra-virgin olive oil**
- **1 onion, finely chopped**
- **3 cloves garlic, finely chopped**
- **1³/₄ cups/350 g short-grain rice**
- **1 small bunch fresh mint, finely chopped**
- **2 cups/500 ml water**
- **8 oz/250 g cooked crabmeat, crumbled**
- **salt and freshly ground black pepper to taste**

*Serves: 4–6*

*Preparation: 15'*

*Cooking: 55'*

*Level of difficulty: 2*

- 6 tbsp extra-virgin olive oil
- 2 medium onions, finely chopped
- 1 green chile bell pepper, seeded and diced
- 4 cloves garlic, finely chopped
- 2 firm-ripe tomatoes, peeled and coarsely chopped
- 1 1/2 lb/750 g squid, cleaned and chopped, ink sacs reserved
- 2 cups/400 g short-grain rice
- 1 quart/1 liter Fish Stock (see page 958)

# BLACK RICE

Heat the oil in a large frying pan over medium heat. Sauté the onions and chile pepper for 8–10 minutes, or until the onions are lightly browned. • Stir in 1 clove of garlic and the tomatoes. Cook for 10–15 minutes, or until the liquid has reduced. • Stir in the squid and reserved ink sacs, which will color the mixture. • Add the rice and stir over high heat for 2–3 minutes. • Pour in the fish stock and bring to a boil. Lower the heat and simmer for 10 minutes. • Add the remaining garlic and cook for 15–20 minutes more, or until the rice and squid is tender. • Serve hot.

# BAKED SHRIMP AND RICE

Preheat the oven to 350°F/180°C/gas 4. •
Butter an ovenproof baking dish. • Cook the
rice in 1 quart (1 liter) of salted, boiling water for
10 minutes. • Drain, reserving the cooking water.
• Mix the shrimp with the onions, yogurt, and a
pinch of salt and pepper. • Melt the butter in a
large frying pan and add the shrimp mixture. Sauté
over high heat until tender. • Add the almonds,
coriander seeds, mint, and 1 cup (250 ml) of the
cooking water from the rice. Cover and cook over
low heat for 5 minutes. • Spoon half the rice into
the prepared dish. Top with the shrimp mixture and
finish with the remaining rice.
• Bake for 15 minutes.
• Serve hot.

- 1$^3$/$_4$ cups/350 g Basmati rice
- 1 lb/500 g shelled shrimp/prawn tails, shelled
- 2 onions, finely chopped
- $^1$/$_2$ cup/125 g plain yogurt
- salt and freshly ground black pepper to taste
- 6 tbsp butter
- 1 tsp coriander seeds
- 1 small bunch fresh mint, finely chopped
- 1 cup/150 g toasted almonds, coarsely chopped

# CAMBODIAN RICE

Serves: 4–6
Preparation: 20'
Cooking: 30'
Level of difficulty: 2

- 4 tbsp extra-virgin olive oil
- 1 onion, finely chopped
- 2 cloves garlic, finely chopped
- 12 oz/350 g pork, cut into small pieces
- 3$^1$/$_2$ oz/100 g chicken breast, cut into small pieces
- 2$^1$/$_2$ oz/75 g peeled shrimp/prawns, cut in half
- 1$^1$/$_4$ cups/250 g Basmati rice
- 1 quart/1 liter Fish Stock (see page 958)
- 2 tbsp vinegar
- pinch of aniseed
- 1 tsp grated ginger root
- $^1$/$_2$ tsp ground cinnamon
- salt and freshly ground black pepper to taste
- 2 eggs
- 2 fresh green chile peppers, finely sliced

Heat the oil in a large frying pan and sauté the the onion and garlic until pale gold. • Add the pork, chicken, and shrimp and cook until browned all over. • Add the rice and cook for 3 minutes, stirring constantly. • Pour in the stock, vinegar, aniseed, ginger, cinnamon, salt, and pepper. Cover and cook over low heat for 20 minutes, or until the rice is tender. • Beat the eggs with a pinch of salt. Fry the eggs in a frying pan until firm. Cut into strips. • Gently mix the fried egg into the rice.
• Garnish with chile pepper. Serve hot.

# CHINESE FRIED RICE

Cook the rice in 1 quart (1 liter) of salted, boiling water for 13–15 minutes, or until tender. • Drain well. • Heat 2 tablespoons of oil in a large frying pan and sauté the rice for 3 minutes. Add the leeks, ham, salt, and pepper and sauté for 1 minute. • Make a well in the center and break in the eggs. Cook until the eggs begin to solidify, then begin to stir, working outward from the center, in increasingly broad circles, blending the eggs and rice. • Sprinkle with the parsley and drizzle with the soy sauce. Stir until the ingredients are well mixed. • Serve hot.

*Serves: 4–6*

*Preparation: 10'*

*Cooking: 25'*

*Level of difficulty: 1*

- 2 cups/400 g long-grain rice
- 2 tbsp extra-virgin olive oil
- 4 leeks, white part only, finely chopped
- 1 cup/125 g diced ham
- salt and freshly ground black pepper to taste
- 2 eggs
- 1 small bunch fresh parsley, finely chopped
- 2 tbsp dark soy sauce

# JAMBALAYA

Serves: 6

Preparation: 20'

Cooking: 45'

Level of difficulty: 1

- 4 tbsp extra-virgin olive oil
- 1 large red onion, finely chopped
- 4 scallions/spring onions, sliced
- 3 cloves garlic, finely chopped
- 3 oz/90 g bacon, finely chopped
- 2 cups/400 g long-grain rice
- 1¹/₂ lb/750 g peeled and chopped tomatoes
- 1 red bell pepper/ capsicum, seeded, cored, and diced
- 5 oz/150 g diced ham
- 1 tsp freshly ground black pepper
- ¹/₂ tsp Tabasco
- 1 tsp dried thyme
- 2 cups/500 ml Chicken Stock (see page 955)
- 2 oz/60 g shrimp/ prawns
- 1 tbsp finely chopped parsley
- salt to taste

Heat the oil in a saucepan over medium heat and cook the onion, scallions, garlic, and bacon for 5 minutes. • Add the rice and cook for 2 minutes, stirring constantly. • Add the tomatoes, bell pepper, ham, pepper, Tabasco, and thyme and cook for 5 minutes. • Add the stock and bring to a boil. Cover and cook over low heat for 30–40 minutes, or until the rice is tender. • Add the shrimp and parsley and toss well. Season with salt. • Serve hot.

*This creole/cajun dish is one of the most famous dishes from the Southern US.*

635

# SPICY LAMB AND PORK PAELLA

Serves: 4–6
Preparation: 20'
Cooking: 40'
Level of difficulty: 2

Blanch the tomatoes in salted, boiling water for 30 seconds. Slip off the skins and chop the flesh coarsely. • Dissolve the saffron in the water. • Season the lamb with salt and pepper. • Heat the oil in a large frying pan and brown the lamb over medium heat for 5 minutes. Remove from the heat and set aside, keeping warm. • Brown the pork in the same oil for 5 minutes. Remove from the heat and set aside, keeping warm. • Sauté the bell peppers and the green beans over low heat for 3 minutes. • Increase the heat and cook the salami, cayenne pepper, and chile pepper for 30 seconds. • Add the rice and cook for 3 minutes, stirring constantly. • Stir in the tomatoes over high heat and cook for 3 minutes. • Add the pork and its cooking juices, the saffron mixture, stock, and salt and pepper. Add the lamb and rosemary and bring to a boil. Cover and cook over medium-low heat for 20 minutes without stirring, shaking the frying pan every so often to prevent the rice from sticking. • When the rice is tender, remove from the heat and allow the paella to rest for 5 minutes before serving.

- 4 firm-ripe tomatoes
- 6 strands saffron, crumbled
- 1 tbsp hot water
- 14 oz/400 g lamb, chopped
- 1 tsp salt
- 1 tsp freshly ground black pepper
- 4 tbsp extra-virgin olive oil
- 8 oz/250 g pork loin, cut in thin strips
- 1 red bell pepper/ capsicum, sliced into thin strips
- 8 oz/250 g green beans
- 4 oz/125 g spicy salami, thinly sliced
- 1 tbsp cayenne pepper
- 1 tsp finely chopped fresh chile pepper
- $1^3/4$ cups/350 g short-grain rice
- $2^1/2$ cups/625 ml boiling Chicken Stock, (see page 955)
- 1 tbsp finely chopped fresh rosemary

# PAELLA WITH OLIVES AND BELL PEPPER

Heat 3 tablespoons of oil in a large frying pan over medium heat and sauté the onion until softened. • Add the garlic and bell pepper and cook for 5 minutes. • Stir in the rice and chile pepper. • Dissolve the saffron in the stock and pour it into the rice. Pour in the wine and stir in the tomatoes. • Bring to a boil, cover and cook over low heat for 15 minutes, or until the rice is tender. • Add the garbanzo beans and remove from the heat. • Mix in the lemon juice, remaining oil, and basil. Season with salt and pepper. Add the olives and parsley and toss well. • Let stand 5 minutes before serving.

- 7 tbsp extra-virgin olive oil
- 1 red onion, finely chopped
- 2 cloves garlic, finely chopped
- 1 red bell pepper/capsicum, seeded, cored, and coarsely chopped
- 1 1/2 cups/300 g long-grain rice
- pinch of chile pepper
- 6 strands saffron, crumbled
- 2 cups/500 ml Vegetable Stock (see page 956)
- 1/2 cup/125 ml dry white wine
- 10 oz/300 g cherry tomatoes, cut in half
- 1 1/2 cups/150 g canned garbanzo beans/chickpeas, drained
- 2 tbsp fresh lemon juice
- 4 leaves basil, torn
- salt and freshly ground black pepper to taste
- 1 1/2 cups/150 g finely chopped black olives
- 4 tbsp finely chopped parsley

# RICE WITH LEMON

*Serves: 4*

*Preparation: 20'*

*Cooking: 25'*

*Level of difficulty: 1*

- 1¹/₃ cups/270 g long-grain rice
- 3 tbsp extra-virgin olive oil
- 1 onion, finely chopped
- 1 lemon
- 1 cup/250 ml dry white wine
- 1 tsp freshly grated ginger root
- salt and freshly ground white pepper to taste
- 3 eggs, lightly beaten
- 2 tbsp freshly grated Parmesan cheese
- 1 small bunch fresh parsley, finely chopped
- 4 leaves fresh basil, torn

Cook the rice in 2 quarts (2 liters) of salted, boiling water for 13–15 minutes, or until tender. • Heat the oil in a large frying pan and sauté the onion until softened. • Grate the zest from 1 lemon and squeeze out the juice. Add the zest to the onion and cook for 1 minute. • Pour in the wine and add the ginger and a pinch of salt. Cook over low heat for 5 minutes. Stir in the beaten eggs, 1 teaspoon of lemon juice, and the Parmesan. Stir quickly and cook for 2 minutes. • Remove from the heat and sprinkle with the parsley and basil. Mix the rice with the sauce and serve hot, sprinkled with lemon zest.

# KEDGEREE

Serves: 4

Preparation: 20'

Cooking: 35'

Level of difficulty: 1

- 2 cups/400 g Basmati rice
- 14 oz/400 g smoked cod
- 1 small piece lemon zest
- 1 bay leaf
- 2 cups/500 ml water
- 4 tbsp butter, cut up
- 1 onion, finely chopped
- 1 tsp curry powder
- 3 hard-boiled eggs, thinly sliced
- 6 tbsp finely chopped fresh parsley
- 2 egg yolks
- $^1/_2$ cup/125 ml heavy/double cream

Cook the rice in 2 quarts (2 liters) of salted, boiling water for 13–15 minutes, or until tender. • Place the cod in a large saucepan with the lemon zest and bay leaf. Pour in enough water to cover. • Bring to a boil over low heat and simmer for 6–8 minutes, or until the fish begins to flake. • Drain the fish, removing the skin and the bones. Cut into small pieces and set aside. • Melt the butter in a large frying pan and sauté the onion and curry for 5 minutes until the onion has softened. • Stir in the hard-boiled eggs, reserving one egg to garnish. • Mix in the rice, cod, parsley, egg yolks, and cream until well blended. Serve hot, garnished with the reserved hard-boiled egg cut into quarters.

# SAUTÉED CHINESE RICE

Serves: 4–6
Preparation: 1 h
Cooking: 30'
Level of difficulty: 2

Soak the mushrooms in 4 tablespoons of boiling water for 20 minutes. Drain, reserving the water. Squeeze the mushrooms dry and slice them. • Slice the meat crosswise, then cut into thin strips. • Mix the reserved mushroom water with the soy sauce, sugar, and corn starch in a small bowl. Add the meat and marinate for 20 minutes. Dry on paper towels, reserving the marinade. • Cook the rice in 2 quarts (2 liters) of salted, boiling water for 13–15 minutes, or until tender. • Drain well and set aside. • Heat the sesame oil and 2 tablespoons of peanut oil in a wok and sauté the garlic and ginger for 3 minutes. • Add the meat, mushrooms, and bacon and sauté over high heat for 3 minutes. • Transfer to a plate and keep warm. • Heat the remaining oil in the wok and sauté the scallions, green beans, celery, and bell pepper over high heat for 4 minutes. • Add the meat mixture and cook for 2 more minutes. • Mix in the rice, stir for 2 minutes, then add the corn, peas, shrimp, and the reserved marinade. • Cook for 2 minutes more and serve hot.

642

- 6 dried Chinese mushrooms
- 6 oz/180 g beef
- 3 tbsp soy sauce
- 1 tsp cane sugar
- 1 tsp corn starch/corn flour
- 1 tbsp sesame oil
- 3 tbsp peanut oil
- 2 cloves garlic, finely chopped
- 2 tsp freshly grated ginger
- 1 cup/125 g diced bacon
- 8 scallions/spring onions, finely sliced
- 4 oz/125 g green beans, finely sliced
- 1 stalk celery, finely sliced
- 1 small green or red bell pepper/capsicum, sliced into thin strips
- 2 cups/400 g long-grain rice
- 1 cup/250 g canned corn cobs, drained and chopped
- 1 cup/125 g fresh or frozen peas
- 4 oz/125 g shrimp/prawns, cooked and shelled

*Serves: 6*

*Preparation: 30' + 2 h to soak rice*

*Cooking: 30'*

*Level of difficulty: 2*

- 1¹/₂ cups/300 g short-grain rice
- 8 dried Chinese mushrooms
- 8 oz/250 g ground beef
- 10 oz/300 g ground pork
- ¹/₃ cup water chestnuts, finely chopped
- 4 scallions/spring onions, finely chopped
- 2 cloves garlic, finely chopped
- 1 tsp freshly grated ginger root
- 1 tbsp soy sauce
- salt to taste
- 1 egg, lightly beaten

**SAUCE**
- 3 tbsp soy sauce
- 2 tbsp cane sugar
- 1 tbsp finely grated ginger root

# CHINESE MEAT AND RICE BALLS

Soak the rice in cold water for at least 2 hours. Drain and dry on a clean cloth. • Soak the mushrooms in hot water for 20 minutes. Drain, then squeeze out excess moisture. Slice very finely. • Mix the mushrooms, beef, pork, water chestnuts, scallions, garlic, ginger, soy sauce, salt, and egg. Divide the mixture into about 20 portions and shape into walnut-sized balls. Roll in the grains of rice until well coated. • Line a Chinese bamboo steaming basket with parchment paper and arrange the balls in it, without crowding (cook them in 2 or 3 batches, depending on the size of the basket). • Place the bamboo basket over a wok or saucepan half-filled with boiling water and steam for 30 minutes. • Sauce: Mix the soy sauce, cane sugar, and ginger in a small bowl. • Serve the rice balls hot, with the sauce on the side.

# TOMATOES AND BELL PEPPERS STUFFED WITH RICE

P reheat the oven to 350°F/180°C/gas 4. •
Grease a large baking dish with oil. • Remove
and set aside the tops of the tomatoes. Use a
teaspoon to hollow them out, placing the flesh in a
small bowl. Place the hollowed out tomatoes
upside down in a colander to drain. • Cut the tops
off the bell peppers, removing the seeds and
cores. • Cook the rice in 2 quarts (2 liters) of
salted, boiling water for 10 minutes. • Drain and
let cool in a large bowl. • Heat 2 tablespoons of oil
in a large frying pan and sauté the onion, garlic,
and oregano until the onion has softened. • Add
the pine nuts and currants and cook for 5 minutes.
• Remove from the heat and mix in the basil and
parsley. Season with salt. • Add the sautéed
mixture and the tomato flesh to the rice and mix
well. Season with salt and pepper. • Stuff the
tomatoes and bell peppers with this mixture. Finish
each bell pepper and tomato and with its own "lid."
• Arrange the bell peppers in the baking dish and
drizzle with the oil. Cover with aluminum foil and
bake for 20 minutes. • Add the tomatoes to the
dish and bake for 30 minutes more. • Serve hot or
at room temperature.

Serves: 4

Preparation: 40'

Cooking: 1 h 20'

Level of difficulty: 2

- **2 large tomatoes**
- **2 red or green bell peppers/ capsicums**
- **1 cup/200 g long-grain rice**
- **6 tbsp extra-virgin olive oil**
- **1 red onion, finely sliced**
- **2 cloves garlic, finely chopped**
- **1 tsp dried oregano**
- **3 tbsp pine nuts**
- **3 tbsp currants**
- **4 tbsp finely chopped fresh basil**
- **3 tbsp finely chopped fresh parsley**
- **salt and freshly ground black pepper to taste**

646

# FISH, RICE, AND ASPARAGUS MOLD

*Serves: 4*

*Preparation: 20'*

*Cooking: 35'*

*Level of difficulty: 1*

- 1 lb/500 g **asparagus stalks**
- 12 leaves fresh **sage**
- 1 egg, lightly **beaten**
- 2 tbsp all-purpose/ **plain flour**
- 4 tbsp **butter**
- 2 leeks, white parts only, finely **chopped**
- 1 shallot, finely **chopped**
- 12 oz/350 g perch (or other fish) **fillets**
- 2 cups/400 g Italian Arborio or Carnaroli **rice**
- 1/2 cup/125 ml dry **white wine**
- 1 quart/1 liter **Fish Stock** (see page 958)
- salt and freshly ground white **pepper to taste**
- 4 tbsp heavy/ **double cream**

Clean the asparagus, trimming the tough ends off the stalks. • Cook the asparagus in salted, boiling water for 5 minutes. Drain, reserving the water, and chop into short lengths. Leave a few tips whole to garnish. • Dip the sage leaves in the egg then dust with the flour. • Melt the butter in a small frying pan and fry the sage leaves until crispy and golden brown. Drain well on paper towels. • Sauté the leeks and shallot in the same butter until softened, adding 2 tablespoons of the cooking water from the asparagus. • Add the fish and cook over high heat for 3 minutes, crumbling with a fork as it cooks. • Add the rice and cook for 3 minutes, stirring constantly. • Pour in the wine and let it evaporate. • Add all the asparagus, except the garnish. • Stir in 1/2 cup (125 ml) of the stock. Cook, stirring often, until the stock is absorbed. Continue adding the stock, 1/2 cup (125 ml) at a time, stirring often until each addition is absorbed, until the rice is tender, 15–18 minutes. • Butter a 6-cup (1.5-liter) fluted mold. • Season the rice mixture with salt and pepper and mix in the cream. • Spoon the rice into the prepared mold, pressing it down firmly. • Turn out onto a serving plate and garnish with the sage and reserved asparagus. Serve hot.

# STUFFED MIXED VEGETABLES

Cook the rice in 2 quarts (2 liters) of salted, boiling water for 13–15 minutes, or until tender. • Drain and transfer to a large bowl. Mix in the onions, meat, herbs, pine nuts, salt, and pepper. • Cut off the tops of the tomatoes and the bell peppers and set aside. Cut a top layer off the eggplants. Use a teaspoon to remove the seeds and filaments from the bell peppers and hollow out the tomatoes. Use a knife and tablespoon to hollow out the eggplants. • Stuff the vegetables with the rice mixture and top each one with its own "lid." Insert pieces of tomato flesh beneath the covers of the eggplants and bell peppers. • Butter a large saucepan, arrange the vegetables in it, and pour in the water. Cover and cook over low heat for 1 hour. • Serve hot.

Serves: 4–6

Preparation: 40'

Cooking: 1 h 20'

Level of difficulty: 2

- 1 1/2 cups/300 g long-grain rice
- 4 onions, finely chopped
- 14 oz/400 g ground lamb or beef
- 1 small bunch mixed aromatic herbs, such as parsley, basil, mint, and wild fennel, finely chopped
- 2 tbsp pine nuts
- salt and freshly ground black pepper to taste
- 4 medium firm-ripe tomatoes
- 4 long eggplants/ aubergines
- 4 green bell peppers/ capsicums
- 2 cups/500 ml water

# RICE WITH SPINACH

Cook the rice in 2 quarts (2 liters) of salted, boiling water for 13–15 minutes, or until tender. • Drain and transfer to a large bowl. • Rinse the spinach and chop finely. • Mix the spinach, garlic, parsley, and oil into the rice. Season with salt and pepper. • Sprinkle with Pecorino, toss well, and serve.

652

*Serves: 4–6*

*Preparation: 15'*

*Cooking: 15'*

*Level of difficulty: 1*

- 1 3/4 cups/350 g long-grain rice
- 12 oz/350 g tender young spinach leaves, stalks removed
- 2 cloves garlic, finely chopped
- 1 small bunch fresh parsley, finely chopped
- 4 tbsp extra-virgin olive oil
- salt and freshly ground black pepper to taste
- 3/4 cup/90 g freshly grated Pecorino cheese

# STUFFED CABBAGE LEAVES

*Serves: 4*

*Preparation: 30'*

*Cooking: 1 h 20'*

*Level of difficulty: 2*

- 1 large cabbage, 8 outer leaves removed and heart discarded
- 2 tbsp extra-virgin olive oil
- 1 onion, finely chopped
- 2 cloves garlic, finely chopped
- 8 oz/250 g ground pork
- 1¼ cups/150 g diced ham
- 1 cup/200 g short-grain rice
- 4 tbsp finely chopped fresh parsley
- 2 tbsp finely chopped capers
- 1 tbsp malt vinegar
- 1 tbsp sugar
- 1 tsp ground allspice
- 1 quantity Tomato Sauce (see page 950)

Preheat the oven to 300°F/150°C/gas 2. • Butter a large ovenproof baking dish. • Blanch the cabbage leaves in salted, boiling water for 2 minutes. Drain and set aside. • Heat the oil in a large frying pan and sauté the onion and the garlic until softened. • Add the pork and cook until browned. • Add the ham and rice and cook, stirring, for 2 minutes. Remove from the heat and place in a large bowl. Add the parsley, capers, vinegar, sugar, and allspice. Divide the mixture into eight parts. • Remove the tough central stalk from the cabbage leaves. • Lay out the leaves and place a portion of filling on each one. Roll up and place, seam-side down, in the prepared baking dish. • Top with the tomato sauce and dot with the butter. • Bake for 1 hour, or until the parcels are tender. • Serve hot.

# RICE WITH CARROTS, WALNUTS, AND FRESH HERBS

Serves: 4

Preparation: 15'

Cooking: 30'

Level of difficulty: 1

- 1¹/₂ cups/300 g long-grain rice
- 4 tbsp extra-virgin olive oil
- 8 oz/250 g carrots, cut in small thin strips
- 1 cup/150 g shelled walnuts
- salt and freshly ground black pepper to taste
- 1 tbsp finely chopped fresh parsley
- 1 tbsp finely chopped fresh marjoram

Cook the rice in 2 quarts (2 liters) of salted, boiling water for 13–15 minutes, or until tender. • Drain and transfer to a large bowl. • Heat the oil in a frying pan and sauté the carrots until lightly golden. Cover and cook over low heat for about 15 minutes. • Toast the walnuts in a frying pan until lightly browned. Transfer to a food processor and chop finely. • Mix the carrots and walnuts into the rice. Season with salt and pepper. Sprinkle with parsley and marjoram and serve hot.

# BROWN RICE WITH ONIONS AND ARUGULA

C ook the rice in 2 quarts (2 liters) of salted, boiling water for 35 minutes, or until tender.
• Drain and transfer to a large bowl. • Heat the oil in a large frying pan and sauté the onions until softened. • Pour in the wine and let it evaporate.
• Cover and cook over medium heat for 5 minutes. • Remove from heat and add the arugula. Season with salt and pepper and toss well. • Serve hot.

*Serves: 4*

*Preparation: 15'*

*Cooking: 40'*

*Level of difficulty: 1*

- 1 3/4 cups/350 g brown rice
- 4 tbsp extra-virgin olive oil
- 2 large onions, finely chopped
- 1/2 cup/125 ml dry white wine
- 5 oz/150 g arugula/rocket, finely shredded
- salt and freshly ground black pepper to taste

656

# BAKED RICE WITH CELERY

*Serves: 4–6*

*Preparation: 15'*

*Cooking: 45'*

*Level of difficulty: 1*

- 1³/₄ cups/350 g long-grain rice
- 4 tbsp extra-virgin olive oil
- 6 stalks celery, finely chopped
- 1 onion, finely chopped
- 1 fresh red chile pepper, finely chopped
- ¹/₂ cup/125 ml dry red wine
- salt to taste
- 1¹/₄ cups/150 g freshly grated Parmesan cheese

Cook the rice in 2 quarts (2 liters) of salted, boiling water for 10 minutes. • Drain and transfer to a large bowl. • Heat 2 tablespoons of oil in a large frying pan and sauté 4 stalks of celery, the onion, and chile until softened. • Pour in the wine and let it evaporate. • Cover and cook over medium heat for about 20 minutes. • Preheat the oven to 400°F/200°C/gas 6. • Remove the celery mixture from heat and mix into the rice. Season with salt and pepper. • Spoon into an ovenproof baking dish, garnishing with the remaining celery. Sprinkle with Parmesan and drizzle with the remaining oil. • Bake for 10 minutes, or until lightly browned. Serve hot.

# NASI GORENG

Heat the oil in a wok and sauté the onions and garlic until pale gold. • Season with salt, pepper, and red pepper flakes. Stir in the ketchup and shrimp. Cover and cook over low heat for 5 minutes. • Cook the rice in 2 quarts (2 liters) of salted, boiling water for 10 minutes. • Drain and mix the rice into the shrimp mixture. Sauté for 2 minutes. Pour in the stock and cook until all the liquid has been absorbed. • Omelette: Heat the oil in a small frying pan and sauté the onion until softened. • Beat the eggs with the salt, pepper, and ginger. • Add the eggs to the frying pan and fry on both sides for 2 minutes. • Cut into thin strips. • Add to the rice just before serving.

*Serves: 4*

*Preparation: 40'*

*Cooking: 30'*

*Level of difficulty: 2*

- 4 tbsp extra-virgin olive oil
- 2 onions, finely chopped
- 1 clove garlic, finely chopped
- salt to taste
- $1/2$ tsp freshly ground black pepper
- 1 tsp red pepper flakes
- 2 tbsp spicy ketchup
- 7 oz/200 g shelled shrimp/prawn
- $1^1/2$ cups/300 g long-grain rice
- 2 cups/500 ml Chicken Stock (see page 955)

**OMELET**

- 1 tbsp extra-virgin olive oil
- 1 onion, finely chopped
- 2 eggs
- salt and freshly ground black pepper to taste
- $1/2$ tsp finely grated ginger root

# RICE WITH BRUSSELS SPROUTS

Serves: 4

Preparation: 15'

Cooking: 25'

Level of difficulty: 1

- 1³/₄ cups/350 g short-grain rice
- 12 oz/350 g Brussels sprouts
- 2 tbsp extra-virgin olive oil
- 3 cloves garlic, finely chopped
- 1 tbsp finely chopped fresh parsley
- salt and freshly ground black pepper to taste
- 4 tbsp freshly grated Parmesan cheese

Cook the rice in 2 quarts (2 liters) of salted, boiling water for 13–15 minutes, or until tender. • Steam the Brussels sprouts for about 10 minutes, or until crunchy-tender. • Heat the oil in a large frying pan and sauté the Brussels sprouts with the garlic and parsley for 5 minutes. • Drain the rice and add it to the Brussels sprouts. Cook for 3 minutes, stirring constantly. • Season with salt and sprinkle with Parmesan. • Serve hot.

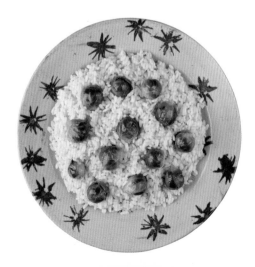

# BAKED RICE WITH MOZZARELLA AND OLIVES

Preheat the oven to 350°F/180°C/gas 4. • Grease a large ovenproof baking dish with oil. • Cook the rice in 2 quarts (2 liters) of salted, boiling water for 10 minutes. • Drain well. • Heat 3 tablespoons of oil in a large frying pan and sauté the garlic and onions until pale gold. • Add the bell peppers and sauté over high heat until softened. • Cover and cook over low heat for 10 minutes. • Stir in the tomatoes and cook for 10 minutes more. • Add the capers, olives, chile pepper, and a pinch of salt. Simmer for 1 minute. Drizzle with the remaining oil and remove from heat. • Spoon a layer of rice into the prepared dish. Cover with a layer of vegetable sauce, Mozzarella, and basil. Top with Parmesan, oregano, and cayenne pepper. • Continue to layer until all the ingredients are in the dish. • Bake for 15 minutes. • Let stand for 5 minutes then serve.

Serves: 4–6

Preparation: 30'

Cooking: 40'

Level of difficulty: 1

- 1³/₄ cups/350 g long-grain rice
- 6 tbsp extra-virgin olive oil
- 2 cloves garlic, finely chopped
- 3 onions, chopped
- 2 yellow bell peppers/ capsicums, seeded, cored, and cut into pieces
- 6 firm-ripe tomatoes, chopped
- 2 tbsp capers, rinsed of salt
- 1¹/₄ cups/150 g black olives, pitted
- 1 fresh red chile pepper, chopped
- salt to taste
- 5 oz/150 g Mozzarella cheese, thinly sliced
- 4 leaves fresh basil, torn
- 1 tsp dried oregano
- ³/₄ cup/90 g freshly grated Parmesan cheese
- ¹/₂ tsp cayenne pepper

# BAKED RICE WITH BROCCOLI

*Serves: 4*

*Preparation: 20'*

*Cooking: 45'*

*Level of difficulty: 1*

- 1³/₄ cups/350 g long-grain rice
- 4 tbsp extra-virgin olive oil
- ¹/₂ cup/60 g fine dry bread crumbs
- 1 onion, finely chopped
- 1 clove garlic, finely chopped
- 12 oz/350 g broccoli, divided into small florets
- 1 cup/125 g freshly grated Parmesan cheese
- ¹/₄ tsp freshly grated nutmeg
- 3 tbsp butter

Preheat the oven to 400°F/200°C/gas 6. • Grease a large ovenproof baking dish with oil and sprinkle with half the bread crumbs. • Cook the rice in 2 quarts (2 liters) of salted, boiling water for 10 minutes. • Drain well. • Heat the oil in a large frying pan and sauté the onion, garlic, and broccoli over medium heat for 15 minutes. • Spoon the rice into the prepared dish. Top with the onions and broccoli, reserving a few florets as a garnish. Sprinkle with Parmesan, remaining bread crumbs, and the nutmeg. Dot with the butter. • Bake for 20–25 minutes, or until golden brown. • Garnish with the reserved broccoli and serve hot

# RICE WITH MIXED VEGETABLES AND LEMON

Heat the oil in a large frying pan and sauté the tomatoes, scallions, garlic, green beans, carrots, peas, mushrooms, and bell pepper for 2 minutes. Cover and cook over low heat for 30 minutes. • Cook the rice in 2 quarts (2 liters) of salted, boiling water for 13–15 minutes, or until tender. • Drain and mix into the vegetables with the olives and saffron. • Cook for 5 minutes more. • Sprinkle with parsley, garnish with the lemon slices, and serve hot.

*Serves: 6–8*

*Preparation: 20'*

*Cooking: 50'*

*Level of difficulty: 1*

- 4 tbsp extra-virgin olive oil
- 12 oz/350 g firm-ripe tomatoes, coarsely chopped
- 3 scallions/spring onions, finely chopped
- 2 cloves garlic, finely chopped
- 8 oz/250 g green beans, cut into short lengths
- 8 oz/250 g carrots, cut into thin strips
- 2 cups/250 g peas
- 7 oz/200 g mushrooms, coarsely chopped
- 1 red bell pepper/capsicum, seeded, cored, and coarsely chopped
- 2 cups/400 g long-grain rice
- 8 black olives
- 4 strands saffron, crumbled
- 1 small bunch parsley, finely chopped
- 1 lemon, cut into slices

# AROMATIC RICE WITH GARBANZO BEANS

Serves: 4–6

Preparation: 40' +
  24 h to soak beans

Cooking: 1 h 45'

Level of difficulty: 2

Soak the garbanzo beans in cold water for 24 hours. • Drain the beans and place in a large saucepan. Pour in enough water to cover the beans by at least twice the volume. • Add the fennel seeds and bay leaves. • Bring to a boil and cover and cook over low heat for about 1$\frac{1}{2}$ hours, or until the beans are tender. • Season with salt at the end of the cooking time. Drain and transfer to a large bowl. • Cook the rice in 2 quarts (2 liters) of salted, boiling water for 13–15 minutes, or until tender. • Drain and mix with the garbanzo beans. Toss with the parsley and garlic and drizzle with the oil. • Serve hot.

- 2 cups/200 g dried garbanzo beans/ chickpeas
- 1 tsp fennel seeds
- 4 bay leaves
- salt to taste
- 1$\frac{1}{2}$ cups/300 g long-grain rice
- 4 tbsp extra-virgin olive oil
- 1 small bunch fresh parsley, finely chopped
- 2 cloves garlic, finely chopped

*Serves: 6*

*Preparation: 20'*

*Cooking: 2 h 15'*

*Level of difficulty: 2*

- 8–10 large cabbage leaves
- 4 tbsp extra-virgin olive oil
- 1 large onion, finely chopped
- 4 oz/125 g bacon, finely chopped
- 1¹/₂ lb/750 g ground pork
- 1 lb/500 g ground ham
- 8 oz/250 g ground beef
- 1 clove garlic, finely chopped
- 1 cup/250 g cooked rice
- salt and freshly ground black pepper to taste
- 1 egg
- 1 quantity Tomato Sauce (see page 950)

# CABBAGE ROLLS

**B**lanch the cabbage leaves in boiling water for 5–10 minutes, or until softened. Drain well. • Preheat the oven to 350°F/180°C/gas 4. • Set out a large baking dish. • Heat the oil in a large saucepan over medium heat. Sauté the onion and bacon for 8–10 minutes, or until lightly browned. • Mix the onion mixture, pork, ham, beef, garlic, and rice in a large bowl. Season with salt and pepper. Add the egg. • Place 3–4 tablespoons of filling in the center of each cabbage leaf. Tuck the ends over the filling and roll up. • Place the cabbage rolls in the pan seam-side down. • Pour in the tomato sauce and cover with aluminum foil. • Bake for about 2 hours, or until tender.

# STEAMED PORK MEATBALLS

Bring a large pan of salted water to a boil. •
Rinse the rice in a strainer and blanch for
2 minutes. Drain and let drip dry. Transfer to a
large plate and set aside. • Mix the pork, water
chestnuts, ginger, rice wine, cornstarch and water,
and salt in a large bowl until well mixed. • Shape
into balls about the size of chestnuts. Roll in the
rice until well coated. • Fill a wok with water and
bring to a boil. • Rinse the leaves of bok choy,
removing the tough stalks, and place in a bamboo
steamer. Arrange the meatballs on top. Balance
the steamer on chopsticks in the wok, so that the
steamer does not touch the water. Cover and
steam for 15 minutes, or until the rice is tender.
• Serve immediately, or the rice will harden.

Serves: 4

Preparation: 30'

Cooking: 20'

Level of difficulty: 2

- 1¹/₂ cups/300 g
  sticky rice
- 1 lb/500 g lean
  ground pork
- 5 oz/150 g water
  chestnuts, finely
  chopped
- 4 thin slices ginger
  root, peeled and
  very finely
  chopped
- 1 tbsp rice wine
- 1 tbsp cornstarch/
  cornflour dissolved
  in 2 tbsp water
- salt to taste
- 5–6 tender leaves
  bok choy

*Serves: 4*

*Preparation: 15'*

*Cooking: 20'*

*Level of difficulty: 1*

- **1 tbsp extra-virgin olive oil**
- **1 cup/150 g unsalted peanuts, shelled and crushed**
- **1 tbsp shredded coconut**
- **1 cup/250 ml coconut milk**
- **2 cups/500 ml water**
- **1 stalk lemon grass, thinly sliced**
- **8 curry leaves**
- **2 scallions/spring onions, thinly sliced**
- **1 tsp ground cumin**
- **$^{1}/_{2}$ tsp ground cardamom**
- **$^{1}/_{2}$ tsp ground turmeric**
- **2 cups/400 g long-grain rice**

# SPICY COCONUT RICE

Heat the oil in a saucepan and sauté the peanuts until golden brown. • Add the coconut, coconut milk, and water. Stir in the lemon grass, curry leaves, and scallions, and bring to a boil. Lower the heat and simmer for 2 minutes. •, Add the cumin, cardamom, and turmeric, and return to a boil. • Add the rice and cook until little steam bubbles begin to appear on the surface. Cover, lower the heat to very low, and simmer for 10–12 minutes, or until the rice is done. • Serve hot.

# RICE WITH CHICKEN LIVER SAUCE

C ook the rice in a large pan of salted, boiling water. • Preheat the oven to 350°F/180°C/ gas 4. • Trim and rinse the livers, drizzle with lemon juice, and set aside. • Heat the oil in a frying pan and sauté the onion and garlic until softened. • Stir in the anchovies until they dissolve in the oil. • Add the livers, stir again, and season with salt and pepper. • Drain the rice when just tender and place in an oiled baking dish. Pour the sauce over the top, toss gently. • Bake for 15 minutes. • Serve hot.

*Serves: 4*

*Preparation: 10'*

*Cooking: 45'*

*Level of difficulty: 1*

- **2 cups/400 g short-grain rice**
- **7 oz/200 g chicken livers**
- **1 lemon**
- **4 tbsp extra-virgin olive oil**
- **1 onion, finely chopped**
- **2 cloves garlic, finely chopped**
- **4 anchovy fillets**
- **salt and freshly ground black pepper to taste**

# RICE WITH ROSEMARY AND CHILE PEPPER

*Serves: 4–6*

*Preparation: 15'*

*Cooking: 25'*

*Level of difficulty: 1*

- 2 cups/400 g short-grain rice
- 6 tbsp extra-virgin olive oil
- 1 small onion
- 3–4 twigs rosemary, finely chopped
- 1 cup/250 ml dry white wine
- salt and freshly ground black pepper to taste
- 1 red chile pepper, thinly sliced
- $^1/_2$ cup/60 g freshly grated Parmesan cheese

Cook the rice in a large pan of salted, boiling water. • Heat the oil in a large frying pan and sauté the onion and rosemary for 5 minutes. • Add the wine and cook for 5 more minutes. • Season with salt and pepper and add the chile pepper. • Drain the rice when just tender and place in a heated serving bowl. • Pour the sauce over the top and toss gently with the Parmesan. • Serve hot.

671

# BLACK RICE WITH FAVA BEANS

Peel the fava beans and rinse under cold running water. Remove the film covering half the beans, and set those beans aside to be used later. • Bring the water to a boil in a small pot. Dissolve the stock cube and keep at a boil. • Place the rice in a large saucepan with just enough water to cover. Cook over medium heat for about 40 minutes, adding stock as needed, and stirring often to ensure that the rice cooks uniformly and does not stick to the pot. • Heat half the oil in a frying pan and sauté the unpeeled garlic cloves until golden, then discard them. • Add the fava beans with the film and cook for 5 minutes. • Add the rice and butter. Season with salt and add a little more stock. • When the rice has completely absorbed the liquids, season with pepper and add the rest of the fava beans. • Add the chile pepper, if using, and serve hot.

*Serves: 4*

*Preparation: 25'*

*Cooking: 1 h*

*Level of difficulty: 1*

- **2 lb/1 kg fresh fava/broad beans**
- **1 quart/1 liter cold water**
- **1 vegetable stock cube**
- **1 1/2 cups/300 g black rice**
- **2 tbsp extra-virgin olive oil**
- **2 cloves garlic**
- **2 tbsp butter**
- **salt and freshly ground black pepper to taste**
- **finely chopped fresh chile pepper (optional)**

# PILAF WITH CHICKEN

Preheat the oven to 350°F/180°C/gas 4. •
Soak the saffron in the water for 10 minutes.
• Heat half the oil in a large frying pan and sauté
the chicken 5–10 minutes, or until nicely browned.
• Drain on paper towels. • Heat the remaining oil in
a large flameproof pan and sauté the onion and bell
peppers until softened. • Add the garlic, chile,
cumin, and coriander and cook for 2–3 minutes.
Stir in the rice and the lemon zest. • Arrange the
chicken on top of the rice. • Mix the saffron into
the stock and pour over the chicken and rice.
Season with salt and pepper. • Cover with
aluminum foil and bake for 50 minutes. • Sprinkle
with the olives and serve.

*Serves: 4*

*Preparation: 30'*

*Cooking: 1 h 10'*

*Level of difficulty: 1*

- 4–6 strands saffron
- 1 tbsp hot water
- 4 tbsp extra-virgin olive oil
- 2 lb/1 kg chicken drumsticks, boned
- 1 red onion, finely chopped
- 2 red bell peppers/ capsicums, seeded and finely chopped
- 3 cloves garlic, finely chopped
- sliced fresh green and red chile pepper to taste
- 2 tsp ground cumin
- 3 tsp ground coriander seeds
- 1 1/4 cups/250 g Basmati rice
- 2 tbsp lemon zest in syrup, finely chopped
- 2 cups/500 ml hot Chicken Stock (see page 955)
- 8 black olives, to garnish

# BAKED RICE WITH WALNUTS

*Serves: 4*

*Preparation: 15'*

*Cooking: 25'*

*Level of difficulty: 1*

- **1³/₄ cups/350 g Italian Arborio rice**
- **¹/₂ cup/125 g Ricotta cheese**
- **¹/₄ tsp dried oregano**
- **1 tbsp extra-virgin olive oil**
- **salt and freshly ground black pepper to taste**
- **¹/₂ cup/60 g diced ham**
- **25 shelled walnuts, finely chopped**
- **5 oz/150 g Mozzarella cheese, cut into small cubes**
- **2 tbsp salted capers, rinsed**

Preheat the oven to 380°F/190°C/gas 5. • Cook the rice in 2 quarts (2 liters) of salted, boiling water for 13–15 minutes, or until tender. • Drain and transfer to a large bowl. Mix in the Ricotta, oregano, oil, ham, half the walnuts, and the Mozzarella. Season with salt and pepper. • Transfer to a baking dish, garnish with the capers and remaining walnuts. • Bake for 10 minutes. • Serve hot.

# LONG-GRAIN LEMON RICE WITH CHICKEN

Heat the oil in a large frying pan and sauté the scallions until softened. • Add the chicken, a few pieces at a time, and cook until browned all over. Remove from the pan. • Add the cumin, coriander, and rice, and cook for 2 minutes. • Return the chicken to the pan. Pour in the stock, lemon juice and zest, and cinnamon, and bring to a boil. • Cover and cook over low heat for 15 minutes, or until the liquid has been absorbed. • Season salt and pepper. Discard the cinnamon stick and serve.

676

*Serves: 4*

*Preparation: 15'*

*Cooking: 30'*

*Level of difficulty: 1*

- **4 tbsp extra-virgin olive oil**
- **2 scallions/spring onions, finely chopped**
- **1 lb/500 g chicken breast, sliced into thin strips**
- **2 tsp cumin seeds**
- **1 tsp ground coriander**
- **2 cups/400 g long-grain rice**
- **1 quart/1 liter Chicken Stock (see page 955)**
- **4 tbsp fresh lemon juice**
- **1 tbsp lemon zest, cut in julienne strips**
- **1 small stick cinnamon**

# MIDDLE EASTERN PILAF

Rinse the rice and let soak in cold water for 1 hour. • Heat the butter in a large saucepan and sauté the onion until softened. • Mix in the cardamom, cumin, peppercorns, turmeric, bay leaf, and salt and stir for 3 minutes. • Drain the rice and add to the pan. Stir over high heat for 2–3 minutes, or until thoroughly coated with butter. • Pour in the stock, a little at a time, and bring to a boil, stirring constantly. • Cook over medium heat for 8–10 minutes, or until nearly all the liquid has been absorbed and the mixture begins to bubble. Cover and cook over low heat for 10–15 minutes, or until the rice is *al dente*. Uncover and cook over low heat for 5 more minutes. • Add the almonds, dates, and apricots, toss well, and serve.

*Serves: 4–6*

*Preparation: 20'*
*+ 1 h to soak*

*Cooking: 35'*

*Level of difficulty: 2*

- 2 cups/400 g Basmati rice
- 6 tbsp butter
- 1 large onion, finely chopped
- 1 tsp crushed cardamom seeds
- 1 tsp cumin seeds
- 6 black peppercorns, lightly crushed
- 1 tsp ground turmeric
- 1 bay leaf
- 1 tsp salt
- 1 quart/1 liter boiling Chicken Stock (see page 955)
- $^1/_2$ cup/50 g almonds, chopped
- $^1/_2$ cup/125 g chopped dates
- $^1/_2$ cup/125 g chopped dried apricots

# RICE PILAF WITH LAMB MEATBALLS

Meatballs: Place the lamb, soaked bread, thyme, mint, parsley, salt, and pepper in a medium bowl and mix well. Shape into marble-sized balls and roll in the flour. • Heat the butter with the sage in a large frying pan and sauté the meatballs in batches until browned all over. Drain on paper towels. • Heat 3 tablespoons of oil in a large frying pan and sauté the mixed vegetables until lightly browned. Remove from the heat and set aside. • Toast the rice in the remaining oil in a large frying pan. Pour in the wine and stir until it evaporates. • Add the sautéed vegetables and season with salt and pepper. • Add the stock, cover the pan, and cook over low heat until the rice is done, about 20 minutes. • Remove from the heat and dot with the butter, letting it melt into the rice. • Toss with the meatballs and serve with the Parmesan passed separately.

*Serves: 4*

*Preparation: 25'*

*Cooking: 40'*

*Level of difficulty: 1*

**MEATBALLS**

- **10 oz/300 g ground lamb**
- **3 slices bread soaked in 4 tbsp milk**
- **1 tbsp each finely chopped thyme, mint, and parsley**
- **salt and freshly ground black pepper to taste**
- **$^1/_3$ cup/50 g all-purpose/plain flour**
- **6 tbsp butter**
- **4 leaves fresh sage**

**PILAF**

- **4 tbsp extra-virgin olive oil**
- **7 oz/200 g diced mixed vegetables,**
- **1$^3/_4$ cups/350 g long-grain rice**
- **4 tbsp dry white wine**
- **3 cups/750 ml boiling Beef Stock (see page 955)**
- **4 tbsp butter, cut up**
- **$^3/_4$ cup/90 g freshly grated Parmesan cheese**

# RICE WITH EGG, CREAM, AND PARMESAN

C ook the rice in 2 quarts (2 liters) of salted, boiling water for 13–15 minutes, or until just tender. • When the rice is almost ready, beat the egg yolks, cream, Parmesan, and a pinch of pepper in a bowl. • Drain the rice and transfer to a heated serving dish. • Pour the sauce over the hot rice, and dot with the butter. Stir quickly and serve.

*Serves: 4*

*Preparation: 5'*

*Cooking: 15'*

*Level of difficulty: 1*

- **2<sup>1</sup>/<sub>4</sub> cups/450 g short-grain rice**
- **3 fresh egg yolks**
- **<sup>1</sup>/<sub>2</sub> cup/125 ml light/single cream**
- **6 tbsp freshly grated Parmesan cheese**
- **freshly ground white pepper to taste**
- **2 tbsp butter**

# BROWN RICE PILAF WITH LEEKS

*Serves: 4*

*Preparation: 30'*

*Cooking: 25'*

*Level of difficulty: 1*

- 1 lb/500 g leeks, thinly sliced
- 1 quantity Béchamel Sauce (see page 946)
- 1 small onion, finely chopped
- 4 tbsp butter
- $1/2$ tsp saffron threads
- $1^1/_2$ cups/350 g brown rice
- 3 cups/750 ml Vegetable Stock (see page 956)
- salt and freshly ground black pepper to taste

Cook the leeks in salted, boiling water for 5–10 minutes, or until tender. Drain well. • Heat the butter in a large heavy-bottomed saucepan over medium heat. Add the onion and sauté until translucent. • Add the rice and stir over high heat for 2 minutes. • Add the stock and saffron and bring to a boil. Season with salt and pepper. Cover the pan with a piece of aluminum foil and simmer over low heat for about 25 minutes, or until the stock has all been absorbed and the rice is tender. • Prepare the Béchamel sauce and stir the leeks into it. • Place the pilaf on a heated serving dish and spoon the leek sauce over the top. • Serve hot.

683

# RICE WITH SEAFOOD

Serves: 6
Preparation: 25'
Cooking: 45'
Level of difficulty: 2

Bring the stock to a boil. • Cut the shrimp into pieces if they are very large. • Heat 2 tablespoons of oil in a large saucepan over medium heat. Sauté the onion for 8–10 minutes, or until pale golden brown. Add the garlic and chile pepper. • Add the squid and cook for 5–7 minutes over medium heat. • Add the tomatoes, season with salt and pepper, and continue cooking over low heat. • Heat the remaining oil in a medium frying pan, add the rice and stir over high heat for 1 minute. • Add the rice to the squid mixture. Pour in the wine and cook until it has evaporated. • Pour in enough stock to generously cover the rice. Lower the heat, cover, and cook for 10–15 minutes, or until the rice is tender. Add the shrimp, mussels, and clams and cook until heated through. When the rice is done, add the butter and garnish with the parsley. • Serve hot.

- 1$^{1}$/$_{2}$ quarts/1.5 liters Fish Stock (see page 958)
- 1$^{3}$/$_{4}$ lb/800 g shrimp, shelled (reserve the shells for the stock)
- 4 tbsp extra-virgin olive oil
- 1 onion, finely chopped
- 2 cloves garlic, finely chopped
- 1 chile pepper
- 14 oz/400 g small squid, cleaned and cut into rings
- 6 tomatoes, peeled and cut into cubes
- salt and freshly ground white pepper to taste
- 2 cups/400 g short-grain rice
- 4 tbsp white wine
- 3 lb/1.5 kg mussels or clams, cooked in a little water to open
- 2 tbsp butter
- 2 tbsp finely chopped parsley

# RICE WITH SQUID

Cook the rice in salted, boiling water for 15–20 minutes, or until tender. • Drain and mix in the saffron. • Heat the oil in a large saucepan over medium heat. • Sauté the squid, onions, garlic, parsley, bay leaves, tomatoes, paprika, ras-al-hanout, cumin, salt, pepper, and tomato paste for a few minutes. • Lower the heat, cover, and cook for 30 minutes, or until the squid is tender. • Spoon the squid stew onto the center of a serving plate and serve with the rice around the edges.

*Serves: 4*

*Preparation: 15'*

*Cooking: 40'*

*Level of difficulty: 1*

- **2 cups/400 g long-grain rice**
- **4–6 threads saffron, crumbled**
- **3 tbsp extra-virgin olive oil**
- **1¹/₄ lb/625 g squid, cleaned and cut into bite-size pieces**
- **2 large onions, chopped**
- **3 cloves garlic, chopped**
- **1 tbsp finely chopped parsley**
- **3 bay leaves**
- **4 tomatoes, chopped**
- **1 tbsp paprika**
- **1 tbsp ras-al-hanout**
- **1 tsp ground cumin**
- **salt and freshly ground black pepper to taste**
- **2 tbsp tomato paste**

# STUFFED TOMATOES

Serves: 4–8

Preparation: 50'

Cooking: 1 h

Level of difficulty: 1

- **8 large tomatoes**
- **salt to taste**
- **6 tbsp extra-virgin olive oil**
- **1 medium onion, finely chopped**
- **1 clove garlic, finely chopped**
- **freshly ground black pepper to taste**
- **1 cup/200 g short-grain rice**
- **3 tbsp finely chopped fresh mint**
- **1 tbsp finely chopped fresh parsley**

Cut the tops off the tomatoes and use a spoon to scoop out the flesh. Reserve the flesh. • Salt the interior of the tomatoes and place upside-down in a colander for 30 minutes. • Preheat the oven to 375°F/190°C/gas 5. • Set out a large baking dish. • Heat 4 tablespoons of oil in a large frying pan. Sauté the onion for 8–10 minutes, or until lightly browned. Add the garlic and stir in the tomato flesh. • Cook for 15–20 minutes, or until the sauce has reduced. • Season with salt and pepper. • Cook the rice in a large pot of salted boiling water for 8–10 minutes, or until the rice is almost tender. • Drain well and add to the sauce. Cook for 5 minutes more. Remove from heat and let cool. • Mix in the mint, parsley, and 1 tablespoon of oil. • Stuff the tomatoes, replace the tops, and arrange in the dish. Drizzle with the remaining oil. • Bake for 35–40 minutes. • Serve hot or at room temperature.

687

# CLASSIC PAELLA

*Serves: 6–8*

*Preparation: 40'*

*Cooking: 45'*

*Level of difficulty: 2*

P reheat the oven to 400°F/200°C/gas 6. • Heat the oil in a paella pan or very large frying pan (about 18 in/45 cm) in diameter. Sauté the garlic over medium heat for 2–3 minutes. • Discard the garlic. • Brown the chicken in the same pan for 5 minutes. • Add the rice and stir until well coated with oil. • Pour in the water and bring to a boil. • Add the snails, artichokes, green beans, peas, mussels, and eel. Season with salt and pepper. Add the bay leaf and saffron. • Continue cooking over medium-high heat until the liquid has almost all been absorbed. The rice grains should still be slightly al dente but there should still be some liquid in the pan. • Bake in the oven, uncovered, for 10 minutes. • Cover the pan with foil or parchment paper and let stand for 10 minutes before serving.

- **4 tbsp extra-virgin olive oil**
- **3 cloves garlic, whole, but lightly crushed**
- **1 chicken (or rabbit), cleaned, boned, and cut into small chunks**
- **3 cups/600 g short-grain rice**
- **1 1/2 quarts/1.5 liters boiling water**
- **2 lb/1 kg snails, cleaned and boiled**
- **2 artichoke hearts, cleaned and chopped**
- **7 oz/200 g green beans, cut in short lengths**
- **7 oz/200 g peas**
- **1 lb/500 g mussels, in shell**
- **1 lb/500 g eel, cleaned and ready to cook**
- **salt and freshly ground black pepper to taste**
- **1 bay leaf**
- **8–10 strands saffron, crumbled**

# STUFFED GRAPE LEAVES

Place the rice in a medium bowl and cover with boiling water. Let soak for 30 minutes. • Drain and set aside. If using fresh leaves, blanch them in a large pot of salted,boiling water for 3 minutes. • Drain well and dry on a clean cloth. • If using brined leaves, soak them in hot water for 1 hour to remove excess salt. • Drain well and pat dry with paper towels. • Heat 4 tablespoons of oil in a large frying pan over medium heat. Sauté the onion for 8–10 minutes, or until lightly browned. Stir in the rice. Lower the heat, cover, and cook for 5 minutes. • Add the mint and dill. Season with salt and pepper. Cover and cook for 5 more minutes over very low heat, making sure that the mixture does not stick to the pan. • Place the grape leaves, shiny-side down on a work surface. Use a tablespoon to spoon the filling onto the center of the leaves. • Fold the sides of each leaf over the filling, then fold over the top and bottom. Roll until slightly flattened. • Place a layer of stuffed leaves seam-side down in a large saucepan. • Pour in the remaining oil, water, and the lemon juice. Cover with a plate to hold the leaves firmly in position. • Cook for 50–60 minutes over medium heat, or until the liquid has reduced. • Serve hot or at room temperature.

Serves: 4

Preparation: 25' + 1 h 30' to soak

Cooking: 50–60'

Level of difficulty: 2

- 1 cup/200 g short-grain rice
- 20 fresh or preserved grape leaves
- 1/2 cup/125 ml extra-virgin olive oil
- 2 large onions, finely chopped
- 3 tbsp finely chopped fresh mint
- 1 tbsp finely chopped fresh dill
- salt and freshly ground black pepper to taste
- 1 cup/250 ml water
- 1 1/2 tbsp fresh lemon juice

# CHICKEN AND APRICOTS WITH RICE

**P**reheat the oven to 350°F/180°C/gas 4. •
Butter an ovenproof baking dish. • Heat the
oil in a large frying pan and sauté the onion until
softened. • Add the chicken and apricots.
Season with salt and pepper. Add the raisins and
cinnamon and pour in enough hot water to cover.
• Cover and cook over low heat until the chicken
is tender. • Meanwhile, cook the rice in 2 quarts
(2 liters) of salted, boiling water for 13–15
minutes, or until tender. • Drain well and spoon
half the rice into the prepared dish. Top with the
chicken and its sauce. Finish with the remaining
rice. • Cover with aluminum foil and bake for
20 minutes. • Serve hot.

Serves: 4–6

Preparation: 25'

Cooking: 1 h

Level of difficulty: 1

- 4 tbsp extra-virgin olive oil
- 1 onion, finely chopped
- 4–6 chicken thighs, boned
- 1/2 cup/125 g coarsely chopped dried apricots
- salt and freshly ground black pepper to taste
- 2 tbsp golden raisins/sultanas
- 1 tsp ground cinnamon
- 1 cup/250 ml water
- 1 1/4 cups/250 g Basmati rice

# RICE WITH ORANGE

Serves: 4

Preparation: 15'

Cooking: 25'

Level of difficulty: 2

- 1¹/₄ cups/250 g short-grain rice
- 2 tbsp extra-virgin olive oil
- 2 tbsp whole-wheat/ wholemeal flour
- 6 tbsp hot water
- grated zest and juice of 2 oranges
- salt to taste
- ¹/₈ tsp dried chile pepper
- 1 egg yolk
- ¹/₈ tsp freshly grated nutmeg

Cook the rice in 2 quarts (2 liters) of salted, boiling water for 13–15 minutes, or until tender. • Drain well. • Meanwhile, heat the oil in a medium frying pan over medium heat and stir in the flour to make a paste. Gradually add the hot water and orange juice, stirring constantly with a wooden spoon until the mixture begins to thicken. Season with salt and chile. • When the mixture is creamy, add the nutmeg and egg yolk, mixing quickly. Remove from the heat. • Spoon the rice into a heated serving plate, and spoon the orange sauce over the top. • Sprinkle with the orange zest and serve hot.

# NEAPOLITAN RICE PIE

Serves: 6–8
Preparation: 30'
Cooking: 1 h 30'
Level of difficulty: 3

694

Sauté the onion in the oil until soft. • Add the tomato paste diluted in 1 cup (250 ml) of stock, the mushrooms and peas. Season with salt and pepper. Cook for 5 minutes, then add the sausage. • Cook for 20 minutes, then remove from heat. Slice the sausage. • Place the beef in a bowl with salt, pepper, 1 egg, 2 tablespoons of bread crumbs, and 1 tablespoon of Parmesan. Shape into small balls and roll in the flour. • Heat the frying oil in a frying pan and fry the meatballs until golden brown. Drain on paper towels. • Heat half the mushroom sauce in a pan. When hot, add the rice. Stir in $^1/_2$ cup (125 ml) of the stock. Cook, stirring often, until the stock is absorbed. Continue adding stock, $^1/_2$ cup (125 ml) at a time, stirring until the rice is tender, 15–18 minutes. • When cooked, stir in 2 oz (60 g) of lard, half the Parmesan, and the remaining eggs. Mix well and set aside to cool. • Add 2 oz (60 g) of lard and the meatballs to the other half of the sauce. Simmer in a saucepan over low heat. • Heat the remaining lard in a small frying pan and sauté the chicken livers. Remove from heat and season with salt. • Butter a large mold and sprinkle with 3 tablespoons of bread crumbs. • Place almost all the rice in the mold. Fill the center with meatballs, sauce, chicken livers, Mozzarella, sausage, and Parmesan. Cover with the remaining rice. Sprinkle with the remaining bread crumbs. • Bake in a preheated oven at 350°F/180°C/gas 4 for 30 minutes. • Let rest for 5 minutes before turning out onto a serving dish.

- 2 oz/60 g dried porcini mushrooms, soaked, and chopped
- 1 small onion, finely chopped
- 3 tbsp extra-virgin olive oil
- 2 tbsp tomato paste
- $1^1/_2$ quarts/1.5 liters Beef Stock (see page 955)
- 8 oz/250 g fresh or frozen peas
- salt and freshly ground black pepper to taste
- 1 Italian pork sausage
- 12 oz/350 g ground beef
- 3 eggs
- $^1/_2$ cup/60 g fine dry bread crumbs
- $^1/_2$ cup/60 g freshly grated Parmesan cheese
- $^1/_2$ cup/75 g all-purpose/plain flour
- 1 cup/250 ml frying oil
- $2^1/_2$ cups/500 g short-grain rice
- 7 oz/200 g lard
- 8 oz/250 g Mozzarella, sliced
- 7 oz/350 g chicken livers, cleaned and chopped

# RICE WITH PESTO

Cook the rice in a large pan of salted, boiling water. • Meanwhile, chop the basil, salt, garlic, pine nuts, Parmesan, and Pecorino in a food processor with the oil until smooth. • Drain the rice, adding 2 tablespoons of cooking water to the pesto. • Place the rice in a heated serving dish. Spoon the pesto over the top, toss well, and serve hot.

*Serves: 4*

*Preparation: 10'*

*Cooking: 15'*

*Level of difficulty: 1*

- 2 cups/400 g short-grain rice
- 2 large bunches basil, rinsed and dried
- salt to taste
- 3 cloves garlic
- 3 tbsp pine nuts
- 2 tbsp freshly grated Parmesan cheese
- 2 tbsp freshly grated Pecorino cheese
- $^1/_2$ cup/125 ml extra-virgin olive oil

# RICE WITH FONTINA

*Serves: 4*

*Preparation: 10'*

*Cooking: 45'*

*Level of difficulty: 1*

- 1¹/₂ cups/300 g short-grain rice
- 4 oz/125 g Fontina cheese, cut into small cubes
- 4 tbsp butter, cut up
- salt to taste

Cook the rice in 2 quarts (2 liters) of salted, boiling water for 13–15 minutes, or until tender. • Drain, reserving 2 tablespoons of the cooking water • Transfer the rice to a large bowl and mix in the Fontina. Stir in the cooking water until the cheese is melted. • Dot with the butter, letting it melt into the rice. • Season with salt, mix again, and serve

# RICE MEATBALLS IN TOMATO SAUCE

**M**eatballs: Hard boil an egg for about ten minutes. Cool under cold running water, peel, and chop finely. • Soak the bread in the milk. • In a fairly large bowl, mix the beef and pork together, then add the rice and the lightly beaten yolks of the 2 remaining eggs. • Season with salt and pepper. • Add the bread soaked in milk, the hard-boiled egg, garlic, mint, and parsley. Knead the ingredients together, then set aide to rest for 3 hours. • Shape the mixture into meatballs about the size of a walnut. • Sauce: Sauté the onion in the oil in a large frying pan until golden brown. • Add the tomatoes. Season with the chile peppers, cumin, salt, and pepper. Stir and cook until the sauce reduces a little. • Pour in the stock and bring to a boil over medium heat. • Add the meatballs and simmer over low heat for 15 more minutes. • Serve hot.

Serves: 4–6

Preparation: 15'
  + 3 h to rest

Cooking: 45'

Level of difficulty: 1

**MEATBALLS**

- 3 eggs
- 3 oz/90 g bread, crusts removed
- 4 tbsp milk
- 15 oz/450 g ground beef
- 15 oz/450 g ground pork
- $1/2$ cup/100 g boiled rice
- salt and freshly ground black pepper to taste
- 2 cloves garlic, finely chopped
- 2 tbsp finely chopped mint
- 2 tbsp finely chopped parsley

**SPICY SAUCE**

- 1 onion, finely chopped
- 6 large tomatoes, peeled and chopped
- 4 tbsp extra-virgin olive oil
- 2 chile peppers, finely chopped
- $1/2$ tsp cumin seeds
- $2/3$ cup/150 ml Beef Stock (see page 955)

# THAI RICE CAKES

Heat 3 tablespoons of oil in a frying pan and sauté the garlic. • Add the bell peppers, half the leeks, and parsley and sauté for 3 minutes. • Add the rice and and cook over high heat. • Pour in enough water to cover. Bring to a boil, turn off heat and cover. Leave until the rice has absorbed the liquid, about 15 minutes. Let cool. • Beat in the egg white and spread the mixture out in a layer about 1 in (2.5 cm) thick. • Cut into 4 in (10 cm) disks. • Heat 2 tablespoons of oil in a frying pan and fry until brown on both sides. Season with salt and pepper. • Cut the remaining leeks in thin strips and fry in the remaining oil. • Garnish the rice with the leeks and serve.

*Serves: 4*

*Preparation: 45'*

*Cooking: 30'*

*Level of difficulty: 1*

- $^1/_2$ cup/125 ml extra-virgin olive oil
- 1 garlic clove, finely chopped
- 1 large red bell pepper/capsicum, finely chopped
- 2 leeks, finely chopped
- 2 tbsp finely chopped parsley
- $1^3/_4$ cups/350 g Thai rice
- 1 egg white
- salt and freshly ground black pepper to taste

# AKED RICE WITH SARDINES

ves: 4–6

paration: 10'

oking: 45'

el of difficulty: 1

1/4 cups/450 g hort-grain rice

tbsp extra-virgin live oil

small bunch arsley

cloves garlic

oz/90 g bread rumbs

round chile epper to taste

alt to taste

4 oz/400 g fresh ardines, filleted

Cook the rice in a large pan of salted, boiling water until tender. • Drain well and toss with 3 tablespoons of oil and a pinch of salt. • Finely chop the parsley and garlic together. Mix with the bread crumbs, a little salt, and the chile pepper. • Preheat the oven to 400° F/200°C/gas 6. • Grease a baking dish. • Spread half the rice over the bottom of the dish and cover with the sardines. Cover with the remaining rice. Sprinkle with the aromatic bread crumbs. • Drizzle with the remaining oil. • Bake for about 25 minutes, or until the top is browned. • Serve hot.

# RISOTTI

# SQUASH AND SHRIMP RISOTTO

M elt 3 tablespoons of butter in a large frying pan and sauté the onion until softened.
• Add the squash and season with salt and pepper. Cook for 5 minutes. • Add the rice and cook for 3 minutes, stirring constantly. • Stir in the shrimp.
• Pour in the wine and let it evaporate. • Stir in $^{1}/_{2}$ cup (125 ml) of the stock. Cook, stirring often, until the stock is absorbed. Continue adding the stock, $^{1}/_{2}$ cup (125 ml) at a time, stirring often until each addition is absorbed, until the rice is tender, 15–18 minutes. • Add the remaining butter and sprinkle with the Parmesan.
• Serve hot.

- 5 tbsp butter
- 1 onion, finely chopped
- 10 oz/300 g winter squash or pumpkin, cut in small cubes
- 16 large shrimp/ prawns, shelled and chopped
- salt and freshly ground black pepper to taste
- 2 cups/400 g Italian Arborio rice
- $^{1}/_{2}$ cup/125 ml dry white wine
- 3 cups/750 ml boiling Vegetable Stock (see page 956)
- $^{1}/_{2}$ cup/60 g freshly grated Parmesan cheese

704

| Serves: 4 |
| Preparation: 10' |
| Cooking: 25' |
| Level of difficulty: 2 |

- 4 tbsp butter
- 2 tbsp finely chopped onion
- 1³/₄ cups/350 g Italian Arborio rice
- ¹/₂ cup/125 ml dry white wine
- 1 quart/1 liter boiling Beef Stock (see page 955)
- ³/₄ cup/90 g freshly grated Parmesan cheese
- salt and freshly ground white pepper to taste
- 3 tbsp cooking juices from roast meat or poultry (optional)
- 2 fresh white truffles, very thinly sliced (optional)

# SIMPLE PARMESAN RISOTTO

Melt half the butter in a large saucepan. Add the onion and cover and cook over low heat until softened. • Add the rice, turn the heat up to high, and cook, stirring constantly, for 3–4 minutes. • Pour in the wine and let it evaporate. • Over medium heat, stir in ¹/₂ cup (125 ml) of the stock. Cook, stirring often, until the stock is absorbed. Continue adding the stock, ¹/₂ cup (125 ml) at a time, stirring often until each addition is absorbed, until the rice is tender, 15–18 minutes. • Stir in half the Parmesan and season with salt and pepper. • Turn off the heat, cover tightly, and let stand for 2 minutes to finish cooking. • Dot with the remaining butter and stir in the remaining cheese. • Add the roast meat juices, if using, and stir. • Serve hot, with shavings of truffle, if liked.

# SCAMPI RISOTTO

Bring the water to a boil in a deep saucepan with the garlic and bay leaf. Boil for 10 minutes. • Add the scampi and simmer for 10 minutes. Remove the scampi with a slotted spoon and peel them, reserving the flesh. • Return the shells and heads to the stock and boil for 20 minutes. • Melt half the butter with the oil in a large saucepan and sauté the shallot until softened. • Add the rice and cook for 3 minutes, stirring constantly. • Pour in the wine and let it evaporate. Season with salt and pepper. • Add the scampi. • Stir in $1/2$ cup (125 ml) of the stock. Cook, stirring often, until the stock is absorbed. Continue adding the stock, $1/2$ cup (125 ml) at a time, stirring often until each addition is absorbed, until the rice is tender, 15–18 minutes. • Remove from the heat. Stir in the remaining butter, sprinkle with Parmesan, and serve.

*Serves: 6*

*Preparation: 50'*

*Cooking: 40'*

*Level of difficulty: 1*

- 1 quart/1 liter cold water
- 1 clove garlic
- 1 bay leaf
- 1 lb/500 g raw scampi, in shell
- 6 tbsp butter
- 4 tbsp extra-virgin olive oil
- 1 shallot, finely chopped
- 2 cups/400 g Italian Arborio rice
- $1/2$ cup/125 ml dry white wine
- salt and freshly ground black pepper to taste
- $3/4$ cup/100 g freshly grated Parmesan cheese

# RISOTTO WITH MASCARPONE AND PROSCIUTTO

Melt half the butter in a large saucepan and sauté the onion until softened. Discard the onion and add the remaining butter. • Add the rice and cook for 3 minutes, stirring constantly. • Pour in the wine and let it evaporate. • Stir in $1/2$ cup (125 ml) of the stock. Cook, stirring often, until the stock is absorbed. Continue adding the stock, $1/2$ cup (125 ml) at a time, stirring often until each addition is absorbed, until the rice is tender, 15–18 minutes. • When the rice is almost cooked, add the prosciutto and season with salt and pepper. Stir in the Mascarpone and drizzle with the oil. • Serve hot.

708

Serves: 4–6

Preparation: 20'

Cooking: 40'

Level of difficulty: 1

- 6 tbsp butter
- 1 onion, cut into quarters
- 2 cups/400 g Italian Arborio rice
- 1 cup/250 ml dry white wine
- 1 quart/1 liter Beef Stock (see page 955)
- 4 oz/125 g prosciutto/Parma ham
- salt and freshly ground black pepper to taste
- $2/3$ cup/150 g Mascarpone cheese
- 4 tbsp extra-virgin olive oil

# SPINACH RISOTTO WITH HAM AND CHEESE

*Serves: 4–6*

*Preparation: 25'*

*Cooking: 40'*

*Level of difficulty: 1*

- **14 oz/400 g spinach leaves**
- **6 tbsp extra-virgin olive oil**
- **2 cloves garlic, finely chopped**
- **3 tbsp butter**
- **$^1/_2$ onion, finely chopped**
- **2 cups/400 g Italian Arborio rice**
- **6 tbsp dry white wine**
- **$1^1/_2$ quarts/1.5 liters boiling Vegetable Stock (see page 956)**
- **$1^1/_2$ cups/180 g diced ham**
- **6 oz/180 g Taleggio or Fontina cheese**
- **salt and freshly ground black pepper to taste**
- **10 leaves fresh basil, torn**

Cook the spinach in a little salted water until tender. Drain well and chop finely. • Heat the oil in a saucepan and sauté the garlic until pale gold. • Add the spinach and cook for 5 minutes. • Melt the butter in a large frying pan and sauté the onion until softened. Remove from heat and add the rice. Return to high heat. Pour in the wine and let it evaporate. • Stir in $^1/_2$ cup (125 ml) of the stock. Cook, stirring often, until the stock is absorbed. Continue adding the stock, $^1/_2$ cup (125 ml) at a time, stirring often until each addition is absorbed, until the rice is tender, 15–18 minutes. • Add the spinach, ham, and cheese. • Season with salt and pepper and sprinkle with the basil. • Serve hot.

# GRILLED SCALLOPS WITH RISOTTO

S eparate the scallops from their coral. Sprinkle with the basil and lemon zest. • Wrap each scallop in a slice of pancetta. • Melt half the butter in a frying pan and sauté the leek until softened. • Melt the remaining butter in a large frying pan. Add the rice and stir for 2 minutes. • Pour in the wine and let it evaporate. • Add the coral. • Stir in $1/2$ cup (125 ml) of the stock. Cook, stirring often, until the stock is absorbed. Continue adding the stock, $1/2$ cup (125 ml) at a time, stirring often, until the rice is tender, 15–18 minutes. Season with salt and pepper. • Broil (grill) the scallops on each side for 2 minutes. Drizzle with the lemon juice. • Stir in the cream and serve hot with the scallops.

*Serves: 6*

*Preparation: 30'*

*Cooking: 50'*

*Level of difficulty: 2*

- **24 scallops, shucked**
- **20 leaves fresh basil, torn**
- **grated zest and juice of 1 lemon**
- **12 slices fatty pancetta or bacon**
- **1 small leek, white part only, thinly sliced**
- **6 tbsp butter**
- **2 cups/400 g Italian Arborio rice**
- **6 tbsp dry white wine**
- **1 quart/1 liter boiling Fish Stock (see page 958)**
- **salt and freshly ground black pepper to taste**
- **6 tbsp heavy/ double cream**

# RICE WITH SQUASH AND BORLOTTI BEANS

*Serves: 4–6*

*Preparation: 15'*

*Cooking: 15'*

*Level of difficulty: 1*

- 1 tbsp butter, cut up
- 2 tbsp extra-virgin olive oil
- 1 small onion, finely chopped
- 7 oz/200 g winter squash or pumpkin, cut into small cubes
- 2 cups/400 g Italian Arborio rice
- salt and freshly ground black pepper to taste
- $^1/_2$ cup/125 ml dry white wine
- $2^1/_2$ cups/625 ml Vegetable Stock (see page 956)
- 2 cups/200 g cooked borlotti beans
- 1 cup/125 freshly grated Parmesan cheese

Heat the butter and oil in a pressure cooker and sauté the onion until softened. • Add the squash and the rice and cook for 3 minutes, stirring constantly. Season with salt and pepper. • Pour in the wine and let it evaporate. • Pour in the stock, close the pressure cooker, and cook for 7 minutes. • Release the steam, open the pressure cooker, and add the beans. • Sprinkle with Parmesan and serve hot.

# ORANGE RISOTTO WITH FONTINA CHEESE

Peel the oranges, taking care to use only the outermost orange layer. Chop the peel into tiny dice. Squeeze the juice and set aside. • Melt three-quarters of the butter in a small saucepan and sauté the onion until softened. • Add the rice and cook for 2 minutes, stirring constantly. • Pour in the wine and let it evaporate. • Stir in $1/2$ cup (125 ml) of the stock. Cook, stirring often, until the stock is absorbed. Continue adding the stock, $1/2$ cup (125 ml) at a time, stirring often until each addition is absorbed, until the rice is tender, 15–18 minutes. • Stir in the Fontina 5 minutes before the rice is cooked. • Season with salt and pepper and pour in the orange juice. Stir well and serve.

*Serves: 4*

*Preparation: 10'*

*Cooking: 30'*

*Level of difficulty: 1*

- **2 large oranges**
- **$1/2$ cup/125 g butter, cut up**
- **1 small onion, finely chopped**
- **2 cups/400 g Italian Arborio rice**
- **$1/2$ cup/125 ml dry white wine**
- **$1^1/2$ quarts/1.5 liters Chicken Stock (see page 955)**
- **4 oz/125 g Fontina cheese, cut into cubes**
- **salt and freshly ground white pepper to taste**

# TOMATO RISOTTO

*Serves: 4*

*Preparation: 15'*

*Cooking: 25'*

*Level of difficulty: 2*

- **6 tbsp butter**
- **1 onion, finely chopped**
- **2 cloves garlic, finely chopped**
- **6 leaves fresh basil, torn**
- **2 tbsp extra-virgin olive oil**
- **1 lb/500 g firm-ripe tomatoes, peeled and chopped**
- **pinch of sugar**
- **salt and freshly ground black pepper to taste**
- **2 cups/400 g Italian Arborio rice**
- **1$^1$/$_4$ quarts/1.25 liters Beef Stock (see page 955)**
- **4 tbsp freshly grated Parmesan cheese**

Melt half the butter with the oil in a large saucepan. Sauté the onion, garlic, and basil over medium heat for 5 minutes, or until the onion has softened. • Stir in the tomatoes, sugar, salt, and pepper. Cook for 5 minutes more. • Add the rice and cook for 2 minutes, stirring constantly. • Stir in $^1$/$_2$ cup (125 ml) of the stock. Cook, stirring often, until the stock is absorbed. Continue adding the stock, $^1$/$_2$ cup (125 ml) at a time, stirring often until each addition is absorbed, until the rice is tender, 15–18 minutes. • Stir in the remaining butter and the Parmesan and serve.

# TOMATO AND PINE NUT RISOTTO

Melt half the butter in a medium saucepan and sauté the basil and garlic until pale gold. • Stir in the tomatoes and season with salt and pepper. Cook over low heat for 15 minutes. • Brown the pine nuts in the oil in a large frying pan over medium-high heat. • Stir in the rice and cook for 2 minutes. • Pour in the wine and let it evaporate. • Stir in $1/2$ cup (125 ml) of the stock. Cook, stirring often, until the stock is absorbed. Continue adding the stock, $1/2$ cup (125 ml) at a time, stirring often until each addition is absorbed, until the rice is tender, 15–18 minutes. • Stir in the tomato sauce about halfway through the cooking time. • Remove from the heat. Stir in the remaining butter and the Pecorino. • Serve hot.

- 6 tbsp butter
- 6 leaves fresh basil, torn
- 2 cloves garlic, finely chopped
- 12 oz/350 g firm-ripe tomatoes, peeled and coarsely chopped
- salt and freshly ground black pepper to taste
- 2 tbsp pine nuts
- 4 tbsp extra-virgin olive oil
- 2 cups/400 g Italian Arborio rice
- 1 cup/250 ml dry white wine
- 1 quart/1 liter Beef Stock (see page 955)
- $1/2$ cup/60 g freshly grated Pecorino cheese

716

Serves: 4

Preparation: 30'

Cooking: 1 h

Level of difficulty: 1

- **14 oz/400 g bell peppers/ capsicum, mixed colors**
- **4 tbsp butter**
- **1 tbsp extra-virgin olive oil**
- **1 onion, finely chopped**
- **12 oz/350 g firm-ripe tomatoes, peeled and coarsely chopped**
- **1 tsp dried oregano**
- **salt and freshly ground black pepper to taste**
- **2 cups/400 g Italian Arborio rice**
- **1 quart/1 liter Beef Stock (see page 956)**
- **4 tbsp freshly grated Parmesan cheese**

# BELL PEPPER RISOTTO

Clean the peppers, removing the seeds and core. Slice each into 4–6 pieces and place under the broiler (grill) until the skins are blackened. Remove the skins and rinse. Cut in thin strips. • Heat half the butter with the oil in a medium saucepan and sauté half the onion until softened. • Stir in the tomatoes, peppers, oregano, salt, and pepper and cook over low heat until the sauce reduces by half. • Melt the remaining butter in a large frying pan and sauté the remaining onion until lightly browned. • Add the rice and stir in $1/2$ cup (125 ml) of the stock. Cook, stirring often, until the stock is absorbed. Continue adding the stock, $1/2$ cup (125 ml) at a time, stirring often until each addition is absorbed, until the rice is tender, 15–18 minutes. • Add the pepper sauce to the rice about halfway through the cooking time. Stir in the Parmesan just before serving.

# RISOTTO WITH APPLES

P eel and dice the apples and soak them in the wine for 20 minutes. • Heat 3 tablespoons of butter and the oil in a large frying pan and sauté the onion until softened. • Add the wine and apples and cook until the wine evaporates. • Add the rice and cook for 3 minutes, stirring often. • Stir in $^1/_2$ cup (125 ml) of the stock. Cook, stirring often, until the stock is absorbed. Continue adding the stock, $^1/_2$ cup (125 ml) at a time, stirring often until each addition is absorbed, until the rice is tender, 15–18 minutes. • Stir in the cream and season with salt. Add the nutmeg and parsley. • Serve hot.

*Serves: 4*

*Preparation: 30'*

*Cooking: 40'*

*Level of difficulty: 1*

- **2 tart apples, such as Granny Smiths**
- **2 cups/500 ml dry white wine**
- **4 tbsp butter**
- **1 tbsp extra-virgin olive oil**
- **1 onion, finely chopped**
- **2 cups/400 g Italian Arborio rice**
- **2 cups/500 ml Vegetable Stock (see page 956)**
- **6 tbsp heavy/ double cream**
- **salt to taste**
- **$^1/_4$ tsp freshly grated nutmeg**
- **1 tbsp finely chopped fresh parsley**

# BROWN RICE, LEEK AND SPINACH PILAF

*Serves: 4*

*Preparation: 20'*

*Cooking: 55'*

*Level of difficulty: 1*

- **2 leeks**
- **4 tbsp extra-virgin olive oil**
- **2 cloves garlic, finely chopped**
- **4 tbsp pine nuts**
- **1 lb/500 g spinach leaves, coarsely chopped**
- **2 cups/400 g brown rice**
- **1 cup/250 ml dry white wine**
- **3 cups/750 ml boiling Beef Stock (see page 955)**
- **salt and freshly ground white pepper to taste**

Clean the leeks and chop finely, using part of the green section as well. • Heat the oil in a large frying pan and sauté the garlic and pine nuts until pale golden brown. • Blanch the spinach in salted, boiling water for 1 minute. Drain well. • Add to the pan with the leeks and cook for 3 minutes. • Add the rice and cook for 3 minutes, stirring constantly. • Pour in the wine and let it evaporate. • Add the stock, cover, and cook over low heat for 40 minutes, or until the rice is tender. • Season with salt and pepper and serve.

# RISOTTO WITH SAUSAGE AND SAVOY CABBAGE

Rinse the cabbage leaves and pat dry. Slice into thin strips. • Melt half the butter in a small saucepan and sauté the onion until softened. • Add the sausage and cook until browned all over. • Add the rice and cook for 3 minutes, stirring constantly. • Pour in the wine and let it evaporate. • Stir in $^1/_2$ cup (125 ml) of the stock. Cook, stirring often, until the stock is absorbed. Continue adding the stock, $^1/_2$ cup (125 ml) at a time, stirring often until each addition is absorbed, until the rice is tender, 15–18 minutes. • Melt the remaining butter in a frying pan and sauté the cabbage over high heat for 3 minutes. Season with salt and pepper and add the nutmeg. • Stir the cabbage into the risotto and remove from the heat. • Sprinkle with the Parmesan and serve hot.

Serves: 4

Preparation: 30'

Cooking: 40'

Level of difficulty: 1

- 10 oz/300 g Savoy cabbage, stalks removed
- 4 tbsp butter
- 1 onion, finely chopped
- 8 oz/250 g Italian sausage, cut into small chunks
- 2 cups/400 g Italian Arborio rice
- 1 tbsp dry white wine
- 1 quart/1 liter boiling Beef Stock (see page 955)
- salt and freshly ground black pepper to taste
- $^1/_4$ tsp freshly grated nutmeg
- $^1/_2$ cup/60 g freshly grated Parmesan cheese

# WHITE GRAPE RISOTTO

Rinse the grapes, drain well, and peel. • Melt the butter in a large frying pan and sauté the onion until softened. • Add the rice and cook for 3 minutes, stirring constantly. • Pour in the wine and cook until evaporated. • Stir in $^{1}/_{2}$ cup (125 ml) of the stock. Cook, stirring often, until the stock is absorbed. Continue adding the stock, $^{1}/_{2}$ cup (125 ml) at a time, stirring often until each addition is absorbed, until the rice is tender, 15–18 minutes. • Add the grapes, chives, and parsley. Season with salt and pepper. Sprinkle with Parmesan and serve.

- 1 bunch white grapes, preferably seedless
- 4 tbsp butter
- 1 onion, finely chopped
- 2 cups/400 g Italian Arborio rice
- 1 cup/250 ml dry white wine
- 1 quart/1 liter boiling Vegetable Stock (see page 956)
- small bunch chives, chopped
- 1 tbsp finely chopped fresh parsley
- salt and freshly ground white pepper to taste
- $^{3}/_{4}$ cup/90 g freshly grated Parmesan cheese

# CREAM AND PINE NUT RISOTTO

- 4 tbsp extra-virgin olive oil
- 4 shallots, finely chopped
- 2 tbsp hot water
- 2 cups/400 g Italian Arborio rice
- $^1/_2$ cup/125 ml dry white wine
- 1 quart/1 liter boiling Vegetable Stock (see page 956)
- salt and freshly ground black pepper to taste
- 4 tbsp heavy/ double cream
- $^1/_2$ cup/60 g Parmesan cheese, in flakes
- 4 tbsp pine nuts, toasted
- basil leaves, to garnish

Heat the oil in a large frying pan and sauté the shallots until softened. Add the hot water and cook for 10 minutes. • Add the rice and cook for 3 minutes, stirring constantly. • Pour in the wine and let it evaporate. • Stir in $^1/_2$ cup (125 ml) of the stock. Cook, stirring often, until the stock is absorbed. Continue adding the stock, $^1/_2$ cup (125 ml) at a time, stirring often until each addition is absorbed, until the rice is tender, 15–18 minutes. • Season with salt and pepper and stir in the cream and Parmesan. • Garnish with the pine nuts and basil and serve hot.

# RISOTTO WITH PROVOLONE AND PISTACHIOS

Serves: 4

Preparation: 15'

Cooking: 30'

Level of difficulty: 1

- 6 tbsp butter
- 3 shallots, finely chopped
- 2 cups/400 g Italian Arborio rice
- salt and freshly ground black pepper to taste
- 1 cup/250 ml dry white wine
- 3 cups/750 ml boiling Beef Stock (see page 955)
- 3 oz/90 g smoked Provolone cheese, cut into cubes
- 3 tbsp coarsely chopped or whole pistachios
- $^1/_2$ cup/60 g freshly grated Parmesan cheese

Melt half the butter in a large frying pan and sauté the shallots until softened. • Add the rice and cook for 3 minutes, stirring constantly. Season with salt and pepper. • Pour in the wine and let it evaporate. • Stir in $^1/_2$ cup (125 ml) of the stock. Cook, stirring often, until the stock is absorbed. Continue adding the stock, $^1/_2$ cup (125 ml) at a time, stirring often until each addition is absorbed, until the rice is tender, 15–18 minutes. •. Add the Provolone and pistachios. Cook for 2 minutes, then remove from the heat. • Add the remaining butter and Parmesan and mix well. Cover the pan and let rest for 2 minutes before serving.

# SAFFRON RISOTTO WITH FAVA BEANS AND SCALLOPS

Shuck the scallops and eliminate the coral. Carefully rinse the shellfish, then chop coarsely. • Blanch the fava beans in salted, boiling water for 5 minutes. Drain well. • Heat the oil in a large frying pan and sauté the leek until softened. • Add the rice and cook for 3 minutes, stirring constantly. • Pour in the wine and let it evaporate. Season with salt and pepper. • Add the saffron, fava beans, and scallops. Stir in $^1/_2$ cup (125 ml) of the stock. Cook, stirring often, until the stock is absorbed. Continue adding the stock, $^1/_2$ cup (125 ml) at a time, stirring often until each addition is absorbed, until the rice is tender, 15–18 minutes. • Dot with the butter and season with extra pepper, if liked. • Serve hot.

Serves: 4

Preparation: 25'

Cooking: 30'

Level of difficulty: 2

- **8 scallops**
- **2 cups/200 g shelled fava/ broad beans**
- **3 tbsp extra-virgin olive oil**
- **1 leek, white part only, finely chopped**
- **2 cups/400 g Italian Arborio rice**
- **6 tbsp dry white wine**
- **salt and freshly ground black pepper to taste**
- **1$^1/_2$ quarts/1.5 boiling Vegetable Stock (see page 956)**
- **4–6 strands saffron, crumbled**
- **4 tbsp butter**

# RISOTTO WITH PEARS AND GORGONZOLA

Serves: 4

Preparation: 20'

Cooking: 25'

Level of difficulty: 2

- 2 firm-ripe pears, peeled and cut in small dice
- 2 tbsp fresh lemon juice
- 2 tbsp butter
- 2 shallots, finely chopped
- 3 stalks celery, finely chopped
- 2 cups/400 g Italian Arborio rice
- $1/2$ cup/125 ml dry white wine
- 1 quart/1 liter boiling Vegetable Stock (see page 956)
- 5 oz/150 g Gorgonzola cheese, cut into small cubes
- salt to taste
- $1/8$ tsp freshly grated nutmeg

Drizzle the pears with the lemon juice. • Melt the butter in a frying pan and sauté the shallots and celery until softened. • Add two-thirds of the pears and cook for 1 minute. • Add the rice and cook for 3 minutes, stirring constantly. • Pour in the wine and let it evaporate. • Stir in $1/2$ cup (125 ml) of the stock. Cook, stirring often, until the stock is absorbed. Continue adding the stock, $1/2$ cup (125 ml) at a time, stirring often until each addition is absorbed, until the rice is tender, 15–18 minutes. • Remove from heat and add the Gorgonzola and remaining pear. Season with the salt and nutmeg, stir well, and serve.

# RISOTTO WITH SALAMI AND PEAS

Heat the oil and butter in a large frying pan and sauté the onion and mushrooms for 5 minutes. • Add the salami and cook for 3 more minutes. • Add the rice and peas and cook for 3 minutes, stirring constantly. • Stir in $1/2$ cup (125 ml) of the stock. Cook, stirring often, until the stock is absorbed. Continue adding the stock, $1/2$ cup (125 ml) at a time, stirring often until each addition is absorbed, until the rice is tender, 15–18 minutes. Season with salt and pepper. • Sprinkle with the Parmesan, and serve.

*Serves: 6*

*Preparation: 20'*

*Cooking: 30'*

*Level of difficulty: 1*

- 2 tbsp extra-virgin olive oil
- 2 tbsp butter
- 1 onion, finely chopped
- 10 oz/300 g sliced mushrooms
- 5 oz/150 g diced salami
- $2^1/4$ cups/450 g Italian Arborio rice
- $1^1/2$ cups/180 g frozen peas, thawed
- $1^1/4$ quarts/1.25 liters boiling Vegetable or Chicken Stock (see pages 955 or 956)
- salt and freshly ground black pepper to taste
- $1/2$ cup/60 g grated Parmesan cheese

# RISOTTO WITH CHICKEN, ARUGULA, AND BELL PEPPERS

*Serves: 4*

*Preparation: 20'*

*Cooking: 40'*

*Level of difficulty: 1*

- 1 red bell pepper/capsicum, quartered and seeded
- 1¹/₂ quarts/1.5 liters Chicken Stock (see page 955), boiled with ³/₄ cup/180 ml dry white wine
- 4 tbsp butter
- 2 tbsp extra-virgin olive oil
- 1 leek, cut into wheels
- 2 cloves garlic, finely chopped
- 2 cups/400 g Italian Arborio rice
- 7 oz/200 g smoked chicken, sliced into thin strips
- small bunch arugula/rocket, shredded
- finely chopped lemon zest, to garnish (optional)

Broil (grill) the bell pepper until blackened. Place in a paper bag for 10 minutes then slip off the skin. Cut in thin strips. • Heat the butter and oil in a large frying pan and sauté the leek and garlic for 5 minutes. • Add the rice and cook for 3 minutes, stirring constantly. • Stir in ¹/₂ cup (125 ml) of the stock and wine. Cook, stirring often, until absorbed. Continue adding the liquid, ¹/₂ cup (125 ml) at a time, stirring often until each addition is absorbed, until the rice is tender, 15–18 minutes. • Stir in the chicken, arugula, bell pepper, and lemon juice. Season with salt and pepper and serve.

731

# TOMATO RISOTTO WITH PESTO

Bring the tomatoes, stock, onion, parsley, and bay leaf to a boil in a medium saucepan. Cover and simmer over low heat for 15 minutes. • Filter the stock. • Add the tomato paste to the wine and stir into the stock. Cover and simmer. • Heat half the oil in a frying pan and sauté the leeks and garlic until pale gold. • Add the rice and cook for 3 minutes, stirring constantly. • Stir in $^1/_2$ cup (125 ml) of the stock. Cook, stirring often, until the stock is absorbed. Continue adding the stock, $^1/_2$ cup (125 ml) at a time, stirring until each addition is absorbed, until the rice is tender, 15–18 minutes. • Remove from heat and add the dried tomatoes and remaining oil. Garnish with the pesto and sprinkle with Parmesan.

*Serves: 4–6*

*Preparation: 20'*

*Cooking: 40'*

*Level of difficulty: 1*

- 1 lb/500 g tomatoes, coarsely chopped
- 2 cups/500 ml Vegetable Stock (see page 956)
- 1 onion, finely chopped
- 3 sprigs fresh parsley
- 1 bay leaf
- 1 tbsp tomato paste/purée
- 1 cup/250 ml dry white wine
- 4 tbsp extra-virgin olive oil
- 1 large leek, sliced
- 1 clove garlic, finely chopped
- $2^1/_4$ cups/450 g Italian Arborio rice
- $3^1/_2$ oz/100 g sundried tomatoes, chopped
- $^1/_2$ cup/125 g Pesto (see page 948
- 2 oz/60 g Parmesan cheese, flaked

# RAISIN RISOTTO

*Serves: 4–6*

*Preparation: 20'*

*Cooking: 40'*

*Level of difficulty: 1*

- **5 oz/150 g raisins**
- **$^1/_2$ cup/125 ml grappa**
- **3 tbsp extra-virgin olive oil**
- **1 large onion, finely chopped**
- **2 cloves garlic, finely chopped**
- **salt and freshly ground black pepper to taste**
- **2 cups/400 g Italian Arborio rice**
- **1 quart/1 liter boiling Beef Stock (see page 955)**
- **$^1/_2$ cup/60 g freshly grated Parmesan cheese**

Soak the raisins in a small bowl with the grappa for 15 minutes. • Heat the oil in a large frying pan and sauté the onion and garlic until softened. • Add the rice and cook over high heat stirring constantly for 3 minutes. Season with salt and pepper. • Stir in $^1/_2$ cup (125 ml) of the stock and wine. Cook, stirring often, until absorbed. Continue adding the liquid, $^1/_2$ cup (125 ml) at a time, stirring often until each addition is absorbed, until the rice is tender, 15–18 minutes. • About 5 minutes before the rice is cooked, stir in the raisins and grappa. • Sprinkle with the Parmesan and serve hot.

733

# RISOTTO WITH LEMON AND MARJORAM

Heat the oil and half the butter in a large frying pan and sauté the onion and garlic for 5 minutes. • Add the rice and cook for 3 minutes, stirring constantly. • Stir in $1/2$ cup (125 ml) of the stock. Cook, stirring often, until the stock is absorbed. Continue adding the stock, $1/2$ cup (125 ml) at a time, stirring often until each addition is absorbed, until the rice is tender, 15–18 minutes. • Remove from the heat and sprinkle with the lemon zest, Parmesan, and marjoram. Dot with the remaining butter, letting it melt into the rice.

*Serves: 6*

*Preparation: 20'*

*Cooking: 25'*

*Level of difficulty: 1*

- 2 tbsp extra-virgin olive oil
- 6 tbsp butter
- 1 onion, finely chopped
- 2 cloves garlic, finely chopped
- $2^1/4$ cups/450 g Italian Arborio rice
- $1^1/2$ quarts/1.5 liters boiling Vegetable Stock (see page 956)
- 1 tbsp finely grated lemon zest
- 3 tbsp fresh marjoram
- 1 cup/125 g freshly grated Parmesan cheese

# RISOTTO WITH SAUSAGES AND BRUSSELS SPROUTS

*Serves: 4–6*

*Preparation: 30'*

*Cooking: 1 h*

*Level of difficulty: 2*

- **14 oz/400 g Brussels sprouts**
- **6 tbsp butter**
- **$1/2$ cup/125 ml heavy/double cream**
- **1 tbsp brandy**
- **8–10 Italian sausages**
- **1 tbsp malt vinegar**
- **1 leaf fresh sage**
- **14 oz/400 g canned tomatoes**
- **4–6 fresh basil leaves, torn**
- **salt and freshly grated black pepper to taste**
- **2 cups/400 g Italian Arborio rice**
- **1 cup/250 ml dry white wine**
- **1 quart/1 liter boiling Beef Stock (see page 955)**
- **$1/3$ cup/50 g freshly grated Parmesan cheese (optional)**

C ook the Brussels sprouts in salted, boiling water until crunchy-tender. Drain and set aside.
• Melt 2 tablespoons of butter in a large frying pan and sauté the Brussels sprouts until lightly golden. Pour in the cream and brandy and bring to a boil. Set aside and keep warm. • Prick the sausages all over and cook in a large pan of boiling water with the vinegar and sage for 20 minutes. Drain and set aside. • Chop the tomatoes and basil with a large knife. • Melt 2 tablespoons of butter in a small saucepan and add the tomatoes. Season with salt and pepper and cook over medium heat for 20 minutes.. • Melt the remining butter in a frying pan. Add the rice and cook for 3 minutes, stirring constantly. • Pour in the wine and let it evaporate. • Stir in $1/2$ cup (125 ml) of the stock. Cook, stirring often, until the stock is absorbed. Continue adding the stock, $1/2$ cup (125 ml) at a time, stirring often until each addition is absorbed, until the rice is tender, 15–18 minutes.
• Remove from the heat and season with pepper. Sprinkle with Parmesan, if using. • Arrange the risotto in the center of a serving plate with the sausages and Brussels sprouts around it.

*This hearty risotto is really a meal in itself.*

# FENNEL AND CHICKEN RISOTTO

Cut the fennel bulbs in thin slices. • Melt 4 tablespoons of butter in a large frying pan and sauté the onion until softened. • Add the fennel and chicken and cook until browned all over. • Pour in half the wine and let it evaporate. Season with salt and pepper, cover, and cook over low heat for at least 30 minutes, adding $1/2$ cup (125 ml) of stock. • Add the rice and cook for 3 minutes, stirring constantly. • Pour in the remaining wine and let it evaporate. • Stir in $1/2$ cup (125 ml) of the stock. Cook, stirring often, until the stock is absorbed. Continue adding the stock, $1/2$ cup (125 ml) at a time, stirring often until each addition is absorbed, until the rice is tender, 15–18 minutes. • Dot with the remaining butter. Serve hot.

*Serves: 4*

*Preparation: 20'*

*Cooking: 1 h*

*Level of difficulty: 2*

- **2 medium fennel bulbs, tough outer leaves removed**
- **6 tbsp butter**
- **1 onion, finely chopped**
- **1 chicken breast, cut into small strips**
- **$1/2$ cup/125 ml dry white wine**
- **salt and freshly ground black pepper to taste**
- **1 quart/1 liter boiling Chicken Stock (see page 955)**
- **$1^3/4$ cups/350 g long-grain rice**

# RISOTTO WITH BELL PEPPERS

*Serves: 4*

*Preparation: 20'*

*Cooking: 25'*

*Level of difficulty: 2*

- **3 bell peppers/
  capsicums, mixed
  colors**
- **6 tbsp butter**
- **1 onion, finely
  chopped**
- **1 1/2 cups/300 g
  Italian Arborio rice**
- **1 tbsp finely
  chopped fresh
  thyme**
- **1 quart/1 liter
  boiling Vegetable
  Stock (see
  page 956)**
- **salt and freshly
  ground black
  pepper to taste**
- **1/3 cup/50 g
  freshly grated
  Parmesan cheese**
- **1 tbsp finely
  chopped fresh
  parsley**

Cut the bell peppers in half and set aside four halves. Chop the rest into small pieces. • Heat 2 tablespoons of butter in a large frying pan and sauté the onion until softened. • Add the rice and cook for 3 minutes, stirring constantly. Add the thyme and diced bell peppers. • Stir in 1/2 cup (125 ml) of the stock. Cook, stirring often, until the stock is absorbed. Continue adding the stock, 1/2 cup (125 ml) at a time, stirring often until each addition is absorbed, until the rice is tender, 15–18 minutes. • Season with salt and pepper and stir in the Parmesan, parsley, and remaining butter. • Spoon the risotto into the reserved bell pepper halves and serve.

# SHRIMP AND ASPARAGUS RISOTTO

740

Cook the asparagus in salted, boiling water for 8–10 minutes, or until just tender. Drain and set aside. • Sauté the prawns, ham, and garlic in the oil over high heat for 5 minutes. Set aside. • Melt the butter in a frying pan and sauté the onion until softened. • Add the rice and stir for 3 minutes. • Pour in the wine and let it evaporate. • Stir in $^1/_2$ cup (125 ml) of the stock. Cook, stirring often, until the stock is absorbed. Continue adding the stock, $^1/_2$ cup (125 ml) at a time, stirring often until each addition is absorbed, until the rice is tender, 15–18 minutes. • Add the prawn mixture, asparagus, and salt. Stir well and serve.

- **12 oz/350 g asparagus tips**
- **2 tbsp extra-virgin olive oil**
- **2 cloves garlic, finely chopped**
- **10 oz/300 g shrimp/prawn tails**
- **3 oz/90 g chopped ham**
- **4 tbsp butter**
- **1 small onion, finely chopped**
- **1$^3/_4$ cups/350 g Italian Arborio rice**
- **1 quart/liter boiling Fish Stock (see page 958)**
- **salt to taste**

*Serves: 4*

*Preparation: 15'*

*Cooking: 35'*

*Level of difficulty: 1*

- 4 tbsp butter
- 1 onion, finely chopped
- 8 oz/250 g mushrooms, finely sliced
- 2 cups/400 g Italian Arborio rice
- 1¹/₂ quarts/1.5 liters boiling Beef Stock (see page 955)
- 2 kiwi fruit, peeled
- ³/₄ cup/90 g freshly grated Parmesan cheese

# MUSHROOM AND KIWI RISOTTO

Melt 2 tablespoons of butter in a large frying pan and sauté the onion until softened. • Stir in the mushrooms and cook until tender. • Add the rice and cook for 3 minutes, stirring constantly. • Stir in ¹/₂ cup (125 ml) of the stock. Cook, stirring often, until the stock is absorbed. Continue adding the stock, ¹/₂ cup (125 ml) at a time, stirring often until each addition is absorbed, until the rice is tender, 15–18 minutes. • Reserve half a kiwi fruit. Mash the remaining kiwi fruit with a fork and stir into the risotto. • Remove from the heat and sprinkle with Parmesan. Dot with the remaining butter. Thinly slice the reserved kiwi fruit and use it as a garnish. Serve hot.

# SAFFRON RISOTTO WITH SHRIMP AND ZUCCHINI

*Serves: 4*

*Preparation: 25'*

*Cooking: 40'*

*Level of difficulty: 2*

- **4 tbsp extra-virgin olive oil**
- **20 shrimp/prawn tails, shelled**
- **3 zucchini/ courgettes, cut into wheels**
- **12 zucchini/ courgette flowers**
- **salt and freshly ground black pepper to taste**
- **1 onion, finely chopped**
- **1³/₄ cups/350 g Italian Arborio rice**
- **¹/₂ cup/125 ml dry white wine**
- **4 strands saffron, crumbled**
- **1 quart/1 liter boiling Vegetable Stock (see page 956)**
- **2 tbsp butter**

Heat half the oil in a large frying pan and sauté the shrimp and zucchini over high heat for 5 minutes. • Add the zucchini flowers, season with salt and pepper, and cook for 2 minutes. • Heat the remaining oil in a large frying pan and sauté the onion until softened. • Add the rice and cook for 2 minutes, stirring constantly. • Pour

743

*With the green zucchini, pink shrimp, and red rice, this dish is especially attractive.*

in the wine and let it evaporate. • Dissolve the saffron in ¹/₂ cup (125 ml) of the stock and stir into the rice. Cook, stirring often, until the stock is absorbed. Continue adding the stock, ¹/₂ cup (125 ml) at a time, stirring often until each addition is absorbed, until the rice is tender, 15–18 minutes. • Stir in the prawns, zucchini, and zucchini flowers with the cooking juices from the pan. • Dot with the butter and serve hot.

# RISOTTO WITH RADICCHIO

Melt 4 tablespoons of butter and the oil in a large frying pan and sauté the onion until softened. • Add the radicchio and cook over low heat until it begins to soften. • Add the rice and cook for 3 minutes, stirring constantly. • Stir in $1/2$ cup (125 ml) of the stock. Cook, stirring often, until the stock is absorbed. Continue adding the stock, $1/2$ cup (125 ml) at a time, stirring often until each addition is absorbed, until the rice is tender, 15–18 minutes. • Season with salt and pepper. Sprinkle with Parmesan and dot with the remaining butter. • Serve hot.

Serves: 4

Preparation: 20'

Cooking: 40'

Level of difficulty: 1

- **6 tbsp butter**
- **2 tbsp extra-virgin olive oil**
- **1 onion, finely chopped**
- **7 oz/200 g radicchio or red chicory, cut in strips**
- **2 cups/400 g Italian Arborio rice**
- **1 quart/1 liter boiling Beef Stock (see page 955)**
- **salt and freshly ground black pepper to taste**
- **$3/4$ cup/90 g freshly grated Parmesan cheese**

# GARLIC, HAM, AND TOMATO RISOTTO

*Serves: 4–6*

*Preparation: 25'*

*Cooking: 40'*

*Level of difficulty: 1*

- **4 tbsp extra-virgin olive oil**
- **6 cloves garlic, finely chopped**
- **2 tbsp finely chopped parsley**
- **salt and freshly ground black pepper to taste**
- **4 oz/125 g firm-ripe tomatoes, peeled and coarsely chopped**
- **²/₃ cup/80 g diced ham**
- **2¹/₂ cups/500 g Italian Arborio rice**
- **1 quart/1 liter boiling Beef Stock (see page 955)**
- **³/₄ cup/90 g freshly grated Parmesan cheese**

H eat the oil in a large frying pan and sauté the garlic and parsley until the garlic is pale gold. Season with salt and pepper. • Add the rice and cook for 3 minutes, stirring constantly. • Stir in the tomatoes and ham and cook for 5 minutes. • Stir in ¹/₂ cup (125 ml) of the stock. Cook, stirring often, until the stock is absorbed. Continue adding the stock, ¹/₂ cup (125 ml) at a time, stirring often until each addition is absorbed, until the rice is tender, 15–18 minutes. • Sprinkle with Parmesan and serve hot.

# CUMIN RISOTTO

Heat half the butter with the oil in a large frying pan and sauté the onions until softened. • Add the cumin, season with salt, and cook for 1 minute. • Pour in the wine and let it evaporate. • Add the rice and cook for 3 minutes, stirring constantly. • Stir in $^1/_2$ cup (125 ml) of the stock. Cook, stirring often, until the stock is absorbed. Continue adding the stock, $^1/_2$ cup (125 ml) at a time, stirring often until each addition is absorbed, until the rice is tender, 15–18 minutes. • Dot with the remaining butter. Serve hot with the Parmesan passed separately.

Serves: 4–6

Preparation: 15'

Cooking: 30'

Level of difficulty: 1

- **5 tbsp butter**
- **2 tbsp extra-virgin olive oil**
- **2 onions, finely chopped**
- **1 tsp crushed cumin seeds**
- **salt to taste**
- **4 tbsp dry white wine**
- **2$^1/_2$ cups/500 g Italian Arborio rice**
- **1 quart/1 liter boiling Beef Stock (see page 955)**
- **$^3/_4$ cup/90 g freshly grated Parmesan cheese**

# RISOTTO WITH CORN

Serves: 4

Preparation: 15'

Cooking: 30'

Level of difficulty: 1

- **4 tbsp butter**
- **salt and freshly ground black pepper to taste**
- **1 onion, finely chopped**
- **2 cups/400 g Italian Arborio rice**
- **1 quart/1 liter boiling Chicken Stock (see page 955)**
- **8 oz/250 g canned corn**
- **³/4 cup/90 g freshly grated Parmesan cheese**

Melt half the butter in a large frying pan and sauté the onion until softened. • Add the rice and cook for 3 minutes, stirring constantly. • Stir in ¹/2 cup (125 ml) of the stock. Cook, stirring often, until the stock is absorbed. Continue adding the stock, ¹/2 cup (125 ml) at a time, stirring often until each addition is absorbed, until the rice is almost tender, 15–18 minutes. • Stir in the corn and cook over high heat for 2 minutes, stirring constantly. • Sprinkle with Parmesan., dot with the remaining butter, and serve.

747

# SIMPLE SAFFRON RISOTTO

Melt 4 tablespoons of butter in a large frying pan and sauté the onion until softened. • Add the rice and cook for 3 minutes, stirring constantly. • Pour in the wine and let it evaporate. • Dissolve the saffron in $^1/_2$ cup (125 ml) of the stock and stir it into the rice. Cook, stirring often, until the stock is absorbed. Continue adding the stock, $^1/_2$ cup (125 ml) at a time, stirring often until each addition is absorbed, until the rice is tender, 15–18 minutes. • Season with salt and pepper. Dot with the remaining butter and sprinkle with Parmesan. • Serve hot.

*Serves: 4*

*Preparation: 10'*

*Cooking: 20'*

*Level of difficulty: 1*

- 6 tbsp butter
- 1 onion, finely chopped
- 2 cups/400 g Italian Arborio rice
- $^3/_4$ cup/180 ml dry white wine
- $3^1/_4$ cups/800 ml Beef Stock (see page 955)
- 6 strands saffron, crumbled
- salt and freshly ground black pepper to taste
- $^1/_2$ cup/60 g freshly grated Parmesan cheese

# RISOTTO WITH GINGER

*Serves: 4*

*Preparation: 25'*

*Cooking: 30'*

*Level of difficulty: 1*

- • 1 lemon
- • 5 tbsp butter
- • 1 onion, finely chopped
- • 1 small piece fresh ginger root, very finely grated
- • 2 cups/400 g Italian Arborio rice
- • 4 tbsp dry white wine
- • 1 quart/1 liter boiling Beef Stock (see page 955)
- • salt and freshly ground black pepper to taste
- • 1/2 cup/60 g freshly grated Parmesan cheese

Peel the lemon and remove the white pith from the zest. Cut the zest into small pieces. • Melt 3 tablespoons of butter in a large frying pan and sauté the onion and ginger until softened. • Add the rice and cook for 3 minutes, stirring constantly. • Pour in the wine and let it evaporate. • Stir in 1/2 cup (125 ml) of the stock. Cook, stirring often, until the stock is absorbed. Continue adding the stock, 1/2 cup (125 ml) at a time, stirring often until each addition is absorbed, until the rice is tender, 15–18 minutes. • Sprinkle with Parmesan, and lemon zest. Dot with the remaining butter and serve hot.

# BAKED EGGPLANT RISOTTO

P lace the eggplants in a colander. Sprinkle with
the coarse sea salt and let drain for 1 hour.
• Heat half the oil in a large frying pan and sauté
the sliced onion until softened. • Add the
tomatoes, parsley, 5 leaves of basil, and salt and
pepper. Simmer over low heat for 20–25 minutes,
or until the tomatoes have broken down. • Heat the
remaining oil in a large frying pan and sauté the
chopped onion until lightly browned. • Add the rice
and cook for 3 minutes, stirring constantly. • Stir in
$^1/_2$ cup (125 ml) of the stock. Cook, stirring often,
until the stock is absorbed. Continue adding the
stock, $^1/_2$ cup (125 ml) at a time, stirring often
until each addition is absorbed, until the rice is
tender, 15–18 minutes. • Remove from the heat
and mix in $2^1/_2$ tablespoons of the Caciocavallo.
• Dip the eggplants in flour until well coated and fry
in hot oil until golden brown all over. • Drain and
pat dry on paper towels. • Preheat the oven to
425°F/220°C/gas 7. • Grease an ovenproof
baking dish with oil. • Line the bottom with one-
third of the eggplants. Spoon in half the risotto,
half the remaining Caciocavallo, and half the sauce.
Sprinkle with the basil and top with half the
remaining eggplants, rice, sauce, and basil,
finishing with eggplant and Caciocavallo. • Bake
for 10 minutes. Serve hot.

Serves: 4–6

Preparation: 20' + 1 h to stand

Cooking: 40'

Level of difficulty: 2

- 2 large eggplants/ aubergines, thinly sliced
- coarse sea salt
- 8 tbsp extra-virgin olive oil
- 1 onion, thinly sliced
- 2 cups/500 g chopped tomatoes
- $1^1/_2$ tbsp finely chopped parsley
- 15 leaves fresh basil, torn
- salt and freshly ground black pepper to taste
- 2 tbsp finely chopped onion
- 2 cups/400 g Italian Arborio rice
- $3^1/_2$ cups/800 ml Vegetable Stock (see page 956)
- 1 cup/125 g freshly grated Caciocavallo cheese
- 2 tbsp all-purpose/ plain white flour
- 1 cup/250 ml olive oil, for frying

# RISOTTO WITH MEATBALLS

Mix the lamb, bread soaked in cream, mint, parsley, salt, and pepper in a medium bowl until smooth. • Scoop up teaspoons of the mixture and shape into small meatballs. • Heat the butter and sage leaves in a large frying pan and fry the meatballs for 7–10 minutes, or until nicely browned all over. • Set aside to drain on paper towels. • Heat 3 tablespoons of oil in a large frying pan and sauté the mixed vegetables for 5 minutes over high heat. Season with salt and pepper and remove from heat. • Heat the remaining oil in a large frying pan and cook the rice over high heat for 3 minutes, stirring constantly. • Pour in the wine and let evaporate. • Stir in $1/2$ cup (125 ml) of the stock. Cook, stirring often, until the stock is absorbed. Continue adding the stock, $1/2$ cup (125 ml) at a time, stirring often until each addition is absorbed, until the rice is tender, 15–18 minutes. • About 5 minutes before the rice is cooked, add the vegetables and meatballs. • Sprinkle with the Parmesan and serve hot.

---

Serves: 4

Preparation: 20'

Cooking: 35'

Level of difficulty: 1

---

- 12 oz/350 g ground lamb
- 3 slices white bread soaked in 4 tbsp fresh cream
- 1 tbsp finely chopped mint
- 1 tbsp finely chopped parsley
- $1/2$ cup/75 g all-purpose/plain flour
- 4 tbsp butter
- 4 leaves sage
- salt and freshly ground black pepper to taste
- 5 tbsp extra-virgin olive oil
- $1^{1}/2$ cups/350 g short-grain rice
- 8 oz/250 g mixed vegetables (peas, carrots, scallions/spring onions, asparagus, zucchini/courgettes), cut in small cubes
- $1/2$ cup/125 ml dry white wine
- $1/2$ cup/60 g freshly grated Parmesan cheese
- $3^{1}/4$ cups/800 ml Vegetable Stock (see page 956)

# RISOTTO WITH TOMATO AND MUSHROOMS

S oak the mushrooms in a bowl of warm water for about 15 minutes. Drain and chop coarsely.
• If using fresh tomatoes, plunge them into a pot of boiling water for 30 seconds, and then into cold. Slip off the skins, cut in half, squeeze to remove some of the seeds, and then chop finely. • If using canned tomatoes, partially drain and chop finely.
• In a heavy-bottomed saucepan, sauté the onion in the oil until soft. Add the mushrooms and, after another minute or so, the tomatoes. • Cook the sauce for 10 minutes, covered, then add the rice and stir well. • When part of the liquid has been absorbed, begin to add the boiling water, pouring it in a little at a time and stirring frequently. • Just before the rice is cooked, season with salt and pepper. • Serve the rice, passing the cheese separately.

*Serves: 4*

*Preparation: 30'*

*Cooking: 35'*

*Level of difficulty: 1*

- $^2/_3$ oz/20 g dried mushrooms
- 14 oz/450 g tomatoes, fresh or canned, peeled and chopped
- 1 small onion, finely chopped
- 6 tbsp extra-virgin olive oil
- 2 cups/400 g short-grain rice
- 1 quart/1 liter boiling water
- salt and freshly ground black pepper to taste
- 6 tbsp freshly grated Pecorino or Parmesan cheese

754

# PISTACHIO RISOTTO

*Serves: 4*

*Preparation: 15'*

*Cooking: 25'*

*Level of difficulty: 2*

- **4 tbsp butter**
- **1 onion, finely chopped**
- **5 oz/150 g pistachios**
- **2 cups/400 g short-grain rice (preferably Italian arborio)**
- **$^1/_2$ cup/125 ml dry white wine**
- **$1^1/_2$ quarts/1.5 liters Vegetable Stock (see page 956)**
- **4 tbsp freshly grated Parmesan cheese**
- **salt and freshly ground white pepper to taste**

Melt half the butter in a large, heavy-bottomed saucepan. Add the onion and sauté over medium heat until transparent. • Add the pistachios and rice, increase the heat, and stir for 2 minutes. • Pour in the wine and let it evaporate. • Stir in $^1/_2$ cup (125 ml) of the stock. Cook, stirring often, until the stock is absorbed. Continue adding the stock, $^1/_2$ cup (125 ml) at a time, stirring often until each addition is absorbed, until the rice is tender, 15–18 minutes. • Add the Parmesan when the rice is almost cooked. • Season with salt and pepper, add the remaining butter, and mix well.

• Serve hot.

# APPLE AND ZUCCHINI RISOTTO

Heat the oil in a large frying pan and sauté the onion, bell pepper, and zucchini over medium heat for 5 minutes. • Increase the heat to high and add the rice. Cook for 2 minutes, stirring constantly. • Begin stirring in the stock, $1/2$ cup (125 ml) at a time. After about 8 minutes, add the apples and potatoes. Add more stock and cook and stir until each addition has been absorbed, until the rice and potatoes are tender, about 15–18 minutes. • Just before the rice is cooked, add the curry powder, saffron, and dill. Season with salt and pepper and stir well. • Serve hot.

*Serves: 4*

*Preparation: 15'*

*Cooking: 20'*

*Level of difficulty: 1*

- **2 tbsp extra-virgin olive oil**
- **1 large onion, finely chopped**
- **1 small red bell pepper/capsicum, cut in small squares**
- **2 large zucchini/ courgettes, cut in small cubes**
- **2 cups/400 g short-grain rice**
- **3 cups/750 ml Vegetable Stock (see page 956)**
- **2 apples), peeled, cored, and thinly sliced, drizzled with 4 tbsp fresh lemon juice**
- **4 small potatoes, cut in small cubes**
- **2 tsp curry powder**
- **1 tsp saffron threads**
- **2 tbsp chopped fresh dill**
- **salt and freshly ground black pepper to taste**

# POPE'S BAKED RISOTTO

Preheat the oven to 400°F/200°C/gas 6. •
Butter the sides of a 10-inch (25-cm) ring
mold. • Melt the butter in a deep-sided frying pan
and sauté the onion until pale gold. • Add the
chicken livers and cook until browned all over.
• Pour in the wine and let it evaporate. • Stir in
the tomatoes and cook for 15
minutes, or until the tomatoes have broken down.
Season with salt and pepper. • Add the rice and
$^1/_2$ cup (125 ml) of stock, stirring constantly.
Cook, stirring often, until the stock is absorbed.
Continue adding the stock, $^1/_2$ cup (125 ml) at a
time, stirring often until each addition is
absorbed, until the rice is tender, 15–18 minutes.
• Remove from the heat and mix in the Parmesan.
• Transfer the rice mixture to the mold, press
down firmly. • Bake for 10 minutes. • Invert the
mold onto a heated platter and serve hot.

*This dish comes from the Eternal City of Rome,
although the origins of its name are not known.*

760

Serves: 4

Preparation: 15'

Cooking: 40'

Level of difficulty: 2

- 4 tbsp butter
- 1 onion, finely
  chopped
- 10 oz/300 g
  chicken livers,
  trimmed and
  coarsely chopped
- 4 tbsp dry white
  wine
- 2 cups/500 g
  chopped tomatoes
- salt and freshly
  ground black
  pepper to taste
- 2 cups/400 g
  short-grain rice
- 1 quart/1 liter
  boiling Beef Stock
  (see page 955)
- 4 tbsp freshly
  grated Parmesan
  cheese

# RISOTTO WITH RED WINE

Melt 3 tablespoons of butter in a large saucepan. Add the onion, celery and carrot, and sauté over low heat for 5 minutes. • Increase the heat slightly, add the rice and cook for 2 minutes, stirring continuously. • Gradually stir in the wine. • When the wine has been absorbed, add $^1/_2$ cup (125 ml) of the stock. Cook, stirring often, until the stock is absorbed. Continue adding the stock, $^1/_2$ cup (125 ml at a time, stirring often until each addition is absorbed, until the rice is tender, 15–18 minutes. • Season with salt and pepper. • Add the remaining butter and the Parmesan just before serving.

*Serves: 4*

*Preparation: 10'*

*Cooking: 25'*

*Level of difficulty: 1*

- **4 tbsp butter**
- **1 small onion, finely chopped**
- **1 stalk celery, finely chopped**
- **1 small carrot, finely chopped**
- **2 cups/400 g short-grain rice**
- **1$^1/_4$ cups/310 ml dry red wine**
- **1$^1/_2$ quarts/1.5 liters Beef Stock (see page 955)**
- **6 tbsp freshly grated Parmesan cheese**
- **salt and freshly ground black pepper to taste**

# RISOTTO WITH EEL

*Serves: 4*

*Preparation: 45'*

*Cooking: 1 h*

*Level of difficulty: 2*

- 1 eel (about
  1 3/4 lb/750 g)
- 1 carrot
- 1 onion
- 1 stalk celery
- 3/4 cup/45 g finely
  chopped parsley
- 1 clove garlic,
  finely chopped
- 3 tbsp butter
- 2 tbsp extra-virgin
  olive oil
- 2 cups/400 g
  Italian Arborio
  risotto rice
- 4 tbsp chopped
  tomatoes
- salt to
  taste

Cook the eel with the carrot, onion, and celery in a large pan of boiling water for 30 minutes.
- Remove the eel flesh from the bone and chop coarsely. Reserve the cooking liquid and onion.
- Sauté the parsley and garlic in half the butter and oil. Add the rice and cook for 2 minutes, stirring constantly. • Pour in 2 cups (500 ml) of the cooking liquid. Cook, stirring frequently, for about 18 minutes, adding more cooking liquid as required. Season with salt. • Slice the reserved onion thinly.
- Heat the remaining butter and oil in a saucepan and sauté the onion. • Add the eel, tomatoes, and 1 cup (250 ml) of cooking liquid. Simmer for 10 minutes. • Stir the eel into the rice and serve hot.

# COOL
# RICE

# RICE SALAD WITH TUNA AND AVOCADO

C ook the rice in 2 quarts (2 liters) of salted, boiling water for 13–15 minutes, or until tender. • Drain and cool under cold running water. Drain well and dry in a clean towel. • Transfer to a salad dish and drizzle with the oil. • Top with the arugula, tuna, avocado, Mozzarella, and parsley. • Beat the lemon juice, oil, and salt in a small bowl until frothy. • Pour the dressing over the salad, toss gently, and serve.

*Serves: 4–6*

*Preparation: 10'*

*Cooking: 15'*

*Level of difficulty: 1*

- **2 cups/400 g long-grain rice**
- **1 small bunch of arugula/rocket, washed and finely shredded**
- **10 oz/300 g canned tuna in oil, drained and crumbled**
- **1 firm-ripe avocado, peeled, pitted, and thinly sliced**
- **5 oz/150 g Mozzarella morsels**
- **1 small bunch fresh parsley, finely chopped**
- **juice of 1 lemon**
- **4 tbsp extra-virgin olive oil**
- **salt to taste**

# COOL CURRY AND SHRIMP RICE CAKES

Serves: 4

Preparation: 30'

Cooking: 1 h

Level of difficulty: 1

- **24 shrimp/prawns, shelled and heads removed**
- **2 cups/500 ml Vegetable Stock (see page 956)**
- **³/₄ cup/90 g frozen peas, thawed**
- **1 green apple**
- **juice of 1 lemon**
- **3 tbsp butter**
- **2 scallions/spring onions, finely chopped**
- **1¹/₂ cups/300 g Camaroli or Vialone rice**
- **1 cup/250 ml champagne or other dry sparkling white wine**
- **2 tsp curry powder**
- **salt and freshly ground black pepper to taste**
- **15 shelled walnuts**
- **2 tbsp extra-virgin olive oil**

Rinse the shrimp shells and heads. Chop the heads into pieces and place them in a medium saucepan with the shells. Pour in the stock and bring to a boil. Simmer over low heat for 30 minutes. • Filter the liquid and set aside. • Cook the peas in salted, boiling water until tender. Drain and set aside. • Cut the apple into small pieces and drizzle with lemon juice to prevent it from turning brown. • Heat 2 tablespoons of butter in a frying pan and sauté the scallions until softened. • Add the rice and cook for 3 minutes, stirring constantly. • Pour in the wine and let it evaporate. • Pour in the filtered stock and cook, stirring, over medium heat for 10 minutes, adding more stock as the mixture starts to dry. • Stir in the curry powder, half the apple, and half the peas. Cook for about 5 minutes, or until the rice is firm to the bite. • Remove from the heat and season with salt and pepper. Mix in the remaining butter, letting it melt into the rice. • Butter four individual molds. Spoon the rice into the molds and place them in a double boiler half-full with warm water. • Sauté the prawns, walnuts, and remaining peas and apple in the oil in a medium frying pan over high heat for 5 minutes. Season with salt and pepper and add a pinch of curry and more stock, if needed. • Turn the rice cakes out onto individual plates and let cool. Serve with the shrimp sauce.

# RICE SALAD WITH SHRIMP

Cook the shrimp in 2 quarts (2 liters) of salted, boiling water and the juice of 1 lemon for 5 minutes. • Drain and let the shrimp cool. Shell the shrimp and devein. Chop off the heads and rinse thoroughly in cold running water. Place in a bowl with 4 tablespoons of oil. • Cook the rice in 2 quarts (2 liters) of salted, boiling water for 13–15 minutes, or until tender. • Drain the rice and pass under cold running water. Drain again and dry in a clean towel. • Place in the bowl with the shrimp. Mix carefully, adding salt and pepper to taste. Add the remaining lemon juice and oil. • Just before serving, add the arugula and mix again.

*Serves: 4*

*Preparation: 30'*

*Cooking: 20'*

*Level of difficulty: 2*

- 1¹/₂ lb/750 g shrimp/prawns, in shell
- juice of 1¹/₂ lemons
- 6 tbsp extra-virgin olive oil
- 2 cups/400 g short-grain rice
- salt and freshly ground white pepper to taste
- 4 tbsp coarsely chopped arugula/ rocket

# BLACK RICE WITH PRAWNS AND CHERRY TOMATOES

Rinse the lemon, cut the zest into thin strips, and squeeze out the juice. • Place the prawn tails in a large bowl with the scallion, garlic, lemon zest and juice, 2 tablespoons of oil, and a grinding of pepper. Mix and let marinate for 15 minutes. • Cook the rice in 2 quarts (2 liters) of salted, boiling water for the time indicated on the package, or until tender. • Drain well and spread out on a clean cloth to cool. • Heat 2 tablespoons of oil in a large frying pan and sauté the cherry tomatoes over high heat for 3 minutes. Season with salt and pepper, add the prawns and their marinade, and cook over high heat until the shrimp are tender. • Transfer the rice to a large bowl and top with the sauce. Sprinkle with the parsley and serve.

*Black rice makes this salad especially eyecatching, but it can also be made with brown or white rice.*

772

*Serves: 4*

*Preparation: 30' + 15' to marinate*

*Cooking: 20'*

*Level of difficulty: 2*

- $1/2$ lemon
- 7 oz/200 g shelled shrimp/prawn tails
- 1 scallion/spring onion, finely sliced
- 2 cloves garlic, finely chopped
- 6 tbsp extra-virgin olive oil
- salt and freshly ground black pepper to taste
- 2 cups/400 g black rice
- 16 cherry tomatoes, cut in half
- 1 small bunch fresh parsley, finely chopped

# BROWN RICE SALAD WITH GREEN BEANS

C ook the rice in 2 quarts (2 liters) of salted, boiling water for 35 minutes, or until tender. Drain and let cool under cold running water. Drain again and dry in a clean towel. • Cook the green beans in salted, boiling water until crunchy-tender. Drain and set aside. • Peel the cucumber and slice

*If preferred, serve the rice salad on a deep bed of arugula (rocket) or other salad greens.* thinly. Place in a colander. Sprinkle

with salt and let drain for 15 minutes. • Mix the rice, green beans, tomatoes, cucumbers, and Fontina in a large bowl. Drizzle with the oil and lemon juice and season with salt and pepper.
• Arrange the lettuce on serving plates and spoon the rice on top.

774

*Serves: 4*

*Preparation: 15' + 15' to drain cucumbers*

*Cooking: 35'*

*Level of difficulty: 1*

- 1 1/2 cups/300 g brown rice
- 14 oz/400 g green beans, topped and tailed
- 1 cucumber
- 10 cherry tomatoes, halved
- 5 oz/150 g Fontina cheese, cut into small cubes
- 1 bunch fresh parsley, finely chopped
- 2 tbsp fresh lemon juice
- 4 tbsp extra-virgin olive oil
- salt and freshly ground black pepper to taste
- 8–10 leaves lettuce. well-washed

# THREE RICE SALAD

*Serves: 6–8*

*Preparation: 25' + 2 h to marinate*

*Cooking: 40'*

*Level of difficulty: 1*

- 1 cup/200 g long-grain rice
- 1 cup/200 g brown rice
- 1/2 cup/100 g black wild rice
- 1 red bell pepper/capsicum
- 1 green bell pepper/capsicum
- 4 tbsp extra-virgin olive oil
- 1 clove garlic, finely chopped
- 2 cups/250 g peas
- 1 tbsp fresh lemon juice
- 1/2 tsp mustard
- salt and freshly ground black pepper to taste
- 4 tomatoes, seeded and chopped
- 4 scallions/spring onions, finely chopped
- 1/2 cup/50 g finely chopped black olives
- 4 tbsp finely chopped parsley

Cook the three types of rice separately in 2 quarts (2 liters) of salted, boiling water for the times indicated on the packages, or until tender. • Cut the bell peppers in half, remove the seeds, and cut into quarters. • Broil (grill) the bell peppers skin-side up for 8–10 minutes, or until blackened. • Transfer the bell peppers to a paper bag and let rest for 5 minutes (this will make it easier to remove the skin). Peel them and cut into small pieces. • Mix the oil, garlic, and bell peppers in a medium bowl. Let marinate for at least 2 hours. • Blanch the peas in salted, boiling water for 2 minutes. Drain and let cool under cold running water. • Drain the bell peppers, reserving the marinade in a small bowl. Mix in the lemon juice and mustard and season with salt and pepper. • Mix the rice, bell peppers, peas, tomatoes, scallions, and olives. Drizzle with the marinade and sprinkle with the parsley. Toss well and serve.

# BROWN RICE SALAD WITH APPLES AND WALNUTS

C ook the rice in 2 quarts (2 liters) of salted, boiling water for 35 minutes, or until tender.
• Drain thoroughly and transfer to a large bowl. Toss with 1 tablespoon of oil and let cool completely. • Mix the rice with the apples, walnuts, and Gruyère. • Beat the oil, lemon juice, honey, garlic, and salt and pepper and drizzle over the rice mixture. Sprinkle with the parsley and serve.

778

*Serves: 4*

*Preparation: 15' + 15' to cool*

*Cooking: 35'*

*Level of difficulty: 1*

- 1 1/3 cups/270 g brown rice
- 4 tbsp extra-virgin olive oil
- 2 tart green apples, such as Granny Smiths, unpeeled and coarsely chopped
- 20 walnuts, coarsely chopped
- 3 oz/90 g Gruyère or Swiss cheese, cut into small cubes
- juice of 1/2 lemon
- 1 tbsp honey, heated
- 2 cloves garlic, finely chopped
- salt and freshly ground black pepper to taste
- 1 small bunch fresh parsley, finely chopped

# RICE SALAD WITH VEGETABLES

C ook the rice in 2 quarts (2 liters) of salted, boiling water for 13–15 minutes, or until tender. Drain and let cool under cold running water. • Cut the bell peppers in half, remove the seeds, and cut into thin strips. • Slice the eggs thinly, reserving a few slices to garnish. • Mix the rice, bell peppers, tomatoes, olives, garlic, Gorgonzola, egg, and mint in a large bowl. Drizzle with the oil and lemon juice and season with salt and pepper. • Garnish with the remaining egg and the sprig of mint.

*Be sure to use a spicy blue cheese rather than a sweet creamy one.*

**780**

Serves: 4–6

Preparation: 20'

Cooking: 15'

Level of difficulty: 1

- 1$^1$/$_2$ cups/300 g long-grain rice
- $^1$/$_2$ green bell pepper/capsicum
- $^1$/$_2$ yellow bell pepper/capsicum
- 2 hard-boiled eggs
- 8–10 cherry tomatoes, halved
- $^1$/$_2$ cup/50 g black olives, pitted and halved
- 2 cloves garlic, finely chopped
- 5 oz/150 g spicy Gorgonzola or other blue cheese, cut into small cubes
- 1 tbsp finely chopped fresh mint, + 1 sprig to garnish
- 2 tbsp fresh lemon juice
- 4 tbsp extra-virgin olive oil
- salt and freshly ground black pepper to taste

# MEDITERRANEAN RICE SALAD

782

Broil (grill) the bell peppers until blackened all over. Place them in a brown paper bag and let cool. Peel and remove the stems, seeds, and filaments. Rinse carefully and dry well. Chop coarsely and place in a large bowl. • Cook the rice in 2 quarts (2 liters) of salted, boiling water for 13–15 minutes, or until tender. • Drain well and let cool. • Mix the rice with the bell peppers, 4 basil leaves, and oil. • Melt the butter in a small frying pan and sauté the garlic until pale gold. • Add the remaining oil and anchovies. Stir until dissolved. • Top the rice with the anchovy sauce. Sprinkle with the remaining basil, mint, and capers and serve.

*Serves: 4*

*Preparation: 30'*

*Cooking: 30'*

*Level of difficulty: 2*

- **1 large yellow bell pepper/capsicum**
- **1 large red bell pepper/capsicum**
- **2 cups/400 g short-grain rice**
- **1 small bunch basil, torn**
- **6 tbsp extra-virgin olive oil**
- **2 tbsp butter**
- **2 cloves garlic, finely chopped**
- **8 anchovy fillets**
- **1 tbsp finely chopped mint**
- **1 tbsp salted capers, rinsed**

# RICE SALAD WITH PICKLED VEGETABLES

*Serves: 4*

*Preparation: 15'*

*Cooking: 15'*

*Level of difficulty: 1*

- 1¹/₂ cups/300 g Italian Arborio rice
- 5 tbsp extra-virgin olive oil
- 2 tbsp fresh lemon juice
- 1 hard-boiled egg yolk
- 2 anchovy fillets, finely chopped
- 8 oz/250 g canned tuna, flaked
- 1 tbsp capers
- 10–12 pitted green olives, thinly sliced
- salt and freshly ground white pepper to taste
- pickled vegetables to garnish

C ook the rice in plenty of salted, boiling water for 13–15 minutes, or until tender. • Drain and place under cold running water. Drain well and dry in a clean cloth. Transfer to a salad bowl. • Pour the oil and lemon juice into a small bowl. Add the egg yolk and use a fork to crush it into the oil and lemon juice. • Add the anchovy then mix to make a well-blended dressing. • Add the tuna, capers, and olives, and season with salt and pepper. • Pour this dressing over the rice and toss gently. Garnish with the pickled vegetables, if liked.

# RICE WITH CASHEWS

Cook the rice in 2 quarts (2 liters) of salted, boiling water for 13–15 minutes, or until tender. • Drain well and place under cold running water. Drain again and dry with a clean cloth. Transfer to a large salad bowl. • Toast the cashews and pine nuts lightly in a frying pan, then chop coarsely. • Heat the oil in a large frying pan and sauté the garlic until pale gold. • Stir in the nuts and cook for 4 minutes. Remove from the heat and sprinkle with the parsley. Add to the rice with the water. Toss well and let cool • Serve at room temperature.

*Serves: 4*

*Preparation: 25'*

*Cooking: 25'*

*Level of difficulty: 1*

- 1 1/2 cups/300 g long-grain rice
- 1/2 cup/75 g cashews, salted and toasted
- 4 tbsp pine nuts, toasted
- 4 tbsp extra-virgin olive oil
- 1 clove garlic, finely chopped
- 1 tbsp finely chopped parsley
- 2 tbsp boiling water

# STUFFED SUMMER TOMATOES

Cut the tomatoes in half horizontally. Squeeze out as many seeds as possible. • Season the tomatoes with salt. Place them upside-down in a colander and let drain for 1 hour. • Cook the rice in 2 quarts (2 liters) of salted, boiling water for 13–15 minutes, or until tender. Drain well and set aside. • Process the chile peppers, garlic, oregano, pinch of salt, and the oil in a food processor until smooth. • Stir the processed mixture into the rice along with the Mozzarella and peas. • Spoon into the drained tomato halves and garnish with a little chile pepper. • Serve chilled or at room temperature.

Serves: 4

Preparation: 25' + 1 h
to drain tomatoes

Cooking: 15'

Level of difficulty: 1

- **8 large firm-ripe tomatoes**
- **salt to taste**
- **1³/₄ cups/350 g short-grain rice**
- **2 fresh spicy chile peppers, seeded**
- **1 clove garlic**
- **1 tsp finely chopped fresh oregano**
- **6 tbsp extra-virgin olive oil**
- **8 oz/250 g Mozzarella cheese, cut into small cubes**
- **1¹/₃ cups/200 g cooked peas**

Serves: 4

Preparation: 30'

Cooking: 15'

Level of difficulty: 1

- 1¹/₄ cups/250 g short-grain rice
- 4 tbsp extra-virgin olive oil
- 2 tbsp lemon juice
- salt and freshly ground white pepper to taste
- 2 medium tomatoes, diced
- 6–8 red radishes, sliced
- 2 stalks celery, sliced
- 6 pickled gherkins, sliced
- 8 small white pickled onions, quartered
- 1 tbsp capers
- 10 green olives, pitted and quartered
- 2 tbsp golden raisins (sultanas), rinsed and drained
- 4 oz/125 g Parmesan cheese, flaked

# RAINBOW RICE SALAD

Bring 2 quarts (2 liters) of salted water to a boil. Add the rice, stir once or twice, and cook for 13–15 minutes, or until tender. • Drain well and pass under cold running water for 30 seconds to stop cooking. Drain again and dry with a clean cloth. Transfer to a large salad bowl. • Season with oil, lemon juice, and pepper to taste. • Just before serving, add the remaining ingredients and toss well.

# RICE SALAD WITH PRAWN TAILS AND ASPARAGUS

Trim the asparagus carefully, removing the tough parts and leaving only the tender parts of the stalks and tips. • Cook in a saucepan of salted, boiling water for 10–12 minutes, or until just tender. The cooking time will depend on the thickness of the stalks and how long ago they were picked. Take care not to overcook; mushy asparagus will spoil the look of your salad. • Drain the asparagus and chop into short lengths. Set aside to cool. • Heat the oil in a large frying pan and sauté the onion and garlic for 5 minutes. • Add the shrimp and sauté over high heat for 4–5 minutes, or until the shrimp are well cooked. Set the pan aside to cool. • Cook the rice in a large pan of salted, boiling water until al dente. • Drain well and place under cold running water. Drain again and dry with a clean kitchen towel. • Rinse and dry the arugula and place on a large salad platter. • Place the rice in a large bowl and add the shrimp mixture and all the juices in the pan and the asparagus. Season with salt and pepper. • Spoon the rice salad onto the arugula on the platter. • If liked, chill for 30 minutes before serving.

Serves: 4

Preparation: 20' + 30' to chill (optional)

Cooking: 25'

Level of difficulty: 1

- 1 lb/500 g asparagus
- 6 tbsp extra-virgin olive oil
- 1 small onion, finely chopped
- 2 cloves garlic, finely chopped
- 12 oz/350 g prawn tails/shrimp tails, shelled and deveined
- 1³/4 cups/350 g short-grain rice
- large bunch fresh arugula/rocket
- salt and freshly ground black pepper to taste

# GNOCCHI

# GNOCCHI

There are two main types of gnocchi—potato gnocchi, made with potatoes and flour, and semolina gnocchi, made with semolina and milk and generally baked in the oven (see page 796). There are also many variations, with additions of spinach, or herbs, or even chocolate to the basic dough. Potato gnocchi were invented in Italy where they are still very popular. The northern city of Verona holds a street festival in their honor every year during Carnival called the "Bacanal del Gnoco" or Gnocchi Feast.

BASIC POTATO GNOCCHI

*Serves: 4–6*

- 1$^{1}/_{2}$ lb/750 g boiling potatoes
- 2 cups/300 g all-purpose/plain flour

**1.** Cook the potatoes in their skins in a pot of salted, boiling water for about 25 minutes, or until tender. Drain and peel while still hot.

**2.** Place the potatoes in a bowl and mash until smooth.

**3.** Transfer to a floured work surface and stir in most of the flour. Mix well, adding more flour as required, until the mixture is soft and smooth, but just slightly sticky.

**4.** Take a piece of the dough and roll it into a long sausage about $1/2$ in (1 cm) in diameter

**5.** Cut into pieces about 1 in (2.5 cm) in length. To give the gnocchi their special grooves, use a gnocchi groover, or twist the gnocchi around the tines of a fork.

**COOKING INSTRUCTIONS**

Set a large pot of salted water to boil. The gnocchi should be cooked in batches. Lower the first batch (20–24 gnocchi) gently into the boiling water. After a few minutes they will rise to the surface. Leave them to bob about for 1–2 minutes, then scoop out with a slotted spoon. Place on a heated serving dish. Repeat until all the gnocchi are cooked.

# BAKED SEMOLINA GNOCCHI

Preheat the oven to 350°F/180°C/gas 4. • Butter an ovenproof baking dish. • Bring the milk to a boil in a large saucepan. • Sprinkle the semolina in little by little, stirring all the time so that no lumps form. Keep stirring energetically for about 30 minutes, or until the mixture is dense. • Remove from heat and season with salt. Stir in half the butter, the egg yolks, half the Parmesan, and the Gruyère. • Spread the mixture out on a lightly floured work surface to a thickness of about 1/2 in (1 cm). Let cool. • Use a glass to cut into disks. • Use the pieces left over from the disks to form a first layer in the dish. Sprinkle with a little of the remaining Parmesan. Lay the disks over the top, one overlapping the next. • Melt the remaining butter and pour over the top. Sprinkle with the remaining Parmesan and dust with pepper. • Bake for about 30 minutes, or until golden brown. • Serve hot.

- 1 quart/1 liter milk
- 1²/₃ cups/250 g semolina
- salt to taste
- 1/2 cup/125 g butter, cut up
- 2 egg yolks
- 1 cup/125 g freshly grated Parmesan
- 4 tbsp freshly grated Gruyère
- freshly ground white pepper to taste

Serves: 6
Preparation: 15'
Cooking: 35'
Level of difficulty: 1

- 3 lb/1.5 kg piece of winter squash or pumpkin
- 2 eggs
- 2²/₃ cups/400 g unbleached all-purpose/strong plain flour
- pinch of salt
- ¹/₃ cup/80 g butter, melted

# SQUASH GNOCCHI

Preheat the oven to 400°F/200°C/gas 6. • Peel the pumpkin and scrape away the seeds and fibrous matter. Cut the flesh into fairly large cubes. Place on a baking sheet and bake for 20 minutes. • Transfer to a bowl and mash until smooth while still hot. • Stir in the eggs, flour, and salt. Mix very thoroughly until smooth and firm, adding a little more flour if needed. • Bring a large pan of salted water to a boil. Shape scant tablespoonfuls of the dough into balls the size of a walnut or a little smaller. • Cook the gnocchi a few at a time for 2–3 minutes, or until they bob to the surface. • Remove with a slotted spoon and transfer to a heated serving dish. Continue until all the gnocchi are cooked. • Drizzle with the butter and serve.

# POTATO GNOCCHI WITH EGGS

W ash the potatoes thoroughly and cook in lightly salted boiling water with their skins on. • Slip off the skins and mash in a large bowl. Stir in the flour and salt. • Use a fork to beat the egg yolks in a small bowl. Mix into the mashed potato mixture and stir until smooth. • Take a handful of the mixture and roll it out on a lightly floured work surface using your hands. It should form a long sausage, about $1/2$ in (1 cm) in diameter. Use a sharp knife to cut the sausage into $3/4$-in (2-cm) lengths. Repeat until all the mixture is used up. Place the gnocchi on a clean cloth and let rest for at least 1 hour before cooking. • Bring a large pan of salted water to a boil. Cook the gnocchi in batches of about 30–40 until they bob to the surface. Cook for 2 minutes more. • Remove with a slotted spoon and transfer to a deep-sided serving bowl. Keep warm. Continue until all gnocchi are cooked. • Drizzle with the melted butter and sprinkle with the Parmesan. Serve hot.

*This is a basic potato gnocchi recipe with the addition of 2 eggs. It is slightly richer than the classic version.*

798

*Serves: 4–6*

*Preparation: 20' + 1 h to rest*

*Cooking: 45'*

*Level of difficulty: 2*

- 3 lb/1.5 kg boiling potatoes
- $3/4$ cup/125 g all-purpose/plain flour
- pinch of salt
- 2 egg yolks
- $1/2$ cup/125 g butter, melted
- 1 cup/125 g freshly grated Parmesan cheese, + extra to serve

# CUNEO POTATO GNOCCHI

Wash the potatoes thoroughly and cook in lightly salted boiling water with their skins on.
• Slip off the skins and mash in a large bowl.
• Beat the egg whites in a large bowl until stiff.
• Use a wooden spoon to fold the egg yolks, egg whites, flour, salt, pepper, nutmeg, into the mashed potatoes. Mix gently but thoroughly.
• Bring a large pan of salted water to a boil and drop small rounded tablespoonfuls of the potato mixture into the water. Cook the gnocchi a few at a time until they bob to the surface. • Remove with a slotted spoon and transfer to a heated serving dish. Sprinkle with the Parmesan. • Melt the butter with the sage in a small saucepan. • Drizzle over the gnocchi and serve hot.

*Serves: 4*

*Preparation: 20'*

*Cooking: 45'*

*Level of difficulty: 2*

- 1 1/2 lb/750 g boiling potatoes
- 3 eggs, separated
- 1 cup/150 g all-purpose/plain flour
- salt and freshly ground white pepper to taste
- 1/8 tsp freshly grated nutmeg
- 4 tbsp freshly grated Parmesan
- 6 tbsp butter
- 6 leaves fresh sage

# POTATO GNOCCHI WITH MELTED BUTTER

*Serves: 4–6*

*Preparation: 35' +*
*1–2 h to rest*

*Cooking: 25'*

*Level of difficulty: 2*

- **2 lb/1 kg boiling potatoes**
- **1²/₃ cups/250 g all-purpose/plain flour**
- **1 tsp salt**
- **1 cup/100 g coarsely grated Fontina cheese**
- **6 tbsp butter, melted**

Wash the potatoes thoroughly and cook in lightly salted boiling water with their skins on. • Slip off the skins and mash in a large bowl. • Stir in the flour and salt. • Sprinkle a work surface lightly with flour. Shape a quarter of the dough into long rolls about ¹/₂ in (1 cm) in diameter. Cut into ³/₄-in (2-cm) lengths. • Press each against the prongs (tines) of a fork (concave side) with your thumb, so that they are slightly hollowed out on one side and ribbed on the other. • Lay the gnocchi out on a lightly floured cloth and let rest for 1–2 hours. • Bring a large pan of salted water to a boil. Cook the gnocchi in batches until they bob to the surface. • Remove with a slotted spoon and transfer to a heated serving dish. Sprinkle with the Fontina, drizzle with the butter, and serve hot.

# SPINACH GNOCCHI

B ring a large pan of salted water to a boil. Add the spinach and cook for 10 minutes. Drain well, squeeze out excess moisture, and chop finely.
• Transfer the spinach to a large bowl and mix in the Ricotta, the egg and egg yolk, half the Parmesan, the nutmeg, and salt and pepper. Mix very thoroughly with a fork until smooth. • Use a tablespoon to shape the mixture into round gnocchi or roll into small balls using floured hands. Coat lightly with flour all over. • Bring a large pan of salted water to a gentle boil. Cook the gnocchi in batches until they bob to the surface. They should simmer rather than boil. • Remove with a slotted spoon and transfer to a heated serving dish.
• Melt the butter with the sage in a small saucepan. • Drizzle over the gnocchi and sprinkle with the remaining Parmesan.
Serve hot.

*Serves: 4*

*Preparation: 25'*

*Cooking: 40'*

*Level of difficulty: 2*

- **1 3/4 lb/800 g trimmed, washed and drained fresh spinach leaves**
- **generous 1 cup/ 250 g very fresh, drained Ricotta cheese**
- **1 egg + 1 egg yolk**
- **3/4 cup/90 g freshly grated Parmesan cheese**
- **1/8 tsp freshly grated nutmeg**
- **salt and freshly ground black pepper to taste**
- **2/3 cup/100 g all-purpose/plain flour**
- **6 tbsp butter**
- **6 leaves fresh sage**

# BAKED GNOCCHI WITH FONTINA

**P**reheat the oven to 400°F/200°C/gas 6. • Butter an ovenproof baking dish. • Wash the potatoes and cook in lightly salted boiling water with their skins on. • Slip off the skins and mash in a large bowl. • Stir in the egg, flour, and salt. • Roll the mixture into long sausages about $3/4$ in (2 cm) in diameter. Cut into 1 in (2.5 cm) lengths. • Bring a large pan of salted water to a boil. Cook the gnocchi a few at a time until they bob to the surface. • Remove with a slotted spoon and transfer to the prepared baking dish. • Top with the Fontina, Parmesan, and butter. Pour in the milk and bake for 15 minutes, or until browned. • Serve hot.

*Serves: 4–6*

*Preparation: 35'*

*Cooking: 40'*

*Level of difficulty: 2*

- **2 lb/1 kg boiling potatoes**
- **1 egg**
- **2 cups/300 g all-purpose/plain flour**
- **1 tsp salt**
- **3 oz/90 g Fontina cheese, sliced**
- **6 tbsp freshly grated Parmesan cheese**
- **$3^1/2$ tbsp butter, cut into flakes**
- **$2/3$ cup/150 ml milk**

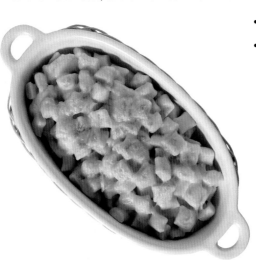

# SPINACH GNOCCHI IN TOMATO AND CREAM SAUCE

*Serves: 4–6*

*Preparation: 35'*

*Cooking: 45'*

*Level of difficulty: 2*

- 1$^{1}/_{2}$ lb/750 g fresh spinach leaves
- $^{1}/_{2}$ cup/125 ml Ricotta cheese
- 1 egg + 1 egg yolk
- 2 cups/250 g freshly grated Parmesan cheese
- $^{2}/_{3}$ cup/100 g all-purpose/plain flour
- $^{1}/_{8}$ tsp freshly grated nutmeg
- salt and freshly ground black pepper to taste
- $^{1}/_{2}$ cup/125 ml heavy/double cream
- 1 quantity Tomato Sauce (see page 950)

Bring a large pan of salted water to a boil. Add the spinach and cook for 10 minutes. Drain well, squeeze out excess moisture, and chop finely. • Transfer the spinach to a large bowl and mix in the Ricotta, egg and egg yolk, Parmesan, flour, and nutmeg. Season with salt and pepper. • Use a tablespoon to shape the mixture into round gnocchi. • Bring a large pan of salted water to a boil. Cook the gnocchi in small batches until they bob to the surface. Remove with a slotted spoon and transfer to a heated serving dish. • Stir the cream into the tomato sauce. Cook over low heat for 2–3 minutes, or until heated through.
• Pour over the gnocchi and serve hot.

# POTATO GNOCCHI WITH SMOKED HAM AND ARTICHOKES

C lean the artichokes by trimming the stem and remove all the tough outer leaves and the fuzzy choke. Slice thinly. • Heat the oil in a frying pan and sauté the garlic and parsley until the garlic is pale gold. • Add the artichokes. Increase the heat and pour in the wine. When the wine has evaporated, stir in the tomatoes. Season with salt and pepper. Cover and cook over low heat until the artichokes are tender, about 15 minutes. • Add the ham and remove from the heat. • Bring a large pan of salted water to a boil. Cook the gnocchi in batches until they bob to the surface. Remove with a slotted spoon and add to the pan with the sauce. Sprinkle with the Pecorino and serve.

Serves: 4–6

Preparation: 35' +
time to make
gnocchi

Cooking: 50'

Level of difficulty: 1

- **6 medium artichokes**
- **7 tbsp extra-virgin olive oil**
- **3 cloves garlic, finely chopped**
- **2 tbsp finely chopped fresh parsley**
- **$^{1}/_{2}$ cup/125 ml dry white wine**
- **2 cups/500 g chopped tomatoes**
- **salt and freshly ground black pepper to taste**
- **$1^{3}/_{4}$ cups/200 g diced smoked ham**
- **1 quantity Basic Potato Gnocchi (see page 794)**
- **1 cup/125 g freshly grated Pecorino cheese**

# POTATO GNOCCHI WITH BROCCOLI AND SPECK

*Serves: 6*

*Preparation: 25' + time to make gnocchi*

*Cooking: 25'*

*Level of difficulty: 1*

- **14 oz/450 g broccoli, broken up into small florets**
- **²/₃ cup/180 ml extra-virgin olive oil**
- **4 cloves garlic, finely chopped**
- **1 fresh red chile pepper, finely chopped**
- **salt and freshly ground black pepper to taste**
- **1 quantity Basic Potato Gnocchi (see page 794)**
- **1¹/₄ cups/150 g diced speck (smoked pork)**
- **¹/₂ cup/60 g freshly grated Pecorino cheese**

Bring a large pan of salted water to a boil. Cook the broccoli until crunchy-tender, about 8 minutes. • Remove the broccoli with a slotted spoon and set aside. • Heat the oil in a frying pan and sauté the garlic and chile until the garlic is pale gold. • Add the broccoli and mix well. Season with salt and pepper and cook for 10 minutes. • Bring the same pan of water used to cook the broccoli to a boil. Cook the gnocchi in small batches until they bob to the surface. • Remove with a slotted spoon and add to the pan with the sauce. • Stir in the speck, sprinkle with the Pecorino, and serve hot.

# SAFFRON GNOCCHI IN MEAT SAUCE

*Serves: 6*

*Preparation: 1 h + 1 h 30' to rest dough*

*Cooking: 40'*

*Level of difficulty: 2*

### GNOCCHI

- 2²/₃ cups/400 g durum-wheat flour
- ¹/₄ tsp ground saffron dissolved in ³/₄ cup/180 ml warm water, + more as needed

### MEAT SAUCE

- 4 tbsp extra-virgin olive oil
- 1 red onion, finely chopped
- ³/₄ cup/90 g diced pancetta
- 10 oz/300 g ground pork
- ¹/₂ cup/125 ml dry red wine
- 3 lb/1.5 kg peeled and chopped tomatoes
- 4 leaves fresh basil, torn
- salt and freshly ground black pepper to taste
- 1 cup/125 g freshly grated Pecorino cheese

Gnocchi: Sift the flour onto a work surface and make a well in the center. Use a wooden spoon to stir in the saffron mixture and enough water to make a smooth dough. Shape the dough into a ball, wrap in plastic wrap, and let rest for 30 minutes. • Meat Sauce: Heat the oil in a Dutch oven (earthenware casserole) and add the onion and pancetta. Cover and cook over low heat for 10 minutes. • Add the pork and sauté over high heat until browned all over. • Pour in the wine and cook until evaporated. • Stir in the tomatoes and basil and season with salt and pepper. Bring to a boil and simmer, partially covered, over low heat for at least 2 hours, adding stock or hot water if the sauce becomes too dry. • Form the dough into logs ¹/₄-in (5-mm) in diameter. Cut into ¹/₂-in (1-cm) lengths. • Lay the gnocchi on a dry cloth dusted with semolina for 1 hour. • Bring a large pan of salted water to a boil. Cook the gnocchi a few at a time until they bob to the surface. • Remove with a slotted spoon and add to the pan with the sauce. Sprinkle with Pecorino and serve.

# CHESTNUT GNOCCHI

**B**ring a large pan of salted water to a boil. Cook the chestnuts with a bay leaf for 35–45 minutes, or until softened. • Drain and transfer to a large bowl. Use a fork or potato masher to mash the chestnuts until smooth. • Mix in the Pecorino and eggs. Season with salt and pepper and add 2–3 tablespoons of semolina flour to form a smooth dough. • Perform a cooking test by breaking off a small ball of dough, dusting it with flour, and cooking it in boiling water. If it breaks during cooking, add more semolina flour. • Form into gnocchi the size of golf-balls. Roll in the semolina flour and lay them out on a plate dusted with flour. • Bring a large pan of salted water to a boil. Cook the gnocchi in small batches until they bob to the surface. • Remove with a slotted spoon and transfer to a serving dish. • Drizzle with the melted butter and garnish with the sage. Serve hot.

*Serves: 4*

*Preparation: 30'*

*Cooking: 1 h 10'*

*Level of difficulty: 2*

- 1¹/₄ lb/650 g peeled chestnuts
- 1 bay leaf
- ¹/₂ cup/60 g freshly grated Pecorino cheese
- 2 eggs
- salt and freshly ground white pepper to taste
- ¹/₂ cup/75 g durum-wheat semolina flour, + more as needed
- 6 tbsp butter, melted
- 1 sprig fresh sage

# POTATO AND NETTLE GNOCCHI

Serves: 4

Preparation: 1 h

Cooking: 1 h

Level of difficulty: 2

- 2 lb/1 kg boiling potatoes
- 3 1/2 oz/100 g cooked, drained nettles, finely chopped
- 1 1/4 cups/200 g rye flour
- 2 eggs
- salt to taste
- 6 tbsp butter
- 4 onions, thinly sliced
- 2 tbsp fresh rye bread crumbs
- 4 oz/125 g Toma (a specialty cheese from Piedmont) or Emmenthal, cut in small thin pieces

Wash the potatoes thoroughly and cook in lightly salted boiling water with their skins on. • Slip off the skins and mash in a large bowl. Spread the potatoes out on a clean work surface. Let cool to lukewarm. • Use a fork to work in the nettles, 1 cup (150 g) of rye flour, and eggs. Season with salt and mix to form a smooth dough. • Form into gnocchi the size of golf balls and set aside on a floured work surface. • Melt the butter in a medium frying pan and sauté the onions over low heat for 30 minutes, or until golden brown. • Preheat the oven to 400°F/200°C/gas 6. • Butter an ovenproof baking dish. • Arrange the cooked onions on the bottom. • Bring a large pan of salted water to a boil. Cook the gnocchi a few at a time until they bob to the surface. • Remove with a slotted spoon and place on the onions in the baking dish. Sprinkle with the bread crumbs. • Bake for 20–25 minutes, or until the bread crumbs are lightly toasted. • Arrange the pieces of Toma on top, letting it melt, and serve piping hot.

# GNOCCHI WITH TWO-CHEESE SAUCE

Two-Cheese Sauce: Bring the milk to a boil in a large heavy-bottomed saucepan. • Mix in the Taleggio and the Fontina cheeses and let them melt. • Melt 1 tablespoon of the butter in a small saucepan and stir in the flour to form a thick paste. Remove from the heat and mix in the egg yolks and salt and pepper. Stir in the melted cheeses.
• Bring a large pan of salted water to a boil. Cook the gnocchi a few at a time until they bob to the surface. • Remove with a slotted spoon and transfer to a frying pan. Add the remaining butter and sauté the gnocchi for 1 minute. • Transfer to serving plates and top with the hot cheese sauce. Season with a generous grinding of pepper and serve hot.

Serves: 6

Preparation: 30' + time to make gnocchi

Cooking: 25'

Level of difficulty: 2

**TWO-CHEESE SAUCE**

- 2$\frac{1}{3}$ cups/580 ml milk
- 5 oz/150 g Taleggio cheese, cut into small cubes
- 5 oz/150 g Fontina cheese, cut into small cubes
- 5 tbsp butter, cut up
- $\frac{3}{4}$ cup/125 g all-purpose/plain flour
- 3 egg yolks
- salt and freshly ground black pepper to taste

- 1 quantity Cuneo Potato Gnocchi (see page 800)

Serves: 4–6

Preparation: 20'

Cooking: 1 h 30'

Level of difficulty: 2

- 7 oz/200 g dried fava/broad beans, soaked overnight and drained
- 3/4 cup/180 g Ricotta cheese
- 1/3 cup/50 g all-purpose/plain flour
- 1 egg
- salt and freshly ground white pepper to taste
- 4 tbsp extra-virgin olive oil
- 4 oz/125 g carrots, thinly sliced into wheels
- 4 oz/125 g zucchini/courgettes, sliced into thin wheels
- 2 oz/60 g mixed fresh herbs (basil, parsley, dill, mint, etc), finely chopped
- 2 oz/60 g celery
- 4 tbsp heavy/double cream
- 2 tbsp butter
- 4 tbsp Vegetable Stock (see page 956)

# FAVA BEAN GNOCCHI WITH VEGETABLES

Cook the fava beans in a large pan of salted, boiling water for about 1 hour, or until tender. • Drain the beans and transfer to a food processor or blender. Chop until smooth. • Transfer to a large bowl and mix in the Ricotta, flour, egg, salt, and pepper. • Bring a large pan of salted water to a boil. Use two teaspoons to shape the gnocchi and drop them into the water. Cook until the gnocchi bob up to the surface then scoop out with a slotted spoon. • Heat the oil in a large frying pan and sauté the carrots, zucchini, celery, and leek until lightly browned. • Add the herbs, stock, cream, butter, salt, and the gnocchi. • Toss gently over high heat for 1 minute. • Serve hot.

# BAKED GNOCCHI WITH MUSHROOMS

Heat 3 tablespoons of oil in a large frying pan and sauté the carrot, celery, and onion until lightly browned. • Add the pork and cook until browned all over. • Stir in the tomato paste, soaked mushrooms, stock, and season with salt and pepper. Cook for 30 minutes, or until the sauce is reduced. • Spread the gnocchi mixture onto a work surface and let cool. • Form tablespoons of the mixture into twelve large gnocchi and stuff with the meat sauce. • Preheat the oven to 400°F/200°C/gas 6. • Butter an ovenproof baking dish. • Heat the remaining oil in a large frying pan and sauté the fresh mushrooms and garlic until the mushrooms are tender. Season with salt and pepper. Remove from the heat, and sprinkle with the parsley. • Prepare the Béchamel sauce and mix in the egg yolks, Fontina, and a pinch of salt. • Layer the gnocchi in the prepared baking dish. Spoon the Béchamel over the top and cover with the mushrooms. Sprinkle with the Parmesan and dot with the butter. • Bake for 10–15 minutes, or until lightly golden. • Serve hot.

Serves: 6
Preparation: 1 h
Cooking: 1 h 30'
Level of difficulty: 2

- 6 tbsp extra-virgin olive oil
- $^1/_2$ stalk celery, chopped
- $^1/_2$ carrot, chopped
- $^1/_2$ onion, chopped
- 8 oz/250 g ground lean pork
- 1 tbsp tomato paste
- $^1/_2$ oz/15 g dried mushrooms, soaked, drained, and chopped
- $^3/_4$ cup/180 ml Beef Stock (see page 955)
- salt and freshly ground black pepper
- 1 quantity Semolina Gnocchi (see page 796)
- 12 oz/350 g fresh mushrooms, sliced
- 1 clove garlic, finely chopped
- 1 tbsp finely chopped parsley
- 1 cup/250 ml Béchamel Sauce (see page 946)
- 2 egg yolks
- 7 oz/200 g Fontina cheese, in cubes
- 1 tbsp butter, cut into flakes
- $^1/_2$ cup/60 g freshly grated Parmesan cheese

# POTATO GNOCCHI WITH HERBS AND DRIED TOMATOES

*Serves: 4–6*

*Preparation: 40'*

*Cooking: 35'*

*Level of difficulty: 2*

- **2 lb/1 kg boiling potatoes**
- **1²/₃ cups/250 g all purpose/plain flour**
- **1 small bunch fresh parsley, finely chopped**
- **1 small bunch chives, finely chopped**
- **2 twigs thyme, finely chopped**
- **2 sprigs fresh mint, finely chopped**
- **salt to taste**
- **5 oz/150 g aged Pecorino cheese, thinly sliced**
- **³/₄ cup/180 ml milk**
- **1 tbsp cornstarch/ cornflour**
- **6 sun-dried tomatoes, packed in oil, drained, and finely chopped**

Wash the potatoes thoroughly and cook in lightly salted boiling water with their skins on. • Slip off the skins and mash in a large bowl. • Stir in 1¹/₃ cups (200 g) of the flour, 2 tablespoons of the mixed chopped herbs, and salt. • Form into logs about ¹/₂ in (1 cm) in diameter. Cut into ³/₄-in (2-cm) lengths. Sprinkle with a little flour. • Melt the Pecorino with 2 tablespoons of milk in a small saucepan over low heat. • Dissolve the cornstarch in the remaining milk. Mix into the melted Pecorino, stirring constantly, and cook for 2 minutes. Remove from the heat and set aside. • Bring a large pan of salted water to a boil. Cook the gnocchi in batches until they bob to the surface. • Remove with a slotted spoon and add to the pan with the cheese sauce. Toss well and arrange on serving plates. • Sprinkle with the remaining chopped herbs and tomatoes. Serve hot.

# GNOCCHI WITH SHRIMP

Heat 1 tablespoon of oil in a large frying pan and sauté the garlic and red pepper flakes until the garlic is pale gold. • Sauté the shrimp over high heat for 2 minutes. • Season with salt and add the brandy. Tilt the pan slightly and set the alcohol alight, holding the pan away from the body. The flame will extinguish as soon as the alcohol has burnt off. Remove from the heat and set the shrimp aside. • Heat the remaining oil in a frying pan with the wine and 1 tablespoon of the stock. Add the leek and carrot. Lower the heat, season with salt, and cook for 10 minutes, adding more stock as the mixture starts to dry. • Stir the cornstarch into the cream and mix into the sauce. Cook for 2 minutes. • Add the shrimp to the sauce. • Bring a pan of salted water to a boil. Cook the gnocchi a few at a time until they bob to the surface. • Remove with a slotted spoon and transfer to the pan with the sauce. Toss well and arrange on serving plates. Serve hot.

*Serves: 4*

*Preparation: 30'
+ time to make
gnocchi*

*Cooking: 30'*

*Level of difficulty: 3*

- **2 tbsp extra-virgin olive oil**
- **1 clove garlic**
- **$1/4$ tsp red pepper flakes**
- **14 oz/400 g shrimp/prawns, cleaned and shelled**
- **salt to taste**
- **4 tbsp brandy**
- **$1/2$ cup/125 ml dry white wine**
- **1 cup/250 ml Vegetable Stock (see page 956)**
- **1 leek, finely chopped**
- **1 carrot, finely chopped**
- **$1/2$ tbsp cornstarch/ cornflour**
- **6 tbsp heavy/ double cream**
- **1 quantity Basic Potato Gnocchi (see page 794)**

# POTATO GNOCCHI WITH BRIE AND ZUCCHINI

*Serves: 4–6*

*Preparation: 20'*
*+ time to make*
*gnocchi*

*Cooking: 25'*

*Level of difficulty: 1*

- **14 oz/400 g Brie cheese**
- **4 tbsp butter**
- **6 tbsp heavy/ double cream**
- **salt and freshly ground black pepper to taste**
- **4 zucchini/ courgettes, cut into thin wheels**
- **1 tbsp finely chopped fresh parsley**
- **1 quantity Basic Potato Gnocchi (see page 794)**

Cut the Brie into small pieces and place in a double boiler over low heat. Add half the butter and the cream and cook until the Brie and cream have melted together. • Season with pepper, remove from the heat, but let stand over the water. • Melt the remaining butter in a large frying pan and sauté the zucchini over high heat until softened. • Season with salt and pepper and sprinkle with the parsley. • Bring a large pan of salted water to a boil. Cook the gnocchi a few at a time until they bob to the surface. • Remove with a slotted spoon and transfer to a large bowl. Add the cheese sauce and the zucchini. Stir delicately and serve.

# BAKED POTATO GNOCCHI WITH TOMATO SAUCE

Wash the potatoes thoroughly and cook in lightly salted boiling water with their skins on. • Slip off the skins and mash in a large bowl. • Mix in the eggs, Pecorino, parsley, and salt and pepper. Form into 3-in (8-cm) long gnocchi. • Preheat the oven to 350°F/180°C/gas 4. • Heat the oil in a small saucepan and sauté the onion until softened. Stir in the tomato sauce, parsley, and salt and cook for 5 minutes. • Spread a small amount of the sauce on the bottom of a baking dish. Arrange the gnocchi on top and cover with the remaining sauce. • Bake for 30 minutes. • Serve piping hot.

*Serves: 6*

*Preparation: 40'*

*Cooking: 45'*

*Level of difficulty: 1*

- 2 lb/1 kg boiling potatoes
- 2 eggs
- 1¹/₃ cups/200 g freshly grated Pecorino cheese
- 1 tbsp finely chopped fresh parsley
- salt and freshly ground black pepper to taste
- 2 tbsp extra-virgin olive oil
- ¹/₂ onion, finely chopped
- 1 quantity Tomato Sauce, (see page 950)

# POTATO GNOCCHI WITH FAVA BEANS AND SHRIMP

Cook the potatoes in their skins in a large pan of salted, boiling water until tender. Drain and slip off the skins. Place in a bowl and mash until smooth. Let cool a little. • Add the egg, salt, pepper, and enough flour to obtain a firm dough. It should not stick to your hands. • Lightly flour a work surface and roll pieces of dough into long "sausage" shapes about $1/2$-inch (1.5-cm) thick. Cut into short lengths. • Shell the fava beans and chop in a food processor with the garlic, mint, and olive oil until smooth. • Place the fava bean mixture in a small bowl and stir in the Pecorino. Season with salt. • Bring a large pan of salted water to the boil and cook the prawn tails and gnocchi in batches. Scoop the gnocchi and shrimp out with a slotted spoon when the gnocchi bob up to the surface and place in a heated serving dish. • Spoon the fava bean sauce over the top and sprinkle with the chile pepper. • Toss gently and serve hot.

Serves: 4–6

Preparation: 40'

Cooking: 45'

Level of difficulty: 1

- 2 lb/1 kg boiling potatoes
- 1 egg
- salt and freshly ground black pepper to taste
- 2 cups/300 g all-purpose/plain flour
- 3 lb/1.5 kg fresh fava/broad beans
- 1 clove garlic, finely chopped
- 10 leaves fresh mint
- 4 tbsp extra-virgin olive oil
- $1/2$ cup/60 g freshly grated Pecorino cheese
- 8 oz/250 shrimp/prawn tails, shelled
- 1 dried chile pepper, crumbled

828

# SEMOLINA GNOCCHI IN STOCK

B ring the milk almost to a boil in a large, deep saucepan. Add the salt and whisk in the semolina. • Bring to a boil and let simmer for 15–20 minutes, stirring constantly with a wooden spoon. If it becomes too thick, add a little boiling water or milk. • When cooked, pour into a large bowl and let cool, stirring occasionally. • Add the egg yolks and butter, mixing well. • Beat the egg whites in a separate bowl until frothy and add them to the mixture. • Form into balls about the size of a marble. • Bring the stock to a boil in a large saucepan. Cook the gnocchi for 3–4 minutes, or until they bob to the surface. • Serve hot sprinkled with the Parmesan.

*Serves: 4–6*

*Preparation: 30'*

*Cooking: 40'*

*Level of difficulty: 2*

- **1 quart/1 liter milk**
- **¹/₈ tsp salt**
- **1²/₃ cups/250 g semolina**
- **2 eggs, separated, + 2 egg yolks**
- **3 tbsp butter, softened**
- **1¹/₂ quarts/1.5 liters Beef Stock (see page 955)**
- **1 cup/125 g freshly grated Parmesan cheese**

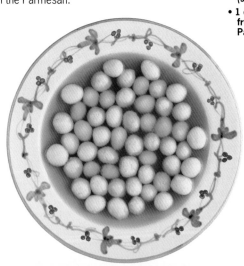

# SEMOLINA GNOCCHI WITH PANCETTA AND GORGONZOLA

*Serves: 6*

*Preparation: 40*

*Cooking: 25'*

*Level of difficulty: 1*

- **2 quarts/2 liters milk**
- **dash of nutmeg**
- **dash of salt**
- **$^2/_3$ cup/150 g butter, cut up**
- **$1^1/_3$ cups/200 g semolina**
- **3 egg yolks**
- **1 cup/125 g freshly grated Parmesan cheese**
- **$1^1/_4$ cups/150 g diced pancetta**
- **4 oz/125 g Gorgonzola dolce cheese, crumbled**

Preheat the oven to 400°F/200°C/gas 6. • Butter an ovenproof baking dish. • Bring the milk to a boil in a large saucepan. Add the nutmeg, salt, and 2 tablespoons of butter. • Sprinkle the semolina in little by little, stirring all the time so that no lumps form. Keep stirring energetically for about 15 minutes, or until the mixture is dense. • Remove from heat and mix in the egg yolks, Parmesan, and pancetta. • Spread the mixture out on a lightly floured work surface to a thickness of about $^1/_2$ in (1 cm). Let cool. • Use a glass to cut into disks. • Lay the disks in the dish, one overlapping the next. Sprinkle with the Gorgonzola. • Bake for 10 minutes. Serve hot.

# BABY GNOCCHI WITH DRIED MULLET ROE

P repare the gnocchi. • Heat the oil in a large frying pan and sauté the garlic for 2–3 minutes. • Chop the zucchini in small cubes and sauté with the garlic for 5 minutes. • Add the bottarga and chives and season with salt and pepper. Cook for 2 more minutes, then turn off heat. • In the meantime, cook the gnocchi in batches in a large pan of salted, boiling water until they bob up to the surface. Scoop them out with a slotted spoon and place in a heated serving dish. • Pour the sauce over the top and sprinkle with the parsley and mint. • Toss gently and serve hot.

*Serves: 4–6*

*Preparation: 30'*
*+ time to make gnocchi*

*Cooking: 20'*

*Level of difficulty: 2*

- **1 quantity Basic Potato Gnocchi (see page 794)**
- **4 tbsp extra-virgin olive oil**
- **1 clove garlic, finely chopped**
- **2 zucchini/ courgettes**
- **2$^1/_2$ oz/75 g bottarga (dried mullet roe), thinly sliced**
- **1 bunch chives; finely chopped**
- **salt and freshly ground black pepper to taste**
- **1 tbsp finely chopped parsley**
- **1 tbsp finely chopped mint**

Serves: 4–6

Preparation: 30'

Cooking: 25'

Level of difficulty: 2

- 1¹⁄₃ cups/200 g durum wheat flour
- 2²⁄₃ cups/400 g all-purpose/plain flour
- salt and freshly ground black pepper to taste
- ²⁄₃ cup/80 g freshly grated Parmesan cheese
- 4 tbsp extra-virgin olive oil
- ¹⁄₃ cup/120 g green olives, pitted and sliced
- 3 oz/100 g bell peppers/capsicums, finely chopped
- 10 basil leaves, torn

# GNOCCHI WITH OLIVES

Mix the two flours with enough water to obtain a fairly stiff dough. • Knead well and shape into thin "sausages", about 15 in/40 cm long. Cut into short pieces and shape into elongated, curved gnocchi. Spread out to dry. • Place 3 tablespoons of Parmesan in a bowl and stir in the oil. • Add the olives, bell peppers, basil, salt, and pepper. Mix well. • Cook the gnocchi in batches in a large pan of salted, boiling water for 3–4 minutes. Scoop out with a slotted spoon and place in a heated serving dish. • Pour the sauce over the top and toss gently. Serve hot sprinkled with the remaining Parmesan.

# BAKED GNOCCHI WITH ASPARAGUS

Heat the Béchamel sauce in a medium saucepan with the cream, saffron, and asparagus. Season with salt and pepper. • Bring the milk to a boil with 5 tablespoons of butter and a pinch of salt. Add the flour and cook over low heat, stirring until the mixture comes away from the sides of the pan. • Remove from heat and let cool completely. • Preheat the oven to 350°F/180°C/gas 4. • Beat in the eggs, one at a time, then stir in 3 oz (90 g) of Gruyère and the nutmeg. • Place the mixture in a piping bag and squeeze gnocchi from it directly into a saucepan of salted, boiling water. Cook the gnocchi in batches until they bob up to the surface. • Scoop them out with a slotted spoon and drain well. • Place in a greased baking dish, layering them with the sauce. • Sprinkle the top layer with the remaining cheese and bake for 10–15 minutes, or until golden brown on top. • Let rest 10 minutes before serving.

834

Serves: 4–6

Preparation: 15'

Cooking: 20'

Level of difficulty: 2

- • 1 quantity Béchamel (see page 946)
- • 2 cups/500 ml heavy/double cream
- • one envelope saffron
- • about 10 stalks cooked asparagus
- • salt and freshly ground black pepper to taste
- • 1$\frac{1}{3}$ cups/350 ml milk
- • 6 tbsp butter
- • 1$\frac{1}{3}$ cups/200 g all-purpose/plain flour
- • 4 eggs
- • 4 oz/125 g grated Gruyère/Swiss or Cheddar cheese
- • $\frac{1}{4}$ tsp freshly grated nutmeg

# RICOTTA GNOCCHI

Place the Ricotta cheese in a large bowl and stir with a wooden spoon until smooth and creamy. Add ³/4 cup (100 g) of Parmesan, the eggs, and pancetta. Season with salt and pepper. • Gradually stir in enough flour to obtain a firm dough. • Shape into balls the size of marbles. Dust with flour. • Heat the butter in a medium frying pan and fry the gnocchi in batches. • Serve hot as is, or add extra melted butter and grated Parmesan.

Serves: 4–6
Preparation: 15'
Cooking: 20'
Level of difficulty: 2

- 1 lb/500 g very fresh Ricotta cheese, drained
- 1¹/3 cups/150 g freshly grated Parmesan cheese
- 3 eggs
- ³/4 cup/100 g pancetta, cut in small cubes
- salt and freshly ground white pepper to taste
- 1¹/3 cups/200 g all-purpose/plain flour
- ²/3 cup/150 g butter

# AROMATIC GNOCCHI

Serves: 4–6

Preparation: 30' + 2 h
to cool

Cooking: 30'

Level of difficulty: 1

- $^1$/$_2$ cup/125 ml milk
- 1$^1$/$_3$ cups/200 g semolina
- 1 onion, stuck with 1 clove
- 1 bay leaf
- 3 oz/100 g freshly grated Emmenthal/ Swiss cheese
- $^1$/$_2$ cup/50 g finely chopped ham
- 1 tbsp finely chopped parsley
- salt and freshly ground white pepper to taste
- 1 egg
- 1 cup/150 g fine dry bread crumbs
- 1 cup/250 ml olive oil, for frying
- slices of fresh lemon, to garnish

Put the milk in a saucepan. Add the onion and bay leaf and bring to a boil. Remove from heat, cover, and let stand for 20 minutes. • Strain the milk and pour it back into the saucepan. • Return to a boil and add the semolina, stirring continuously with a wooden spoon. When the mixture begins to thicken, lower heat and cook, stirring continuously, for 10–15 minutes. Remove from heat and add the cheese, ham, parsley, salt, and pepper. • Pour into a greased rectangular pan sprinkled with bread crumbs and let cool. • Cut into 8 rectangles, dip in the beaten egg and bread crumbs, and fry in very hot oil until golden. • Serve hot with the lemon.

# SPATZLY WITH VEGETABLE SAUCE

Place the flour, milk, eggs, salt, pepper, and nutmeg in a bowl and beat until a smooth and quite firm dough forms. • Prepare the spatzly using a spatlzy-maker (or prepare very small potato gnocchi, following the instructions on page 796). • Cook the spatzly in a large pan of salted, boiling water for 3–4 minutes. Drain well and place in a bowl with 2 tablespoons of oil. Toss gently so that the oil stops them from sticking together. • Blanch the zucchini and bell pepper together in a pan of salted, boiling water for 2–3 minutes. • Heat the remaining oil in a large frying pan and toast the pine nuts for 5 minutes over high heat. • Add the bell peppers, zucchini, and tomatoes. Season with salt and pepper and add the olives, capers, basil, and chile pepper. • Add the spatzly to the pan and toss gently over medium heat for 1–2 minutes. • Serve hot.

838

*Serves: 4*

*Preparation: 30'*

*Cooking: 30'*

*Level of difficulty: 2*

- 1²/₃ cups/250 g all-purpose/plain flour
- ¹/₂ cup/125 ml milk
- 2 eggs
- salt and freshly ground black pepper to taste
- ¹/₄ tsp freshly grated nutmeg
- 2 tbsp extra-virgin olive oil
- 1 large zucchini/courgettes, cut in small cubes
- ¹/₂ small yellow bell pepper/capsicum, cut in small pieces
- 2 tbsp pine nuts
- 12 cherry tomatoes, cut in half
- 2 tbsp pitted black olives
- 1 tbsp salted capers, rinsed
- 6 leaves basil, torn
- 1 dried chile pepper, crumbled

# GRAINS & BEANS

# GRAINS AND BEANS

This chapter includes a wide-ranging selection of recipes for different types of grains and beans. On these pages we have included step-by-step instructions for making a delicious Italian dish based on cornmeal, called polenta. Making polenta by hand can be hard work, although nowadays precooked varieties are available that only require 8–10 minutes stirring.

BASIC POLENTA

Serves: 6–8

- 4 quarts/4 liters cold water
- 2 tbsp coarse sea salt
- 3 1/2 cups/450 g coarse-grain yellow cornmeal

**1.** Bring the water and salt to a boil in a large heavy-bottomed pan.

**2.** Add the cornmeal gradually, stirring continuously so that no lumps form.

**3.** Stir the polenta over medium heat with a long, wooden spoon. The polenta should be stirred almost continuously for the 40–45 minutes it takes to cook. Quantities and method are the same when using an electric polenta cauldron. Stir the cornmeal into the boiling water gradually, then turn on the mixer. Leave for 40–45 minutes.

**4.** Pour the cooked polenta onto a serving platter and serve hot with sauce, or leave to cool to make fried or baked polenta crostini.

# POLENTA WITH BEANS AND PANCETTA

S oak the beans overnight in a large bowl of water. Drain and set aside. • Heat the oil in a large frying pan and sauté the pancetta and onion until crispy. • Add the beans and sage and pour in the water. Bring to a boil and cover and simmer over low heat for 1 hour. • When the beans are almost tender, season with salt. Gradually sprinkle in the cornmeal, stirring constantly. • Cook over low heat for 45 minutes, adding a little warm water as the mixture begins to dry out. The polenta should be fairly soft, not stiff. • Turn out onto a board or platter and serve.

844

*Serves: 6*

*Preparation: 20'*
  *+ 12 h to soak*

*Cooking: 2 h*

*Level of difficulty: 1*

- 1$^{1}$/$_{3}$ cups/250 g dried borlotti or pinto beans
- 1 tbsp extra-virgin olive oil
- $^{1}$/$_{2}$ cup/60 g diced pancetta or bacon
- $^{1}$/$_{2}$ onion, finely chopped
- salt to taste
- 2$^{1}$/$_{4}$ cups/350 g coarse-grain yellow cornmeal
- 4 leaves fresh sage, torn
- 1$^{1}$/$_{4}$ quarts/1.25 liters water

# BUCKWHEAT POLENTA WITH ANCHOVIES AND CHEESE

*Serves: 4–6*

*Preparation: 25'*
*+ 30' to cool*

*Cooking: 1 h 20'*

*Level of difficulty: 1*

- 1¹/₂ quarts/1.5 liters water
- 1 tbsp coarse sea salt
- 1¹/₃ cups/200 g coarse-grain yellow cornmeal
- 1 cup/150 g buckwheat flour
- ¹/₂ cup/125 g butter, cut up
- 3¹/₂ oz/100 g salted anchovies, rinsed and boned
- 8 oz/250 g Fontina cheese, thinly sliced

Bring the water to a boil with the salt in a large pan. Sprinkle in the cornmeal and buckwheat flour, stirring constantly with a balloon whisk to prevent any lumps from forming. • Cook over medium heat, stirring almost constantly for about 45 minutes. • When the polenta is ready (it should be stiff), turn it out onto a cutting board and let cool for 30 minutes. • Melt three-quarters of the butter in a small saucepan. • Preheat the oven to 400°F/200°C/gas 6. • Use the remaining butter to grease a deep ovenproof dish. • Slice the polenta about ³/₄ in (2 cm) thick and arrange one-third of in the prepared dish. Sprinkle with one-third of the anchovies, cheese, and half the remaining melted butter. Top with the remaining polenta and drizzle with the remaining butter. Bake for 20–25 minutes, or until golden brown on top. • Serve hot.

# POLENTA WITH SAUSAGE

Melt the lard in a frying pan and sauté the onion, celery, carrot, and parsley over medium heat until the vegetables have softened. • Pour in the tomato concentrate and water. Season with salt and cover and cook over medium-low heat for 30 minutes. • Add the sausage and cook for 15 minutes. • Bring the water to a boil with the salt in a large pan. Gradually sprinkle in the cornmeal, stirring constantly with a large balloon whisk to prevent any lumps from forming. Cook over low heat, stirring almost constantly for about 45 minutes. • When the polenta is ready (it should be stiff), turn it out onto a cutting board and let cool for 30 minutes. • Spoon the sauce over the top. Serve hot.

*Serves: 6*

*Preparation: 25' + 30' to cool*

*Cooking: 1 h 40'*

*Level of difficulty: 2*

- **3 tbsp lard or butter**
- **1 onion, finely chopped**
- **1 stalk celery, finely chopped**
- **1 small carrot, finely chopped**
- **2 tbsp finely chopped flat-leaf parsley**
- **1 tbsp tomato concentrate/ purée dissolved in $1/2$ cup/125 ml cold water**
- **salt to taste**
- **12 oz/350 g Italian sausage, peeled and coarsely chopped**
- **3 quarts/3 liters cold water**
- **1 tbsp coarse sea salt**
- **$3^1/3$ cups/500 g coarse-grain yellow cornmeal**

# POLENTA GNOCCHI

**B**ring the water to a boil with the salt in a large pan. Gradually sprinkle in the cornmeal, stirring constantly with a large balloon whisk to prevent any lumps from forming. Cook over low heat, stirring almost constantly, for about 45 minutes, or until the polenta is stiff. • Stir in the butter and remove from the heat. • Preheat the oven to 400°F/200°C/gas 6. • Use a tablespoon to make oval dumplings, dipping the spoon in cold water to prevent the polenta from sticking. Don't worry if the dumplings look rather untidy. • Arrange a layer of dumplings in a deep ovenproof dish. Spoon some meat sauce over the top and cover with another layer of polenta dumplings. Continue until all the polenta and meat sauce are in the dish. Sprinkle with the Parmesan. • Bake for 10 minutes, or until the topping is golden brown. Serve hot.

| |
|---|
| *Serves: 6* |
| *Preparation: 25'* |
| *Cooking: 1 h* |
| *Level of difficulty: 2* |

- 2 quarts/2 liters water
- 1 heaped tbsp coarse sea salt
- 3$^1$/₃ cups/500 g coarse-grain yellow cornmeal
- 4 tbsp butter
- 1 quantity Meat Sauce (see page 952)
- 1$^1$/₄ cups/150 g freshly grated Parmesan cheese

# BAKED POLENTA IN CHEESE SAUCE

*Serves: 4*

*Preparation: 20' + 4 h for the polenta*

*Cooking: 30'*

*Level of difficulty: 2*

- • 1 quantity **Basic Polenta (see pages 842)**
- • 2 tbsp butter
- • 1 tbsp all-purpose/ **plain flour**
- • 1 cup/250 ml milk
- • pinch of nutmeg
- • 6 oz/180 g **Gorgonzola cheese, chopped**
- • 6 oz/180 g **Emmental (or Gruyère) cheese, thinly sliced**
- • $^1/_2$ cup/60 g **freshly grated Parmesan cheese**
- • 1 tbsp butter

Prepare the polenta. Set aside to cool for at least 3 hours. • Preheat the oven to 400°F/200°C/gas 6. • Melt the butter in a saucepan. Add the flour and cook over low heat for 1–2 minutes, stirring continuously. • Begin adding the milk, a little at a time, stirring continuously until the sauce is smooth. Season with a little nutmeg. • Turn up the heat and add the Gorgonzola, Emmental, and Parmesan, a handful at a time, stirring constantly until smooth. • Use the butter to grease an ovenproof baking dish large enough to hold the polenta and sauce in a layer about 2 in/5 cm thick. • Cut the polenta into $^3/_4$-in/2-cm cubes. • Cover the bottom of the dish with half the polenta and pour half the sauce over the top. Put the remaining polenta on top and cover with the remaining sauce. • Bake for 25–30 minutes, or until the top is golden brown.

# ITALIAN SAUSAGE WITH POLENTA

*Serves: 4–6*

*Preparation: 25'*

*Cooking: 50'*

*Level of difficulty: 2*

- 1 quart/1 liter water
- 1 tbsp coarse sea salt
- 2 cups/300 g coarse-grain yellow cornmeal
- 2 tbsp butter
- 1 tbsp extra-virgin olive oil
- 1 small twig rosemary + extra, to garnish
- 1 lb/500 g very fresh thin Italian pork sausages
- 1 cup/250 ml dry white or red wine

**B**ring the water to a boil with the salt in a large pan. Gradually add the cornmeal, stirring constantly with a large balloon whisk to prevent lumps from forming. Cook over low heat, stirring almost constantly for about 45 minutes. • About 20 minutes before the polenta is cooked, use a toothpick to prick holes in the sausages. • Melt the butter with the oil in a large frying pan over medium heat. Add the rosemary and sausages and cook for 3–4 minutes, or until browned all over. • Pour in the wine, cover and cook over low heat for about 10 minutes, turning the sausages halfway through. • Cut the sausages into 2-in (5-cm) pieces. • Spoon the polenta into serving dishes and arrange the sausage on top. Garnish with the rosemary and drizzle with the cooking juices. Serve hot.

Serves: 6–8

Preparation: 20'
+ 2 h to marinate

Cooking: 1 h

Level of difficulty: 2

- 2 lb/1 kg rump or topside beef, cut into small chunks
- 1 tsp minced ginger
- 2 tbsp finely chopped thyme
- 6 bay leaves
- 2 cloves garlic, finely chopped
- 1 sprig rosemary, chopped
- 4 leaves sage, finely chopped
- 1 tsp red pepper flakes
- $^1/_2$ cup/125 ml extra-virgin olive oil
- juice and grated zest of 2 lemons
- salt and freshly ground black pepper to taste
- 8 oz/250 g leeks, thinly sliced
- 2 cups/250 g diced pancetta or bacon
- 1 cup/250 ml dry white wine
- 1 quantity Basic Polenta (see pages 842)
- 3 tbsp butter

# POLENTA WITH VEAL AND PANCETTA

Mix the veal, ginger, thyme, bay leaves, garlic, rosemary, sage, and red pepper flakes in a bowl. Pour in one-third of the oil and half the lemon juice. Season with salt and pepper. Let marinate for 2 hours. • Heat the remaining oil in a large frying pan and sauté the leeks over high heat until cooked but still crisp. Remove and set aside. • Sauté the pancetta in the same oil for 3–4 minutes. • Add the marinated veal and spices and cook until browned all over. • Pour in the wine and let it evaporate. • Add the lemon zest and remaining juice and cook until the meat is tender. • Meanwhile, prepare the polenta. • Melt the butter into the cooked polenta and spoon it into individual serving dishes. • Top with the veal, leeks, and pancetta. Serve hot.

# WHEAT WITH MEAT SAUCE

Soak the wheat in cold water for 12 hours. •
Drain and transfer to a large saucepan. Pour in
enough hot water to cover the wheat with double
the volume. • Bring to a boil and cook for 1–2
hours, or until tender. • Meanwhile, sauté the garlic
and chile in the oil in a heavy-bottomed saucepan
until the garlic is
pale gold. •
Discard the garlic. • Add the lamb and beef and
cook over high heat until browned all over. • Stir in
the tomatoes and season with salt. Cover and
simmer over low heat for 2 hours. • Drain the
wheat when tender and place in a heated serving
dish. Top with the meat sauce and serve hot.

*Nutritious wheat takes a while to prepare.
Cook a double quantity and freeze half for salads.*

852

*Serves: 4–6*

*Preparation: 30'*
*+ 12 h to soak*

*Cooking: 2 h 30'*

*Level of difficulty: 1*

- **14 oz/400 g wheat berries**
- **2 cloves garlic, lightly crushed but whole**
- **1 dried red chile pepper, crumbled**
- **2 tbsp extra-virgin olive oil**
- **7 oz/200 g ground lamb**
- **7 oz/200 g ground beef**
- **1 lb/500 g tomatoes, peeled and finely chopped**
- **salt to taste**

# WHEAT WITH ZUCCHINI, WALNUTS, AND PARMESAN

*Serves: 4–6*

*Preparation: 20'*
*+ 12 h to soak*

*Cooking: 1–2 h 15'*

*Level of difficulty: 1*

- 10 oz/300 g wheat berries
- 4 zucchini/courgettes
- salt and freshly ground black pepper to taste
- 20 walnuts, shelled, chopped, and toasted
- 2 tbsp finely chopped parsley
- 1 tbsp finely chopped mint + extra leaves to garnish
- 3 oz/100 g Parmesan cheese, in thin flakes
- 6 tbsp extra-virgin olive oil
- 1 tbsp freshly squeezed lemon juice

Soak the wheat in cold water for 12 hours. • Drain and transfer to a large saucepan. Pour in enough hot water to cover the wheat with double the volume. • Bring to a boil and cook for 1–2 hours, or until tender. • Rinse the zucchini, pat them dry, and slice thinly. Grill on a red-hot griddle for 30 seconds on each side. • Transfer to a bowl, salt and pepper them generously, and drizzle with 2 tablespoons of the oil. Sprinkle the parsley and mint over the top. • Drain the wheat thoroughly and set aside. Let cool. • Place the zucchini on a large serving dish and spoon the wheat over the top. Drizzle with the remaining oil and the lemon juice. • Add the toasted walnuts, Parmesan cheese and, if liked, a few more leaves of fresh mint.

# COUSCOUS WITH MIXED VEGETABLES

Place the couscous in a large bowl. Pour in the boiling water and add 2 tablespoons of oil. Let stand for 10 minutes, or until the couscous has absorbed the water. Break it up with a fork and drizzle with the lemon juice and mint. • Heat the remaining oil in a large frying pan and sauté the onions, carrots, zucchini, and cumin until lightly browned. • Pour in half the stock and cook for 10 minutes. • Stir in the garbanzo beans and peas. • Dissolve the saffron in the remaining stock and pour it into the pan. Season with salt and pepper and cook for 10 minutes more. Remove from the heat. • Spoon the couscous onto the center of a serving plate, surround with the vegetables with their cooking sauce, and serve hot.

Serves: 4

Preparation: 30' + 10' to soak

Cooking: 30'

Level of difficulty: 1

- 14 oz/400 g precooked couscous
- 1 1/4 cups/310 ml boiling water
- 5 tbsp extra-virgin olive oil
- juice of 1/2 lemon
- 1 sprig fresh mint, finely chopped
- 2 red onions, finely sliced
- 2 carrots, cut into short lengths
- 3 zucchini/courgettes, cut into short lengths
- 1/2 tsp cumin seeds
- scant 1/2 cup/100 ml Vegetable Stock (see page 956)
- 2/3 cup/100 g frozen peas
- 8 oz/250 g boiled garbanzo beans (chickpeas), drained
- 4 strands saffron, crumbled
- salt and freshly ground black pepper to taste

# BARLEY AND VEGETABLE SALAD

Serves: 4
Preparation: 20'
Cooking: 1 h
Level of difficulty: 2

10 oz/300 g pearl barley

2 quarts/2 liters water

salt to taste

6 tbsp extra-virgin olive oil

1 clove garlic, lightly crushed but whole

2 zucchini/ courgettes, cut in very small pieces

1 carrot, cut in very small pieces

3 scallions/spring onions, finely chopped

$^1/_2$ tsp red pepper flakes

2 eggplants/ aubergines, finely chopped

2 tbsp finely torn fresh basil

2 tbsp finely chopped fresh mint

juice of 1 lemon

Rinse the barley and place in a saucepan. Pour in the water and bring to a boil. Cover and cook over low heat for 30 minutes. Season with salt. • Heat 4 tablespoons of oil in a large frying pan and sauté the garlic until pale gold. • Discard the garlic. Sauté the zucchini, carrot, and scallions in the same oil until lightly browned. • Add the red pepper flakes and season with salt. Cook for 10 minutes, stirring often. • Transfer the vegetables to a large bowl and set aside, keeping them warm. • Add the remaining 2 tablespoons of oil to the same pan. Sauté the eggplants for 10 minutes over low heat. Season with salt. • Remove from the heat, mix with the other vegetables, and sprinkle with basil and mint. • Drain the barley and add to the vegetables. Drizzle with the lemon juice and mix well. • Serve warm or at room temperature.

# SPELT SALAD WITH VEGETABLES

C ook the spelt in a large pan of salted, boiling water for about 45 minutes, or until tender.
• Heat the oil in a large frying pan and sauté the zucchini, eggplant, onion, bell pepper, and garlic. Season with salt and cover and cook over medium heat for 10 minutes. • Stir in the tomatoes and cook over high heat for 3 minutes.
• Add the capers and basil. Mix in the mustard.
• Drain the spelt when tender and add to the pan.
• Stir carefully and serve at room temperature or during the summer slightly chilled.

*Serves: 4*

*Preparation: 20'*

*Cooking: 1 h*

*Level of difficulty: 1*

• 10 oz/300 g spelt
• 4 tbsp extra-virgin olive oil
• 2 zucchini/ courgettes, thinly sliced
• 1 eggplant/ aubergine, thinly sliced
• 1 onion, finely chopped
• 1 green or yellow bell pepper/ capsicum, seeded and finely chopped
• 1 clove garlic, finely chopped
• salt and freshly ground black pepper to taste
• 8–10 cherry tomatoes, halved
• 2 tbsp salted capers, rinsed
• 1 bunch fresh basil, torn
• 1 tbsp mustard dissolved in 1 tbsp warm water

# SPELT, ARUGULA, AND APPLES WITH GORGONZOLA AND HONEY

*Serves: 4*

*Preparation: 45'*

*Cooking: 45'*

*Level of difficulty: 2*

- 14 oz/400 g spelt
- 1 bunch of arugula/rocket
- 2 Granny Smith apples
- 2 tbsp honey
- 4 oz/125 g spicy Gorgonzola cheese
- 1 tbsp wine vinegar
- 6 tbsp extra-virgin olive oil
- salt and freshly ground black pepper to taste

Rinse the spelt and boil it in plenty of salted water for about 45 minutes, or until tender. Drain, allow to cool, and transfer to a large serving bowl. • Mix the oil in a small bowl with the vinegar, honey, a pinch of salt, and a generous grinding of black pepper. Stir thoroughly and set aside. • Rinse the arugula and drain well. Chop coarsely. • Cut the cheese into small pieces. • Rinse the apples but don't peel them. Pat dry, remove the core, and slice thinly. • Add the arugula, apple, and Gorgonzola to the bowl with the spelt. • Drizzle with the honey sauce, toss gently, and serve.

*If liked, add a few toasted almonds and 1 teaspoon of cumin seeds to the salad.*

863

# QUENELLE WITH CRESS

Soak the bread crumbs in the milk for 15 minutes, or until all the milk is absorbed.
• Drain, squeezing out the excess milk. • Mix the chicken, soaked bread crumbs, cream, ham, egg, parsley, and salt and pepper until smooth. Form into large quenelle (or gnocchi). • Cook the quenelle in small batches in a large pan of salted, boiling water for about 2 minutes, or until they bob to the surface. • Remove with a slotted spoon and set aside, keeping them warm. • Blanch the cress in salted, boiling salted water for 1 minute. Drain, squeezing it dry, and chop it finely. • Melt the butter in a large frying pan and sauté the cress for 1 minute. Pour in the stock and season with salt and pepper. • Transfer to a food processor or blender and process until smooth. • Pour the sauce over the hot quenelle. Sprinkle with Parmesan and serve hot.

*Serves: 4*

*Preparation: 40'*
  *+ 15' to soak*

*Cooking: 20'*

*Level of difficulty: 1*

- 7 oz/200 g fresh bread crumbs
- 6 tbsp milk
- 5 oz/150 g ground chicken
- $^2$/3 cup/150 g heavy/double cream
- 1$^1$/4 cups/150 g diced ham
- 1 egg
- 1 tbsp finely chopped fresh parsley
- salt and freshly ground black pepper to taste
- 8 oz/250 g watercress
- 4 tbsp butter
- 4 tbsp Vegetable Stock (see page 956)
- 1 cup/125 g freshly grated Parmesan cheese

# BAKED BREAD WITH PEARS AND GORGONZOLA

*Serves: 4*

*Preparation: 40'*

*Cooking: 1 h*

*Level of difficulty: 2*

- 1 heart celery
- 2 tbsp butter
- 1 bay leaf
- 1/2 cup/125 ml Vegetable Stock (see page 956)
- 2 pears, preferably Williams, cored and quartered
- salt and freshly ground black pepper to taste
- 12 large slices flavorful whole-wheat bread
- 1 cup/250 g Gorgonzola cheese, thinly sliced
- 1 cup/125 g freshly grated Parmesan cheese

Clean the celery, setting aside the leaves. Rinse and cut into short lengths. • Melt 1 tablespoon of butter in a large frying pan and add the celery and bay leaf. Cook over medium heat for 5 minutes. • Pour in the stock and cover and cook for 15 minutes. • Add the pears and cook over high heat for 3 minutes. Season with salt and pepper. Discard the bay leaf. • Use a slotted spoon to remove the celery and pears. Reserve the cooking juices. • Cut the crusts off four slices of bread, then flatten them with a rolling pin and cut them into triangles. • Preheat the oven to 400°F/200°C/gas 6. • Butter a baking dish and line with the slices of bread that still have crusts. • Drizzle with the reserved cooking juices and top with the celery and pears. Sprinkle with Gorgonzola and arrange the triangles of bread on top. Sprinkle with Parmesan and top with the remaining butter. • Bake for 30–35 minutes, or until the pears have softened and the cheeses have melted. • Serve hot.

# ASPARAGUS AND BREAD GRATIN

Serves: 6

Preparation: 40'

Cooking: 50'

Level of difficulty: 1

Cook the asparagus in a large pan of salted, boiling water for 10 minutes, or until crunchy-tender. • Drain, discarding the tough stalks. • Melt 2 tablespoons of butter in a large frying pan and sauté the asparagus over low heat for 5 minutes. • Preheat the oven to 350°F/180°C/gas 4. • Butter a baking dish and arrange the bread on the bottom, overlapping slightly. • Slice 10 oz (300 g) of Fontina thinly and coarsely grate the remainder. • Top the bread with the sliced Fontina and asparagus. • Beat the eggs and egg yolk in a small bowl until frothy. Add the milk, cream, nutmeg, salt, and pepper. • Pour into the baking dish. Let stand for 10 minutes, so that the egg mixture is almost completely absorbed. • Sprinkle with the grated Fontina and dot with the remaining butter. • Bake for 25–30 minutes, or until lightly golden. • Serve hot.

- 1³/₄ lb/800 g asparagus, trimmed
- 4 tbsp butter
- 12 oz/350 g white firm-textured bread, thinly sliced
- 14 oz/400 g Fontina or Gruyère cheese
- 2 eggs + 1 egg yolk
- 1 cup/250 ml milk
- 1 cup/250 ml heavy/double cream
- ¹/₈ tsp freshly grated nutmeg
- salt and freshly ground black pepper to taste

Serves: 6

Preparation: 40'
+ 12 h to soak

Cooking: 3 h

Level of difficulty: 2

- 3 cups/300 g dried fava/broad beans, soaked overnight
- 1 potato, thickly sliced
- 2 quarts/2 liters water, + more as needed
- 1/4 cup/50 g short-grain rice
- 4 tbsp extra-virgin olive oil
- 1/2 small onion, finely chopped
- 2 tomatoes, peeled and finely chopped
- 1 dried red chile pepper, crumbled (optional)
- 1 1/3 cups/200 g wheat semolina

# FAVA BEAN PURÉE WITH SEMOLINA

Place the potato in a large pan and add the fava beans. Add enough water to cover the beans. Cover and cook over low heat for 30 minutes. • Drain the cooking water and replace with very hot water to cover the surface of the fava beans. Season with salt. Cover and cook over low heat for 2 hours, or until very soft. • Add the rice and cook for 13–15 minutes, or until tender. • Drizzle with 1 tablespoon of oil. • Heat the remaining oil in a large frying pan and sauté the onion until browned. • Stir in the tomatoes and chile, if using. Cook for 5 minutes. • Pour in 1/2 cup (125 ml) of water and bring to a boil. Season with salt and gradually sprinkle in the semolina. Cook, stirring constantly, until cooked. • Add the semolina to the fava bean purée and mix well. Serve hot.

# MOZZARELLA BITES WITH FAVA BEANS

Process the Mozzarella in a food processor or blender with the egg, Parmesan, parsley, basil, and mint until smooth. Season with salt and pepper. • Shape the mixture into balls the size of walnuts. Roll in the bread crumbs until well coated. • Heat the oil in a large frying pan and sauté the lemon quarters over high heat for 2 minutes, turning them often. Remove and set aside. • Sauté the Mozzarella balls in small batches in the same oil for 5–7 minutes, or until golden brown all over. • Add the fava beans and cook for 5 minutes. Add the lemon slices to the pan, cook for 1 minute, and serve.

*Serves: 4*

*Preparation: 30'*

*Cooking: 15'*

*Level of difficulty: 1*

- 12 oz/350 g Mozzarella cheese
- 1 egg
- 1 cup/125 g freshly grated Parmesan cheese
- 1 bunch fresh parsley
- 6 leaves fresh basil, torn
- 1 sprig fresh mint
- salt and freshly ground black pepper to taste
- $1/2$ cup/60 g fine dry bread crumbs
- 6–7 tbsp extra-virgin olive oil
- 1 lemon, quartered
- $1^3/4$ lb/800 g freshly hulled fava/broad beans

Serves: 6

Preparation: 1 h

Cooking: 40'

Level of difficulty: 3

## CRÊPES

- 5 eggs
- 1 1/3 cups/200 g garbanzo bean/chickpea flour
- 1 cup/150 g plain/all-purpose flour
- 1/8 tsp salt
- 2 cups/500 ml milk
- 4 tbsp water
- 2 tbsp butter

## FILLING

- 4 tbsp extra-virgin olive oil
- 1 onion, chopped
- 1 carrot, chopped
- 1 stalk celery, chopped
- 2 artichokes, cleaned and finely chopped
- 3/4 cup/180 g heavy/double cream
- salt and freshly ground black pepper to taste
- 1 1/4 cups/150 g diced ham
- 1/2 cup/60 g freshly grated Parmesan cheese

# FILLED GARBANZO BEAN CRÊPES

C rêpes: Beat the eggs in a large bowl. Use a balloon whisk to beat in the garbanzo bean and all-purpose flours and salt until smooth. • Pour in the milk and water, mixing constantly. • Melt a small amount of butter in a small frying pan. Pour in a small amount of batter and, tilting the frying pan, distribute the batter over the pan bottom. Cook the crêpe for 2–3 minutes, turning so that both sides are cooked. Remove from the heat and keep warm. • Prepare the other crêpes (you should get 15 in all) in the same manner, stacking them as you go, until you have used up all the batter. • Filling: Heat the oil in a large frying pan and sauté the onion, carrot, and celery until lightly browned. • Add the artichokes and cook until tender. • Pour in the cream and season with salt and pepper. Cook over low heat for 20 minutes, or until reduced by half. • Add the ham and 2 tablespoons of Parmesan to the vegetables. • Spoon the filling into the center of nine crêpes, then roll them up. Slice each crêpe about 1/2-in (1.5-cm) thick. • Shape the remaining crêpes around six small fluted tartlet molds and place in a hot oven until crisp. Remove the crêpes from the molds. • Fill them with the slices of stuffed crêpes and sprinkle with the remaining Parmesan. • Broil (grill) the crêpes until the cheese has melted. Serve hot.

# MIXED VEGETABLES WITH PANCETTA AND BREAD

Place the potatoes and vegetables in a large Dutch oven (earthenware saucepan). Pour in enough water to cover the vegetables completely. Season with salt. Bring to a boil and cover and cook over low heat for about 2 hours. • Heat the oil in a large frying pan and sauté the onion, pancetta, and chile until the onion and pancetta are lightly browned. • Add the sautéed mixture to the vegetables and cook for 3 minutes, stirring well. • Add the bread and cook for 10 minutes, stirring frequently. • Serve hot.

Serves: 6

Preparation: 30'

Cooking: 2 h 30'

Level of difficulty: 1

- 10 oz/300 g potatoes, cut into small chunks
- 1 3/4 lb/800 g mixed vegetables, such as green beans, zucchini/courgettes, and tomatoes, finely chopped
- 2 quarts/2 liters water, + more as needed
- salt to taste
- 4 tbsp extra-virgin olive oil
- 1 onion, finely chopped
- 3/4 cup/90 g diced pancetta
- 1 small dried chile pepper, crumbled (optional)
- 6 slices day-old bread, coarsely chopped

# FAVA BEAN PURÉE WITH BROILED BELL PEPPERS

Serves: 6

Preparation: 30' + 12 h to soak

Cooking: 2 h 30'

Level of difficulty: 1

- 2 1/2 cups/250 g dried fava/broad beans
- 1 potato, coarsely chopped
- 2 quarts/2 liters water, + more as needed
- 3 tbsp extra-virgin olive oil
- 1 red bell pepper/ capsicum
- 1 yellow bell pepper/capsicum

Soak the fava beans overnight. • Drain and rinse well. • Arrange the potato on the bottom of a large pan and add the fava beans. Pour in enough water to cover the beans. Cover and cook over medium-low heat for 30 minutes. • Drain the cooking water and replace with very hot water to cover the surface of the fava beans. Season with salt. Cover and cook over low heat for 2 hours, adding water if the beans begin to dry. • Drizzle with the oil and mix with a wooden spoon until dense and creamy. • Clean the peppers, removing the seeds and core. Slice each into 4–6 pieces and place under the broiler (grill) until the skins are blackened. Remove the skins and rinse the peppers. • Cut into thin strips and arrange on top of the purée.

# FAVA BEAN PURÉE WITH TOMATOES AND BREAD

Soak the fava beans overnight. • Drain and rinse well. • Arrange the potato on the bottom of a large pan and add the fava beans. Pour in enough water to cover the beans. Cover and cook over medium-low heat for 30 minutes. • Drain the cooking water and replace with very hot water to cover the surface of the fava beans. Season with salt. Cover and cook over low heat for 2 hours, adding water if the beans begin to dry. • Remove from the heat and set aside. • Heat the oil in a large frying pan and sauté the onion until lightly browned. Stir in the tomatoes and season with salt. Cook over low heat for about 5 minutes, or until the tomatoes begin to break down. • Stir in the fava bean puree and mix well. • Add half the bread and cook over low heat for 5 minutes, stirring constantly. • Crumble the remaining bread and sprinkle over the puree. Serve hot.

*Serves: 6*

*Preparation: 30'*
*+ 12 h to soak*

*Cooking: 2 h 50'*

*Level of difficulty: 1*

- **3 cups/300 g dried fava/broad beans**
- **2 quarts/2 liters water, + more as needed**
- **salt to taste**
- **4 tbsp extra-virgin olive oil**
- **1 onion, finely chopped**
- **2 firm-ripe tomatoes, peeled, seeded, and coarsely chopped**
- **4 slices day-old bread, cut into small pieces**

# FATTOUSH

*Serves: 4–6*

*Preparation: 20'*

*Cooking: 5'*

*Level of difficulty: 1*

- **8 slices firm-textured bread**
- **1 medium cucumber, finely chopped**
- **3 firm-ripe tomatoes, finely chopped**
- **1 onion, finely chopped**
- **1 small bunch fresh parsley, finely chopped**
- **1 small bunch fresh mint, finely chopped**
- **1 small bunch fresh cilantro/coriander,. finely chopped**
- **2 cloves garlic, finely chopped**
- **juice of 2 lemons**
- **$^1/_2$ cup/125 ml extra-virgin olive oil**
- **salt and freshly ground white pepper to taste**
- **seeds from 1 pomegranate**

Remove the crusts from the slices of bread. Chop coarsely and toast in a hot oven until golden brown and crisp. • Transfer to a large bowl and mix in the cucumber, tomatoes, onion, parsley, mint, cilantro, and garlic. • Drizzle with the lemon juice and oil and toss well. Season with salt and pepper. • Sprinkle with the pomegranate seeds and serve.

# SICILIAN COUSCOUS

B oil the fish stock with the onion, garlic, oil, parsley, saffron, cinnamon, lemon, and salt for about 30 minutes. • Carefully clean the fish, fillet it, and remove all the small bones. • Sauté the onion, bay leaf, and cinnamon in 4 tablespoons of the oil in a Dutch oven (earthenware casserole) over low heat for 10 minutes. • Add the garlic, tomato concentrate, lemon zest, and 1 cup (250 ml) water. Bring to a boil and gently add the filleted fish. • Pour in enough water to cover the fish completely. Season with salt and cover and cook over very low heat for about 1 hour. • Place the couscous in a large saucepan. Filter the fish stock and pour it, still boiling, over the couscous. Stir, making sure that the couscous is completely covered. Cover and let rest for 10 minutes. • Place on the heat and add the remaining 4 tablespoons of oil to prevent clumping. Stir for 5 minutes, adding more stock as required, then transfer to a large, deep serving dish. Stir and cover with a kitchen cloth. • Let rest for about 20 minutes before serving with the fish sauce spooned over the top.

Serves: 6

Preparation: 1 h

Cooking: 1 h

Level of difficulty: 2

- 1 1/2 quarts/1.5 liters Fish Stock (see page 958)
- 1 onion, cut into quarters
- 2 cloves garlic, crushed but whole
- 4 tbsp extra-virgin olive oil
- 1 tbsp finely chopped parsley
- 1/2 tsp saffron threads, crumbled
- 1 small stick cinnamon
- 1/2 lemon, chopped
- salt to taste
- 3 lb/1.5 kg mixed fish, such as mullet, snapper, grouper, and cod
- 1 red onion, finely chopped
- 1 bay leaf
- 1 small stick cinnamon
- 1/2 cup/125 ml extra-virgin olive oil
- 2 cloves garlic, finely chopped
- 2 tbsp tomato concentrate/puree
- grated zest of 1/2 lemon
- 3 cups/750 ml water
- 2 lb/1 kg instant couscous

# SOUPS

# CHEESE DUMPLING SOUP

Mix the Parmesan with the bread crumbs and eggs in a large bowl. • Melt the butter in a small saucepan and add to the bread crumb mixture. • Add the nutmeg, lemon zest, and salt and set aside for 30 minutes. • Press the mixture through a food mill fitted with the disk with the largest holes, to produce short, cylindrical dumplings, about $1^1/_2$ in (4 cm) long. Cut them off with the tip of a sharp knife as they are squeezed out of the mill. If the mixture is too stiff, add a little stock; if too soft, add some more bread crumbs. • Let the little worm-shaped dumplings fall directly into a saucepan of boiling stock and simmer until they bob up to the surface. Turn off the heat; leave to stand for a few minutes and serve.

*Serves: 4*

*Preparation: 25' + 30' to rest*

*Cooking: 5'*

*Level of difficulty: 2*

- 1 cup/125 g freshly grated Parmesan cheese
- $1^1/_4$ cups/150 g fine dry bread crumbs
- 3 eggs
- 2 tbsp butter
- dash of freshly grated nutmeg
- finely grated zest of 1 lemon
- salt to taste
- $1^1/_2$ quarts/1.5 liters Beef Stock (see page 955)

# BROCCOLI AND TAGLIATELLE SOUP

Serves: 4
Preparation: 10'
Cooking: 25'
Level of difficulty: 1

- 1 lb/500 g broccoli
- 2 tbsp extra-virgin olive oil
- 3 oz/90 g pork fat, diced
- 2 cloves garlic, finely chopped
- 2 tbsp finely chopped parsley
- 1 tbsp tomato paste
- 3 cups/750 ml boiling water
- salt to taste
- 10 oz/300 g tagliatelle, broken or cut into pieces
- 6 tbsp freshly grated Parmesan cheese

Wash the broccoli and trim the tough parts off the stalk. Dice the stalk and divide the tops into florets. • Heat the oil in a large saucepan and sauté the pork fat, garlic, and parsley for 5 minutes. • Add the broccoli and cook for about 5 minutes, then add the tomato paste and water. Season with salt and pepper, then partially cover and cook a over medium-low heat for about 15 minutes, or until the broccoli is almost cooked. • Add the tagliatelle and cook until al dente. • Turn off the heat and leave for 3–4 minutes. Serve hot with the Parmesan passed separately.

*Serves: 4–6*

*Preparation: 30' +
time to make pasta*

*Cooking: 2 h 30'*

*Level of difficulty: 1*

**PASTA**

- $1/2$ **quantity
  Plain Pasta dough
  (see page 286)**

**SOUP**

- $1^1/2$ **cups/300 g
  dried and soaked,
  (or 2 lb/1 kg fresh)
  borlotti or red
  kidney beans**
- **1 small onion,
  peeled**
- **1 carrot, trimmed
  and peeled**
- **1 stalk celery,
  trimmed and
  washed**
- **salt to taste**
- **1 clove garlic,
  peeled and lightly
  crushed**
- $1/2$ **cup/125 ml
  extra-virgin olive
  oil + extra to serve**
- **1 tbsp finely
  chopped parsley**
- **1 cup/250 g fresh
  or canned
  tomatoes**
- **4–6 tbsp freshly
  grated Parmesan
  cheese**

# PASTA AND RED BEAN SOUP

Prepare the pasta dough. Shape into a ball and set aside to rest for about 1 hour, wrapped in plastic wrap (cling film). • Roll the dough out into a thin sheet. Cut into uneven diamond shapes by first cutting it diagonally into strips, then cutting in the opposite direction. (In the past, when fresh pasta was made every day, leftover pieces and offcuts of pasta were used in this dish). • Place the beans in a deep saucepan with enough cold water to cover. Then add the onion, carrot, and celery, but no salt at this stage. Bring to a boil and simmer gently for about 2 hours. • When the beans are very tender, chop half in a food processor until smooth. Add salt to taste. Reserve the remaining beans and cooking liquid. • Sauté the garlic in the oil in a large, heavy-bottomed pan until it starts to color, then discard it. • Add the parsley and tomatoes to the flavored oil. Cook, uncovered, to reduce and thicken. Then add the bean purée, the whole beans, and the cooking liquid. Bring this thick soup to a boil, then add the pasta. It will take 3–4 minutes to cook. • Serve hot, adding a trickle of extra-virgin olive oil and 1 tablespoon of Parmesan to each serving.

# PASTA AND BEAN SOUP

S oak the beans overnight in a large bowl of water. • Drain and transfer to a saucepan with enough unsalted cold water to cover. Simmer for about 2 hours, or until tender. • When the beans are cooked, do not drain. Remove one-third with a slotted spoon and purée in a food processor. Return the purée to the pan and stir. • Heat the oil in a frying pan and sauté the onion, garlic, carrot, celery, and rosemary with the pancetta until lightly browned. Stir this mixture into the beans. • Season with salt. • Bring the beans back to a boil. Add the pasta, cook for 5 minutes, then remove from heat. Leave to stand for 20 minutes. • Reheat and serve with a grinding of pepper and a trickle of oil.

*Serves: 4–6*

*Preparation: 30' + time to soak beans*

*Cooking: 2 h 20'*

*Level of difficulty: 1*

- 1½ cups/300 g dried cannellini or white kidney beans
- 2 tbsp extra-virgin olive oil
- 1 onion, finely chopped
- 1 clove garlic, finely chopped
- 1 carrot, finely chopped
- 1 stalk celery, finely chopped
- 1 sprig fresh rosemary, finely chopped
- 5 oz/150 g finely chopped pancetta
- salt to taste
- 5 oz/150 g soup pasta
- freshly ground black pepper

390

# CLEAR SOUP WITH PASTA

*Serves: 4*

*Preparation: 10'*

*Cooking: 5–10'*

*Level of difficulty: 1*

- **1 quart/1 liter Beef, Chicken, or Vegetable Stock (see pages 955, 956)**
- **10 oz /300 g small soup pasta**
- **1 cup/125 g freshly grated Parmesan cheese**

**B**ring the stock to a boil in a large pot. • Add the pasta and cook until it is al dente. • Ladle the soup into heated serving bowls. • Sprinkle with the cheese and serve immediately.

# FAVA BEAN SOUP

S oak the fava beans in enough cold water to cover for 12 hours. • Drain the beans and combine with 2 tablespoons of the oil, the tomatoes, onion, and celery in a heavy-bottomed pan or earthenware pot. Add the water. • Partially cover and cook over low heat for 3 hours, stirring frequently and mashing the fava beans with a fork. They should be soft and mushy. • When cooked, add salt, pepper, and the remaining oil. • Sprinkle with the Pecorino, if using, and serve hot.

Serves: 4–6

Preparation: 15' + time to soak the fava beans

Cooking: 3 h

Level of difficulty: 1

- 1$^1$/$_2$ cups/300 g dried fava/broad beans
- 4 tbsp extra-virgin olive oil
- 1 lb/500 g peeled and chopped fresh or canned tomatoes
- 1 large onion, thinly sliced
- 3 celery stalks, finely chopped
- 2 quarts/2 liters cold water
- salt and freshly ground black pepper to taste
- 16 tbsp freshly grated Pecorino cheese (optional)

| Serves: 4 |
| --- |
| Preparation: 10' |
| Cooking: 30' |
| Level of difficulty: 2 |

- 3 eggs
- 1 cup/125 g freshly grated Parmesan cheese
- 1 tbsp finely chopped parsley
- salt to taste
- pinch of nutmeg
- $^2/_3$ cup/180 ml whole milk
- $^2/_3$ cup/100 g all-purpose/plain flour
- 4 tbsp butter
- $1^1/_4$ quarts/ 1.25 liters boiling Chicken Stock (see page 955)

# CRÊPES IN CHICKEN STOCK

Beat the eggs in a bowl with 2 tablespoons of the cheese, the parsley, salt, nutmeg, and half the milk. • Gradually stir in the flour and remaining milk. The batter should be fairly liquid. • Heat 1 tablespoon of butter in a small frying pan and add a ladleful of batter. Tip the pan and rotate, so that the batter spreads evenly into a very thin crêpe. After 1 minute, flip the crêpe and cook for 1 minute on the other side. • Slip it onto a plate and repeat, adding a dab of butter to the pan each time, until all the batter has been used. Stack the crêpes up in a pile. • Sprinkle each crêpe with Parmesan, then roll up loosely. Slice into ribbons. Divide equally among 4 individual soup bowls. Pour the boiling stock over the top.
• Serve hot.

# RYE DUMPLINGS WITH BACON IN MEAT STOCK

*Serves: 4*

*Preparation: 30'*
*+ 1 h to rest*

*Cooking: 30'*

*Level: of difficulty 2*

- 10 oz/300 g rye bread, crusts removed and sliced
- 1¹/₂ cups/180 g finely chopped bacon
- 1 small red onion, finely chopped
- 1 large leek, white part only, finely chopped
- 1 clove garlic, finely chopped
- 3 tbsp milk
- 3 tbsp water
- salt to taste
- 4 tbsp finely ground cornmeal
- ¹/₂ cup/75 g all-purpose/plain flour
- 1¹/₄ quarts/1.25 liters Beef Stock (see page 955)

Place the bread in a large bowl and mix in the pancetta, onion, leek, and garlic. • Mix the milk, water, and salt in a small bowl. • Pour the milk mixture over the bread mixture and let rest for 1 hour. • Stir in the cornmeal and use your hands to shape the mixture into 1¹/₂-inch (4-cm) balls. Dust lightly with flour. • Bring the stock to a boil in a large saucepan and cook the rye bread balls for 20 minutes over low heat. • Serve hot.

# 89

# POTATO SOUP WITH PASTA

Place all the chopped vegetables in a large saucepan with the oil and salt. Pour in the water and bring to a boil over low heat. Simmer for 45 minutes. • Run the soup through a food mill or process in a food processor or blender.
If it seems too dense, dilute with boiling water.
• Return to the heat and bring to a boil. Add the pasta and cook for the time indicated on the package. • Season with pepper, a drizzle of oil, and the Parmesan. • Serve hot.

Serves: 4–6

Preparation: 20'

Cooking: 1 h

Level of difficulty: 1

- 1 1/4 lb/625 g starchy potatoes, peeled and cut into chunks
- 1 firm-ripe tomato, coarsely chopped
- 1 red onion, finely chopped
- 1 stalk celery, finely chopped
- 2 tbsp finely chopped parsley
- 3 tbsp extra-virgin olive oil
- 1/2 tsp salt
- 2 quarts/2 liters water
- 7 oz/200 g soup pasta
- freshly ground black pepper to taste
- 8 tbsp freshly grated Parmesan cheese

# BEAN SOUP WITH HERBS AND PASTA

Serves: 4

Preparation: 20'

Cooking: 1 h 15'

Level of difficulty: 1

- 2 cups/400 g canned borlotti beans
- 1 quart/1 liter Vegetable Stock (see page 956)
- 3 tbsp tomato paste
- 4 tbsp extra-virgin olive oil
- $1/2$ cup/50 g finely chopped prosciutto/ Parma ham
- $1/2$ cup/50 g finely chopped pancetta or bacon
- 2 cloves garlic, finely chopped
- 1 bunch parsley, finely chopped
- 10 leaves fresh basil, torn
- 4 leaves fresh sage, finely chopped
- 1 sprig rosemary
- 7 oz/200 g soup pasta
- salt and freshly ground black pepper to taste

Place the beans in a large saucepan and pour in enough of the stock to cover them completely. • Dissolve the tomato paste in the remaining stock and stir it into the beans. • Bring to a boil over low heat and transfer half the mixture to a food processor or blender. Process until puréed. • Stir into the bean mixture in the saucepan. • Heat the oil in a frying pan and sauté the prosciutto and pancetta over very low heat until crispy. • Add the garlic, parsley, basil, sage, and rosemary and sauté for 10 minutes. • Transfer the sautéed mixture to the bean soup and mix well. • Bring to a boil, add the pasta, and cook until al dente. • Remove from the heat and season with salt and pepper. Serve hot or warm with a drizzle of oil.

# PASTA, VEGETABLE, AND LEGUME SOUP

S oak the legumes in cold water for 12 hours. •
Drain and transfer to a large saucepan. Pour in
enough water to cover completely. Bring to a boil
over low heat and simmer for about 90 minutes, or
until they are almost tender. • Heat the oil in a
Dutch oven (casserole) and sauté the pancetta
over low heat for 5 minutes. • Add the onion and
cook for 5 minutes. • Stir in the herbs and
tomatoes and cook until reduced by half. • Pour in
the water and add the ham bone. Bring to a boil
and season with salt. Add the vegetables and cook
over medium heat for 30 minutes. • Mix in the
legumes and their cooking liquid. • Finely chop the
garlic and lard and add to the soup. • Simmer for
about 30 minutes. • Add the pasta and cook until
al dente. • If the soup is too dense, add more
boiling water. • Season with pepper and sprinkle
with the Pecorino. Serve hot.

*Serves: 4–6*

*Preparation: 1 h + time to soak legumes*

*Cooking: 3 h*

*Level of difficulty: 2*

- 1 cup/200 g mixed dried legumes
- 4 tbsp extra-virgin olive oil
- $^1/_2$ cup/60 g finely chopped pancetta or bacon
- 1 onion, finely chopped
- 3 tbsp finely chopped herbs
- 1 cup/250 ml canned tomatoes
- 2 quarts/2 liters water
- 1 ham bone
- salt and freshly ground black pepper to taste
- 1 lb/500 g mixed vegetables, finely chopped
- 2 cloves garlic
- 3 tbsp lard
- 7 oz/200 g mixed short pasta
- 6 tbsp freshly grated Pecorino cheese

# SPELT SOUP

Place the carrot, onion, leek, and celery in a large saucepan. • Add the beef and ham bone. Pour in the water, season with salt, and add the peppercorns. Bring to a boil and simmer over medium heat for about 2 hours. • Remove the beef and set aside for another use. • Skim the fat from the stock and pour the stock into a large pan. • Add the spelt and cook over low heat for 45 minutes, or until tender. • Transfer half the spelt to a food processor. Process until puréed. • Stir into the pan with the remaining spelt. Add 2 tablespoons of oil and cook for 15 minutes more. • Cook the pasta in a large pan of salted, boiling water until al dente. • Drain and add to the soup. Simmer for 5 minutes. • Sprinkle with the mint, drizzle with the remaining oil, and serve over the toasted bread.

Serves: 4–6

Preparation: 25'

Cooking: 3 h 10'

Level of difficulty: 1

- 1 carrot, finely chopped
- 1 onion, finely chopped
- $^1/_2$ leek, white part only, finely chopped
- 1 stalk celery, finely chopped
- $1^1/_2$ lb/750 g mixed beef cuts
- 1 ham bone
- 3 quarts/3 liters water
- salt to taste
- 4 black peppercorns
- $1^1/_2$ cups/300 g spelt
- 5 oz/150 g short pasta
- 4 tbsp extra-virgin olive oil
- 2 sprigs fresh mint
- 2–4 slices firm-textured bread, toasted and, if liked, rubbed with garlic

# PASTA, VEGETABLES, AND BEAN MINESTRONE

Serves: 4

Preparation: 20'

Cooking: 35'

Level of difficulty: 1

- **2 tbsp extra-virgin olive oil**
- **1 onion, finely chopped**
- **$^1/_2$ cauliflower, cut into florets**
- **3 oz/100 g French beans/green beans, topped and tailed**
- **2 small carrots, finely chopped**
- **1 small potato, finely chopped**
- **$1^1/_2$ quarts/1.5 liters hot water**
- **salt and freshly ground black pepper to taste**
- **$2^1/_2$ cups/250 g canned cannellini beans**
- **8 oz/250 g spaghetti, broken into short lengths**

Heat 1 tablespoon of oil in a large frying pan and sauté the onion over low heat for 5 minutes.
• Add the vegetables and sauté over low heat for 5 more minutes. • Pour in 2 cups (500 ml) of the water, cover, and cook for about 15 minutes.
• Pour in the remaining water. Bring to a boil and season with salt. • Stir in the beans and mix well.
• Add the spaghetti and cook until al dente.
• Ladle the soup into heated serving bowls and season with pepper. Drizzle with the remaining oil and serve hot.

# CREAM OF CHARD SOUP WITH PASSATELLI

Heat the oil in a large frying pan and sauté the shallots and bay leaves for 5 minutes. • Add the Swiss chard, cover, and cook for 2 minutes. • Discard the bay leaves. • Add the flour and butter and cook with the beets until light brown. • Pour in the milk and 2 cups (500 ml) of stock. Bring to a boil and cook, stirring constantly, until thick. • Chop in a food processor or blender until smooth. Season with salt. • Passatelli: Knead the bread crumbs, Parmesan, egg and egg yolks. Add the salt and lemon zest and knead to form a smooth dough. Use a passatelli maker to make the pasta (or roll by hand into fat spaghetti and cut into short lengths with a knife). • Bring the remaining stock to a boil in a large saucepan and cook for 2–3 minutes. • Serve hot with the soup.

*Serves: 4*

*Preparation: 30'*

*Cooking: 30'*

*Level of difficulty: 2*

- **4 tbsp extra-virgin olive oil**
- **2 shallots, finely chopped**
- **2 bay leaves**
- **10 oz/300 g Swiss chard, stalks removed**
- **2 tbsp all-purpose/plain flour**
- **3 tbsp butter**
- **2 cups/500 ml milk**
- **1¹/₂ quarts/ 1.5 liters Vegetable Stock (see page 956)**
- **salt to taste**

PASSATELLI

- **1¹/₂ cups/90 g fresh bread crumbs**
- **³/₄ cup/75 g freshly grated Parmesan cheese**
- **1 egg + 3 egg yolks**
- **pinch of salt**
- **¹/₂ tsp finely grated lemon zest**

02

# CORN SOUP WITH CRAB MEAT

Serves: 4
Preparation: 20'
Cooking: 10'
Level of difficulty: 1

- 1 tbsp extra-virgin olive oil
- 2 cloves garlic, finely chopped
- 14 oz/400 g canned corn/ sweetcorn
- 1 tsp finely grated ginger root
- 3 cups/750 ml Chicken Stock (see page 955)
- 1 tsp fish sauce
- 5 oz/150 g canned crab meat, drained
- 1 egg
- 1 tbsp finely chopped cilantro/ coriander
- $1/4$ tsp paprika
- salt and freshly ground black pepper to taste

Heat the oil in a large, heavy-bottomed saucepan and sauté the garlic until pale. • Add the corn, ginger, and stock and bring to a boil. • Stir in the fish sauce and crab meat, and season with salt and pepper. • Beat the egg in a small bowl then slowly beat it into the soup. • Cook for about 30 seconds, or until the egg begins to set. • Add the cilantro and paprika. • Remove from heat and serve hot.

903

# SPELT AND BEAN SOUP

*Serves: 6*

*Preparation: 30' +*
*time to soak beans*

*Cooking: 1 h 20'*

*Level of difficulty: 2*

- 1 cup/200 g dried borlotti beans
- 1³/₄/350 g spelt
- 1 quart/1 liter water
- 1 bay leaf
- 1 clove garlic, lightly crushed but whole
- 4 tbsp extra-virgin olive oil
- 10 oz/300 g leeks, white parts only, cut into wheels
- 5 oz/150 g pancetta or bacon, finely chopped
- 1¹/₂ quarts/ 1.5 liters Vegetable Stock (see page 956)
- salt to taste
- 1 tbsp finely chopped parsley

S oak the beans overnight. Drain the beans and transfer to a pressure cooker. Pour in enough water to cover completely. Add the bay leaf and garlic, close the lid, and cook for 45 minutes, or until the beans are tender. • Drain the beans and discard the bay leaf and garlic. • Heat 3 tablespoons of oil in a large frying pan and sauté the leeks and pancetta until the leeks are translucent. • Transfer to the soup and add the boiled beans and spelt. Pour in the vegetable stock and season with salt. Close and seal the pressure cooker. Cook for 25 minutes, or until the spelt is tender. • Drizzle with the remaining oil and sprinkle with the parsley. Serve hot.

# FRENCH BEAN AND POTATO MINESTRONE

Heat the oil in a large, heavy-bottomed saucepan and sauté the garlic until pale gold. • Discard the garlic and add the tomatoes. Cook until the tomatoes have broken down completely. • Add the potatoes, French beans, and celery. Season with salt. Cover and cook over low heat for about 10 minutes. • Pour in the water, add the basil, and season with salt. Bring to a boil then simmer over low heat until the potatoes and beans are tender. • Serve hot.

*Serves: 6*

*Preparation: 20'*

*Cooking: 30'*

*Level of difficulty: 1*

- 3 tbsp extra-virgin olive oil
- 2 cloves garlic, lightly crushed but whole
- 4–5 large tomatoes, peeled, seeded, and coarsely chopped
- 1 lb/500 g potatoes, diced
- 1 lb/500 g French beans/green beans, topped and tailed and finely chopped
- 1 stalk celery, finely chopped
- salt to taste
- 1 cup/250 ml water
- 4 leaves fresh basil, torn

# PASTA AND GARBANZO BEANS

S oak the garbanzo beans overnight in lightly salted water. • Drain and place in a large saucepan. Pour in enough water to cover them completely. Add the celery, garlic, onion, and bay leaves and season with salt. • Bring to a boil and simmer over low heat for about 2 hours, or until tender. • Cook the pasta in a large pan of salted, boiling water until al dente. • Drain and add to the bean soup. Season with pepper and drizzle with the oil. • Serve hot.

*Serves: 4–6*

*Preparation: 30' + time to soak beans*

*Cooking: 2 h*

*Level of difficulty: 1*

- **2 cups/400 g garbanzo beans/ chickpeas**
- **2 quarts/2 liters water**
- **2 stalks celery, finely chopped**
- **2 cloves garlic, finely chopped**
- **1 onion, finely chopped**
- **salt and freshly ground black pepper to taste**
- **2 bay leaves**
- **7 oz/200 g small pasta tubes**
- **3 tbsp extra-virgin olive oil**

# CHICKEN AND BELL PEPPER SOUP

*Serves: 4*

*Preparation: 30'*

*Cooking: 40'*

*Level of difficulty: 1*

- **6 medium tomatoes**
- **2 spicy chile peppers, finely chopped**
- **1 small onion**
- **2 scallions/spring onions, finely chopped**
- **1¹/₂ cups/300 g Basmati rice**
- **2¹/₃ cups/600 ml Chicken Stock (see page 955)**
- **1 lb/500 g chicken breast, boiled, boned, and diced**
- **6 oz/180 g corn kernels**
- **¹/₂ tsp cumin seeds**
- **¹/₄ tsp ground red chile pepper**
- **3 tbsp green chile pepper sauce**

Plunge the tomatoes into boiling water for 2–3 minutes, then slip off the skins. • Transfer the tomatoes to a food processor or blender with the green chile peppers, onion, and 1 scallion. Process until smooth. • Cook the rice in salted, boiling water until firm to the bite. • Drain and set aside. • Mix the puréed tomato mixture and stock in a large saucepan. Bring to a boil and add the diced chicken. Mix in the rice and corn. Season with the cumin, red chile pepper, and green chile pepper sauce. • When the soup returns to a boil, remove from the heat and serve, garnished with the remaining scallion.

# ZESTY SHRIMP SOUP

S hell the shrimp and remove the heads, setting the shells aside. • Heat the oil in a large frying pan and sauté the shrimp shells for 3–4 minutes. • Add the lemon grass, lime leaves, green chile pepper, lime zest, and stock. • Bring to a boil and simmer over low heat for about 20 minutes. • Filter the liquid and pour it back into the pan. • Add the lime juice and fish sauce. Season with salt and pepper. • Bring to a boil, add the shrimp, and boil for 3 minutes. Add the red chile pepper and scallion. • Serve hot, garnished with the cilantro.

*Serves: 4*

*Preparation: 25'*

*Cooking: 30'*

*Level of difficulty: 1*

- **10 oz/300 g shrimp/prawns**
- **1 tbsp extra-virgin olive oil**
- **1 stalk lemon grass, coarsely chopped**
- **2 lime leaves, shredded**
- **1 green chile pepper, seeded and finely chopped**
- **grated zest and juice of 1 lime**
- **1 1/4 quarts/ 1.25 liters Chicken Stock (see page 955)**
- **1 tbsp fish sauce**
- **1 red chile pepper, finely sliced**
- **1 scallion/spring onion, thinly sliced**
- **salt and freshly ground black pepper to taste**
- **1 tbsp finely chopped cilantro/ coriander**

# CHICKEN STOCK WITH VERMICELLI

Serves: 4–6

Preparation: 15'

Cooking: 15'

Level of difficulty: 1

- **2 quarts/2 liters Beef Stock (see page 955)**
- **7 oz/200 g chicken, cooked and diced**
- **7 oz/200 g Chinese vermicelli, broken up into short lengths**
- **$^1/_2$ cup/60 g finely chopped parsley**
- **freshly ground pepper to taste**

Pour the stock into a large saucepan and bring to a boil. Add the chicken and boil for about 1 minute. • Add the vermicelli and cook until tender. • Season with pepper, garnish with parsley, and serve hot.

# 91

# THAI SQUASH SOUP

*Serves: 6*

*Preparation: 20'*

*Cooking: 40'*

*Level of difficulty: 1*

- 2 lb/1 kg squash/
  pumpkin
- 1 tbsp peanut oil
- 1 tsp yellow
  mustard seeds
- 2 cloves garlic,
  crushed
- 1 large onion, finely
  chopped
- 1 stalk celery,
  finely chopped
- 1 small red chile
  pepper, finely
  chopped
- 1 quart/1 liter
  Vegetable Stock
  (see page 956)
- 1 tbsp dried shrimp
  paste
- $^1/_2$ cup/125 ml
  cream of coconut
- salt and freshly
  ground black
  pepper to taste

Cut the squash in half and remove the seeds. Peel and dice the flesh. • Heat the oil in a large saucepan and sauté the mustard seeds until they begin to pop. • Add the garlic, onion, celery, and half the chile pepper and sauté for 2 minutes. • Add the squash, stock, and dried shrimp paste. Bring to a boil. Cover and simmer over low heat for about 30 minutes, or until all the ingredients have softened. • Transfer the mixture to a food processor or blender and process until puréed. Return to the saucepan and mix in the cream of coconut. • Season with salt and pepper and sprinkle with the remaining chile pepper. • Serve hot.

913

# CHILLED CREAM OF AVOCADO SOUP

**C**ut the avocados in half lengthwise and twist each half so that the large pit breaks free from the flesh. Remove the rind and scrape out the flesh. • Process the avocado flesh with the onion, garlic, cilantro, mint, lime juice, and $1/2$ cups (375 ml) of the stock in a food processor or blender until smooth. • Pour in the remaining stock, the rice vinegar, and soy sauce. Season with salt and pepper. • Cover with plastic wrap and refrigerate for at least 2 hours. • Garnish with lime zest and serve cold.

914

*Serves: 4–6*

*Preparation: 30'*
 *+ 2 h to chill*

*Level of difficulty: 1*

- **2 firm-ripe avocados**
- **1 small onion, finely chopped**
- **1 clove garlic, lightly crushed but whole**
- **2 tbsp finely chopped fresh cilantro/coriander**
- **1 tbsp finely chopped fresh mint**
- **2 tbsp fresh lime juice**
- **3 cups/750 ml Vegetable Stock (see page 956)**
- **1 tbsp rice vinegar**
- **1 tbsp light soy sauce**
- **salt and freshly ground black pepper to taste**
- **shredded lime zest, to garnish**

# HAM, MORTADELLA, AND SPINACH SOUP

Bring the stock to a boil in a large saucepan. Add the ham, mortadella, spinach, garlic, onion, parsley, and basil. Simmer over low heat for 10 minutes. • Add the pasta and cook until al dente. • Stir in the cream, brandy, and peas. Cook over medium heat until the peas are cooked. • Add the butter and remove from the heat. • Sprinkle with the Parmesan and serve hot.

*Serves: 4*

*Preparation: 15'*

*Cooking: 20'*

*Level of difficulty: 1*

- **2 quarts/2 liters Vegetable Stock (see page 956)**
- **7 oz/200 g diced ham**
- **7 oz/200 g diced mortadella**
- **8 oz/250 g spinach, tough stalks removed**
- 1 clove garlic, finely chopped
- 1 onion, finely chopped
- 1 small bunch parsley, finely chopped
- 1 small bunch basil, torn
- 10 oz/300 g soup pasta
- $^1/_2$ cup/125 ml heavy/double cream
- 4 tbsp brandy
- 1 cup/200 g peas
- 4 tbsp butter

# CHICKEN AND CORN SOUP

*Serves: 4*

*Preparation: 15'*

*Cooking: 15'*

*Level of difficulty: 1*

- **4 large corn/ sweetcorn cobs**
- **1¹/₂ quarts/ 1.5 liters Chicken Stock (see page 956)**
- **7 oz/200 g chicken, cooked and diced**
- **2 tbsp finely ground cornmeal**
- **1 piece of fresh peeled ginger, 1 in/2 cm long, finely grated**
- **8 scallions/spring onions, finely chopped**
- **6 tbsp water**
- **1 tsp sesame oil**
- **salt and freshly ground black pepper to taste**
- **1 tbsp finely chopped parsley**

Cook the corn cobs in a steamer until tender. Let cool, then scrape off the kernels with a knife. • Bring the stock to a boil in a medium saucepan. Add the corn kernels, chicken, and ginger. Cook over low heat for 5 minutes. • Mix the cornmeal and water until smooth and stir into the soup until thickened. • Add the scallions and sesame oil and mix well. Season with salt, pepper, and parsley. • Serve hot.

# MULLIGATAWNY SOUP

Serves: 6

Preparation: 30'

Cooking: 1 h 10'

Level of difficulty: 1

- 2 tbsp all-purpose/ plain flour
- 2 tsp curry powder
- 1 tsp ground turmeric
- 1/2 tsp ground ginger
- 2 lb/1 kg chicken breasts
- 4 tbsp butter
- 6 cloves
- 12 black peppercorns
- 1 large apple, peeled and diced
- 1 1/2 quarts/ 1.5 liters Chicken Stock (see page 955)
- 2 tbsp fresh lemon juice
- 1/2 cup/125 ml heavy/double cream

Mix the flour, curry, turmeric, and ginger in small bowl. Sprinkle the chicken with the resulting powder. • Melt the butter in a large saucepan and sauté the pieces of chicken until tender. • Crush the cloves and peppercorns and place them in a muslin (cheesecloth) bag. Tie it securely and add to the chicken with the apple. Pour in the stock. Bring to a boil and simmer over low heat for 1 hour. • Remove the chicken from the saucepan and remove the muslin bag. Cut the chicken into small pieces. • Skim the fat from the stock. • Return the chicken to the saucepan. Add the lemon juice and the cream and cook over low heat until the soup is just boiling. • Serve hot.

# CHINESE SWEET AND SOUR SOUP

Soak the mushrooms in a bowl with enough hot water to cover for 30 minutes. Drain, squeezing out the excess moisture, and chop finely. • Bring the stock to a boil in a large saucepan. • Add the mushrooms, noodles, chicken, bamboo shoots, and ginger. • Cook over low heat for 5 minutes. • Mix the cornstarch and water in a small bowl to form a smooth paste and stir the paste into the soup. Gradually drizzle in the beaten egg, stirring constantly. • Remove from the heat and mix in the tomato sauce, soy sauce, vinegar, sesame oil, and scallions. Season with salt and pepper. Garnish with thinly sliced scallion and serve hot.

Serves: 6

Preparation: 30' + 30' to soak mushrooms

Cooking: 20'

Level of difficulty: 1

- 4 dried Chinese mushrooms
- 1 quart/1 liter Chicken Stock (see page 955)
- 2 oz/60 g Chinese noodles
- 7 oz/200 g chicken, cooked and diced
- 8 oz/250 g bamboo sprouts, finely chopped
- 1 tsp finely grated ginger root
- 1 tbsp cornstarch/ cornflour
- 6 tbsp cold water
- 1 egg, lightly beaten
- 1 tbsp tomato sauce
- 1 tbsp soy sauce
- 1 tbsp rice vinegar
- 2 tsp sesame oil
- 2 scallions/spring onions, finely chopped
- salt and freshly ground black pepper to taste

# CREAM OF CARROT AND POTATO SOUP

*Serves: 6–8*

*Preparation: 25'*

*Cooking: 50'*

*Level of difficulty: 1*

- 2 tbsp butter
- 3 carrots, coarsely chopped
- 3 leeks, white parts only, coarsely chopped
- 1¼ lb/600 g potatoes, coarsely chopped
- 2 quarts/2 liters boiling water or Chicken Stock (see page 955)
- 1 tsp sugar
- salt and freshly ground black pepper to taste
- ½ cup/125 ml heavy/double cream
- 1 bunch parsley or chervil, finely chopped

Melt the butter in a large saucepan and sauté the carrots and leeks until softened. • Add the potatoes and stir thoroughly until well coated with the butter. • Pour in the water and add the sugar. Season with salt and pepper. • Cover and cook for 30–40 minutes, or until the potatoes have softened. • Transfer to a food processor or blender and chop until smooth. • Return the soup to the saucepan. Stir in the cream and cook over low heat until heated through. • Garnish with the parsley and serve hot.

# GARBANZO BEAN AND PANCETTA SOUP

S oak the garbanzo beans overnight in cold water. • Drain and rinse under cold running water. Transfer to a large saucepan with the water, onion, pancetta, garlic, and bay leaf. Season with salt and pepper. • Bring to a boil and simmer over low heat for at least 2 hours, or until the garbanzo beans are very tender. • Garnish with the chopped egg and parsley and serve hot.

924

*Serves: 4*

*Preparation: 25' + time to soak beans*

*Cooking: 2 h*

*Level of difficulty: 1*

- 2$^1$/$_2$ cups/250 g dried garbanzo beans/chickpeas
- 1 quart/1 liter cold water
- 1 small onion, finely chopped
- $^1$/$_2$ cup/60 g diced pancetta or bacon
- 2 cloves garlic, lightly crushed but whole
- 1 bay leaf
- salt and freshly ground black pepper to taste
- 1 hard-boiled egg, finely chopped
- 1 tbsp finely chopped fresh parsley

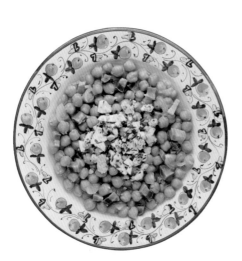

# RICE AND LENTIL SOUP

*Serves: 4*

*Preparation: 30' + 12 h to soak lentils*

*Cooking: 45'*

*Level of difficulty: 1*

- **2 cups/200 g lentils**
- **2 onions**
- **2 stalks celery**
- **1¹/₂ quarts/1.5 liters hot water**
- **salt and freshly ground black pepper to taste**
- **¹/₂ cup/60 g diced pancetta or bacon**
- **1 clove garlic**
- **1 bunch parsley**
- **4 tbsp extra-virgin olive oil**
- **2 tbsp tomato paste dissolved in 1 cup/ 250 ml water**
- **1 cup/200 g rice**

Soak the lentils in cold water for 12 hours. • Drain and rinse under cold running water. Transfer to a large saucepan and add 1 onion and 1 stalk of celery. Pour in the water and season with salt. Cook over medium heat for 30 minutes. • Finely chop together the pancetta, garlic, remaining onion, remaining celery, and the parsley. • Heat the oil in a large saucepan and sauté the chopped mixture until golden. • Stir in the tomato paste mixture until the soup begins to thicken. • Transfer the lentils and their cooking liquid to the tomato mixture and return to a boil. • Add the rice and cook until tender, stirring often. • Season with pepper and serve hot.

# RICE AND ZUCCHINI SOUP

Heat the oil in a large, heavy-bottomed pan and sauté the onion until softened. • Stir in the tomatoes, zucchini, and potatoes. • Cook over medium heat until all the vegetables turn golden brown. • Pour in the stock. • Cook over medium heat for 5 minutes. • Add the rice and cook until tender. • Garnish with the parsley and nutmeg. • Serve hot.

Serves: 4–6

Preparation: 20'

Cooking: 35'

Level of difficulty: 1

- 4 tbsp extra-virgin olive oil
- 1 onion, finely chopped
- 12 tomatoes, peeled and coarsely chopped
- 8 zucchini/ courgettes, diced
- 2 potatoes, diced
- 2 quarts/2 liters Vegetable Stock (see page 956)
- 2 cups/400 g rice
- 1 bunch parsley, finely chopped
- $1/8$ tsp freshly grated nutmeg

# COOL YOGURT AND CUCUMBER SOUP

*Serves: 4*

*Preparation: 15' + 3 h to chill*

*Level of difficulty: 1*

- 2 large cucumbers
- 1 quart/1 liter plain yogurt
- 4 tbsp ice water
- salt and freshly ground white pepper to taste
- 4 scallions/spring onions with the green stalks, finely chopped
- 12 leaves fresh mint, finely chopped

Peel the cucumbers and cut them into thin slices lengthwise. Use a spoon to remove the seeds and cut them into very thin sections. • Place the yogurt in a large bowl. • Mix in the ice water and add the cucumbers. Season with salt and pepper. Add the scallions and mint. • Refrigerate for at least 3 hours. • Serve chilled.

# MEXICAN GAZPACHO

C ut the avocado in half lengthwise and twist each half so that the large pit breaks free from the flesh. Remove the rind and scrape out the flesh. • Mix the avocado flesh with the lime juice in a medium bowl. • Process the avocado mixture, tomatoes, cucumber, bell pepper, scallions, garlic, parsley, basil, oil, and water in a food processor or blender until smooth. Season with salt and pepper. Refrigerate for 2 hours. • Serve chilled.

*Serves: 4*

*Preparation: 20' + 2 h to chill*

*Level of difficulty: 1*

- 1 firm-ripe avocado
- juice of 1 lime
- 3 large firm-ripe tomatoes, peeled and finely chopped
- 1 medium cucumber, peeled and finely chopped
- 1 green bell pepper/capsicum, seeded and finely chopped
- 4 scallions/spring onions, finely chopped
- 1 clove garlic, finely chopped
- 1 bunch parsley, finely chopped
- 6 leaves fresh basil, torn
- 2 tbsp extra-virgin olive oil
- 2 cups/500 ml water
- salt and freshly ground white pepper to taste

# FAVA BEAN SOUP WITH RICE

Cook the rice in a large pan of salted, boiling water for 12–15 minutes, or until tender.
• Drain and set aside. • Remove the tough outer leaves and trim stalks from the artichokes. Remove any fuzzy choke and cut into thin slices. • Heat 3 tablespoons of oil in a large saucepan and sauté the onion until softened. • Stir in the tomatoes, fava beans, peas, zucchini, potato, and artichokes. • Pour in the water and season with salt. • Cook over medium heat for 30 minutes. • Stir in the rice and cook for 5 minutes. • Garnish with the parsley and basil and sprinkle with the Pecorino. Drizzle with the remaining tablespoon of oil. Serve hot.

*Serves: 4–6*

*Preparation: 25'*

*Cooking: 45'*

*Level of difficulty: 1*

- 1 cup/200 g rice
- 2 artichokes
- 4 tbsp extra-virgin olive oil
- 1 onion, finely chopped
- 1 cup/250 g chopped tomatoes
- $1^1/2$ cups/300 g fresh shelled fava/broad beans
- 2 cups/250 g fresh peas
- 1 zucchini/ courgette, diced
- 1 potato, diced
- $1^1/2$ quarts/1.5 liters boiling water
- salt to taste
- 1 small bunch parsley, finely chopped
- 5 leaves fresh basil, torn
- $1/3$ cup/50 g freshly grated Pecorino cheese

# LEEK SOUP WITH RICE

Serves: 4–6

Preparation: 30'

Cooking: 30'

Level of difficulty: 1

- 1¹/₂ cups/300 g rice
- 4 tbsp extra-virgin olive oil
- 12 oz/350 g leeks, white parts only, cut into thin wheels
- 5 oz/150 g potatoes, thinly sliced
- 2 quarts/2 liters Vegetable Stock (see page 956)
- 1 small bunch parsley, finely chopped
- salt and freshly ground white pepper to taste

C ook the rice in a large pan of salted, boiling water for 12–15 minutes, or until tender.
• Drain and set aside. • Heat 3 tablespoons of oil in a large saucepan and sauté the leeks until softened. • Add the potatoes and pour in the stock. Cook over low heat for 5 minutes.
• Transfer the soup to a food processor or blender. Process until smooth . Season with salt and pepper. Return to the saucepan and bring to a boil. Cover and cook over medium-low heat. • Stir in the rice and cook over low heat for 5 minutes. • Garnish with the parsley and drizzle with the remaining tablespoons of oil. • Serve hot.

933

# LEGUME AND PASTA SOUP

*Serves: 4*

*Preparation: 1 h + time
to soak legumes*

*Cooking: 3 h*

*Level of difficulty: 1*

- **7 oz/200 g mixed
  dried legumes**
- **2 quarts/2 liters
  water**
- **salt and freshly
  ground black
  pepper to taste**
- **1/2 oz/15 g dried
  mushrooms**
- **4 tbsp extra-virgin
  olive oil**
- **2 cloves garlic,
  finely chopped**
- **1/2 cup/60 g diced
  pancetta or bacon**
- **1 onion, finely
  chopped**
- **1 stalk celery,
  finely chopped**
- **1/2 small Savoy
  cabbage, about
  10 oz/300 g,
  finely shredded**
- **7 oz/200 g soup
  pasta**
- **4 tbsp freshly
  grated Pecorino
  cheese**

Soak the legumes in cold water overnight. •
Drain and place in a large saucepan. Pour in
enough water to cover the legumes with double
the volume of water. • Cook over low heat for
about 2 hours, or until the legumes are tender.
Season with salt. • Drain, reserving the cooking
liquid. • Soak the mushrooms in a bowl with
enough hot water to cover for 30 minutes. Drain,
squeezing out the excess moisture, and chop
finely. • Heat the oil in a large frying pan and sauté
the garlic and pancetta until pale gold. • Add the
onion, celery, mushrooms, and Savoy cabbage
and sauté for 3 minutes. Pour in enough of the
reserved cooking liquid to cover the vegetables.
Cook for about 30 minutes, or until all the
vegetables are tender. • Add the legumes and
cook for 10 minutes. • Add the pasta and cook
until al dente. • Season with salt and pepper and
sprinkle with the Pecorino. • Serve hot.

# SQUASH AND PASTA SOUP

Cook the squash in a large pan of salted, boiling water for 30 minutes, or until tender. • Drain and set aside. • Melt the butter in a large saucepan and sauté the leeks and celery until softened. • Add the cloves. Pour in the milk and water. Bring to a boil, season with salt, and cook over low heat for 10 minutes. • Stir in the squash and pasta and cook until al dente. • Sprinkle with the Parmesan. Serve hot.

*Serves: 4*

*Preparation: 25'*

*Cooking: 40'*

*Level of difficulty: 1*

- 1¹/₄ lb/600 g winter squash or pumpkin, cut into small cubes
- 4 tbsp butter
- 2 leeks, finely chopped
- 1 stalk celery, finely chopped
- 2 cloves
- 1 quart/1 liter milk
- 1 quart/1 liter water
- salt to taste
- 8 oz/250 g pasta tubes
- ¹/₂ cup/60 g freshly grated Parmesan cheese

# ZUCCHINI SOUP

Serves: 4
Preparation: 20'
Cooking: 40'
Level of difficulty: 1

- 4 tbsp extra-virgin olive oil
- 1¹/₂ lb/750 g zucchini/courgettes, finely chopped
- 1 firm-ripe tomato, peeled, seeded, and coarsely chopped
- salt and freshly ground black pepper to taste
- 1 bunch fresh parsley, finely chopped
- 1 quart/1 liter boiling Vegetable Stock (see page 956)
- 8 slices firm-textured bread

Heat the oil in a large, heavy-bottomed saucepan and sauté the zucchini until golden. • Add the tomato and season with salt and pepper. Stir in the parsley and cook over medium heat for 5 minutes. • Pour in the stock and simmer over medium heat for about 30 minutes. • Place two slices of bread in each bowl and pour over the soup.

937

# TAPIOCA SOUP

Beat the butter, egg yolk, and cream in a medium bowl until well blended. Season with salt and pepper. • Bring the stock to a boil in a large saucepan and gradually sift in the tapioca. • Cook over medium heat for about 15 minutes, stirring constantly. • Mix in the butter mixture and cook for 5 minutes. • Serve hot.

*Serves: 4*

*Preparation: 10'*

*Cooking: 25'*

*Level of difficulty: 1*

- **2 tbsp butter, softened**
- **1 egg yolk**
- **1 cup/250 ml heavy/double cream**
- **salt and freshly ground white pepper to taste**
- **1$^1$/$_2$ quarts/ 1.5 liters Vegetable Stock (see page 956)**
- **10 tbsp tapioca**

# SWEET POTATO SOUP

Serves: 6–8

Preparation: 25'

Cooking: 30'

Level of difficulty: 1

- 1¹/₄ lb/600 g sweet potatoes
- 2 quarts/2 liters Vegetable Stock (see page 956)
- 4 tbsp butter

Peel the potatoes and cut into quarters. • Boil the potatoes in the stock in a large saucepan for 15–25 minutes, or until tender. • Process the potatoes and stock in a food processor. • Mix in the butter and return to the saucepan. • Bring to a boil and simmer for 2 minutes. • Serve hot.

# RICE AND GARBANZO BEAN SOUP

S oak the garbanzo beans overnight in cold water. • Drain and rinse under cold, running water. Transfer them to a large saucepan with the water. Bring to a boil and simmer over low heat for at least 2 hours, or until the garbanzo beans are very tender. • Cook the rice in a large pan of salted, boiling water for 12–15 minutes, or until tender. • Drain and add to the garbanzo beans. Stir in the tomatoes and cook for 5 minutes more. • Mix in parsley, garlic, Worcestershire sauce, oil, and ground chile pepper. Season with salt and pepper and serve hot.

*Serves: 4–6*

*Preparation: 30' + time to soak beans*

*Cooking: 2 h 20'*

*Level of difficulty: 1*

- ³/4 cup/150 g dried garbanzo beans/chickpeas
- 1 quart/1 liter water
- 1 cup/200 g rice
- ¹/2 cup/125 g chopped tomatoes
- 1 small bunch parsley, finely chopped
- 2 cloves garlic, finely chopped
- 2 tbsp Worcestershire sauce
- 4 tbsp extra-virgin olive oil
- 1 red chile pepper, crumbled
- salt and freshly ground black pepper to taste

# CONSOMMÉ WITH SMALL RAVIOLI

Consommé: Place the beef, carrot, leek, celery, and egg white in a medium saucepan. Pour in 2 cups (500 ml) of stock. Bring to a boil, stirring gently until the liquid begins to evaporate. Stop stirring and wait for the egg white to come to the surface, filtering the impurities. Boil for 3 minutes, then strain through a cloth without breaking the egg white. • Return to the heat and bring to a boil. Remove from the heat and pour in the wine. • Place the remaining stock over high heat. Cover and bring to a boil. • Cook the ravioli in the boiling stock for 3 minutes. • Drain the pasta well and place in the clarified stock. Serve hot.

Serves: 4

Preparation: 1 h

Cooking: 30'

Level of difficulty: 1

- 1 quart/1 liter Beef Stock (see page 955)
- 2 oz/60 g ground beef
- $1/2$ carrot, finely chopped
- $1/2$ leek, finely chopped
- $1/2$ stalk celery, finely chopped
- 1 egg white
- 2 cups/500 ml dry white wine
- 14 oz/400 g Ricotta-filled ravioli

# BASIC
# RECIPES

# BÉCHAMEL SAUCE

Heat the milk in a saucepan until it is almost boiling. • In a heavy-bottomed saucepan, melt the butter with the flour over low heat, stirring rapidly with a wooden spoon. Cook for about 1 minute. • Remove from heat and add half the hot milk, stirring constantly. Return to low heat and stir until the sauce starts to thicken. • Add the rest of the milk gradually and continue stirring until it comes to a boil. • Season with salt and nutmeg, if using. Continue stirring until the béchamel is thick and creamy. • If any lumps form, beat the sauce rapidly with a balloon whisk until they dissolve.

946

| Makes: about 2 cups/ 500 ml |
| --- |
| Preparation: 5' |
| Cooking: 10' |
| Level of difficulty: 1 |

- 2 cups/500 ml milk
- 6 tbsp butter
- 6 tbsp all-purpose/ plain flour
- salt to taste
- 1/4 tsp freshly grated nutmeg (optional)

# PESTO

Place the basil, pine nuts, cheeses, garlic, oil, and salt in a food processor and chop until creamy. • Drain well and place in a heated serving dish. When serving with pasta, add 2 tablespoons of the cooking water. • Serve with all kinds of fresh and dried pasta, and potato gnocchi.

*Makes: about 1 cup/ 250 ml*

*Preparation: 15'*

*Level of difficulty: 1*

- **large bunch fresh basil leaves**
- **4 tbsp toasted pine nuts**
- **2 tbsp each freshly grated Parmesan and Pecorino cheese**
- **2 cloves garlic**
- **²/₃ cup/150 ml extra-virgin olive oil**
- **salt to taste**

948

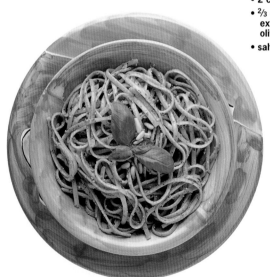

# MEDITERRANEAN SAUCE

Makes: about 1 cup/
250 ml

Preparation: 15'

Cooking: 10'

Level of difficulty: 1

- **6 tbsp extra-virgin olive oil**
- **4 cloves garlic, finely chopped**
- **8 tbsp dry bread crumbs**
- **12 sundried tomatoes, packed in oil, drained, and coarsely chopped**
- **2 tbsp finely chopped parsley**
- **salt to taste**

Heat 5 tablespoons of oil in a large frying pan and sauté the garlic for 2–3 minutes. • Heat the remaining oil in a small frying pan and toast the bread crumbs until golden brown. • Drain on paper towels then place in a small bowl with the tomatoes. • When serving with pasta, add 2 tablespoons of the cooking water. • Add the garlic and oil, parsley, and the bread crumbs and tomatoes. • Serve with all kinds of fresh and dried pasta, and potato gnocchi.

# TOMATO SAUCE

Heat the oil in a large frying pan and sauté the onion, carrot, celery, garlic, parsley, and basil for 5 minutes. • Add the tomatoes and season with salt, pepper, and sugar. Cover and cook over low heat for about 45 minutes, or until the tomato and oil begin to separate. • For a smoother sauce, press the mixture through a food mill or chop in a food processor. • Serve with all kinds of fresh and dried pasta, and potato gnocchi.

Makes: about 1 quart/ 1 liter

Preparation: 15'

Cooking: 50'

Level of difficulty: 1

- 4 tbsp extra-virgin olive oil
- 4 lb/2 kg peeled and coarsely chopped fresh or canned tomatoes
- 1 large onion, finely chopped
- 1 large carrot, finely chopped
- 1 stalk celery, finely chopped
- 1 clove garlic, finely chopped
- 1 tbsp finely chopped parsley
- 8 fresh basil leaves, torn
- salt and freshly ground black pepper to taste
- 1 tsp sugar

# MEAT SAUCE

Makes: about 1 quart/
1 liter

Preparation: 25'

Cooking: 2 h 30'

Level of difficulty: 1

Place 3 tablespoons of oil, 3 cloves of garlic, the sage, rosemary, beef, pork, and sausages in a large heavy-bottomed pan and sauté for about 15 minutes. • When the meat is almost cooked (browned, with no red blood visible), remove from the pan and set aside on a plate. • Heat the remaining oil in the same pan and add the carrots, onion, celery, and remaining garlic. Sauté for about 5 minutes, or until softened. • In the meantime, chop the meat mixture finely in a food processor or with a sharp knife. • Pour the wine over the vegetables in the pan and cook for 10 more minutes. • Add the meat and brandy and cook until the brandy evaporates. • Add the milk and simmer for 5 minutes, then add the tomatoes. • Season with salt and pepper, turn the heat to low, and simmer, partially covered, for about 2 hours. • Stir the sauce from time to time so that it doesn't stick to the bottom of the pan. • After $1^1/2$ hours, add the basil and taste to see if there is enough salt. • If, after 2 hours, the sauce is too watery, uncover and simmer for 10–15 minutes more. • When cooked, add the butter and remove from the heat.

- $1/2$ cup/125 ml extra-virgin olive oil
- 5 cloves garlic, finely chopped
- 1 sprig fresh sage
- 2 twigs fresh rosemary
- 12 oz/350 g lean beef, coarsely chopped
- 14 oz/450 g lean pork, coarsely chopped
- 3 Italian pork sausages, skinned and crumbled
- 2 large carrots, 1 large onion, 2 large stalks celery, all finely chopped
- $1^1/4$ cups/310 ml dry white wine
- $1/2$ cup/125 ml brandy
- 2 cups/500 ml milk
- $3^1/2$ lb/1.8 kg tomatoes
- salt and freshly ground black pepper to taste
- 40 leaves basil, torn
- 3 tbsp butter

| | |
|---|---|
| *Makes: about 2 quarts/2 liters* | # BEEF STOCK |
| *Preparation: 10'* | |
| *Cooking: 2 h* | |
| *Level of difficulty: 1* | |

- **1 large carrot**
- **1 medium onion**
- **1 large stalk celery**
- **4 small tomatoes**
- **5 sprigs parsley**
- **10 leaves basil**
- **2 lb/1 kg lean boiling beef + 2 lb/ 1 kg beef bones**
- **1–2 tsp salt**
- **3 quarts/3 liters water**

Put all the vegetables, the meat, bones, and salt in a large pot with the water. • Bring to a boil over high heat. Lower heat to medium-low and simmer for about 2 hours. • Remove the bones and meat. Set the meat aside. • As the stock cools, fat will form on top and can be scooped off and discarded. • Use the stock as indicated in the recipes .

---

| | |
|---|---|
| *Makes: about 2 quarts/2 liters* | # CHICKEN STOCK |
| *Preparation: 10' + 2 h* | |
| *Cooking: 3 h* | |
| *Level of difficulty: 1* | |

- **1 chicken (about 4 lb/2 kg)**
- **2 medium carrots**
- **1 onion, studded with 5 cloves**
- **1 large stalk celery**
- **4 small tomatoes**
- **5 sprigs parsley**
- **1–2 tsp salt**
- **5 peppercorns**
- **3 quarts/3 liters water**

Put the chicken, whole, in a very large pot. Add the carrots, onion, celery, tomatoes, parsley, salt, and peppercorns. Cover with the cold water and simmer over medium-low heat for 3 hours. The water should barely move. • Strain the stock, discarding the vegetables. • To remove the fat, in part or completely, let the stock cool, then refrigerate for about 2 hours. The fat will solidify on the top and can easily be scooped off.

These stocks can be prepared in advance and frozen. Freeze in ice-cube trays so that you will always have fresh homemade stock on hand.

# VEGETABLE STOCK

Heat the oil in a medium saucepan. Add the onion, carrot, leek, celery, tomato, and parsley. • Cover and sauté over low heat for about 5 minutes. • Add the peppercorns, and bay leaf. Season with salt. • Pour in the water, cover, and simmer over low heat for about 1 hour.
• Strain through a fine mesh strainer and discard the vegetables.

Makes: about 1¹/₂ quarts/1.5 liters

Preparation: 10'

Cooking: 1 h

Level of difficulty: 1

- 2 tbsp extra-virgin olive oil
- 1 medium onion
- 1 carrot
- 1 leek, trimmed and cut in 4 pieces
- 2 celery stalks with their leaves
- 1 small tomato
- 6 sprigs parsley
- 5 peppercorns
- 1 bay leaf
- 1 tsp salt
- 2 quarts/2 liters water

# FISH STOCK

P ut the water in a large pot and add the fish trimmings, onion, carrot, celery, tomato, parsley, bay leaf, lemon slice, wine, coarse salt, and peppercorns. • Bring to a boil over medium-high heat, then lower the heat to medium and cook for 20 minutes, removing the foam at regular intervals with a slotted spoon. • Strain the stock and use as indicated in the recipes.

958

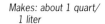

*Makes: about 1 quart/ 1 liter*

*Preparation: 15'*

*Cooking: 50'*

*Level of difficulty: 1*

- **2 quarts/2 liters water**
- **1 lb/500 g fish trimmings (heads, scales, skin, shells)**
- **1 onion, chopped**
- **1 carrot, chopped**
- **1 stalk celery**
- **1 medium tomato**
- **1 bunch parsley**
- **1 bay leaf**
- **1 large slice lemon**
- **$^1/_2$ cup/125 ml dry white wine**
- **1 tsp salt**
- **6 peppercorns**

# Index

967

975